KT-394-656

Mozambique

THE BRADT TRAVEL GUIDE
Third Edition

Philip Briggs
Ross Velton

Bradt Travel Guides Ltd, UK
The Globe Pequot Press Inc, USA

CORK CITY LIBRARY

Reprinted with amendments September 2005
Reprinted June 2006
Third edition 2002
First published 1997

Bradt Travel Guides Ltd
23 High Street, Chalfont St Peter, Bucks SL9 9QE, England
Published in the USA by The Globe Pequot Press Inc, 246 Goose Lane,
PO Box 480, Guilford, Connecticut 06475-0480

54 01 400

BISHOPSTOWN
LIBRARY

Text copyright © 2002 Philip Briggs
Maps copyright © 2002 Bradt Travel Guides Ltd
Photographs © 2002 Ariadne Van Zandbergen

The author and publisher have made every effort to ensure the accuracy of the
information in this book at the time of going to press. However, they cannot accept any
responsibility for any loss, injury or inconvenience resulting from the use of information
contained in this guide.

All rights reserved. No part of this publication may be reproduced, stored in a retrieval
system, or transmitted in any form or by any means, electronic, mechanical, photocopying,
recording or otherwise without the prior consent of the publishers.
Requests for permission should be addressed to Bradt Travel Guides Ltd,
19 High Street, Chalfont St Peter, Bucks SL9 9QE in the UK;
or to The Globe Pequot Press Inc,
246 Goose Lane, PO Box 480, Guilford, Connecticut 06475-0480
in North and South America.

British Library Cataloguing in Publication Data
A catalogue record for this book is available from the British Library

ISBN-10: 1 84162 042 4
ISBN-13: 978 1 84162 042 8

Photographs Ariadne Van Zandbergen
Illustrations Annabel Milne
Maps Alan Whitaker

Typeset from the author's disc by Wakewing
Printed and bound in Italy by Legoprint SpA, Lavis (TN)

Authors/Photographer

AUTHORS

Philip Briggs (philari@hixnet.co.za) is a travel writer and tour leader specialising in East and southern Africa. Born in Britain and raised in South Africa, Philip started travelling in East Africa in 1986 and has since spent the equivalent of four years exploring the highways and backroads of the subcontinent. His first book, *Guide to South Africa*, was published by Bradt in 1991. Since then, he has written Bradt guides to *Tanzania*, *Uganda*, *Ethiopia* and *Malawi* and *East and Southern Africa: The Backpacker's Manual,* and has co-authored the Bradt guide to *Rwanda*. He is also a frequent contributor to British and South African periodicals.

Ross Velton (rvelton@yahoo.com) is a travel writer and freelance journalist. He has written two previous books for Bradt Travel Guides, *Haiti and the Dominican Republic: The Island of Hispaniola* and *Mali: The Bradt Travel Guide*, as well as numerous travel features for magazines and newspapers including *The Times* of London. His other writing credits include a website about extreme sports and adventure travel in the Dominican Republic (www.DRpure.com), and articles on subjects ranging from the sex clubs of Paris to soccer in Albania. Ross has been travelling independently for 12 years, in which time he has visited around 70 countries on all continents except for Antarctica. His experience of African travel includes hitchhiking across the Sahara Desert and several trips to various West African countries.

PHOTOGRAPHER

Ariadne Van Zandbergen (philari@hixnet.co.za), who took the photographs for this book, is a freelance photographer and tour guide. Born and raised in Belgium, she travelled through Africa from Morocco to South Africa in 1994/5 and is now resident in Johannesburg. She has visited 19 African countries in total, and her photographs have appeared in several books, periodicals and pamphlets.

Contents

LIST OF MAPS

Bradt Travel Guides is a partner to the new 'know before you go' campaign, recently launched by the UK Foreign and Commonwealth Office. By combining the up-to-date advice of the FCO with the in-depth knowledge of Bradt authors, you'll ensure that your trip will be as trouble-free as possible.

www.fco.gov.uk/knowbeforeyougo

Acknowledgements

The authors have depended on the help and support of many people to write this book.

Philip Briggs would like to thank Bernhard Skrodski, the original author of the Bradt *Guide to Mozambique*; the travellers who wrote to Bernhard with update material, including Andrew Chilton, Jackie Nee, Julle Tulianen, B P Rawlins, the Co-ordinator of Projects at the Diocese of Lichinga and Iain Jackson; Hans van Well, Sally Crook, Vincent Parker and Bob de Lacy Smith, all of whom contributed to the text of this guide; Andre Kleynhans and Pedro Commissario of LAM for their outstandingly positive attitude to this project; David Ankers of Hotel Polana and John Elliot of the Hotel Cardosa in Maputo; Margie McDuff, Gilbert Bouic, Derek Schuurman, Mike Slater, Tracey Naughton and Don Beswick, all of whom made a significant contribution. Last, but never least, all my love and gratitude to Ariadne for being a true companion, both while we were on the road and when at home.

Ross Velton would like to thank Daniel Albano at TAP Air Portugal in London, and Armando Miguel Bango, Cláudio Banze and Sarita Adade Muage at LAM in Maputo for their positive attitude and invaluable practical assistance. Help was also provided in different ways by the following: Vicente Simango, John Elliot, Jónia Chilusse and Paul Norman in Maputo; Fanie and Debbie Van Rensburg in Chidenguele; Colin Jefferies and the Pisces Dive Centre in Jangamo; Margie Toens in Vilankulo; Benguerra Lodge on Benguerra Island; Detlef Kalus and Christina Klusmann in Cuamba; Kate Robertson and Mariette Asselbergs in Lichinga; and Fiona Ashton in Cabo Delgado. Thanks also to Tuija Paukkonen for making some important introductions. The hospitality of Neil Carter and Samantha Allen during the creative stages of this book was also much appreciated.

This amended reprint has benefited from information provided by Kaskazini Tourism Services (Pemba), Quilálea Marketing, Steppes Travel, Expert Africa (formerly Sunvil Africa), Unusual Destinations and WildLife Adventures, as well as by individual travellers.

Introduction

Visit Mozambique today, and you'll probably find it difficult to imagine that only 20 years ago this now rather obscure country attracted a greater volume of tourists than South Africa and Rhodesia combined; that less than ten years ago the country was in the closing stages of a civil war which claimed the lives of 100,000 people; that in February 2000 large tracts of land in the southern part of the country were submerged by 8m of water; and that nowadays, of all the countries in the world, nowhere is tourism developing as quickly as it is in Mozambique. So, where and when will this rollercoaster ride end? Is Mozambique heading full circle back to the good old days of the early 1970s, or do more hard times lie ahead?

Mozambique is no longer a country at war, nor is it one of those countries that you sense might return to war at the slightest provocation. It is also in the process of trying to rehabilitate the coastal resorts and game reserves that once made it one of Africa's most popular tourist destinations. This, inevitably, will be a slow process. South African and Zimbabwean holidaymakers are returning to the resorts that line the coast between Maputo and Beira, but word of Mozambique's revival as a tourist destination has yet to spread much beyond its immediate neighbours. And, while you need only spend a few days at any backpackers' hostel in Malawi and Zimbabwe to realise that Mozambique has become the most talked-about off-the-beaten-track destination in eastern and southern Africa, the fact is that very few backpackers are prepared do more than talk about visiting a country for which relatively little reliable travel information is available.

So far as tourists are concerned, Mozambique might almost as well be two countries. Linked only by the solitary motor ferry that crosses the mighty Zambezi River at Caia, and divided by the more than 1,000km of rutted road that connects Beira to Nampula, southern Mozambique and northern Mozambique offer entirely different experiences to visitors. The two parts of the country have in common the widespread use of Portuguese and a quite startlingly beautiful coastline. The difference is that the south coast of Mozambique is already establishing itself as a tourist destination, with rapidly improving facilities and a ready-made market in the form of its eastern neighbours. The north, by contrast, has few facilities for tourists.

The majority of people who buy this guide will probably confine their travels to southern Mozambique. Not only does this part of the country offer good roads, reasonable public transport, some exceptional restaurants, and any number of beach resorts suitable for all tastes and budgets, but it is within a day's drive of Johannesburg, the subcontinent's largest city and major international transport hub. The south coast of Mozambique is exceptionally beautiful – truly the achetype of palm-lined tropical beach nirvana – as well as boasting snorkelling, diving and game fishing to rank with the very best in the world. Add to this Maputo and Beira, two of Africa's most attractive cities, not to mention the old-world gem that is Inhambane town, and you are looking at a stretch of coast as varied and attractive as any in Africa. If southern Mozambique lacks one thing, it is a notable game reserve, but even this should be rectified when the Transfrontier Wildlife Park, combining South Africa's Kruger National Park and the Banhine National Park in Mozambique, opens in 2002.

Any honest description of northern Mozambique is bound to repel visitors seeking comfort, predictability or packaged entertainment. Equally, it is likely to whet the appetite of travellers looking for an adventurous trip through one of southern Africa's least-explored regions. The northeastern provinces of Zambézia, Niassa, Nampula and Cabo Delgado have a remote, isolated and self-contained feel – not surprising when you consider that they are collectively bordered by the unbridged Rovuma River and the undeveloped southeastern quarter of Tanzania to the north, and by the vast watery expanses of the Indian Ocean and Lago Niassa to the east and west.

Little visited even by backpackers, northern Mozambique offers the sort of challenging travel that recalls conditions in countries like Zambia, Tanzania and Uganda in the mid-1980s – but exacerbated by linguistic barriers, humidity levels that reach intolerable proportions in summer, relatively high costs, and a public transport system that in places defies rational comprehension. But, if travelling through much of northern Mozambique is more or less travel for its own sake (a great deal of bumpy motion with relatively few highlights) it cannot be denied that the area boasts two historical attractions of quite compelling singularity, namely the former Portuguese capital on Ilha do Moçambique and the ancient island town of Ibo. These, alone, are worth any number of days on the back of a dusty truck and nights in a smelly, sweaty pensão room.

Mozambique may not be the easiest country in which to travel; in the northeast it can be downright frustrating. But this will change, and even as things stand Mozambique is not a country without rewards. Looking to the future, I wish Mozambicans every bit of success in redeveloping their country and its tourist industry, and I hope very much that by writing this book I will encourage more people to visit them. For now, not the least of Mozambique's attractions is that it still offers ample scope for genuinely exploratory travel; it is that rare country that adventurous travellers can experience entirely for themselves, without the distorting medium of a developed tourist industry.

ABOUT THIS BOOK

Philip Briggs and Ross Velton have written the text of this book, even though the first person has been used throughout. This means that the personal opinions and experiences that are given are those of either Philip or Ross – if not both of them.

The prices in the guide were collected in late 2001 and have been quoted in US dollars using the exchange rate of US$1 = 20,000MT, which is slightly lower than the official exchange rate at the time of writing. Consequently, most of the prices are an overestimation of what was actually payable. Of course, by the time you visit Mozambique the US dollar value of the notoriously volatile metical may have changed considerably.

At the time of this amended reprint (2005), the rate is around 24,000 meticais to US$1, and costs in Mozambique have inevitably risen, in some cases considerably. In a reprint (rather than a new edition) we can't adjust all individual prices, so, if budgeting is important to you, do obtain the latest information before you travel.

Tourism in Mozambique is developing very rapidly. New lodges are opening and new facilities are starting up. We have reflected the main innovations (particularly in the Quirimbas Archipelago) but there will be many more by the time you read this book. Currently of note is the fact that extra digits have just been added to all the phone numbers – see details on pages 73 and 75.

The fourth, newly researched and fully updated edition of *Mozambique: The Bradt Travel Guide* should hit the bookstores early in 2007 – check the Bradt website (www.bradtguides.com) nearer the time for more on this.

Part One

General Information

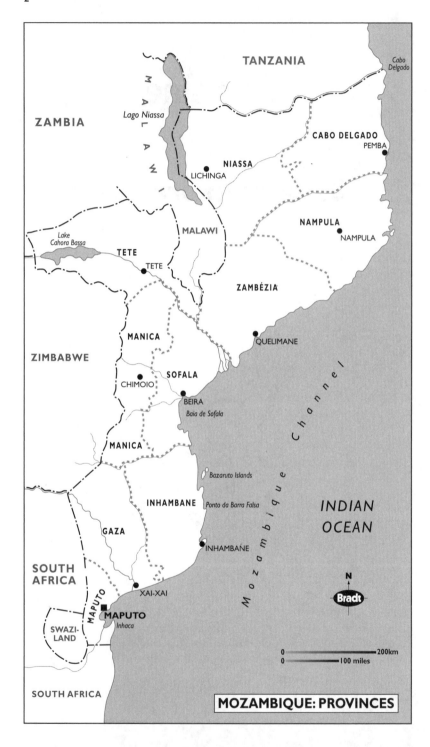

MOZAMBIQUE: PROVINCES

Background

FACTS AND FIGURES
Location
Mozambique extends for 2,500km along the east coast of Africa, between latitudes 11° and 26° south and longitudes 30° and 40° east. It is bordered by the Indian Ocean to the east, and by South Africa to the south. The north of the country is bisected by Malawi, which forms the eastern border of Niassa and Zambézia provinces and the western border of Tete Province. The northern border east of Malawi is shared with Tanzania, while the northwestern border west of Malawi is shared by Zambia. The eastern border south of Malawi and Zambia is shared with Zimbabwe, South Africa and Swaziland.

Size
Mozambique covers an area of approximately 799,380km^2, of which 13,000km^2 is water. It is the 16th-largest country in Africa, roughly two-thirds the size of the neighbouring Republic of South Africa, about three times the size of Great Britain, and slightly larger than the state of Texas.

Principal cities
The capital city is Maputo, known in colonial times as Lourenço Marques. Maputo lies in the far south of the country, 430km east of Johannesburg by road. It has a population of roughly one million people, or two million if you include the surrounding areas. The next four largest cities in Mozambique, listed in order of estimated population, are as follows: Beira (300,000), Nampula (200,000), Quelimane (135,000) and Chimoio (80,000).

Provinces
Mozambique is divided into ten provinces. Each province is divided into districts, further subdivided into administrative areas and civil parishes. Zambézia and Nampula provinces in the northern half of the country contain the richest agricultural land and 40% of the population of the country, whereas the three southern provinces of Gaza, Inhambane and Maputo are mostly arid and previously served as labour reserves for Mozambique's industries and for mines and farms in South Africa.

Time
Two hours ahead of GMT

MOZAMBIQUE: PROVINCE BY PROVINCE

Province	Capital	Area (km²)	Population (2000)
Cabo Delgado	Pemba	82,625	1,465,537
Gaza	Xai-Xai	75,709	1,203,294
Inhambane	Inhambane	68,615	1,256,139
Manica	Chimoio	61,661	1,137,448
Maputo	Maputo	26,358	933,951
Nampula	Nampula	81,606	3,265,854
Niassa	Lichinga	129,056	870,544
Sofala	Beira	68,018	1,453,928
Tete	Tete	100,724	1,319,904
Zambézia	Quelimane	105,008	3,316,703

Flag

The national flag consists of three horizontal bands: from top, green, white-edged black and yellow. There is a red triangle on hoist side, centred around a yellow star bearing an open white book on which are depicted a crossed rifle and a hoe in black.

Population

The population of Mozambique was estimated to be 17,242,240 in 2000, and is expected to exceed 30 million by 2020. The average life expectancy lies at between 45 and 50 years. Approximately 67% of the population live in rural areas, but there is an ongoing trend of gravitation to the cities.

Mozambique has one of the lowest population densities in southern and eastern Africa, currently standing at roughly 23 inhabitants per km². Excluding the desert countries of Namibia and Botswana, Zambia is the only country in the region more thinly populated than Mozambique. It has been suggested that the low population density was due to the protracted civil war. In fact, the interior of Mozambique has always been sparsely populated, and the population has grown by more than 50% in the twenty years since independence. The most densely populated provinces are Zambézia, Nampula and Maputo.

Minority population groups include Indians and Pakistanis, particularly around Nampula, and Portuguese, who are concentrated in the cities of Maputo and Beira.

HISTORY
To AD1500
The interior

It is widely agreed that humanity evolved in East Africa. Mozambique itself has yielded few notable hominid fossils, but it is nevertheless reasonable to assume that it has supported human life for millions of years. Southeast Africa has incurred two major population influxes from West Africa in the last few millennia. The first occurred roughly 3,000 years ago, when the lightly built Batwa hunter-gathererers – similar in appearance and culture to the modern bushmen of Namibia – spread throughout the region. Roughly 1,000 years later, the Bantu-speakers who still occupy most of the region started to expand into eastern Africa, reaching the Indian Ocean coast in about AD400, an influx which broadly coincided with the spread of iron-age culture in the region. Although there is little concrete evidence of the mechanisms of this so-called Bantu migration, the records of early Portuguese adventurers leave us with a good idea of the main Bantu-speaking groupings of the southeast African interior at around AD1500.

The low-lying, relatively dry and disease-prone Mozambican lowveld was then, as it is now, relatively thinly populated, with the dominant ethno-linguistic groupings being the Makua north of the Zambezi River, the Tonga between the Zambezi and the Inhambane area, and the Nguni south of Inhambane into modern-day South Africa. The three main ethno-linguistic groups of the lowveld had discrete social and economic systems: the Makua had a matrilineal social structure as opposed to the patrilineal system favoured further south, while the Nguni had a cattle-based economy and the Tonga a mixed farming economy supplemented by revenue raised from the trade routes passing through their territory.

What the people of the lowveld had in common was a decentralised political structure, based around fragmented local chieftaincies. In direct contrast, the Karonga (or Shona) who occupied the highveld of what is now Zimbabwe had a highly centralised political structure with an ancient tradition of stone building that evidently dates to around AD1000. At the centre of this region stood the extensive and magnificent city of Great Zimbabwe, which is thought to have had a population of more than 10,000 at its peak. The economy of Karangaland was probably based around cattle-ownership, but its external relations were shaped by the coastal trade in gold, which has been mined in the Zimbabwean highlands since around AD900.

Karangaland appears to have gone through a major political upheaval in the second half of the 15th century. Great Zimbabwe was abandoned in roughly 1450, for reasons that remain a matter of speculation, but are probably linked to local environmental degradation or a secession struggle. Whatever the cause, the abandonment of Great Zimbabwe coincided with a northerly reorientation of the highland kingdoms and a corresponding shift in the main trade routes. During the 15th century, the trade routes fanning from the Zambezi assumed greater importance, while the established route inland of Sofala along the Buzi River appears to have diminished in use. It is highly probable that the Karonga kingdoms known to the earliest Portuguese explorers were relatively new creations resulting from the upheavals of the late 15th century.

By 1500, the three main kingdoms of the highveld were Butua in what is now the Bulawayo area of Zimbabwe; Monomotapa in what is now central Zimbabwe; and Manica in the highlands of what is now the Zimbabwe–Mozambique border area. The upheavals also resulted in two Karanga chieftaincies being established in what had formerly been Tonga territory: Barue in the lowveld south of the Zambezi and west of Sena, and Kiteve in the lowveld between the Pungue and Buzi Rivers. Of these five main kingdoms, Butua was the only one to retain the stone-building tradition, while Monomotapa established itself as the paramount dynasty in the region.

The coast

The East African coast has long been a centre of international trade. Starting in around 2500BC, the ancient Egyptians evidently entered into spasmodic trade with an East African port they knew as Punt. From about 600BC, the Phoenicians and Romans are known to have traded with an East African port called Rhapta. The location of Punt remains a matter of pure speculation, but detailed references to Rhapta in Ptolemy's 4th-century *Geography* and in an older Phoenician document *Periplus of the Ancient Sea* point to a location somewhere in present-day Tanzania, possibly near the mouth of the Pangani River.

The collapse of the Roman empire signalled a temporary end to maritime trade with the East African coast, and it presumably forced the closure of any contemporary trade routes into the African interior. Ptolemy claims that a Greek explorer called Diogenes saw two snow-capped mountains 25 days upriver from Rhapta and that he was told by other traders of vast lakes further inland, which indicates that 4th-century trade routes must have penetrated the interior as far as Mount Kenya and Kilimanjaro, and possibly also Lakes Victoria and Tanganyika.

The rise of Islam in the 7th century AD revived the maritime trade with East Africa. The writings of Ali Masudi in AD947 make it clear that Arab mariners had by this time entered into regular trade with Madagascar and that they were aware that the main source of Africa's gold was Sofala, near the mouth of the Buzi River in what is now central Mozambique. The presence of 9th-century Islamic ruins on Manda Island off the Kenya coast indicates that Arabic traders started settling in East Africa at a very early point in this era of trade. The 12th-century geographer Al Idrisi refers to Sofala as an important source of iron, gold and animal skins, and he indicates that by this time China and India were both trading with East Africa. By the 13th century, the coast between Somalia and Central Mozambique was dotted with some 30 or 40 Swahili city-states, among the most important of which were Mogadishu, Malindi, Mombasa, Pangani, Zanzibar, Kilwa and Sofala.

Although many of these ancient Swahili cities have survived into the modern era, our best idea of what they must have looked like comes from the extensive ruins of those that haven't – notably Kilwa in southern Tanzania and Gedi in Kenya. The impressive rag coral architecture and overwhelming Muslim influence of such places has led many popular accounts to treat them as little more than Arabic implants. However, most modern historians are agreed that this is an outdated interpretation, and that there was a high level of integration between Arabic settlers and the indigenous peoples of the coast. It is true that the Islamic religion was adopted all along the coast, but then so was the Swahili language, which is self-evidently Bantu in origin, and which adopted elements of Arabic vocabulary only after the arrival of the Omani Arabs in the 18th century.

Several modern Mozambican ports have been built over medieval Swahili trade settlements – most notably Ilha do Mozambique, but also Angoche, Ibo and possibly Inhambane. However, the most important port south of Kilwa in medieval times, Sofala, is no longer in existence. The port of Sofala is thought to have been founded as a trading post in the 9th century, as a result of an Arabic ship being blown off course to hit land south of the Zambezi. Sofala is said to have had a population of around 10,000 by the 15th century. The absence of suitable building material meant that the medieval cities of Mozambique were never built as durably as those located further north, so little physical evidence of Sofala remains. Even if Sofala had been a stone city, it would now be submerged off the ever-mutating sandy shoreline south of the Buzi River.

Despite the absence of tangible ruins at Sofala, one should not underestimate its importance in medieval times, when it formed the pivotal link between the gold mines of Karangaland and Manica and the port of Kilwa. Sofala was best known to Arabs as the source of Kilwa's gold, but it was also an important trade centre in its own right, with direct maritime links to Madagascar and indirect links via Madagascar to India and Indonesia. Sofala's main exports, apart from gold, were worked iron, copper, ivory and cotton – the latter grown as far south as Inhambane by the 15th century.

There is strong evidence to suggest that Arabic vessels explored the Zambezi as far inland as Cahora Bassa. It also seems highly probable that Muslim traders settled along the Zambezi long before the arrival of the Portuguese. Despite the oft-repeated assertion that Portugal founded the river ports at Sena and Tete in 1531, the greater probability is that Portuguese traders occupied existing Muslim settlements at these locations. Particularly compelling evidence of this comes from a 12th-century Arab document that refers to a town called Seyouna located near the confluence of two large rivers and a large mountain – the similarity in name and the geographical details would point to Seyouna and Sena being one and the same place. It has also been suggested that a town referred to as Dendema in a 14th-century document was in the same locality as present-day Tete.

Portuguese occupation of East Africa 1488–1530

The well-established trade links that bonded East Africa to the Gulf and to Asia were to alter dramatically in the 16th century following the arrival of the Portuguese on the Indian Ocean. Throughout the 15th century, Portugal attempted to find a route around Africa, with the main impetus of establishing direct control over the eastern spice trade. After Portugal captured the Moroccan port of Ceuta in 1415, it also became conscious of the fact that somewhere in Africa lay the source of the gold traded in that city. Furthermore, the Portuguese Crown was eager to establish the whereabouts of the legendary kingdom of Prester John (the name by which they knew Ethiopia) and to forge links with this isolated Christian empire.

It took Portugal almost a century to circumnavigate Africa, quite simply because they underestimated the continent's size. Nevertheless, Portuguese explorers had sailed as far south as Senegal by 1444; they reached the Gambia River in 1446; Sierra Leone in 1460; and São Tomé in 1474. In 1485, under King João II, an expedition led by Cão sailed up the Congo River as far as it was navigable, then continued south as far as Cape Cross in present-day Namibia. Cão died near Cape Cross, but when the survivors of his journey returned to Portugal, King João ordered Bartholomew Diaz to continue where he left off. Diaz set sail in August 1487, and in early 1488 he unwittingly rounded the Cape of Good Hope into the Indian Ocean, eventually sailing to roughly 50km past where the city of Port Elizabeth stands today. At the same time as Diaz was exploring the route via West Africa, another Portuguese explorer, Pero da Covilham, made his way overland and along the East African coastline to Kilwa and Sofala. The two routes of exploration finally connected in 1498, when Vasco da Gama sailed around Africa, stopping at Mozambique Island before continuing as far north as Malindi and, with the help of a Swahili navigator, crossing the Indian Ocean to India.

In 1505, the Portuguese decided to occupy the East African coast. In July, Kilwa was captured and a friendly sheikh installed on its throne. Two months after that, a Portuguese boat landed at Sofala and was given permission by the local sheikh to erect a fort and trading factory – however, the sheikh and his allies attacked the Portuguese stockade within a year of its foundation, resulting in the sheikh being killed and replaced by a Portuguese puppet. In 1507, a permanent Portuguese settlement was established on Mozambique Island, which so rapidly became the centre of Portuguese operations that Kilwa was abandoned by its colonisers in 1513.

Portugal also set about attacking rival Muslim centres of commerce: Oja, Bravo and Socatra on the north coast were sacked in 1507, and the islands of Mafia, Pemba and Zanzibar followed in 1509. Several Muslims from Mozambique Island and Sofala were forced to relocate to Angoche and Querimba Island, where they started a clandestine trade which was temporarily halted when Portugal razed Angoche in 1511 and Querimba in 1522. By 1530, practically the whole East African coast north of Sofala was under Portuguese control.

The East African coast 1530–1600

The boundaries of modern Mozambique were in many instances shaped by events during the first four centuries of the Portuguese occupation of the coast, but Mozambique as we know it is in essence a 20th-century entity. The expansions and contractions of Portuguese influence between 1500 and 1890 don't really reflect a considered policy, but rather a haphazard sequence of largely unsuccessful attempts at formal expansion from a few coastal strongholds.

The Portuguese presence in East Africa was characterised by a high level of disunity. The interests of the Crown and the appointed Captain of Mozambique (who prior to 1670 ran the 'colony' as a private trade enterprise) were often in conflict, as were those of the many Portuguese deserters who fled from the few formal Portuguese settlements to intermarry with locals and form a distinct group of mixed-race *mazungos*. Contrary to popular perception, Mozambique prior to 1890 was not so much a Portuguese territory as it was a patchwork of endlessly mutating and fragmenting fiefdoms, some of which were under the nominal or real rule of the Portuguese Crown, but the greater number of which were lorded over by self-appointed despots, be they renegade *mazungos*, indigenous chiefs or Muslim sheikhs.

In the early years of the Portuguese occupation, the kingdom of Monomotapa (more accurately transcribed as Mwene Mutapa, that is the state of the Mutapa dynasty) took on legendary proportions in the mind of its would-be conquerors. For centuries, it has been assumed that Monomotapa was a vast and all-powerful homogenous empire covering most of modern-day Zimbabwe as well as parts of Botswana and Mozambique. Modern academics, however, believe that the kingdom's size and importance was exaggerated by Portugal, and that the Mutapa dynasty ruled over what was merely one of many loosely defined Karanga kingdoms. Quite how Monomotapa's mythical status arose is an open question, but it is fairly certain that it would have suited Portuguese interests to perpetuate the myth that the whole interior was one vast centralised kingdom – especially after 1607, when Portugal signed a treaty with the Mutapa giving it full access to all gold, copper and silver mines in his kingdom.

The earliest sanctioned exploration of the Mozambican interior was made by Antonio Fernandes, who reported on the main gold trade routes over three journeys between 1511 and 1513, and who was probably the first Portuguese to visit the capital of Monomotapa in the Cahora Bassa Region. However, Fernandes' findings did not result in the official occupation of the interior – on the contrary, the Portuguese Crown appears to have been content to trade with local chiefs from its coastal fortresses. The disruption caused to the gold trade by the upheavals in Karangaland and the clandestine approach of the Muslim gold traders at places like Angoche forced the Portuguese to turn their attention to ivory, which by 1530 had replaced gold as the main item of export. The Portuguese fortresses on the coast also required large amounts of food, which created a secondary trade network between the representatives of the Crown and established chiefs. Despite initial tensions, the market for food and ivory eventually created a mutual dependency and stable relations.

Once Portugal realised that it would be unable to wrest control of the elusive gold trade from the Muslim traders by force, it attempted to take control of the routes to the interior by occupying the existing Muslim settlements at Tete, Sena and Quelimane in 1531.

The only concerted effort made by the Crown to conquer Monomotapa in the 16th century was an expedition of 1,000 men led by Francisco Barreto, which arrived at Sena in December 1571. Hundreds of Barreto's men had died of fever along the way and – ignorant of tsetse fly and mosquito-borne diseases – Barreto blamed his losses on the black magic of the Muslims at Sena. The Portuguese troops attacked Sena, killing most of its Muslim population and capturing the 19 men they identified as their leaders, who were then tortured to death at the rate of two a day. In July 1572, Barreto marched towards Tete with 650 men, but before he could reach his destination, his troops were attacked by a force of 16,000 Africans led by a Maravi king known as Mambo. Barreto's men were forced to turn back after killing some 4,000 of their attackers. Only 180 of the men who left Sena returned there alive, and Barreto himself died of fever on the way. Two years later, another group of soldiers marched 450km inland, defeating the Kiteve capital but achieving little else before they returned to the coast, with their numbers reduced by two-thirds due to malaria.

The Portuguese occupation of Mozambique should not be seen as colonisation in the way we understand it today. Most of the infiltration of the interior and the coast away from the fortress towns was the work of Afro-Portuguese half-castes (*mazungos*), many of whom were refugees from the Crown. Armed with muskets, many of these refugees married into local communities and assumed the role of surrogate chiefs, building up their own private armies and trade empires. During the 16th century, not only did various *mazungos* establish themselves at practically every port and island along the coast, but they also settled along the southern bank of the Zambezi as far as Tete, setting up what were in effect minor chieftaincies over the local Tonga people – basically, the forerunners of the *prazo* land grants of the 17th and 18th centuries.

Ironically, it could be argued that the most successful expansionists in 16th-century Mozambique were not of European but African origin. Probably as a result of a drought, cannibalistic Zimba warbands from the Maravi Kingdom of the Shire Highlands (in Malawi) swept into Mozambique in the late 1560s. The Zimba attacked Tete in the 1560s, they halted Barreto's progress in 1572, and they then continued northwards, razing Kilwa and Mombasa and eating many of their occupants. The Zimba were eventually defeated near Malindi in 1587, but the survivors returned southwards to settle in the area between the Rovuma and Zambezi Rivers, practically all of which was ruled over by one or other Maravi chieftaincy at the beginning of the 17th century.

Towards the end of the century, Portugal's dominance in the region was threatened by Turks, for which reason the fortifications of Mozambique Island and Mombasa were vastly improved and the coast was divided into two administrative regions with Cabo Delgado as the boundary. This border has remained significant ever since and now separates Tanzania from Mozambique.

The East African Coast 1600–1800

In the early 17th century, Portugal experienced the first serious rivalry to its status as the dominant European power in the Indian Ocean. In 1602, barely a decade after the first Dutch and British ships had rounded the Cape of Good Hope, the Dutch East India Company (VOC) was formed with the intent of taking over Portugal's Indian Ocean trade. In 1607, the Dutch made a concerted effort to capture the Portuguese capital on Mozambique Island, a six-week siege which failed only because the invaders were unable to take the

Portuguese fortress. After a second attempt at ousting Portugal in 1608, the Dutch fleets left Mozambique Island alone, but in alliance with English ships they captured several other Portuguese territories in the Indian Ocean. This period of instability ended in the late 1630s, when treaties were signed between the three countries.

The beginning of the 17th century also saw Karangaland fall into an extended period of instability following the death of the Monomotapa in 1597. The succeeding Monomotapa, Gatse Lucere, became dependent on the protection of the *mazungo* Diego Madeira's armies to retain control over his kingdom, which Madeira saw as more or less an invitation to take over Karangaland following the signing of a mineral rights treaty in 1607. Gatse Lucere died in 1623, to be succeeded by Inhamba, who in 1628 murdered the Portuguese envoy to his capital, prompting a full-scale war with Portugal. Inhamba was driven from his capital, and a baptised Mutapa was installed in his place. However, this puppet ruler had little support, and so in 1631 Inhamba led an uprising in which he recaptured the Crown and killed several hundreds of Portuguese and their supporters. Meanwhile, the Maravi took advantage of the chaos in Monomotapa to capture Quelimane.

In 1632, Portugal had one of its few successful military forays in the Mozambican interior. Under the leadership of Sousa de Menesis, 2,000 troops landed at Quelimane, where they booted out the Maravi, then marched to Karangaland, destroyed Inhamba's army, and installed a vassal Monomotapa. So began a 60-year period in which Portugal was to have its only sustained control of Karangaland. During this time, major Portuguese settlements grew up around the various gold fairs of the interior, notably Dambarare (near modern-day Harare) and Masekesa (on the site of Manica town).

The Crown's tenuous supremacy in Karangaland ended in 1693, when a Changamire chief called Dombo attacked Dambarare and killed all its Portuguese inhabitants. Other Portuguese settlements in Karangaland were evacuated and the Changamire proceeded to attack all the gold fairs in Manica. As things settled down, the Changamire took effective control of the highlands to found the Rozvi Kingdom, while the Portuguese kept control of the lowveld. This boundary is reflected in the modern one between Mozambique and Zimbabwe.

Events on the coast in the late 17th century reinforced what was eventually to become the northern border of modern Mozambique. In 1650, Muscat was captured by Omani Arabs and used as a base from which to launch an attack on the East African coast. Omani ships attacked Zanzibar in 1652 and Mombasa in 1661. Ten years later, Mozambique Island was looted by Omani sailors, and once again it was only the fortress of São Sebastão that prevented Portugal being ousted from their East African capital. The Omani never again attempted to attack Portuguese settlements in what is now Mozambique, but in 1698 they captured Mombasa. The coast north of Cabo Delgado was lost to Portugal forever.

The period between 1650 and 1800 saw the informal *mazungo* chieftaincies of the Zambezi Valley formalised into a network of *prazo* estates – large tracts of land granted to settlers and wealthy traders by the Portuguese Crown. The *prazo* leases were good for three generations, and they were inherited by females, presumably as a way of encouraging wealthy Portuguese to settle in the Zambezi Valley. In theory, no person was allowed to own more than one *prazo*, but in reality large blocks of *prazos* were linked by marriage. The holders of the leases, known as *prazeros*, ruled over their estates with absolute authority. In effect, the *prazos* were run as small feudal empires, and the *prazeros* derived most of their income by forcing tributes from people living on their estate rather than by developing the estate for agriculture.

Mozambique in the 19th century

The early part of the 19th century was a time of great hardship in southeastern Africa, as the region was gripped by severe droughts between 1794 and 1802 and again between 1817 and 1832. These droughts were to have far-reaching effects on Mozambique and many other parts of southeast Africa, most significantly amongst the Nguni people of southern Mozambique and the east coast of South Africa. During the first years of the drought, the Nguni became increasingly dependent on cattle raids to support themselves, which led to a high degree of militarisation and eventually to the centralisation of the Nguni into three main kingdoms: the Zulu, Swazi and Ndandwe. The Zulus, who emerged as the most powerful of these kingdoms under the leadership of Shaka, raided and looted surrounding territories, causing vast tracts of the South African highveld to become depopulated and forcing many people to migrate to other areas.

In 1819, the Zulus conquered the Ndandwe Kingdom, causing the survivors to emigrate from the area in a number of large warbands which grew in size as they raided and plundered the villages that they passed through. The warband that was to have the greatest effect on Mozambique was that led by Nxaba, who attacked Inhambane in 1824 and conquered many of the chieftaincies of Manica in 1827. In the early 1830s, with the drought at its peak, Nxaba was based around the Gorongosa area, and in 1836 he plundered Sofala. Following a Nguni leadership battle in 1837, Nxaba and his followers were forced to flee Mozambique, while the victor, Shoshangane, founded the Gaza Kingdom, which covered most of Mozambique south of the Zambezi between 1840 and its conquest by Portugal in 1895.

Elsewhere, the Rozvi Empire of the Zimbabwean highlands was destroyed and the Changamire killed by a Nguni warband, and eastern Zimbabwe was eventually settled by the Matabele, another Nguni offshoot. Within Mozambique, a Nguni leader called Maseko established a kingdom north of Tete, while another called Gwangwara established himself along what is now the Tanzanian border. The Nguni invasion made travel in the interior unsafe, and Nguni warbands destroyed many of the gold fairs, practically forcing the closure of the gold trade.

Another significant feature of the first half of the 19th century, one that was not entirely unrelated to the drop in the gold trade, was a rapid increase in slave trading along the East African coast. Prior to the mid-18th century, slaves formed only a small part of the Indian Ocean trade network, but this started to change after the 1770s with the emergence of clandestine trade between the Muslims of Ibo and the French sugar plantations of the Indian Ocean Islands. In the 1770s, the number of slaves being exported from Mozambique was still relatively low – fewer than 2,000 annually – but as increasing restrictions were imposed on the trade out of West Africa, prices rose and so did the volume of slaves being exported from the ports of East Africa. Between 1825 and 1830, around 20,000 slaves were shipped out of Mozambique annually, to destinations as far afield as the USA and Brazil. It has been estimated that more than a million Africans were shipped out of the ports of Mozambique in the 19th century.

Britain persuaded Portugal to abolish the slave trade in 1836, in effect driving it underground – the number of slaves shipped out in the 1850s probably exceeded that in the 1830s. Public attention was drawn to this clandestine trade when the Scots missionary David Livingstone published reports of his Zambezi expedition of 1858–64. Following Livingstone's death in 1875, several Scots missions were established in the Shire Highlands (a part of modern-day Malawi that would otherwise almost certainly have been incorporated in Mozambique later in the century).

The great droughts undermined the agricultural base of the Zambezi Valley, forcing many *prazeros* to abandon their estates. By the mid-19th century, power in this important area had become consolidated under five large feudal fiefdoms ruled over by powerful *mazungo* families or other settlers. The Zambezi Valley became a lawless zone, characterised by inter-family feuds and mini-wars, starting in 1840 with a unsuccessful attack on the Pereira family by the Portuguese authorities, and reaching a peak in 1867–69 with four abortive and bloody attempts to capture the Da Cruz family stockade at Massangano. The Zambezi Valley was only fully brought under government control in 1887, when Massangano was captured by the governor of Manica.

An important feature of 19th-century Mozambique was the strong British influence on the East African coast following its successful take-over of the Cape Colony in 1806 and Mauritius in 1810. In 1820, the British flag was raised on the southern part of Delagoa Bay, initiating a protracted period of disputes between Britain, Portugal and the Boer Republic of the Transvaal over the control of this strategic possession. This dispute was only resolved in 1875, when French arbitrators gave the whole bay to Mozambique. Meanwhile, as the so-called Scramble for Africa approached its climax, the Beira Corridor area became something of a battleground between the British imperialist and founder of Rhodesia, Cecil Rhodes, and his Portuguese counterpart Paiva de Andrada.

After a couple of years of haggling over boundaries and disputed territories, Britain and Portugal signed a treaty in May 1891 and Mozambique took its modern shape. The northern boundary with German East Africa (Tanzania) simply followed the border established centuries before between the administrative regions of Mombasa and Mozambique Island. The northwestern borders were more keenly contested, but they were basically settled in favour of the power that had the higher presence in each area – hence northern Mozambique was bisected by the Scots-settled area that is now southern Malawi. The southwestern borders followed well-established divides: the border with Zimbabwe was similar to the one that separated the Rozvi and Portuguese spheres of influence between around 1700 and 1840; the western borders with the Transvaal followed the one agreed to in the Boer–Portuguese treaty of 1869; and the southern border with the British colony of Natal had been determined by French arbitration in 1875.

The colonial period 1890–1975

Mozambique is less arbitrarily delineated than many other countries in Africa. Nevertheless, Mozambique was anything but a cohesive entity at the time its boundaries were defined, and parts of the country remained entirely independent of Portugal as late as 1914. As an indication of the weakness of Portuguese colonial rule during the closing decade of the 19th century, it is interesting to note that Britain and Germany signed a secret treaty determining how Mozambique and Angola should be divided in the event of their being abandoned by Portugal.

Only four of Mozambique's ten modern-day provinces were directly administered by the colonial authorities. The area south of the Save River – basically the modern provinces of Maputo, Inhambane and Gaza – was given a reasonable degree of political coherence by the Gaza monarchy, who were conquered by Portugal between 1895 and 1897. The other part of the country that fell under direct colonial rule was the area around of Mozambique Island (modern-day Nampula Province), but the Portuguese presence in much of this area was rather tenuous until around the time of the outbreak of World War I. In 1904, the Portuguese in this area were attacked by a collection of Muslim and African chiefs, and they were forced to take refuge on Mozambique Island.

The rest of the country fell under indirect rule. The present-day provinces of Niassa and Cabo Delgado were leased to the Niassa Company between 1894 and 1929. The Niassa Company was almost totally ineffective until 1908, when it was taken over by a South African Company and started to make its presence felt in the northern interior. The Yoa capital at Mwende was captured by the Niassa Company in 1912, but the Makonde Plateau remained independent until after World War I. Meanwhile, most of what are now Tete and Zambézia Provinces were controlled by *prazeros*, while the area now incorporated into the provinces of Sofala and Manica was leased to the Mozambique Company from 1891 to 1941.

A significant trend in the first decade of formal colonialism was the rising economic importance of southern Mozambique. This was directly due to the proximity of Lourenço Marques to the gold mines of the Witwatersrand in South Africa. Following the completion of the rail link to the Witwatersrand in 1894, the port at Lourenço Marques exported roughly a third of this wealthy area's minerals.

No less significant was the volume of migrant labour from southern Mozambique to the mines of Witwatersrand. The Witwatersrand Native Labour

Association employed between 50,000 and 100,000 Mozambicans annually between the end of the Boer War and start of World War II. In some years, the tax contributed by the migrant workers of Southern Mozambique amounted to more than half of the total revenue raised by the colonial government.

At around the turn of the century, Lourenco Marques was made the official capital of Mozambique, replacing the former capital of Mozambique Island after almost four centuries (strangely, every new source that I check to confirm the exact year when the capital was transferred has thrown up a different date, and I now have the choice of 1886, 1897, 1898, 1902 or 1907 – the year 1898 as quoted by the official Lourenço Marques city guide published in 1964 seems most plausible).

Migrant labour had been an important factor in the Mozambican economy even before 1890, but the volume of workers increased dramatically following the Colonial Labour Law of 1899. Not only did this decree divide Mozambicans into two classes, Indigenous and Non-indigenous, but it also required that all indigenous males and females aged between 14 and 60 had to work and had to pay hut tax. It can be argued that the Labour Law rescued Mozambique from the bleak economic future that many had predicted at the time of its formal colonisation, but it is equally true that by imposing the obligation to work on the indigenous population it allowed them to be exploited in a manner that was little better than slavery. Paradoxically, it was the people who lived in the *prazos* and company concessions who were most ruthlessly exploited – until the 1930s, people in these areas were regularly press-ganged into 'employment'. The migrant labour of southern Mozambique was socially disruptive, but it also meant better wages and a lower cost of living; so that even as late as 1967, roughly half a million Mozambicans (out of a total population of eight million) were working in South Africa or Rhodesia.

In 1926, Portugal's Republican Government was overthrown in a military coup, leading to the so-called 'New State', a dictatorship dominated by the figure of Antonio Salazar, Prime Minister of Portugal from 1932 to 1968. Salazar envisaged a future wherein Portugal and it colonies would form a self-sufficient closed economy with the mother country serving as the industrial core and the dependencies providing the agricultural produce and raw materials. Salazar outlawed the company concessions and *prazos* which had until then practically ruled two-thirds of Mozambique, and he was largely successful in his efforts to create a more unitary administration. Forced labour was replaced by forced agricultural schemes, leading to a tenfold increase in Mozambique's cotton and rice production between 1930 and 1950. As a result, Mozambique enjoyed something of an economic boom, particularly during World War II when Portugal's neutral stance allowed Mozambique to concentrate on food production and benefit from a 500% increase in the value of its exports during the years 1939–45. However, the war also meant a decrease in the activity of the mines of South Africa and Rhodesia, and the return of large numbers of migrant labourers, one result of which was the introduction of population control rulings that mimicked the South African Pass Laws.

The post-war period saw greater economic diversification in Mozambique, with the development of secondary industries, particularly in Lourenço Marques and Beira, and a boom in incoming tourism from South Africa and Rhodesia. The outcome of the war encouraged Salazar to drop his more fascist policies and to enter into NATO in 1949, one result of which was the admittedly rather semantic change in Mozambique's status from a colony to an Overseas Province.

After World War II, almost all of Europe's African colonies experienced a vociferous and sometimes violent campaign for independence. Generally, these calls for liberation were initiated by African soldiers who had fought for democracy in Europe and then returned home to find that they remained second-class citizens in the country of their birth. That no significant liberation movement existed in Mozambique prior to 1960 can probably be attributed to Portugal's neutrality during the war. Nevertheless, following a violent uprising in Angola in February 1961, the ever-astute Salazar decided to try to forestall the inevitable, firstly by allowing Portugal's Overseas Provinces to be represented in the Lisbon government, and secondly by bestowing full citizenship on the indigenous population. In December of that year, Portugal's three colonial enclaves in Asia were reclaimed by India. Following this, Salazar decided that he would oppose similar calls from his African colonies with force.

Mozambique's first broad-based liberation movement was formed in exile in 1963, when President Nyerere of Tanzania persuaded a number of small-time liberation groups to amalgamate into an organisation called the Front for the Liberation of Mozambique (Frelimo), held together by the powerful leadership of Eduardo Mondlane, a Mozambican academic living in the USA. In 1964, Frelimo decided on a militant policy, and by the end of 1965 it had captured much of Cabo Delgado and Niassa Provinces. Portugal responded by arresting 1,500 Frelimo agents in southern Mozambique, effectively destroying the organisation in this part of the country. Meanwhile, Frelimo started to factionalise in the north, with the educated leadership on the one side and the traditionalist chiefs on the other. In 1968, the Frelimo offices in Dar es Salaam were raided by traditionalists, and rioting in the Frelimo-run school in Dar es Salaam forced its closure. In February 1969, Mondlane was assassinated using a letter-bomb. The ensuing power struggle within the party forced out the traditionalists and saw the military commander, Samora Machel, take over the party presidency in May 1970.

Machel faced an immediate challenge in the form of 35,000 troops sent by the government to clear Frelimo out of northern Mozambique and to attack its bases in Tanzania. Instead of fighting, Frelimo evacuated the north, slipped through Malawi, and relocated its centre of internal operations to the area north of Tete. With the support of the local Chewa people, Frelimo attempted to destabilise the Tete and Beira Corridors and to disrupt the construction of the Cahora Bassa Dam, a policy that culminated in the derailing of trains to Beira in 1974.

The extent to which Frelimo's limited attacks influenced Mozambique's eventual independence is debatable. At least as significant were the concurrent political changes in Portugal. Upon entering the European Common Market in 1970, Portugal was forced to dismantle its rigid trade agreements with Mozambique. The result was an almost immediate realignment of the Mozambican economy towards South Africa – by 1974, South Africa had already become the main investor in Mozambique, as well as its principal trading partner. Even more critical to Mozambique's future was the left-wing coup that took place in Lisbon in April 1974. Within two months, the new government of Portugal had entered into negotiations with Frelimo. In September 1974, the two sides signed the Lusaka Accord: Mozambique would be granted independence after a mere nine months of interim government, and power would transfer to Frelimo without even the pretence of a referendum or election.

Independent Mozambique

Three factors were to prove critical in shaping Mozambique during the first two decades of independence: the mess left behind by the colonisers, the leadership of Frelimo, and the destabilising policies of South Africa's nationalist government.

It would be easy enough to see the first fifteen years of Frelimo government as typical of the sort of Marxist dictatorship that has characterised post-independence Africa. It would also be rather simplistic. Frelimo assumed a dictatorial role through circumstance as much as intent – there simply *was* no viable opposition in the decade following independence – and its progressive, humanitarian ideals were a far cry from the self-serving, repressive policies enacted by many of its peers. Frelimo's undeniable failures can be attributed partly to unfortunate circumstance, but most of all to its intellectual and interventionist policies – idealistic grand schemes which failed to take into account the importance of ethnicity, tradition and religion in rural African societies, and which ultimately alienated the peasantry.

Frelimo's most notable successes were on the social front. In the first few years of independence, primary school attendance doubled and enrolment at secondary schools increased sevenfold. The new government attempted to combat the quite appalling literacy rate of less than 5% at the time of independence by initiating an adult literacy scheme that benefited hundreds of thousands of Mozambicans, and it sought to undermine the problem of ethnicity by spreading the use of Portuguese as a common language. Despite there being fewer than 100 trained doctors in the country in 1975, Frelimo launched an ambitious programme of immunisations, praised by the World Health Organisation (WHO) as one of the most successful ever initiated in Africa. The scheme reached 90% of the population in the first five years of Frelimo rule, resulting in a 20% drop in infant mortality. Frelimo's emphasis on sexual equality was underscored by the fact that 28% of the people elected to popular assemblies in 1977 were women – a higher figure that almost anywhere else in the world.

Frelimo's critical failing was on the economic front, though it should be recognised that the post-independence collapse of Mozambique's economy was precipitated by several factors that were beyond Frelimo's control.

Mozambique attained independence during the global depression that followed the 1973 Oil Crisis, which aside from having a direct effect on the economy also caused the South African gold mines to lay off two-thirds of their Mozambican workers in 1976, leading to an immense loss in Mozambique's foreign earnings. Worse still was the mass exodus of skilled Portuguese settlers and the related outflow of capital and asset-stripping that caused the collapse of many secondary industries within a year of independence. Frelimo attempted to abate this outflow by nationalising a number of industries, but at a pace that only caused the situation to spiral, and which gave many Portuguese settlers a pretext for destroying anything that they couldn't take out of the country. Meanwhile, Frelimo's ambitious agricultural schemes were to some extent thwarted by climatic factors; disastrous floods hit the main agricultural areas in the summer of 1977/8, to be followed by four years of nation-wide drought.

Finally, Frelimo had to contend with South Africa's policy of 'destabilisation' and its support of a guerrilla organisation called the Mozambican National Resistance (Renamo), which was founded by the Rhodesian Special Branch shortly after Mozambique's independence. Aided by several former members of the Portuguese Security Police, the Rhodesians conceived of Renamo as a fifth column to attack strategic bases in Mozambique, which at that time was allowing the Zimbabwean liberation movements to operate out of Manica. When Zimbabwe achieved independence in 1980, the South African Defence Force (SADF) took over Renamo and retrained its soldiers at Phalaborwa in the northern Transvaal. Renamo enjoyed considerable success with SADF backing – most notably by blowing up the Zambezi rail bridge in 1983 – and it boosted its ranks by kidnapping young boys in rural areas. With the assistance of various anti-Marxist American groups, South Africa managed to give its sponsored outlaws some sort of credibility by establishing Renamo offices in several capital cities, most of them manned by non-Africans.

On March 16 1984, Mozambique and South Africa signed the Nkomati Accord, an agreement that neither country would support elements hostile to the other. Mozambique abided by the accord, but the SADF continued to give clandestine and possibly unofficial support to Renamo, helped by Malawi's President Banda, who allowed the organisation to operate out of his country. In September 1986, President Samora Machel of Mozambique, along with the presidents of Zimbabwe and Zambia, held a summit with Banda in Malawi and persuaded him to boot out Renamo. On the return flight to Maputo, Machel's plane was diverted by a South African radio signal and crashed in South African territory, killing everybody on board. Conspiracy theories abound, the most likely being that of South African sabotage. Indeed, after an inquiry launched in May 1998, South Africa's Truth and Reconciliation Committee decided that the incident raised questions that merited further investigation by an appropriate body.

In December 1986, Malawi signed a mutual security agreement with Mozambique's recently installed President Joaquim Chissano. Left with nowhere else to run, Renamo was forced to base itself permanently in Mozambique, where it took on a life of its own. Formerly, Renamo had limited its activities to occasional raids on strategic targets. From 1987 onwards, Renamo warbands roamed through the Mozambican countryside, supporting themselves with random raids on rural villages in what an official of the US State Department described as 'one of the most brutal holocausts against ordinary human beings since World War II'. By 1990, Frelimo's control barely extended beyond the main towns. It has been estimated that Renamo killed 100,000 Mozambicans during this period, and that as many as one-third of Mozambique's human population was displaced or forced into exile by the raiding warbands. The country's economic infrastructure, already crippled by the post-independence withdrawal of skills and funds, then by years of misplaced Marxist policies, was practically destroyed. Frelimo's social achievements were reduced to cinders along with roughly 2,500 primary schools and 800 clinics and hospitals. Teachers, doctors and educated administrative staff who hadn't managed to flee the country in time were systematically executed by Renamo.

In November 1990, pressured by overseas aid donors, Frelimo unveiled a new constitution denouncing its former Marxist policies and allowing for multi-party elections. However, the civil war continued into 1992, when the Rome Conference in October resulted in a cease-fire being signed by President Chissano and the Renamo leader Afonso Dhlakama. Mozambique's first democratic elections, which achieved an 85% turnout, were held in October 1994, with Chissano obtaining 53% of the presidential vote and Dhlakama 34%. Neither party achieved an absolute majority in the parliamentary elections, with Frelimo picking up 44% of the vote to Renamo's 38%. The strongest Renamo support came from the central provinces of Nampula, Zambézia, Sofala, Manica, and Tete, where it attained a majority of parliamentary seats, while the northern and southern provinces went to Frelimo. Renamo's relative success in the election came as a surprise to many, considering its history and the fact that it had no real policies other than being anti-Frelimo. The good showing was probably due to Frelimo's low-key campaigning and failure to connect with the populace at grassroots level rather than any inherent virtues seen to be attached to Renamo.

The remainder of the 1990s was characterised by an uneasy peace and the jostling for political power that invariably follows a protracted civil war. After the 1994 parliamentary election, Renamo asserted the right to the governorships in the provinces where it had won majorities, a claim that was swiftly rejected by Chissano. Frelimo further bolstered its authority in the May 1998 local elections – boycotted by Renamo and 16 other opposition parties – in which it won almost everything up for grabs. It came as little surprise, then, that in general elections held in December 1999, Chissano was re-elected president for a further five-year term, Frelimo won an outright majority of parliamentary seats, and Renamo contested the result on the basis that the voting had been fraudulent. Although international monitors declared that the election had been free and fair, Renamo threatened unilaterally to establish a parallel government in the central and northern regions unless the vote was recounted or new elections held. As Mozambique moved into the new century, however, it continued to be governed by a single authority which, although by no means perfect, could at least claim to exercise effective and legitimate control in a country where such a feat has never been easy to achieve.

Welcome to the 21st century

In February 2000, attention was detracted from the Frelimo–Renamo soap opera by the worst flooding in Mozambique for nearly 50 years. After weeks of heavy rains and, as if this weren't enough, a wet and windy cyclone, rivers in southern and central parts of the country burst their banks. In the resulting floods, hundreds lost their lives and thousands more their homes and livelihoods. Television sets the world over broadcast the unforgettably tragic images of families hanging from treetops, their homes submerged under muddy waters, as helicopters tried to save what was left of their broken lives. The rainy season the following year caused similar damage, although on a slightly lesser scale.

The main areas of flooding were in the valleys of the Zambezi and Limpopo Rivers, which had burst their banks after the combined effects of weeks of torrential rain and the 260kmph winds of Cyclone Eline. Floodplains along these two rivers were, at some points, 5km wide, and the water level was 7m higher than usual. The waters began to recede in the beginning of March, leaving the country to count the costs of its worst flooding in nearly 50 years. Some 700 people had died and 500,000 more had been made homeless. There was also colossal material and infrastructural damage. Roads, bridges and railway lines had been destroyed, an estimated quarter of the country's agriculture had been damaged, and 80% of the livestock in Mozambique had perished. The floodwaters had also dislodged land mines laid during the civil war, re-depositing them elsewhere.

Meanwhile President Chissano remained in power. In September 2004, having declared that he would not stand for a third term, he made a farewell tour of all the country's eleven provinces, by which time over nine million people had registered to vote in the forthcoming election. In December 2004, Armando Guebuza, secretary-general of Mozambique's ruling Frelimo party, was elected president. In May 2005, Joaquim Chissano was named the UN's new top official for Guinea Bissau.

ECONOMY

Mozambique is a country with tremendous economic potential. There is no shortage of arable land, water resources, or woodland. Extensive tracts of tropical hardwoods still exist in many places and, if managed responsibly, also offer possibilities. The country has considerable mineral reserves, and modern ports linked to a rail network constructed for the transportation of goods to and from the states of southern central Africa. The sea has plentiful supplies of fish, and the islands and coastline are ideally suited to tourism. This economic potential has never been developed to the full, either in Portuguese colonial times or since.

During the civil war Mozambique's economic development was predictably sluggish, and a shortage of skilled labour and Frelimo's rigid, centrally planned economic policies didn't exactly help the situation. Since the cease-fire in 1992, however, agricultural production has been increasing gradually, and Frelimo has instigated market-orientated reforms, including privatisation in several important industrial sectors. In June 1999 the International Monetary Fund (IMF) and World Bank agreed to reduce Mozambique's public debt by two-thirds, which, along with other debt-relief programmes, augured well for the country's continued economic improvement. Then came the floods in February 2000 (see *Welcome to the 21st century* opposite), which washed away over 100,000ha of crops, killed more than 40,000 heads of cattle and caused considerable infrastructural damage. The extent to which the country's economic recovery will continue following this setback is dependent on the foreign assistance made available to repair the damage.

The country's economy is based on **agriculture**, which contributes almost 45% of the gross domestic product. The main export crops are shrimps, prawns, cotton, cashew nuts, sugar cane and copra, while the principal subsistence crops are cassava, corn and wet rice grown in the floodplains of the country's many rivers. An estimated 80% of Mozambique's population relies on subsistence agriculture and fishing to survive, although the enduring effects of the war, droughts and floods continue to hinder the country's efforts to regain self-sufficiency in food production.

The second major contributor to the economy is **industry**, primarily food processing, beverages and tobacco, textiles, edible oils, soaps and other consumer goods. During Portuguese times, Mozambique was the fourth industrial power in Africa, although, considering the relatively low rate of industrialisation of the continent, this is no great claim. In the first ten years after independence the country's industrial sector came to an almost total standstill, primarily brought about because most whites had fled the country in fear of Frelimo and the uncertainty of its policies during the transitional phase to independence. Companies were deserted by their owners, machinery often destroyed.

The exodus of the settler population meant the loss of management expertise, skilled workers and capital. Both Frelimo's new economic policy, which concentrated solely on agriculture, particularly on the creation of large-scale mechanised State collective farms, and the civil war against Renamo contributed to the downfall of the country's industries. At the end of the 1980s industry had ground to an almost complete halt. Frelimo embarked on a policy of privatisation after the end of the civil war in an attempt to kick-start the industrial sector, and during the 1990s hundreds of enterprises were bought by private investors. Past problems have doomed some of these privatisations to failure; others – particularly those backed by foreign investment – have been more successful.

Foreign investment

The Mozambican economy is dependent on foreign investment, and the government is trying hard to improve conditions and attract foreign money. In Maputo there is a Chamber of Commerce (Câmara de Comércio de Moçambique, Rue Mateus Sansão Mathemba 452, CP 1836, Maputo; tel: 258 1 491970; fax: 258 1 492211) and a government agency to encourage foreign investment (Centro de Promoção de Investimentos, Avenida 25 de Setembro 2049, CP 4635, Maputo; tel: 258 1 422456/7; fax: 258 1 422459).

Private banks, both local and foreign, are now permitted to operate in the country and private farmland that was brought under state control during the revolutionary years is now being returned to its Portuguese and South African owners. There are 'industrial free zones' in Maputo, Beira, Mocuba and Nacala intended to encourage investors to come to the country. In these zones, certain taxes and duties are waived in favour of a small royalty on sales.

Certain businesses, previously state-owned, have been offered for sale by tender. In 1994, for instance, a short list of about a dozen enterprises covered a range of industries from plastics to pasta, from transport to tea – over US$60 million of sales turnover. Arguably the largest carrots for foreign investors are the transportation 'corridors' linking the land-locked countries of southern Africa to the Mozambican ports of Maputo, Beira and Nacala (see *Corridors of power* on page 68). In January 2000, for example, a consortium led by South African, Portuguese and US companies was granted a concession to manage the port of Nacala and the Malawi–Nacala railway; and negotiations for similar concessions for the Maputo and Beira Corridors were also underway. Inevitably, fears have been expressed in the country of a sell-out of Mozambican resources to foreign countries. But without foreign investment Mozambique will have very little chance of ever getting back on its feet economically.

Without doubt, the most influential of all Mozambique's trading partners is South Africa, whose business people seem to be buying up everything – factories, mines, breweries, hotels, transport concerns and so on.

Foreign exchange

During Portuguese colonial times the main sources of foreign exchange were the export of agricultural produce; rail transport and provision of ports for South Africa, northern Rhodesia (Zambia), southern Rhodesia (Zimbabwe), Nyasaland (Malawi) and Swaziland; income from the supply of manpower to South African and Rhodesian mines and plantations; and tourism from South Africa and Rhodesia.

Except for agricultural exports, these sources of income have since more or less disappeared, although tourism is slowly beginning to re-emerge, particularly south of Beira. Rail transportation to neighbouring countries is now only possible on a small scale due to the effects of the civil war. After the government's severing of trade links with South Africa at the beginning of the 1980s, South Africa terminated the existing agreement on the employment of Mozambican workers by the South African mines. This agreement between

Portugal and South Africa, dating from 1928, had been particularly lucrative for Mozambique since it meant that 60% of the salaries were paid at a fixed gold price.

Nowadays, since the rehabilitation of the Cahora Bassa hydroelectric plant in 1997 and the beginning of construction of a new plant some 70km downstream of Cahora Bassa, Mozambique can expect to earn a considerable amount of its foreign exchange from the export of electricity to neighbouring countries.

Natural resources

During colonial times there was almost no exploitation of the country's large mineral deposits. At this time very little in the way of geological exploration had been conducted in Mozambique: it is estimated that more geological investigations were conducted in Mozambique between 1977 and 1983 than during the entire colonial period. In the course of these investigations, rich deposits of coal, salt, iron ore and phosphate, as well as gold, tantalum, chromium, copper, bauxite, nickel and many other minerals, were discovered. At present, only coal and salt are mined in significant quantities, although bauxite and, since 1994, graphite are starting to be exploited at commercially viable levels. Other resources with potential include titanium, the world's largest reserve of which was discovered in Gaza Province in 1999, and gas, found principally in Inhambane Province. Once again, the exploitation of these natural resources is dependent on large amounts of foreign investment.

FACIM Trade Fair

Mozambique's window on the world, economically speaking, is the Feria Internacional de Maputo, or FACIM. It is the most important, in fact the only real, trade fair in Mozambique and attracts considerable international participation. It is held in Maputo annually towards the end of August. For further information, contact:

FACIM/Maputo Trade Fair PO Box 1761, Av do Sarges; tel: 258 1 423713/427151; fax: 258 1 427129; web: www.facimfair.com

TOURISM

Prior to independence, Mozambique was one of the most popular tourist destinations in southern Africa. In those days, thousands of Rhodesians and South Africans flocked to the beaches and offshore islands in the south, and Gorongosa National Park was one of the region's major attractions. The bottom fell out of the industry after independence, and the outbreak of civil war hardly helped to bring the tourists back. The statistics speak for themselves: in 1972, 292,000 people visited Mozambique; by 1981, this number had fallen to just 1,000. It was never in much doubt, however, that once a semblance of stability had returned to the country, tourism would, once again, play an important economic role. And sure enough, by the end of the 1990s, tourism was the fastest growing sector of the Mozambican economy.

As an indication of the importance attached to encouraging this industry, the post of Minister for Tourism was created following the 1999 election. Then came the National Policy of Tourism, outlining the way in which the government would like to see tourism develop in the near future. The areas prioritised for immediate 'exploration' were, predictably, the beach resorts near Maputo and Beira. The formerly renowned Gorongosa National Park was also earmarked for major rehabilitation.

NATURAL HISTORY
Geography
The topography of eastern Mozambique is dominated by a low-lying coastal belt that widens from north to south to account for almost half of the country's surface area. The coastal plain rises gradually towards the west to meet a high plateau of 500 to 1,000m. Mozambique is generally characterised by relatively flat terrain, though much of the northwest is mountainous and several areas of the western plateaux are dotted with isolated granite inselbergs known in southern Africa as koppies.

In the areas bordering Malawi and Zimbabwe, there are a few mountains that rise to an altitude of above 1,800m. Mount Binga in the Chimanimani Range on the Zimbabwe border is Mozambique's highest peak at 2,436m (the *Time Out* map shows a 2,593m peak in the highlands west of the Chimoio–Tete road, but this is presumably a misplacement of Inyanga peak on the Zimbabwe side of the border). Other notable mountains include the massive inselberg of Gorongosa (1,862m) in Sofala Province; Mount Domue (2,095m) near Bragança in Tete Province; Mount Chiperone (2,052m) near Milange and Mount Namuli (2,419m) near Gurué in Zambézia; and Mount Txitonga (1,848m) and Mount Jeci (1,836m) on the Rift Valley escarpment north of Lichinga in Niassa Province.

Mozambique is traversed by several major river systems, all of which flow eastwards into the Indian Ocean. The mouths of these rivers have played a significant role in Mozambican history: many of the country's older towns are situated on large river mouths, and the rivers themselves often formed important trade routes into the interior. The Zambezi is Africa's fourth-largest river and the Limpopo its tenth-largest. The Zambezi basin, at 1,330,000km^2 is the third-largest drainage system in Africa (after the Zaire and the Nile) and the 13th-largest in the world. Of the 820km-long Mozambican section of the Zambezi, 460km are navigable.

Other main river systems are the Rovuma on the Tanzania border; the Lúrio on the border of Cabo Delgado and Nampula provinces; the Save on the border of Sofala and Inhambane Provinces; and the Lebombo in the south of the country.

Roughly 200km of the eastern shore of Africa's third-largest freshwater body, Lake Malawi, lies in Mozambique, where it is known as Lago Niassa. Further south, the lake formed by the Cahora Bassa Dam is one of the 15 largest in Africa, its exact ranking depending on the effects of rainy seasons and swamp flooding at three other lakes.

MOZAMBIQUE'S CLIMATE

		Temperature	Rainfall	Humidity
January	Maputo	21–30°C	130mm	73%
	Beira	24–32°C	270mm	75%
July	Maputo	13–25°C	15mm	73%
	Beira	16–25°C	30mm	79%

Climate

The climate in most of Mozambique is tropical and warm with a dry cooler season from April until September and a wet hot season with temperatures of around 28°C at the coast from October until April. In winter the weather at the coast is sunny and pleasantly warm (the average temperature in Maputo in June and July is 19°C). The dry and relatively cool winter months between April and September offer the most comfortable and easy travel conditions.

Temperatures and rainfall figures vary widely across the country. The hottest and most humid parts of the country are the northeastern coast and the upper Zambezi Valley, while the coolest areas are those at higher altitudes, such as the highlands of Niassa and Nampula Provinces. Most of northeastern and central Mozambique has an annual average rainfall in excess of 1,000mm, with the wettest part of the country being the highlands east of Malawi, where several areas experience almost 2,000mm of rain annually. The south is generally much drier, with coastal regions south of Beira generally receiving around 900mm of rain and some parts of the interior of Gaza Province dropping to an average of below 500mm annually. The rainy season in the south runs from October to March, while north of the Zambezi it tends to start and end a month or two later.

Vegetation

Most of Mozambique is covered in savannah, a rather loosely applied term that can be used to cover practically any wooded habitat that doesn't have a closed canopy. The main savannah type in Mozambique is brachystegia woodland (named after the most common tree), and characteristically this is much more densely wooded than are similar habitats in Zimbabwe and South Africa, and the trees are much taller. Brachystegia woodland is the dominant vegetation type throughout northern Mozambique, in the Zimbabwe and Zambia border areas, and along the coastal belt north of the Limpopo. In total, brachystegia woodland covers about 70% of the country, but it is replaced by mopane woodland in drier areas such as Tete Province south of the Zambezi and the interior of Gaza Province, and by acacia woodland in parts of the south and along the main watercourses of the north.

The beaches of the coast are typically covered in dense, scrubby thickets and palm groves, the latter particularly impressive around Inhambane and

Quelimane. The flood plains of major rivers such as the Limpopo, Zambezi and Pungue, and the area near Lake Chilwa on the Malawi border, are covered in alluvial grasslands and marshes. The largest alluvial plain in Mozambique is the Zambezi Delta, a vast marshy area of thick grassland and borassus palms that stretches for 120km along the coast and covers an area of roughly 8,000km².

Only a tiny portion of Mozambique is covered in true forest. Moist rain forests occur on the upper reaches of a few mountains, notably Mount Gorongosa in Sofala, the Chimanimani and Inyanga Highlands on the Zimbabwe border, and Mount Murrumbala, Namuli and Chiperone in western Zambézia. Dry lowland forest occurs in patches in some coastal areas, notably in northern Cabo Delgado and around Dondo near Beira, while several rivers support thin belts of riparian forest.

Wildlife conservation

Mozambique's formerly abundant wildlife has been severely depleted by years of civil war and associated poaching – the elephant population, for instance, has dropped from 65,000 to no more than 15,000. Despite the fact that some 11% percent of the country's surface area has been gazetted as protected areas, little of this land is readily accessible to visitors.

Mozambique's five **national parks** are Gorongosa to the north of the Beira Corridor; Zivane on the southern bank of the Save River; Banhine in the centre of Gaza Province; Bazaruto off the coast opposite Vilankulo and Inhassoro; and the Quirimbas Park, opened in 2002 in Cabo Delgado province (see page 230). Only Bazaruto and Quirimbas have tourist facilities. The five **game reserves** are Niassa on the Tanzanian border, Gile southeast of Nampula, Marromeu at the Zambezi Delta, Pomene on the coast between Inhambane and Vilankulo, and the Maputo Elephant Reserve on the coast to the south of the capital. Low-key and off-the-beaten-track tourism is starting to develop at the Niassa National Reserve, while there are ambitious plans (there have been for some time now) to restock and develop tourist facilities at the Maputo Elephant Reserve with a view to combining safari trips with beach holidays at the nearby resorts of Inhaca Island and Ponta do Ouro.

Without a large-scale programme of reintroducing animals, it is unlikely that any of Mozambique's reserves will replenish their wildlife stocks in the next decade to the extent that they become viable tourist attractions. In the Maputo Elephant Reserve, for instance, most large game species have been poached to extinction during the last decade, while the formerly prolific elephant population has been reduced to two breeding herds of around 30 heads each.

African buffalo

The picture at Marromeu Game Reserve is only slightly better. The elephant population of the Zambezi Delta dropped from 1,500 to 300 animals between 1988 and 1990, and the buffalo population dropped from over 55,000 in the 1970s to 4,000 in

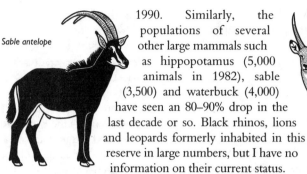

Sable antelope

Common waterbuck

1990. Similarly, the populations of several other large mammals such as hippopotamus (5,000 animals in 1982), sable (3,500) and waterbuck (4,000) have seen an 80–90% drop in the last decade or so. Black rhinos, lions and leopards formerly inhabited in this reserve in large numbers, but I have no information on their current status.

Gorongosa National Park, formerly regarded as one of southern Africa's finest reserves, is similarly depleted of animals, largely because it formed the focus of hostilities during periods of the civil war. On a more upbeat note, there are said still to be large herds of game in the far north of the country, especially away from the main roads in Cabo Delgado, Niassa and northern Tete.

Leopard

Turning conservation areas into earners of foreign exchange is a priority of the Mozambican government, and with this in mind the international game fence between the Banhine National Park in Gaza Province and the Kruger National Park in South Africa has been taken down to create one of the largest wildlife reserves in the world. Sections of the Transfrontier Wildlife Park, or the 'peace park', which will later be extended to include the Gonarezhou National Park in Zimbabwe, are to be opened in April 2002, with most of the tourist traffic entering and leaving the park via Kruger. The entrance on the Mozambican side is at the town of Massingir, which the authorities plan to develop into a regional service centre. Time will tell whether these plans become reality or suffer the same fate as several others relating to Mozambican wildlife conservation.

Birds

Mozambique's excellent birdlife has been little affected by the civil war, though, as elsewhere in Africa, forest dwelling species are increasing threatened by environmental encroachment, as are several species attached to wetland environments.

Mozambique is an important destination for southern African birders. Of the 850-odd bird species that are resident in or regular migrants to Africa south of the Zambezi, roughly 30 have been recorded only in Mozambique or else have their main concentration there. Some of the birds fitting into one of these categories are the Madagascar squacco heron, eastern saw-wing swallow, Boehm's bee-eater, palmnut vulture, silvery-cheeked hornbill, green tinker barbet, little spotted woodpecker, green-headed oriole, slender bulbul, stripe-

BIRDING IN MOZAMBIQUE
Vincent Parker

Of all the bird species resident in southern Africa, possibly the one that has been seen by fewest birdwatchers is the olive-headed weaver. A patch of tall brachystegia woodland just south of the town of Panda (60km inland of Inharrime in Inhambane Province) is the only locality in the region where the birder has a chance of seeing it. This may not be for long, as the continued presence of the species is threatened by extensive wood cutting in the area.

Other exciting birds to be seen in the brachystegia woodlands of the Mozambican interior south of the Save River include chestnut-fronted helmet shrike, racquet-tailed roller, mottled spinetail, Rudd's apalis, Livingstone's flycatcher, blue-throated sunbird, Neergard's sunbird and pink-throated twinspot.

Visitors to southern Mozambique seldom stray away from the coast. Exciting birds to be seen along the coast include crab plovers, which are seen regularly in and around the Bazaruto Archipelago in summer, and occasionally as far south as Inhaca Island near Maputo. One of the rarest birds in the world, Eleanora's falcon, has been seen at Vilankulo and Pomene. Vast flocks of migrant waders include bar-tailed godwit, terek sandpiper and great sandplover. The very rare gull-billed tern has recently been seen at freshwater lakes in three localities.

Indigenous woodland is very scarce along the coast, having been largely replaced by exotic coconut palms and cashew trees. However, the red-throated twinspot, Livingstone's loerie and brown robin can still be found near Xai-Xai.

In central Mozambique, two localities of great interest to birders are Gorongoza Mountain (near Gorongoza National Park) and the forests north of Dondo. Species that cannot be seen elsewhere in Southern Africa include green-headed oriole and Gunning's akalat.

cheeked bulbul, white-breasted alethe, Swynnerton's robin, Gunning's robin, Chirinda apalis, black-headed apalis, moustached warbler, Robert's prinia, mashona hylotia, yellow-breasted hylotia, Vanga flycatcher, Woodward's batis, Mozambique batis, Livingstone's flycatcher, marsh tchagra, chestnut-fronted helmetshrike, red-headed quelea, cardinal quelea, olive-headed weaver, Nyasa seedcracker, East African swee and lemon-breasted canary.

Also of interest to southern African birders are the few dozen species present in northern Mozambique that aren't on the southern Africa checklist or which have only been recorded in southern Africa as vagrants – see the box on *Birding in Mozambique* for more details.

PEOPLE AND SOCIETY

Over 98% of the people in Mozambique are African, which I suppose stands to reason. The remainder is made up of Europeans (mainly Portuguese),

Northern Mozambique is particularly alluring to birders, since many areas have yet to be thoroughly explored and birdwatchers are likely to find species that are new to the Mozambique list – and possibly even new to science! Birders in northern Mozambique will certainly encounter species that are not included in southern African field guides, so they will need to refer to a second field guide (see *Appendix 2, Further Reading*).

Some of the birds that are known to occur in northern Mozambique but not in southern Africa are pale-billed hornbill; brown-breasted barbet; mountain, little, grey-olive, Fischer's and Canabis' greenbuls; Thyolo alethe; central bearded scrub robin; evergreen and red-capped forest warblers; Kretchmar's longbill; white-winged and long-billed apalises; white-tailed blue flycatcher, mountain babbler, red-and-blue and eastern double-collared sunbirds; Bertram's weaver; Zanzibar red bishop; African citril and stripe-breasted canary.

Vincent Parker is in charge of the Mozambique Atlas Bird Project, the first attempt to atlas the avifauna of this relatively unexplored country. All birders visiting Mozambique are invited to contribute their observations to the project. Contributors should keep a list of all species encountered at each locality they visit. Ideally, each locality should correspond with a Quarter Degree Square (15 minutes longitude by 15 minutes latitude). Contributors who are unfamiliar with a Quarter Degree Square should provide the latitude and longitude of each locality and include any species encountered within 5km of the central locality. Further information and field cards can be obtained from Vincent Parker of the Mozambique Bird Atlas Project at FNP, PO Box 4203, Maputo; fax: 42 2434; email: vinparker@yahoo.com; web: www.uct.ac.za/depts/stats/adu; or c/o Endangered Wildlife Trust, Private Bag XII, Parkview 2122, South Africa; tel: (+2711) 486 1102.

Indians, East Asians and *mestiços* (people of mixed African–European ancestry). As in most of Africa, the tribes living in Mozambique share cultural and linguistic similarities with their counterparts in neighbouring states.

The basic tribal pattern in Mozambique is a result of pre-19th-century migrations from the north and west, and the fleeing of people in the early 19th century from the violent Zulu kingdom in South Africa. This has left a north–south split, with the Zambezi River as the dividing line. The tribes north of the Zambezi are predominantly agriculturists and have matrilineal societies. The two largest tribes, the Makua and the Lomwe, which are concentrated in Zambézia, Nampula, Niassa and Cabo Delgado provinces, together make up about 35% of the total Mozambican population. Another northern tribe worth knowing is the Makonde, famous for its art and its wooden statues and masks, which lives on both the Mozambican and Tanzanian sides of the Rovuma River. The tribes south of the Zambezi River

BOOK CITY LIBRARY

are mainly cattle rearing and have patrilineal societies. The most important is the Thonga, the country's second-largest ethnic group, which is concentrated in the area south of the Save River and makes up around 23% of the population. The majority of Africans in Maputo are Thonga. Meanwhile, most of Sofala and Manica Provinces are inhabited by Shona, a tribe whose numbers have grown due to migrations into Mozambique of Shona from Zimbabwe and South Africa. In addition to the tribal differences north and south of the Zambezi River, a third distinct region is formed by the Zambezi Valley itself, which has historically been influenced by the Portuguese and Arabs who used the river to access the interior.

Language

Portuguese is the official language of Mozambique, but it is generally only spoken by the 25% of the population who have been to school. This creates serious problems: the economic, business and legal language is Portuguese; tuition in high schools, colleges and universities is exclusively in Portuguese and thus debars the many who have had no chance to learn it at primary education stages; many of the younger people grew up in refugee camps and have had little formal education, let alone in what is essentially a foreign tongue, and three-quarters of the people are illiterate, despite considerable efforts (by themselves and by the government). The problems with education, both in languages and in general, have become so acute that some schools have started to work a shift system: children of one age group go to school every day for a few hours in the morning, children of another in the afternoon.

All of Mozambique's indigenous languages belong to the Bantu family. The root Bantu language is thought to have spread through eastern and southern Africa during the first half of the first millennium AD, since when it has diversified into many linguistic subfamilies and several hundred distinct languages and closely related dialects. Roughly 60 distinct languages and dialects are spoken in Mozambique. The various dialects of Makua-Lomwe are spoken only north of the Zambezi, but they nevertheless account for the home language of around 40% of the total population of Mozambique. In the south, the majority of people speak dialects of Tsonga, a language that is also spoken in South Africa. Various Tonga and Shona dialects are spoken in central Mozambique.

In northern coastal regions, some people speak KiSwahili, a simplified Bantu language with some Arabic influences that became the *lingua franca* of coastal trading centres between Mogadishu and Sofala in medieval times.

Visitors who are unfamiliar with Portuguese and Bantu languages will find that most Mozambicans are extremely helpful and will do what they can to overcome your language barrier. The mixing of the people during the war has made them adept at getting along and making themselves understood in a variety of communication forms: a bit of gesturing and drawing in the dirt with a stick can overcome many barriers. Often, people will simply lead you to where you want to go. For practical information on speaking Portuguese, see *Appendix 1*, page 245.

Concern has recently been expressed in Lisbon that the end of apartheid and the democratisation of South Africa will lead to the anglicisation of Mozambique. Since Portuguese is not an indigenous language and all of Mozambique's neighbours and SADCC partners (Angola excepted) use English as an official language, as do most donor countries, there would be a certain logic to displacing Portuguese with English as the main language of education and government. That said, I would place as high a priority on having KiSwahili (one of the simplest and most widely spoken Bantu languages) taught in schools throughout southern and eastern Africa, in order to help overcome the vast linguistic barriers to inter-regional trade and communication.

Religion
Roughly 50% of Mozambicans follow traditional African religions. These beliefs, along with traditional hierarchies and medicines, were suppressed during the communist era, being seen as backward and unscientific, but are now enjoying something of a resurgence, encouraged by the resumption of authority of many local chiefs in the absence of any other effective 'management'. Traditional healers are also enjoying a comeback as part of this cultural renaissance.

There are large Christian and Muslim minorities in Mozambique (25–30% and 20–25% respectively). Christianity is more common in urban areas while the Muslim faith is predominantly confined to the north. This has led to the incorporation of one or more elements of Christianity in most traditional beliefs. As in other African countries, the reverse is also true – there are often traditional elements in the way that Christianity is applied.

FOOD AND DRINK
Depending on where you are in Mozambique, the choice of food will often boil down to seafood or chicken, both accompanied by either rice (*arroz*) or chips (*batata fritas*). Along the coast the meals of choice are, naturally, seafood-based. Choose from a variety of locally caught fish (*peixe*), calamari (*lulas*), crab (*caranguejo*) and some of the finest lobster (*lagosta*) and prawns (*camarão*) in the world. Inland, chicken (*galinha* or *frango*) and, particularly in towns near the Zimbabwe border, beef (*bife* or *carne*) are more common. Whatever the main ingredient of your meal, the likelihood is that it will be cooked using a spicy red-pepper sauce called *piri-piri*. If chicken is cooked in this way, it might be described as *frango a calria*: 'chicken, the African way'. Other traditional Mozambican dishes to look out for, although by no means at every restaurant you visit, include *matapa*, a clam and peanut stew made with pumpkin leaves, *mu-kwane*, a coastal dish made from coconut mixed with the leaves of the cassava plant, and *ncima* or *posho*, a maize porridge popular in the interior. The Portuguese influence has also made its mark on Mozambican cuisine, and in the more upscale restaurants of major towns such as Maputo and Beira you will find dishes made with wines and Port. Snacks include sandwiches (*petiscoes*) – typically egg (*ovo*), cheese (*queijo*) and spicy sausage (*chouriço*) – steak rolls (*prego no pao*) and hamburgers (*amburque*).

The usual brand-name soft drinks are widely available in the whole of Mozambique, while south of the Zambezi River locally produced alternatives are easy to find. If the fizzy stuff doesn't appeal, you can buy imported South African fruit juice at supermarkets in large towns throughout the country. There are tea plantations in Zambézia Province, although most of the tea that you'll drink will probably be of the imported variety. Bottled water is common, but make sure that the seals on the bottles have not been broken. The most widespread alcoholic drink is beer. The local brands are 2M (pronounced *dozyem*), which tastes like a watered-down, Continental-style dark larger, and Manica, a slightly stronger and sweeter tasting alternative to 2M, while imported South African beers such as Castle, Lion and Carling Black Label can also be found. Portuguese wines, Port and a variety of spirits are sold at the larger supermarkets and in most tourist-class hotels and bars.

WildLife Adventures is a leading specialist tour operator to Mozambique.

Your choice of operator is one of the most important decisions when planning your holiday to Mozambique. WildLife Adventures has over 10 years' experience operating and designing travel in Africa, and the Indian Ocean Islands and has specialized in Mozambique since 1996.

- WildLife Adventures owns and operates Ibo Island Lodge on historic Ibo in the breathtaking Quirimbas Archipelago. Contact us for bookings and specials combining radical Ibo Island

- Competitive rates and excellent options for all boutique hotels, luxury lodges, islands, resort hotels, safari lodges, tented camps, guesthouses, eco and community lodges and adventure camps throughout Mozambique

- Tailor-made, personalized holidays combine Mozambique with South Africa, Botswana, Zambia, Malawi, Tanzania, Kenya and Zanzibar Island for the ultimate beach and bush (safari) experience

- Luxury yacht charters, game and fly fishing, scuba diving, live-aboards, traditional sailing safaris, and kayak safaris throughout Mozambique

- Honeymoons, individuals, families, special interest group safaris, fishing or diving groups, expeditions, cultural and heritage, all planned with meticulous attention and to suit all budgets and requirements.

WildLife Adventures Central Reservations:
PO Box 30661, Tokai, 7966.
25 Bell Crescent, Westlake Business Park. Cape Town, South Africa
Tel: ++ (27 21) 702 0643 Fax: ++ (27 21) 702 0644
Email: office@wildlifeadventures.co.za

www.wildlifeadventures.co.za

Planning and Preparation

TOURIST INFORMATION

Helpful websites giving practical and up-to-date information are www.mocambiqueturismo.co.mz and www.futur.org.mz. The official (and efficient) Mozambique National Tourist Company (MNTC) is based in Johannesburg, South Africa: their office is in Noswal Hall on the corner of Bertha and Stiemens Streets in Braamfontein, and the postal address is PO Box 31991 Braamfontein 2017; tel: (011) 339 7275, 339 4900, 339 7281; fax (011) 339 7295; email moz-tour@netactive.co.za. They can make bookings for most upmarket hotels and beach resorts within the country, and will organise visas and coach bookings between Johannesburg and Maputo. Tourists coming from Portugal might like to contact the Agéncia de Informação de Mozambique at Avenida Infante Santo 23, 4xP-1300, Lisbon.

HIGHLIGHTS OF MOZAMBIQUE

It must be said that most people who visit Mozambique, whether they're from South Africa, Zimbabwe or farther afield, do so for the country's coastal attractions. Indeed, there are few other countries in the world with such an extensive, beautiful and largely undeveloped coastline. This means that travellers will find truly **deserted beaches**, many of which stretch for kilometres on end, even at the more built-up resorts. Once you have made the effort to get to these beaches, the opportunities for **diving** and **fishing** are among the best in southern Africa. Once again, the infrastructure underpinning these activities is still in its infancy, which means that dive sites are uncrowded and the fish varied and plentiful. Another attraction of the southern Mozambican coastline is the very high probability of seeing **humpback whales** between about September and the middle of November as they head north with their newly born calves.

Nature lovers, especially birdwatchers, will find plenty to see on dry land provided that they are prepared to make the effort to get to the country's remote and relatively inaccessible **national parks** and **reserves**. The reward once they have arrived is an animal population which, although less numerous than the well-stocked parks in neighbouring countries, is 100% wild. In Mozambique, when you see a lion in Niassa Province, for example, the likelihood is that it will not have seen another human being in its life before you. Electrifying for some, terrifying for others!

And then there are the towns. The sleepy and historic **Inhambane** would be a highlight on any African itinerary, and should not be missed by travellers to Mozambique. **Ilha do Mozambique** and **Ibo Island** are equally historic and equally compelling, although it will take slightly more effort to get to them. **Maputo**, meanwhile, is as clean and safe a city as you'll find in Africa; and with an increasing number of quality hotels, restaurants and other facilities, it's the perfect base for a trip around Mozambique.

However, the main highlight of a trip to Mozambique is the **people**. Generally unassuming, helpful, funny and honest, the Mozambicans are what really makes Mozambique one of the greatest travel destinations in Africa.

WHEN TO VISIT

The coastal regions of Mozambique are best visited in the dry winter months of May through to October, when daytime temperatures are generally around 20–25°C. There is no major obstacle to visiting Mozambique during the summer months of November to April, but you'll find that climatic conditions are oppressively hot and humid at this time of year, especially along the north coast. Because most of the country's rain falls during the summer months, there is also an increased risk of contracting malaria and of dirt roads being washed out.

Unless you are a South African with children at school, it is emphatically worth avoiding the south coast of Mozambique during South African school holidays, when campsites as far north as Vilankulo tend to be very crowded and hotels are often fully booked. The exact dates of South African school holidays vary slightly on a provincial basis, but the main ones to avoid are those for Gauteng (the province that includes Johannesburg, South Africa's most populous city and only a day's drive from Maputo). To give a rough idea of the periods to avoid, there are four annual school holidays in Gauteng: a three-week holiday that starts in the last week of March and ends in the middle of April, a month-long holiday running from late June to late July, a two-week holiday starting in late September, and a six-week holiday from early December to mid-January. Any South African embassy will be able to supply the exact dates of school holidays for any given year. If you do visit southern Mozambique during school holidays, then you should make reservations for all the hotels and campsites at which you plan to stay.

School holidays in landlocked Zimbabwe see a substantial influx of Zimbabwean tourists into southern Mozambique, so that most resorts between Beira and Xai-Xai are more crowded than usual. Provided that you have a tent, you shouldn't get stuck during these periods.

Few South Africans or Zimbabweans currently venture north of the Beira Corridor (the road and railway line linking Beira to the Zimbabwe border town of Mutare), so school holidays have no notable effect on tourist patterns in northern Mozambique.

RED TAPE

A valid passport is required to enter Mozambique. The date of expiry should be at least six months after you intend to end your travels; if it is likely to expire before that, get a new passport.

Visas

Visas are required by all visitors. They must be bought in advance at a Mozambican embassy, high commission or through the National Tourist Company in Johannesburg. You do occasionally hear of people managing to buy a visa at an overland border, but this is not normal procedure and the chances are that you'll simply be refused entry if you arrive at a border or at the airport without a visa. Visa fees will depend on where you are applying. In London, for example, you'll pay more than in Paris, where you'll pay more than in Washington. In general, however, prices range from about US$20–50 for a single-entry visa and US$40–100 for a multiple-entry visa. These prices can drop considerably if you buy your visa from an embassy or consulate in a neighbouring country. At the time of writing, for instance, the Mozambican consulate in Nelspruit, South Africa, was only charging US$10 for a single-entry visa – which, moreover, was issued in one day. Harare in Zimbabwe is apparently another cheap place in the region to obtain a Mozambican visa. As with the fee, the time it takes to issue the visa will vary from one embassy to another. Budget on at least a week, and don't forget to allow more time if you are applying by post. Express services are often available, but they cost considerably more than the basic fee. To apply for a visa, you'll need a passport with a minimum of six months' validity, one or two photographs and, at least at embassies in countries that do not share a land border with Mozambique, a copy of your airline ticket. You must enter the country within one month (sometimes two) of the date your visa is issued. After initial entry, visas will generally be valid for 30 days (although, once again, some embassies will give you twice as long), but can be extended to a maximum of 90 days at any immigration office (there is one in each of the provincial capitals). Note that if, in addition to other travels in Mozambique, you plan on using the Tete Corridor to get between Zimbabwe and Malawi, then you should apply for a multiple-entry visa.

Embassies and high commissions abroad

There are Mozambican high commissions or embassies in the following countries:

Belgium Blvd Saint Michel 97, B-1040 Brussels; tel: (2) 7362564/7360096/7322632; telex: 65478 EMOBRU B; email: embamoc.bru@euvronet.be

France 82 Rue Laugier, F-75017 Paris; tel: (1) 47649132; fax: (1) 42673828; telex: 641527 EMBMOXBF; email: embamocparis@compuserve.com

Germany Adenauerallee 46, D 53113 Bonn; tel: (228) 262993; fax: (228) 213920; telex: 2283631 EMBAMOC; or Auaenstelle Berlin, Clara-Zetkin-Str 97/IV, D 10117 Berlin; tel: (030) 2291751/2291413; telex: 115074 EUMM DD; email: emoza@aol.com

Italy Via Filippo Corridoni 14, Rome; tel: (6) 37514675; email: embmozambiqueitalia@excalhq.it

Malawi Commercial Bank Building, PO Box 30579, Lilongwe 3; tel: (265) 784100/784696; telex: 4793 EMBMOQ MI; email: mozambique@malawi.net. Also on Kamuzu Highway, Blantyre (Limbe). (People requiring transit visas should get to the consulate before 08.30 so that their permit is ready to collect later on the same day. Other visas take three or more working days to issue.)

Portugal 7 Av Berna, P-1000 Lisbon; tel: (1) 7961672; telex: 13641 EMBAMOC P

Russia Ul Gilyarovskovo 20, Moscow; tel: (095) 2844007/2843654/2844319; telex: 413369 EMMOC SU

Swaziland Princess Drive Rd, PO Box 1212, Mbabane; tel: (268) 43700; telex: 2248 WD

Sweden Sturegatan 46, PO Box 5801, 10248 Stockholm; tel: (8) 6660350

Tanzania PO Box 15274, 25 Garden Av, Dar-Es-Salaam; tel: (51) 116502; telex: 41214 EMBAMOC

UK 21 Fitzroy Square, London W1P 5HJ; tel: (020) 7383 3800; fax: (020) 7383 3801; email: mozalon@compuserve.com

USA 1990 M St, NW #570, Washington 20036-3404; tel: (202) 2937146/8; fax: (202) 8350245; telex: 248530 AMOC UR; email: embamoc@aol.com; web: www.embamoc-usa.org

Zambia PO Box 34877, 9592 Kacha Rd, Northhead, Lusaka; tel: (1) 220333; telex: 42690/45900 EMBAMOC ZA; email: mozhclsk@zamnet.zm

Zimbabwe PO Box 4608, 152 Herbert Chitepo Av, Harare; tel: (4) 790837/9, 793653/7; telex: 4466; email: embamoc@utande.co.zw

A list of foreign embassies in Mozambique itself is given in the *Maputo* chapter.

Consulates in South Africa

Cape Town 45 Castle St, 7th floor; tel: (021) 262944/5; fax: (021) 262946

Durban 320 West St, 5th floor; tel: (031) 304 0222; fax: (031) 304 0774

Johannesburg 252 Jeppe St, Cape York Building, 7th floor; tel: (011) 336 1819/22/24; fax: (011) 336 9921

Nelspruit 43 Brown St; tel: (013) 752 7396; fax: (013) 753 2088

Pretoria (013) 343 7840/0957

Bringing a vehicle to Mozambique

The amount of paperwork involved in bringing a vehicle into Mozambique isn't overwhelmingly great, but you will have problems if your papers aren't in order, particularly if you're entering the country from South Africa. To take a vehicle out of South Africa, you must have the original registration papers to show at the customs office, and a letter of authorisation if the vehicle is not being driven by the registered owner.

At the Mozambican customs, you will need to show the temporary export permit given to you by South African customs, and to pay for third-party insurance (*seguros*). Expect to pay the equivalent of about US$20 for the temporary export permit and insurance, plus a tax of around US$10 per person. The procedure is much the same at the Zimbabwe and Malawi border crossings.

Once you are through the two customs posts, you will have accumulated a ream of papers (temporary import permit, insurance chit, etc), which you should retain at all times, since you'll be asked to show them at every roadblock, along with a valid driver's licence (an international driver's licence is a good idea, since most officials cannot read English).

Readers who are driving into Mozambique should carry the obvious spares (fan-belt, second spare tyre and rim). They should also carry two hazard triangles (the absence of one of these is a favoured pretext for extracting bribes from drivers) and ensure that seatbelts on the driver's and passengers' seats are working properly (see page 63 for further advice).

MONEY MATTERS
Organising your finances
However safe they may be, unfortunately travellers' cheques are currently (mid 2005) very hard to cash and can incur high charges. Normally the US dollar and the rand are widely accepted, but some recent visitors had trouble using anything but meticais in rural areas, so stock up with these when you're near a bank. Other main international currencies should be easy to exchange in larger towns but less so if you're off the beaten track. We recommend that you get the latest news on this from your tour operator or embassy before travelling. Also see pages 67–8.

Credit cards are gaining ground, and are accepted in the larger hotels and main centres. If you pre-book your accommodation, check this at the same time. Some lodges will charge substantial levies for payments by credit cards – sometimes 5%. Also you can draw cash against credit cards in some banks in Maputo. The most popular is Visa. Some main banks also have ATMs. It's good to bring a small amount of cash with you (say around US$200), preferably in small denominations, in case you need to change it in a hotel or on the street if you arrive when banks are closed. Be very cautious about pavement money-changers and try to avoid them unless you're streetwise; not all are dishonest, but... some are. If you're changing or drawing money in a bank, you're likely to get the best rate for cash.

Western Union is now active in Mozambique, with agencies in all main towns and some minor ones, so you can have cash sent quickly (although not cheaply) from home if you run out. Normally it's a trouble-free process, although there could be local quirks. A useful website for checking the value of the metical against your own currency is www.xe.com; unlike some sites it covers *all* world currencies.

At present the most sensible combination to take with you seems to be a mix of credit cards (preferably Visa) and cash (preferably US$ or rand). But check before travelling. And be cautious when you use cash machines or emerge from banks, because the risk of petty theft (and pickpockets) does exist.

Carrying money and valuables
It is advisable to carry all your hard currency as well as your passport and other important documentation in a money belt. The ideal money belt for Africa is one that can be hidden beneath your clothing. Externally worn money belts may be fashionable, but wearing one in Africa is as good as

telling thieves that all your valuables are there for the taking. Use a money belt made of cotton or another natural fabric; bear in mind that such fabrics tend to soak up a lot of sweat, so you will need to wrap plastic around everything inside the money belt.

Budgeting

Although Mozambique is not an expensive country by Western standards, visitors should accept that their day to day expenses will be considerably higher than they would be in most other countries in East or southern Africa. By any standards, Mozambique offers poor value for money – what might be described as African standards at Western prices. The cheap-and-cheerful, two-dollar-a-night African-style lodges that exist in neighbouring countries (especially Malawi) are few and far between in Mozambique. It is more likely that you'll fork out up to US$15 for a basic room with communal bucket showers and no lightbulb. The same goes for eating out: you'll regularly pay the sort of sum that would buy a good steak or two large pizzas in a South African restaurant for a plate of chicken or fish and chips that could most kindly be described as ordinary.

With Mozambique, as elsewhere, any budget will depend greatly on how and where you travel, but the following guidelines might be useful to people trying to keep costs to a minimum. If you travel widely in Mozambique, it will be difficult to keep your basic travel expenses (food, transport, accommodation and drink) to much below US$20 per day for one person or US$30 per day for a couple. Your main expense will probably be accommodation: in many towns, you'll be lucky to get away with less than US$15 for a double room, and there are plenty of places where even camping costs around US$5 per person. A meal in a restaurant will typically cost between US$4 and US$6 per head, though you can save considerably by putting together your own food or eating at market stalls. Transport costs will probably work out at around US$3–4 daily, assuming that you're on the move every other day or thereabouts. Drinks are reasonably priced, with a bottle of soda rarely costing more than 50 cents and a bottle of beer US$1.

This said, budget travellers can travel more cheaply if they carry a tent, are selective about where they visit, and stay put in cheaper places for a few days. In the south, Vilankulo and Tofo Beach have good backpacker facilities that make them much cheaper than the other beach resorts – a full week at Vilankulo needn't work out at more than around US$50 per person.

See page 68 for further currency information.

WHAT TO TAKE
Luggage

If you intend to use public transport or to hike, you will want to carry your luggage on your back. There are three ways of doing this: with a purpose-made backpack, with a suitcase that converts to a rucksack, or with a large daypack.

The choice between a convertible suitcase or a purpose-built backpack rests mainly on your style of travel. If you intend to do a lot of hiking, you're definitely best off with a proper backpack. If, on the other hand, you'll be doing things where it might be a good idea to shake off the sometimes negative image attached to backpackers, there are obvious advantages in being able to convert your backpack to a conventional suitcase. Otherwise, it doesn't really matter much which you use.

After having undertaken several backpacking trips in Africa, my own preference is for a large daypack. The advantages of keeping your luggage as light and compact as possible are manifold. For starters, you can rest it on your lap on buses, thus avoiding complications such as extra charges for luggage, arguments about where your bag should be stored, and the slight but real risk of theft if your luggage ends up on the roof. A compact bag also makes for greater mobility, whether you're hiking or looking for a hotel in town.

The sacrifice you need to make in order to use a daypack is not to carry camping equipment and a sleeping bag. This will affect your budget, as camping can save you a fair amount of money over an extended stay in Mozambique, but there are few instances where you really *need* camping equipment. For non-camping purposes, a light sheet sleeping bag is almost as useful as the real thing (a sheet sleeping bag still performs the important role of enclosing and insulating your body; it is only in really cold conditions that it will fail you – and then you can cover up with extra clothing). During my last few African trips, I've managed to fit everything I truly need as well as a few luxuries in a 35cl daypack weighing around 8kg. And, having made the conversion from a bulkier, heavier rucksack, I can highly recommend it to other travellers.

Clothing

If you're carrying your luggage on your back, you'll want to restrict your clothes to the minimum. In my opinion, this is one or two pairs of trousers and/or skirts, and one pair of shorts; three shirts or T-shirts; at least one sweater (or similar) depending on when you are visiting the country and where you intend to go; enough socks and underwear to last five to seven days; and one or two pairs of shoes.

Trousers Jeans are less than ideal for African travel. They are bulky and heavy to carry, hot to wear, and they take ages to dry. Far better to bring light cotton trousers. If you intend spending a while in montane regions, instead of bringing a second pair of trousers, you might prefer to carry tracksuit bottoms. These can serve as thermal underwear and as extra cover on chilly nights, and they can also be worn over shorts on chilly mornings.

Skirts Like trousers, these are best made of a light natural fabric such as cotton. For reasons of protocol, it is advisable to wear skirts that go below the knee: short skirts will cause needless offence to many Mozambicans (especially Muslims) and, whether you like it or not, they may be perceived as provocative in some quarters.

Shirts T-shirts are a better idea than button-up shirts because they are lighter and less bulky. That said, I've found that the top pocket of a shirt (particularly if the pocket buttons up) is a good place to carry my spending money in markets and bus stations, as it's easier to keep an eye on than trousers pockets. A long-sleeved shirt will help fend off mosquitoes in the evenings.

Sweaters Mozambique is generally warm at night, though at higher altitudes it can cool down in the evening. For general purposes, one warm sweater or sweatshirt should be adequate. In summer, a light waterproof jacket will be useful .

Socks and underwear These *must* be made from natural fabrics, and bear in mind that re-using them when sweaty will encourage fungal infections such as athlete's foot, as well as prickly heat in the groin region. Socks and underpants are light and compact enough for it to be worth bringing a week's supply.

Shoes Unless you're serious about off-road hiking, bulky hiking boot are probably over the top in Mozambique. They're also very heavy, whether they are on your feet or in your pack. A good pair of walking shoes, preferably made of leather and with some ankle support, is a good compromise. It's also useful to carry sandals, thongs or other light, waterproof shoes.

Camping equipment
There is a strong case for carrying a tent to Mozambique, particularly if you are on a tight budget or have private transport. Campsites exist in most of Mozambique's more popular resorts. Travellers who intend doing a fair bit of off-the-beaten-track hiking or driving will find a tent a useful fallback where no other accommodation exists.

Backpackers who decide to carry camping equipment should look for the lightest available gear. It is now possible to buy a lightweight tent weighing little more than 2kg, but make sure that the one you buy is reasonably mosquito proof. Usable sleeping bags weighing even less than 2kg can be bought, but, especially as many lightweight sleeping bags are not particularly warm, my own preference is for a sheet sleeping bag, supplemented by wearing heavy clothes in cold weather. Also essential is a roll-mat, which will serve both as insulation and padding.

Cooking utensils
In Mozambique, there is no real need for backpackers to carry a stove, since firewood is available at most campsites where meals cannot be bought. If you do carry a stove, it's worth knowing that Camping Gaz cylinders are not readily available, so being a good supply of spare canisters. If you are camping in the rainy season, a box of firelighter blocks will help get a fire going in the most unpromising conditions. It would also be advisable to carry a pot, plate, cup and cutlery – lightweight cooking utensils are available at most camping shops in Western countries.

People who are driving into Mozambique are obviously in a position to carry far more equipment than people using public transport. Recommended cooking accessories are a grid and tongs for barbecues, a gas cooker and an adequate supply of canisters, a water container and pots, foil for baking potatoes, and a selection of spices. A less obvious luxury that you'll probably be glad of is a device for squeezing citrus fruit; oranges and tangerines are available cheaply everywhere in Mozambique and fresh fruit juice is a welcome respite from fizzy drinks. If you don't like instant coffee, take some device for making fresh coffee (detaching the filter from a percolator is good enough) as well as a stock of ground coffee.

Photography

For photographs of people and scenery, an ordinary 50mm lens or – better for scenic shots – 28–70mm zoom should be adequate. If you expect to take photographs of animals or birds, a 70–300mm or similar zoom will be more appropriate. Low-speed 50 or 100 ASA films are ideal for most circumstances. You can buy 400 ASA print film in most large towns. If you want to use colour print film of other speeds, or any slide film or black-and-white print film, then bring all that you need with you.

I'm generally uncomfortable about taking photographs of people when I travel. Partly, this is because I've travelled so much in Muslim parts of Africa, and partly because I think flashing cameras in any social situation is rude and obtrusive. Another factor is that I get so fed up with being asked to take people's photos, I actually can't be bothered to carry a camera most of the time. However, nothing in our experience suggested that there is any cause to be edgy about taking photographs of people in Mozambique – on the contrary, the majority of Mozambicans go completely crazy in the nicest possible way when there's a camera around, and a flash can cause something close to mass hysteria. Nevertheless, some people definitely don't like to be photographed, and it would be very rude not to ask permission before you start snapping away, particularly in Muslim areas.

In markets and similar places, you may well find that people are initially reluctant to let you photograph them, but that as soon as one person agrees to be photographed then everybody else wants a bit of the action. Couples travelling together should take note that Mozambican women are less likely to object to being photographed by another woman than by a man. See page 46 for more about cultural sensitivity when travelling in Mozambique.

Other useful items

Binoculars are essential for getting a good look at animals, especially birds. Compact binoculars have a crisper image than the traditional variety, they are much more backpack-friendly, and these days you can find adequate brands that are not significantly more expensive than traditional binoculars. The one drawback of compact binoculars is their restricted field of vision, which can make it difficult to pick up birds in thick bush. For most purposes, 7x35 traditional binoculars or 7x21 compact binoculars are fine, but birdwatchers will find a 10x magnification more useful.

If you are thinking of doing much snorkelling in Mozambique, it is certainly worth bringing your own equipment – not only because it will save

PHOTOGRAPHIC TIPS

Ariadne Van Zandbergen

Equipment

Although with some thought and an eye for composition
you can make nice photos with a 'point-and-shoot' camera, you need an SLR
camera with one or more lenses if you are at all serious about photography.
If you carry only one lens in Mozambique, a 28—70mm or similar zoom
should be ideal. For a second lens, a 80—200mm or 70–300mm or similar
will be excellent for candid shots and for varying your composition.

Film

Print film is the preference of most casual photographers, slide film of
professionals and some dedicated amateurs. Slide film is more expensive than
print film, but this is broadly compensated for by cheaper development costs.
Most photographers working outdoors in Africa favour Fujichrome slide film,
in particular Sensia 100, Provia 100 (the professional equivalent to Sensia) or
Velvia 50. Slow films (ie: those with a low ASA/ISO rating) produce less grainy
and sharper images than fast films, but can be tricky without a tripod in low
light. Velvia 50 is extremely fine-grained and shows stunning colour saturation;
it is the film I normally use in soft, even light or overcast weather. Sensia or
Provia may be preferable in low light, since 100 ASA allows you to work at a
faster shutter speed than 50 ASA. Because 100 ASA is more tolerant of
contrast, it is also preferable in harsh light. It is worthwhile bringing a few fast
films like Fuji's Provia 400 ASA to be prepared for very low light situations.

For print photography, a combination of 100 or 200 ASA film should be
ideal. For the best results it is advisable to stick to recognised brands.
Fujicolor produces excellent print films, with the Superia 100 and 200
recommended.

Some basics

The automatic programmes provided with many cameras are limited in the
sense that the camera cannot think, but only make calculations. A better
investment than any amount of electronic wizardry would be to read a
photographic manual for beginners and get to grips with such basics as the
relationship between aperture and shutter speed.

Beginners should also note that a low shutter speed can result in camera
shake and therefore a blurred image. For hand-held photographs of static
subjects using a low magnification lens (eg: 28–70), select a shutter speed
of at least 1/60th of a second. For lenses of higher magnification, the rule of
thumb is that the shutter speed should be at least the inverse of the
magnification (for instance, a speed of 1/300 or faster on a 300
magnification lens). You can use lower shutter speeds with a tripod.

Most modern cameras include a built-in light meter, and give users the
choice of three types of metering: matrix, centre-weighted or spot metering.

You will need to understand how these different systems work to make proper use of them. Built-in light meters are reliable in most circumstances, but in uneven light, or where there is a lot of sky, you may want to take your metering selectively, for instance by taking a spot reading on the main subject. The meter will tend to under- or overexpose when pointed at an almost white or black subject. This can be countered by taking a reading against an 18% grey card, or a substitute such as grass or light-grey rocks — basically anything that isn't almost black, almost white or highly reflective.

Dust and heat

Dust and heat are often a problem in Africa. Keep your equipment in a sealed bag, stow films in an airtight container (such as a small cooler bag), leave used films in your hotel room, and avoid changing film in dusty conditions. On rough roads, I always carry my camera equipment on my lap to protect against vibration and bumps. Never stow camera equipment or film in a car boot (it will bake), or let it stand in direct sunlight.

Light

The light in Africa is much harsher than in Europe or North America, for which reason the most striking outdoor photographs are often taken during the hour or two of 'golden light' after dawn and before sunset. Shooting in low light may enforce the use of very low shutter speeds, in which case a tripod (ideally) or monopod (lighter) will be required to avoid camera shake. Be alert to the long shadows cast by a low sun; these show up more on photographs than to the naked eye.

With careful handling, side lighting and backlighting can produce stunning effects, especially in soft light and at sunrise or sunset. Generally, however, it is best to shoot with the sun behind you. Because of this, most buildings and landscapes are essentially a 'morning shot' or 'afternoon shot', depending on the direction in which they face. When you spend a couple of nights in one place, you'll improve your results by planning the best time to take pictures of static subjects (a compass can come in handy).

When photographing people or animals in the harsh midday sun, images taken in light but even shade are likely to look nicer than those taken in direct sunlight or patchy shade, since the latter conditions create too much contrast. Fill-in flash is almost essential if you want to capture facial detail of dark-skinned people in harsh or contrasting light.

Protocol

Except in general street or market scenes, it is unacceptable to photograph people without permission. Expect some people to refuse or to ask for a donation. Even the most willing subject will often pose stiffly when a camera is pointed at them; relax them by making a joke, and take a few shots in quick succession to improve the odds of capturing a natural pose.

you money in the long run, but also because snorkelling equipment is only available for hire at a handful of resorts.

If you stay in local hotels, it is best to carry your own padlock – many places don't supply them. You should also carry a towel, soap, shampoo, and any other toiletries you need. Washing powder to wash your clothes as you dirty them is also worth considering. Adopting a 'wash-and-wear' approach allows you to economise on the number of clothes you pack in the first place, and the more powder you use, the lighter your bag becomes.

People who wear contact lenses should be aware that the various fluids are not readily available in Mozambique. Bring enough to last the whole trip. Many people find the intense sun and dry climate in some African countries irritates their eyes, though this might not apply so much to Mozambique, which is generally moist and humid. Nevertheless, you could also think about reverting to glasses for the duration of your trip, if only because carrying contact lens fluids will add considerable weight and bulk to your luggage. Alternatively, you could bring enough one-day contact lenses (which you throw away on a daily basis) for the duration of your travels. This will cut out the need for cleaning fluids, but could be costly if your trip is a long one.

Toilet paper is widely available and cheap, but many communal toilets don't have any (this includes some upper-range hotels). Always carry a spare roll with you.

Sanitary towels are available in most large towns, but it is advisable to carry some spares. Tampons are imported and available in cities only.

English-language reading material of any description is difficult to get hold of. Books are also very expensive, and there are few second-hand book stalls around. Bring a good stock with you – and, if you're remotely interested in what's happening in the world, you might also think about carrying a short-wave radio, as the only newspapers are Portuguese.

A torch is useful if you are camping or staying in towns where there is no electricity, and a travel alarm clock is absolutely essential for catching early-morning buses.

TOUR OPERATORS AND TRAVEL AGENTS
Travel agents
London is a good source of travel agencies offering cheap airfares to Africa. Generally they also provide other travel needs such as insurance and health advice. The following is just a small selection.

Africa Travel Centre 4 Medway Court, Leigh Street, London WC1H 9QX; tel: 0845 450 1543; email: info@africatravel.co.uk; web: www.africatravel.co.uk
Bridge The World 47 Chalk Farm Rd, London NW1 8AN; tel: 020 7911 0900; fax: 020 7813 3350; email: sales@bridge-the-world.co.uk; web: www.b-t-w.co.uk
Flight Centre Tel: 0870499 0040; web: www.flightcentre.com. Offices in London and elsewhere in UK, also Australia, New Zealand, South Africa, USA.
STA Travel Tel: (sales) 0870 1 600599; email: enquiries@statravel.co.uk; web: www.statravel.co.uk. Has 65 branches in UK and over 450 worldwide.

Trailfinders Tel: 020 7938 3939; web: www.trailfinders.com; travel shop 194 Kensington High St, London W8 7RG. Also in Ireland, Australia etc.

Tour operators
In the UK
Aardvark Safaris RBL House, Ordnance Rd, Tidworth SP9 7QD; tel: 01980 849160; fax: 01980 849161; email: mail@aardvarksafaris.com; web: www.aardvarksafaris.com

Africa Explorer 5 Strand on the Green, London W4 3PQ; tel: 020 8987 8742; fax: 020 8994 6264; email: africa.explorer@easynet.co.uk; web: africa-explorer.co.uk

Expert Africa (formerly Sunvil Africa) Sunvil House, Upper Square, Old Isleworth, Middx TW7 7BJ; tel: 020 8232 9777; fax: 020 8568 8330; email: info@expertafrica.com; web: www.expertafrica.com

Explore Worldwide 1 Frederick St, Aldershot, Hants GU11 1LQ; tel: 01252 319448; fax: 01252 760001; email: info@explore.co.uk; web: www.explore.co.uk

Rainbow Tours 305 Upper St, London N1 2TU; tel: 020 7226 1004; fax: 020 7226 2621; email: info@rainbowtours.co.uk; web: www.rainbowtours.co.uk

Steppes Travel 51 Castle St, Cirencester GL7 1QD; tel: 01285 880980; fax: 01285 885888; email: africa@steppestravel.co.uk; web: www.steppestravel.co.uk

In the USA
Ker & Downey 6703 Highway Bvd, Katy, TX 77494; tel: 281 371 2500; or toll-free US & Canada (800) 423 4236; email: info@kerdowney.com; web: www.kerdowney.com

In South Africa
Mozambique Connection PO Box 2861, Rivonia 2128; tel: 011 803 4185; fax: 011 803 3861; email: bookings@mozcon.com; web: www.mozambiqueconnection.co.za
Mozambique Travel Services Johannesburg; tel: 011 659 1766; fax: 082 890 6393; email: moztrav@mweb.co.za

Unusual Destinations Johannesburg; tel: 011 706 1991; email: info@unusualdestinations.com; web: www.unusualdestinations.com.

WildLife Adventures PO Box 30661, Tokai 7966; tel: 021 702 0643; fax: 021 702 0644; email: office@wildlifeadventures.co.za; web: www.wildlifeadventures.co.za, www.iboisland.com

RESPONSIBLE TOURISM
Before you leave
If you want to swot up beforehand on what it means to be a responsible tourist, a UK-based source of information is **Tourism Concern** (tel: 020 7753 3330; fax: 020 7753 3331; email: info@tourismconcern.org.uk; web: www.tourismconcern.org.uk). It's also good to do some research about the country you're about to visit – not just its weather and its costs and its hotels, but also what makes it tick: its history, culture, achievements, failures and so on. It can help to break the ice with local people if you know something (anything!) about their country and way of life.

In Mozambique

Fancy terms such as 'cultural sensitivity' and 'low-impact tourism' just boil down to good old-fashioned respect and common sense. As a visitor, you should be willing to adapt to and respect local customs and traditions. For example, learn a bit of the local language, seek the permission of the community leader before roaming through villages, and ask before you take photographs. In conservative rural areas, note how the local people dress and don't expose parts of yourself that they keep hidden. Of course pick up your litter – well, we know you will! - or don't drop it in the first place, and don't uproot plants and flowers. Also be careful to use energy resources such as water and electricity efficiently, not to wash in lakes or rivers (regardless of local practices, because of pollution) or get too close to the wildlife.

Shop locally and use the services of local people whenever possible. Buy souvenirs from the craftspeople who made them rather than via middlemen who will siphon off profits, and patronise small street vendors rather than big supermarkets. Don't bargain unreasonably; the difference may be the cost of a drink to you but a whole family meal to the vendor. Use the services of a local guide, or a child who wants to help, and pay a fair rate.

If you have spent time in a village and become friendly with its inhabitants, why not consider donating pens, crayons and notebooks to the local primary school? It's easy to buy stationery in local markets. Ask to meet the schoolteacher, so that he/she can receive and officially distribute the gift. Offer to spend some time in the school, being questioned by the children about your home country.

A warning: travellers often collect up pens/biros at home beforehand and bring them over to donate – but, in this case, *please* check that they work and have plenty of ink before handing them over. To an impoverished rural child, a new pen is a huge and thrilling gift. He/she is so proud and happy – and then so bitterly disappointed when it stops working after only a few hours. And do bear in mind the damage you can do by giving little gifts (coins, sweets, pens, cookies or whatever) to a child or youngster who comes up and begs, however cutely. If the begging bears fruit (and if the gift isn't immediately grabbed by a bigger child), he/she will start to pester all visitors. Or begging may appear more profitable than going to school.

Back at home

After you've returned home, try to be an ambassador. Share your experiences, and keep in touch with the people you've met on your travels. Mozambique's international image has been rather negative in recent years, and simply by talking about the country's beauty and many positive aspects you can help to dispel misconceptions.

If you've enjoyed Mozambique and feel that you'd like to stay in touch with the country or to put something back into it, here are a few suggestions.

If you'd like to return as a **volunteer** and have some relevant skills, check out **Voluntary Service Overseas** (www.vso.org.uk). They also welcome donations, from small amounts up to the cost of maintaining a volunteer in a developing country. Then there's **International Voluntary Service** (www.ivs-gb.org.uk), which doesn't always require specific skills or qualifications.

A way to volunteer without leaving home is via the **Online Volunteering Service** (www.onlinevolunteering.org); it's managed by the United Nations Volunteers Programme (UNV), which is the volunteer arm of the United Nations. Volunteers need reliable access to a computer and the internet, and some relevant skill or experience. Also check out **Netaid** on www.netaid.org.

It's sometimes hard to remember that the work of the massive international **charities** does reach down to benefit the poorest, and that they do need our small donations. But it does, and they do. For making a general donation you could do far worse. Check which come closest to your interests. If it's wildlife that appeals to you, then you'll already know about the **Worldwide Fund for Nature** – WWF – which has a big presence in Mozambique and particularly in the new Quirimbas National Park (see Chapter 14). Below are some smaller ones.

Computer Aid International (www.computeraid.org) Since starting up in 1998, it has shipped over 45,000 PCs to more than 90 countries. Over 25,000 of them have gone to educational institutions and the rest to community organisations working in fields as diverse as HIV/AIDS, environment, human rights, and primary healthcare. Donations of funds and computers are welcomed, plus (in the UK) volunteers with technical skills to help check and refurbish used machines.

Practical Action (www.practicalaction.org) Formerly the Independent Technology Group, founded in 1966 by the radical economist Dr E F Schumacher (www.itdg.org), Practical Action works to show that correctly chosen technologies can help people to find lasting, appropriate solutions to poverty, and that a small-scale approach can bring results that benefit whole communities long into the future. It enables poor communities to discover how new technologies, adapted in the right way, can improve their lives.

Save the Children (www.savethechildren.org.uk) One of the bigger charities, it started work in Mozambique in 1984. Its aim is to improve the lives of children and young people and to ensure that they have access to good-quality basic services. It works in partnership with the government, donors, local and international NGOs and local communities.

SOS Children's Villages (www.soschildrensvillages.org.uk) constructed its first community in Mozambique in 1987, in Tete, for children who had lost their parents in the war. Since then it has opened villages and/or centres in Maputo and Pemba. These include schools, medical centres and vocational training. Contact details for SOS Children's Villages in Mozambique are Aldeia de Criancas de Moçambiqué, Avenida 24 de Julho No 3260, CP 2062, Bairro do Laulane, Maputo; tel: 1 400 443; fax: 1 400 848; email: jaimesos@tropical.co.mz.

WaterAid (www.wateraid.org.uk) This much-praised charity is dedicated to the provision of safe domestic water, sanitation and hygiene education to the world's poorest people. WaterAid's partner in Mozambique, ESTAMOS, has won the Mozambique Development Prize for its work in ecological sanitation.

Fly to
MOZAMBIQUE

We'll promise you a great time

If you have never been to Mozambique you do not know the magic you are missing.

All the wild life and idyllic islands and long beaches we have to offer.
Mozambique Airlines has the pleasure to present you to the truly Mozambican way and spirit the minute you check into one of our aircrafts.
For further information please contact us:
Maputo - Mozambique • Tel. 00.258.1.426001/4

International Flights to Johannesburg, Harare, Lisbon with connections to America, Asia and Europe

Mozambique Airlines
COME FLY WITH US

www.lam.co.mz

Getting to Mozambique

This chapter discusses the various ways of getting to Mozambique, a subject that warrants its own chapter for a number of reasons. The first is quite simply that Mozambique's size and unusual shape means there are an abnormally large number of different border crossings into the country. The second is that many of these crossings are rather difficult on public transport, and the section on the crossing from Tanzania in particular needs to include a fair amount of detail on that country. The third is to highlight the reality that northern and southern Mozambique are in some respects best treated as different countries. It may not be obvious from looking at a map, but crucial to planning any trip to Mozambique is the realisation that the provinces of Niassa, Cabo Delgado and Nampula form a discrete travel unit, one that is separated from the provinces of Tete and Sofala by the poorly maintained 1,000km of road that connects Beira to Nampula via Zambézia Province and its capital city Quelimane.

BY AIR
Europe and North America
There are no direct flights to Mozambique from the UK. The main European gateway city for flights to Maputo – indeed, the *only* gateway city – is the Portuguese capital, Lisbon. TAP Air Portugal fly direct to Maputo from Lisbon, as does the Mozambican national carrier, LAM. TAP, meanwhile, has connections between Lisbon and London, as well as several other European cities. The most common way for UK-based travellers to get to southern Mozambique is via South Africa, and for northern Mozambique is via Tanzania, from Dar es Salaam to Pemba. There are plenty of flights between London and Johannesburg, from where it's easy enough to travel to Maputo either by air or land. South African Airlines do the London–Johannesburg route, and have connecting flights to Maputo. There are also flights with Kenyan Airways from Amsterdam and London, changing at Nairobi: see *Africa* page 51.

From North America, the procedure for getting to Mozambique is very much the same as from Europe: you will either have to travel via Lisbon, South Africa or Nairobi.

Flying from London to Johannesburg and then continuing on to Maputo by land will be the cheapest option by virtue of the relatively large number of airlines plying this route. Alternatively, since crossing the land borders that

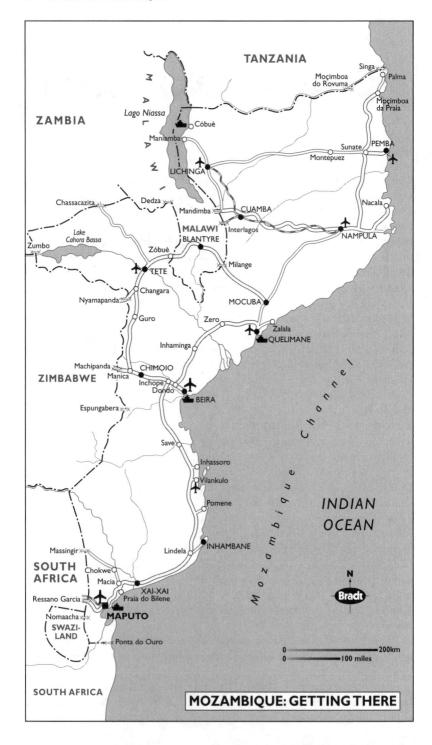

MOZAMBIQUE: GETTING THERE

separate Mozambique from its neighbours is relatively straightforward, you could fly to Zimbabwe, Malawi or Tanzania (once again, probably cheaper than a direct flight to Maputo) before continuing to Mozambique by land. See page 44 for travel agents offering low fares.

Africa

Mozambique is well connected to the rest of Africa, though mainly via Johannesburg or Dar es Salaam. South African Airlines, for instance, has a wide African network with connections in Jo'burg to Maputo. Another option is LAM, which, in addition to its Lisbon route, flies from Maputo and Beira to Jo'burg and Harare and from both Dar es Salaam and Jo'burg to Pemba. Currently all LAM flights from Jo'burg to Pemba leave Jo'burg at 08.40 on Wed and Fri, have a one-hour stop in Maputo and arrive in Pemba at 13.40. Flights from Pemba to Jo'burg on Wed and Fri leave at 13.30 and arrive in Jo'burg at 18.30. There's also a Sunday flight. Flights from Dar es Salaam to Pemba go on Mon, Tue and Sat; and from Pemba to Dar on Mon, Tue, Wed, Thur and Sat.

In 2005, Kenya Airways launched twice-weekly (Thur and Sun) flights from Nairobi to Maputo, leaving at 07.55, arriving at 12.40 and returning to Nairobi one hour later. These connect with the Kenya Airways flights from/to Heathrow and/or Amsterdam.

Pelican Air has daily flights from Jo'burg to Vilanculos and also (not daily) from Nelspruit KMIA to Vilanculos. Charlan Air (www.charlanair.co.za) flies between Lanseria and Vilanculos on Mon and Fri; Swazi Express (www.swaziexpress.com) flies between Durban and Vilanculos on Wed and Fri.

Arriving at Maputo-Mavalane International Airport

Provided that you have a valid passport and visa, and a return ticket, you should whiz through the entrance formalities at the airport with a minimum of fuss. The only reason why a fly-in visitor would be likely to arrive in Mozambique without a return ticket is because of an intention to travel more widely in Africa, an unlikely scenario given that it's far cheaper to fly to Nairobi, Harare or Johannesburg and start an extended African trip from one of these cities. Nevertheless, if for some reason you will be arriving with a one-way ticket, there is a small but real possibility that you will be given a rough time by immigration officials. Basically, what they will be concerned about is that you won't have enough funds to buy a flight out of the country. Obviously, the more money you have, the less likely they are to query your finances. And a credit card will almost certainly convince them to let you in. Assuming that you do intend to travel to neighbouring countries, you can underline this intention by arranging a visa or visitor's pass for the next country.before you land in Mozambique.

The very worst that can happen if you arrive without a return ticket is that you will have to buy a ticket back to your home country before being allowed entry. Assuming that you intend to leave overland, it is important that you check with the relevant airline that this ticket will be refundable, and also that you select a departure date that will give you time to get to a country where you can organise the refund.

See *Maputo: Getting there and away* on page 103 for information about other facilities available at Maputo-Mavalane International Airport, as well as transportation from the airport to Maputo centre.

Airport tax

An airport tax of US$20 is payable in hard currency on flying out of the country. A tax of US$5 is charged for domestic flights; some airports will insist that you pay in hard currency.

Main airline offices

Air Mauritius Tel: 49 9534; web: www.airmauritius.com

Air Zimbabwe Web: www.airzimbabwe.com

LAM Av Karl Marx and Av Mao Tse Tung; tel: 46 5810/4; email: reservas@lam.co.mz; web: www.lam.co.mz

Pelican Air Tel: +27 11 395 3054; web: www.pelicanair.co.za

South African Airlines Av Samora Machel 16–17, Mavalane Airport; tel: 42 0740; web: www.flysaa.co.za

TAP Air Portugal Hotel Rovuma Carlton; tel: 30 3927; fax: 30 3947; web: www.tap-airportugal.pt

TTA Rua de Tchamba 405; tel: 49 0430; fax: 49 1763

Airline security

At the time of writing, airport security is high following terrorist activity. Whether or not it relaxes, be aware that you might have problems if you pack in your hand luggage any toy or replica guns, cutlery, catapults/slingshots, razor blades, knives, tools, darts, scissors, nail files, tweezers and nail clippers, hypodermic syringes (unless for a valid medical reason), knitting needles, sports bats and clubs.

ARRIVING OVERLAND

Provided that arrive at the border with a visa, you should have no problem entering Mozambique overland, nor is there a serious likelihood of being asked about onward tickets, funds or vaccination certificates. About the worst you can expect at customs is a cursory search of your luggage (see *Customs reform* on page 62).

At most overland borders there is nowhere to change money legally, which means that you may have to change money with a private individual. Although this is not strictly legal, it is perfectly open at most borders – though obviously it would be wise to be discreet in the presence of officialdom. Generally, the rates you get at borders are lower than they would be elsewhere. This is because the people who change money at borders are simply providing a service to travellers, and they need to make a profit on transactions in both directions. At some borders, there's a lot of hustle attached to changing money privately, and especially along the Beira Corridor there is a real risk of being conned.

One solution would be to arrange in advance to be carrying money for the country you are entering – ask travellers coming in the opposite direction if they have any left-over cash to swap. If you can't do this, try to carry a small surplus of the currency from the country you are leaving (say around US$20) and to change this at the border rather than using up your hard currency. Whatever else you do, you should try to establish the rough exchange rate in advance and avoid changing significantly more money than you will need to get you through until you can go to a bank. It is a good idea to keep the money you intend to change separate from the rest of your hard currency and travellers' cheques.

Overland routes into southern Mozambique

Southern and central Mozambique can be entered overland from five countries: South Africa, Swaziland, Zimbabwe, Zambia and Malawi. The majority of visitors who enter or leave Mozambique overland do so at the borders with South Africa, Zimbabwe or Malawi, but it is also straightforward to enter Mozambique from Swaziland. The border with Zambia is more remote and little used.

To/from South Africa

The most normal crossing is the Komatipoort/Ressano Garcia border post between Johannesburg and Maputo. It is also possible to enter Mozambique from Swaziland using the Namaacha border. People driving to Maputo from KwaZulu-Natal can enter Mozambique at Ponto do Ouro in the south, though they will need a 4WD if they intend to continue north to Maputo. Backpackers coming from KwaZulu-Natal can use the thrice-weekly bus service between Durban and Maputo via Swaziland.

Johannesburg to Maputo (Ressano Garcia crossing)

Komatipoort lies 470km east of Johannesburg, a four to five hour drive along the well-maintained N12 and N4 through Nelspruit. If you want to spend the night in Komatipoort (not a bad idea if the alternative is arriving in Maputo in the late afternoon and absolutely a good idea if the alternative is driving part of the road to Maputo in the dark) there is a municipal campsite and a hotel in the town centre, and a more attractive resort on a dam about 3km out of town (signposted from the Nelspruit road) where you can camp for the rand equivalent of US$10/site or rent a bungalow for the equivalent of US$30/double. The border post lies about 5km out of Komatipoort – it's a simple crossing provided that all your papers are in order – after which it's a 108km drive along a good, recently resurfaced road through to Maputo.

If you are dependent on public transport, you have the choice of trains, buses and minibuses. A train service runs daily between Johannesburg and Maputo, leaving Johannesburg at 06.10 and Maputo at 11.00. The journey takes about 17 hours, a major advantage of which is that you will arrive at your destination in the morning, giving you plenty of time to find a room.

A company called Panthera Azul runs a regular coach service between Johannesburg and Maputo. Coaches leave Johannesburg from the corner of

Kerk and Polly Streets at 07.30 every day. In the opposite direction, buses to Johannesburg leave Maputo from in front of the Panthera Azul office on the corner of Avenida Julius Nyerere and Avenida 24 de Julho at 08.00 every day. The journey takes around seven and a half hours and costs US$27.

Minibuses are cheaper than buses and they leave on a fill-up-and-go basis from the Joubert Park minibus rank in Johannesburg and from the corner of Rua Albert Lithuli and Avenido 25 de Setembro in Maputo. Note that Joubert Park is one of the most risky parts of Johannesburg in terms of mugging and theft.

Hitching between Johannesburg and Maputo is feasible, though finding a lift out of Johannesburg itself is problematic and arguably rather dangerous – best to use public transport at least some of the way. On the Mozambican side of the border, there are minibuses through to Maputo. In the opposite direction, minibuses to the Ressano Garcia border leave Maputo from the same place as minibuses to Johannesburg. Once you're at the border, hitching on to Johannesburg should be easy enough.

Durban to Maputo (Ponta do Ouro crossing)
The other main crossing between South Africa and Mozambique is at Ponta do Ouro in the far south of Mozambique where it borders KwaZulu-Natal. This is the best border to use if you are coming from Durban and have a private 4WD vehicle. It's not of much to backpackers, since there is no public transport and hitching would be slow. It is normally possible to get to Ponta do Ouro itself in a saloon car from Durban, but the road between there and Maputo requires a 4WD.

Panthera Azul runs a thrice-weekly bus service between Durban and Maputo. These buses leave Durban at 07.00 on Tuesdays, Fridays and Sundays, and Maputo at 07.30 on Mondays, Thursdays and Saturdays. The trip takes about 12 hours and costs US$45 one way. Buses out of Durban leave from the main bus station in the city centre. Bookings can be made by ringing Durban 309 7798.

To/from Swaziland (Namaacha crossing)
The Namaacha border post in Swaziland has no advantages over the Komatipoort border, unless you are already in Swaziland. The road from Mbabane (the capital of Swaziland) to Namaacha is in good condition, as is the road to Maputo except for a potholed stretch of a few kilometres after Namaacha; it's navigable in any vehicle. There are buses from Mbabane to Manzini, from Manzini to Namaacha, and from Namaacha to Maputo. Each leg costs a little more than a dollar and takes up to two hours. Panthera Azul coaches between Durban and Maputo stop at Mbabane.

To/from Zimbabwe
Mutare to Chimoio (Machipanda crossing)
The most widely used border post is the one on the Beira Corridor, 10km east of Mutare in Zimbabwe and about 20km west of Manica township. The 300km road between Mutare and Beira is surfaced and mostly in excellent

condition; you should be able to drive it in less than five hours in any motorised vehicle. There are regular buses along this route, and hitching is a possibility. Trains between Mutare and Beira take about 12 to 15 hours and they run in either direction every other day, stopping at Manica and Chimoio. If you're thinking of leaving Mutare by road late in the day, bear in mind that there is no accommodation in Manica, though there is a campsite and chalet complex about 20km further towards Beira at the Chicamba Real Dam (see page 175), as well as accommodation in Chimoio another 50km towards Beira.

In a private 4WD, a scenic option is the Selinda/Espungabera border post south of the Chimanimani Mountains. So far as I'm aware, there is no public transport along this route, and hitching is unlikely to be a realistic option.

Harare to Tete (Nyamapanda crossing)
It's difficult to see why anybody would want to use the Nyamapanda border post between Harare and Tete unless they were crossing directly to Malawi via the Tete Corridor. If you decide to go this way, it's straightforward enough: any bus between Harare and Blantyre can drop you at Tete, from where there are daily buses to Maputo and Beira via Chimoio.

To/from Zambia
In practice, it's probably only possible to cross between Zambia and Mozambique if you have private transport, using the **Chassacazita** border post 290km north of Tete and 53km south of the main Lusaka–Chipata Road. I've never met a traveller who has used this route, but the last time I was in Zambia (1995) I did talk to a local who had cycled to Petauke from Tete and who claimed there is nothing in the way of public transport along this road. You could, presumably, get through in a 4WD (or on a bicycle!). If you're mad enough to try hitching, any bus heading between Lusaka and Chipata can drop you at Petauke or Katete townships, both of which have basic local lodgings for around US$4/room. I'd be interested to hear from anybody who uses this route.

The other possibility is the border post at **Zumbo** on the western edge of the Cahora Bassa Dam. This could be an interesting route, since both Zumbo and the village on the Zambian side of the river were formerly important Portuguese towns, but it would also be rather challenging. There is no vehicle ferry here, as far as I'm aware, and although backpackers could certainly find a boat to take them across the dam, there is little transport out of Zumbo. Again, it would be good to hear from anybody daring enough to give it a try.

To/from Malawi
Assuming that you are confining your Mozambican travels to Tete, Beira and points further south, then the best place to cross into Mozambique from Malawi is the **Zóbuè** border post between Blantyre and Tete. The road from Blantyre and Tete is surfaced and well maintained. In a private vehicle, you should get through in three to four hours, depending on delays at the border. If you're driving yourself, it's worth bearing in mind that the border becomes

completely chaotic during the hour after the first Blantyre to Harare bus pulls in – I'd plan your trip so that you arrive at the border before 07.30 or after 09.30.

The easiest way to get from Blantyre to Tete is to use one of the buses that cross daily between Blantyre and Harare via the Tete Corridor. Several such buses leave Blantyre at around 06.00 every morning, arriving in Tete before midday. The only problem with using the buses to Harare is that they aren't licensed to drop off passengers in Mozambique – they'll drop you in Tete, no problem, but they will have to charge you the full fare of roughly US$15 to Harare. The alternative to using a Harare-bound bus is to catch a local bus from Blantyre to the border town of Mwanza, and then to cross into Mozambique on foot. At Zóbuè, the town on the Mozambican side of the border, there are at least two hotels within 100m of the border post. From Zóbuè you could either try to hitch or else board one of the regular passenger trucks to Tete. There are a few resthouses in Mwanza if for some reason you want to spend the night there before crossing into Mozambique.

An alternative route to Zóbuè, more direct if you're driving from Lilongwe as opposed to Blantyre, is via the **Dedza** border post. The road from Dedza to the Tete Corridor is in fair condition, and any vehicle should make it through except perhaps after heavy rain. There is no public transport along this route, and hitching could be very slow.

Overland routes to northern Mozambique

Northern Mozambique can be approached from two countries: Malawi and Tanzania. It can also be approached from southern Mozambique, along the 1,000km road between Beira and Nampula. The latter trip will take two to three days in a private vehicle. If you are backpacking, it will take at least four days, and you will probably be dependent on getting lifts with trucks (for further details see *Quelimane: Getting there and away*, page 189), so there is a good case for flying from Beira to one of the towns in the north. There are no international flights into northern Mozambique.

To/from Malawi

There are at least four ways of crossing between Malawi and northern Mozambique: by rail from Liwonde to Cuamba; by road from Mangochi to Mandimba; by road from Mulanje to Milange; or by boat from Likoma Island to Cóbuè. The best route to use depends largely on which parts of Mozambique you intend to visit, bearing in mind that getting around Malawi is much easier and cheaper than getting around Mozambique.

Mangochi to Mandimba (Mandimba crossing)

This is the best crossing for motorists, who should be able to manage it in any vehicle with reasonable clearance, except after rain. It is also the most straightforward route in most other circumstances, and even though it is less well known to backpackers than the rail crossing further south, it is undoubtedly more efficient. To give some idea, I was able to travel the 405km between Lichinga and Blantyre via Mandimba in roughly ten hours using public transport – excellent time anywhere in Africa, and particularly for a trip punctuated by a border crossing and several changes of vehicle. Using this route, you could reasonably expect to get between Cuamba or Lichinga and most parts of southern Malawi between Cape Maclear and Blantyre in a day.

The first step in getting to Mozambique via Mandimba is to get to Mangochi, a medium-sized town on the Shire River roughly 250km north of Blantyre and 70km south of Monkey Bay. Any bus heading between Monkey Bay and Blantyre can drop you at Mangochi. There are also regular minibuses between Blantyre and Mangochi, leaving Blantyre from Limbe bus station and taking about three hours. There are several resthouses to choose from in Mangochi if you want to spend the night there.

Transport to the border leaves Mangochi from the bus station a few hundred metres from the PTC supermarket. If you can't find a vehicle heading all the way, then hop on the next vehicle heading to Namwera, a sizeable town with several resthouses where you can easily pick up another vehicle covering the last 10km to the border post. The road between Mangochi and Namwera is very scenic, crossing a couple of densely wooded hills and with some great views back to Lake Malombe.

After exiting Malawi, it's a good 7km or so to the Mozambican border post at Mandimba. You may be lucky and catch a lift, but it's more likely you'll have to arrange a bicycle-taxi. The bikes are very uncomfortable and the road is hilly enough that it would speed things up to organise separate bikes to carry yourself and your pack. Once you've crossed into Mozambique, you're no more than 100m from the main Lichinga–Cuamba road, and provided you arrive before around 14.00 you should be able to find transport out of Mandimba in either direction. Alternatively, there's a pleasant little resthouse with double rooms for under US$10 and an acceptable restaurant just behind the filling station on the main road through the town.

Liwonde to Cuamba (Interlagos crossing)

The most popular crossing with backpackers is the series of train services connecting Liwonde to Cuamba and eventually Nampula. This route involves three different train journeys: one from Liwonde to the Nayuchi border post; another from the border to Cuamba (where you have the option of going north by road or rail to Lichinga); and then the recently opened passenger service from Cuamba to Nampula.

Liwonde, the starting point for this trip, is a small town with several resthouses lying about 1km off the main road between Blantyre and Monkey Bay. Any bus covering this route can drop you at the turn-off. Trains to the Nayuchi border leave Liwonde at 08.00 on Monday and Thurday, and arrive at the border about three hours later. From the Malawian border post, it's about 20 minutes' walk to its Mozambican counterpart – just follow the crowd. It's easy to change excess kwachas into meticais with people coming in the opposite direction, and you'll get a much better rate than you will from professional money-changers.

On the Mozambican side of the border, there is a basic restaurant and a small pensão in the small town of Interlagos (positioned exactly halfway between Lakes Chilwa and Chiuta). However, if all goes to plan, you should be able to pick up a train to Cuamba on the day you arrive – the services are scheduled to connect with each other. The train journey from Interlagos to Cuamba should take around six hours, though on a bad day it might take as long as eight hours. Coming in the opposite direction, trains from Cuamba to Interlagos also leave on Mondays, Wednesdays and Fridays at 04.30, arriving in Interlagos at 10.40 if all goes well. From Cuamba, there is a daily passenger train to Nampula, and a daily bus north to Lichinga (see *Cuamba: Getting there and away*, page 201).

Likoma to Cóbuè (Cóbuè crossing)
Currently a rather obscure option, the crossing between Likoma Island and Cóbuè on the shores of Lake Malawi (Niassa) is used by some travellers.

Likoma Island is a part of Malawi entirely enclosed by Mozambican waters. Lake ferries run between most major ports on the Malawian section of the lake and Likoma, and there are several places to stay on the island. From Likoma, fishing dhows operate as a ferry service to Cóbuè, taking roughly one hour to cover the 10km stretch of water. At Cóbuè, the Australian run Hotel Santo Miguel has clean rooms for US$10 and facilities for camping. However, the best and quickest way of travelling between Malawi and Mozambique via Lake Niassa is by the Malawian ferry, which does a circuit of the lake twice a week. On Tuesday mornings it arrives in Likoma from Nkhata Bay on the Malawian side of the lake, from where it continues on to Cóbuè, Metangula and finally Nkhotakota back on the Malawian side. On Saturdays it does the same trip in reverse, arriving in Metangula in the morning and Cóbuè in the afternoon. The immigration offices in Metangula and Cóbuè send people to meet the boat, so those arriving from Malawi can get their passports stamped. Otherwise, this formality can be done at the immigration office in Lichinga.

At present, anybody can visit Cóbuè as an overnight trip from Likoma. No visa is required for a stay of 24 hours or less, but you do need a visa for a longer stay, or if you plan to travel further into Mozambique.

Mulanje Mocuba (Milange crossing)
This is the most southerly border crossing between Malawi and northern Mozambique, and it is only worth thinking about if you're determined to visit Quelimane. The Muloza/Milange border post connects Blantyre and Mulanje in Malawi to Mocuba and Quelimane in Mozambique. A fair 120km tar road connects Blantyre to Mulanje town and the border post. The 190km road from the border to Mocuba is rocky and sandy in stretches, but provided that you drive carefully and it hasn't rained recently even an ordinary saloon car should make it through. The road from Mocuba south to Quelimane is better – pristine tar for 46km to Malei, then firm dirt for 33km to Namacurra, and finally 66km of pot-holed tar to Quelimane. If you are travelling in the opposite direction, note that the turn off to Milange at Mocuba isn't signposted.

If you're doing the same route on public transport, there are plenty of buses from Blantyre to Mulanje town, about 20km before the border. The trip takes three to four hours, depending on whether you catch an express bus or a stopping bus. Some buses to Mulanje continue on to the border, but if you arrive in Mulanje late in the day, you're advised to stay put for the night and to continue travelling on the following day. The Council Rest House opposite Mulanje market has clean rooms for less than US$2 and the Mulanje View Hotel on the main road to Blantyre has motel-style rooms for around US$5. At Milange town, immediately after crossing into Mozambique, the Pensão Esplanada is relatively poor value, as it charges around US$10 for an indifferent single.

Getting between Milange and Mocuba may prove problematic. Public transport along this road is sporadic, and you should count yourself lucky if you find a *chapa* (a truck customised to carry passengers) heading from Milange to Mocuba. Hitching is just as much of a lottery, and what you most certainly don't want to do is take a lift unless it's going the whole way to Mocuba, as there is no accommodation along the way. Once at Mocuba, there are two pensãos and regular trucks heading towards Quelimane or Nampula.

To/from Tanzania

The overland trip from Dar es Salaam, the Tanzanian capital, to northern Mozambique is one of the most interesting and exhausting in this part of Africa. The town you want to head for is Mtwara, which lies about 30km north of the Rovuma River on the border with Mozambique, and there are three ways of getting there: by boat from Dar es Salaam, by road from Dar es Salaam, or by road from Mbeya. More extensive coverage of this area is included in *Tanzania: The Bradt Travel Guide* (4th edition), from which the following brief notes are drawn.

Getting to Mtwara

The easiest way to travel between Dar es Salaam and Mtwara is **by air**. Air Tanzania flies this route thrice-weekly and a one-way ticket is cheaper than you might expect – comfortably less than US$100 in early 2002. Another option is **by boat**, assuming that one is running. The vessel that used to cover this route regularly was the *Canadian Spirit*, but this is out of commission, and no regular substitute has emerged. Your best bet is to check at the harbour at Dar es Salaam (or at Mtwara, if you're heading in the opposite direction) for any boat that might be running. It is unusual for a boat to cover this trip more often than once per fortnight.

The third option is to travel **by bus**. Direct buses are available, but, with a travel time of up to 24 hours, there is much to be said for breaking up the trip. This will also allow you to explore what is undoubtedly the highlight of Tanzania's southern coast, the ruined city of **Kilwa Kisiwani**. Lying on an island about 2km offshore, Kilwa was the focus of the Swahili Coast's gold trade prior to the arrival of the Portuguese in 1500. The ruined city includes some beautiful mosques, a house with a swimming pool, and a sunken audience court, as well as a fort dating to the Portuguese area.

Except during the rainy season, when the roads along the south coast are often impassable, buses run every day between Dar es Salaam and **Kilwa Masoko**, the mainland settlement opposite Kilwa Kisiwani. This trip used to take up to 15 rough hours, but these days it often takes no more than eight hours, a timing that is likely to be reduced further when the mooted bridge across the Rufiji River is completed (hopefully before the end of 2002). You could also catch a bus heading to Lindi or Mtwara (these leave Dar es Salaam from the more central Morogoro Road bus station) and ask to be deposited at the junction town of **Nangurukuru**, from where there are regular pick-up trucks to Kilwa Masoko, taking about 20 minutes. Once in Kilwa Masoko, there are several inexpensive local guesthouses to choose from, with the New Mjaka probably the best, charging between US$2 and US$5 for rooms ranging from a basic single to a self-contained double chalet with fan. It's easy to organise a local fishing dhow to take you across to Kilwa Kisiwani for the day, though you must pay a visit – and nominal fee – to the local council office first. Also worth a look is **Kilwa Kivinje**, a fascinating small town which served as the terminus of the Lake Malawi slave caravan route for much of the 19th century. Pick-up trucks run back and forth between Kilwa Masoko and Kilwa Kivinje throughout the day, taking about half an hour in either direction, and there are a few very basic guesthouses in Kilwa Kivinje.

When you're ready to head south from Kilwa Masoko, catch an early morning pick-up truck to Nangurukuru to wait for transport coming from Dar es Salaam. The next main town is Lindi, an agreeable if rather run-down place situated on a beautiful bay. If you want to stay overnight in **Lindi**, the Nankolwa Hotel is about the best place in town, charging slightly less than US$10 for a self-contained double. In the US$3–4 range, I can recommend the Town and South Honour guesthouses, though if you arrive early enough in the day, you could head directly to Mtwara – the two towns are connected by a good tar road, and buses take no longer than three hours.

The other road route to Mtwara is from Mbeya near the Zambian border. This is a really rough trip, which can take several days. There are regular buses along a good tar road from Mtwara to **Njombe** and from Njombe to **Songea**, with each leg taking around five hours. In Njombe, the Lutheran Centre Hostel has clean and inexpensive dormitory accommodation, and the Milimani Hotel has comfortable self-contained doubles, with nets and hot showers, for well under US$10. In Songea, the OK Hotel has reasonably priced self-contained doubles and a good restaurant, and there are several cheaper guesthouses of which the Deluxe and New Star stand out. There are no buses along the appalling 370km road that connects Songea to Masasi – a lift on a truck costs US$12 and a lift in a 4WD costs US$20. The journey normally takes two days, with an overnight stop at **Tunduru** where you can find a basic room for US$6. Once at **Masasi**, the principal town on the Makonde Plateau, you'll find that there are regular buses on a good tar road to Mtwara. If you need to spend the night in Masasi, there are several guesthouses on the road between the bus station and the Masasi Hotel. The Masasi Hotel itself used to be very good value – a large self-contained room with nets and fans cost less than US$4 in 1993 – but I've heard no recent reports.

Mtwara itself is something of a let down – a rather bland, sprawling port built to service a post-war groundnut scheme that never got off the ground. There are quite a few basic lodgings dotted around town: the Pro Rata Guesthouse, Kwa Limo Motel and Lutheran Guesthouse are all decent places, clocking in at comfortably less than US$10 for a double room. More interesting than Mtwara is **Mikindani**, which is sprawled along the main road 10km back towards Lindi, and is also where Livingstone started his final journey into the African interior. The British-owned, backpacker-oriented Ten Degrees South Lodge (www.tendegreessouth.com) in Mikindani charges US$10 for acceptable double rooms, and has great food. You can also eat well and at a reasonable price at the restored Old Boma around the corner, though at prices from US$89 for a double, full board, the lovely rooms here will be beyond the range of most backpackers.

Mtwara to Palma

When you are ready to leave Tanzania, you have three options: to cross directly overland via Mwambo, to catch an ocean-going dhow between Msimbati and Palma, or to use the very obscure Moçimboa do Rovuma border between Masasi and Mueda.

If you want to use the direct overland route, the first thing you must do is catch a Land-Rover to Mwambo and visit the immigration office to get an exit stamp. From Mwambo, you'll probably have to walk the 5km to a village on the north bank of the Rovuma River where you can pick up a dugout canoe into Mozambique. Since June 2000 a motorised ferry able to carry four small vehicles or one overland truck has been operating between the Tanzanian and Mozambican sides of the Rovuma. Tickets cost US$0.50. Once across the river, it's about 200m to the immigration office at Singa, from where you can catch a *chapa* to Palma. Note that this road is sometimes swampy from January to May and cuts through deep bush. Consequently, the 40-odd kilometres might take as long as three hours.

Another option is to catch a fishing dhow from Tanzania directly to Palma or Moçimboa da Praia. The important thing to know if you are doing this is that the dhows don't leave from Mtwara itself, but from a nearby village called Msimbati. There are buses between Mtwara and Msimbati, and there is an immigration office once you're there. The dhows are private fishing boats: they leave when the weather and tides are right, and fares are negotiable (around US$6–7 per person feels about right). It's worth asking the immigration officer if he can help you find a dhow heading south. The trip shouldn't take more than ten hours, depending on the weather and where the boat is heading to. Bear in mind that the dhow will probably be heading to where the sailors live; if you are lucky, you'll be dropped right at Palma or Moçimboa da Praia, but you may also be dropped at a village on a beach about three hours walk from Palma – a tricky route, for which you'll need to adopt a local as a guide. You can complete your entry formalities at Palma. If you are heading in the opposite direction, things are much simpler insofar as you can pick up a dhow at either Palma or Moçimboa da Praia, and you'll almost certainly be dropped at Msimbati.

The route between Masasi and Mueda is definitely for the adventurous only, with the compensation that this must be among the most remote roads anywhere in East Africa, and it passes through some wildly beautiful scenery. The easiest bit of this trip is to get to Newala, a small Makonde town that lies 40km from the border. Buses run to Newala daily, both from Masasi and from Mtwara, and there are a couple of adequate resthouses when you arrive. From Newala, expect to walk the 40km to the border post (the road is impassable other than on foot or bicycle), where a dugout canoe will take you across the river to **Moçimboa do Rovuma**. There's not a great deal of transport along the 90km road between Moçimboa do Rovuma and Mueda – I have a secondhand report of a volunteer who claimed, quite plausibly, to be the first European to cross this way in more than two years, and who waited two days for a tractor ride.

CUSTOMS REFORM

Vigorous steps have been taken recently to eradicate corruption in the Mozambique customs service. New staff have been recruited and trained, and there is even a special authority to deal with officials who attempt to solicit bribes during the course of their duties. Those who have a legitimate complaint should contact the Internal Irregularities Unit in Maputo (tel: 30 8584), taking note of the fact that *offering* or *paying* a bribe is also a criminal offence.

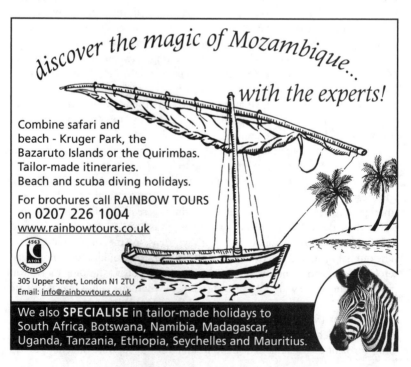

discover the magic of Mozambique...
with the experts!

Combine safari and beach - Kruger Park, the Bazaruto Islands or the Quirimbas. Tailor-made itineraries. Beach and scuba diving holidays.

For brochures call RAINBOW TOURS on **0207 226 1004**
www.rainbowtours.co.uk

305 Upper Street, London N1 2TU
Email: info@rainbowtours.co.uk

We also **SPECIALISE** in tailor-made holidays to South Africa, Botswana, Namibia, Madagascar, Uganda, Tanzania, Ethiopia, Seychelles and Mauritius.

Travelling in Mozambique

GETTING AROUND
By air
LAM has a domestic flight network that links the following Mozambican towns: Maputo, Beira, Quelimane, Nampula, Pemba, Tete and Vilankulo. Most of the flights originate and terminate in Maputo after having done a circuit of the country in a relatively spacious Boeing 737. One or two flights start in Beira, in which case they'll probably be in a much smaller aircraft.

Booking tickets can be done at LAM offices or travel agents. It is very important to reconfirm your flight 72 hours before departure since certain routes are regularly over-booked. Having said this, however, LAM seems to function relatively smoothly when compared to some other airlines in similarly impoverished African countries. This is not to say that tickets are especially cheap. For example, a Maputo–Beira costs US$165 one way, a Beira–Quelimane US$97 one way, and a Maputo–Pemba US$262 one way. There are sizeable reductions, however, for travellers who are under 25 and over 59 years of age.

By boat
There are regular ferries between Maputo and Catembe. Boats must also be used to get between Vilankulo or Inhassoro and the islands of the Bazaruto Archipelago, to Ibo Island in northern Mozambique, and to cross some of the country's main rivers and inland waterways (the Zambezi River, Rovuma River and Lake Niassa, for instance). If travelling by sea is your thing, you might be able to find the odd trawler plying the coast between Beira and Quelimane; and note that in the far north near the Tanzanian border, private fishing dhows are a legitimate alternative to travelling by road.

By rail
Apart from the train between Maputo and Johannesburg (see pages 53 and 104), the only rail service of any interest to travellers in Mozambique is the one that links Nampula, Cuamba and the Malawian border. It is possible to travel by train to some other destinations (along the Beira Corridor, for instance), although the options by road are infinitely quicker and more practical.

By road
Driving in Mozambique
From a commercial point of view, Mozambique has always been a country dominated by its railways rather than its roads. Add to this the destruction

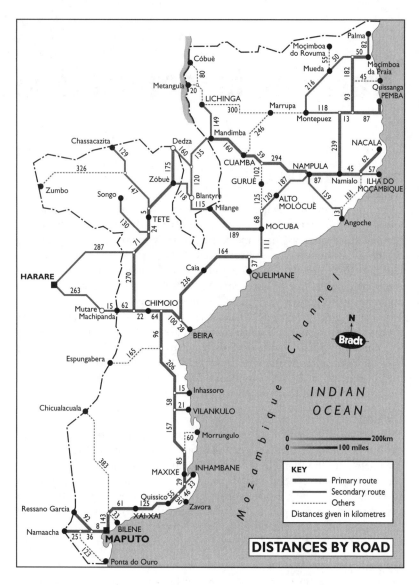

DISTANCES BY ROAD

caused first by the civil war and then by the February 2000 floods, and it is
no surprise that driving in Mozambique is not always as straightforward as
it could be. A five-year, multi-million-dollar project to rehabilitate the
country's roads was set back severely by the floods, which destroyed several
sections of the EN1 (the Maputo–Beira road), as well as bridges over the
Save and Limpopo Rivers. The reparation of such damage will no doubt
take priority over other road improvement schemes, such as the
construction of a paved road from Pemba all the way to the Tanzanian
border.

The main roads in Mozambique are penetration lines towards the country's borders. Therefore, you should have no problem travelling from Maputo to Komatipoort in South Africa, Beira to Chimoio and the Zimbabwe border, and Tete to the Malawi and Zimbabwe borders in any saloon car. Other relatively good, tarred roads include Maputo to Inhassoro (the flood damage notwithstanding), Chimoio to Tete, and Nampula (or at least Namialo) to Pemba, all of which are suitable for almost any type of vehicle.

The road between Inhassoro and Beira is passable in a saloon car provided that you go very slowly, your vehicle has good clearance, and it hasn't rained for a while. Elsewhere in the country, a 4WD is practically essential – bear in mind that even where roads are in good condition, you will generally need to use rougher roads to get to them.

The main hazard to your vehicle on Mozambican roads comes from pot-holes. You are advised to keep your eyes glued to the road ahead and to slow down for oncoming traffic, since a vehicle passing in the opposite direction will impede your ability to manoeuvre around an unexpected pot-hole. If you are driving in a vehicle with an unprotected sump, it is probably worth carrying a spare one. It's also a sensible precaution to carry an extra spare tyre and rim (you can pick up spares like this cheaply at a scrapyard in South Africa). Livestock and pedestrians frequently wander into the middle of the road, and motorists tend to be more reckless, not to mention inebriated, than in Europe, so drive more defensively than you would at home. Driving at night is inadvisable, partly for security reasons, but also because the general chaos on the road is exacerbated by vehicles lacking headlights.

Frequent roadblocks are part and parcel of driving in Mozambique. You can expect to be stopped at most roadblocks and asked to produce your driving licence, vehicle registration and temporary import papers. You may also be required to show that you have traffic triangles stashed away somewhere in the vehicle, and you could be in for a heated discussion if you're not wearing a seatbelt. Otherwise, contrary to all the horror stories about officiousness that you may have heard of in advance, you should not normally be detained for longer than a couple of minutes at a roadblock.

Good maps are hard to come by and those generated from aerial photographs can be downright misleading – a lot of the old Portuguese routes and structures are no longer used, but still show up as stripes on these pictures rather better than do the more organic African tracks and settlements. Also, the massive movements of people during and since the war have led to places marked on maps being not much more than memories and settlements of a few thousand people not being recorded at all. Particularly in off-the-beaten-track areas, believe the roads you can see and believe the tyre tracks, navigate with your eyes looking through the windscreen and not with your head buried in some chart! Having said this, see page 75 for some recommended maps of Mozambique.

Land mines still pose a threat to anybody who wants to indulge in some off-road driving, so stick to the track. For ecological reasons, drivers are strongly urged against driving along dunes and beaches.

Petrol costs roughly the same in Mozambique as it does in South Africa, around US$0.50 per litre.

Hiring a vehicle

Having a 4WD vehicle at your disposal is a definite luxury, permitting you to forget the hassles of public transport and navigate the more difficult tracks to out-of-the-way places. This luxury, however, comes at a hefty price. A 4WD, for example, rarely costs much less than US$100 per day, and quite often considerably more. A saloon car is cheaper, with the most basic models starting at around US$30 per day. The larger hotels and most travel agents can arrange car-hire. Alternatively, go directly to the car rental agencies, most of which are based at the country's larger airports (ie: Maputo, Beira and Nampula).

Avis Maputo, tel: 46 5497; Beira: 30 1263
Europcar Maputo, tel: 49 7338
Hertz Maputo, tel: 49 4982
Imperial Maputo, tel: 49 3543; Beira: 32 8395; Nampula: 21 5761

Buses and chapas

Reasonably reliable bus services connect Maputo, Beira, Chimoio, Tete and points in between. The recommended lines for long-hauls between these towns are Oliviera's and TSL, but there are also several local bus companies that connect the various towns between Maputo and Beira. The Mozambican word for bus is *machimbombo*.

Just about anywhere in Mozambique can be reached on a *chapa*. This term is the Mozambican equivalent of the East African *matatu*, and it is evidently applied to just about any vehicle apart from a bus that will carry passengers, be it an open truck or pick-up truck or minibus. The most common type of *chapa* is a large truck with caged sides, a canvas or plastic 'roof', and inward-facing benches around the sides. In the south, the only instance where you regularly need to use *chapas* is along the short roads connecting places like Bilene and Inhambane to the EN1 between Maputo and Beira.

Chapas are a more important form of transport in the northeastern provinces of Zambézia, Nampula, Niassa and Cabo Delgado, where there are fewer buses. The main bus company in this region, Transnorte, covers the roads connecting Pemba, Nacala and Nampula, as well as the road between Cuamba and Lichinga. There is also a bus service between Nampula and Quelimane. Elsewhere, you'll be dependent on *chapas* and trucks.

On most routes through the north, the bulk of public transport leaves at 05.00. Travellers coming from elsewhere in Africa will be used to being told that buses leave at 05.00, only to arrive at the bus station and find that they have to sit around for an hour or two before anything actually leaves. Things work differently in Mozambique: when people tell you that buses or *chapas* leave at 05.00, there's every chance that they'll all have gone if you aren't in position a good 10 to 15 minutes earlier.

Getting around Mozambique is complicated by the fact that few places have central bus or *chapa* stations. Instead, there is an informally agreed departure

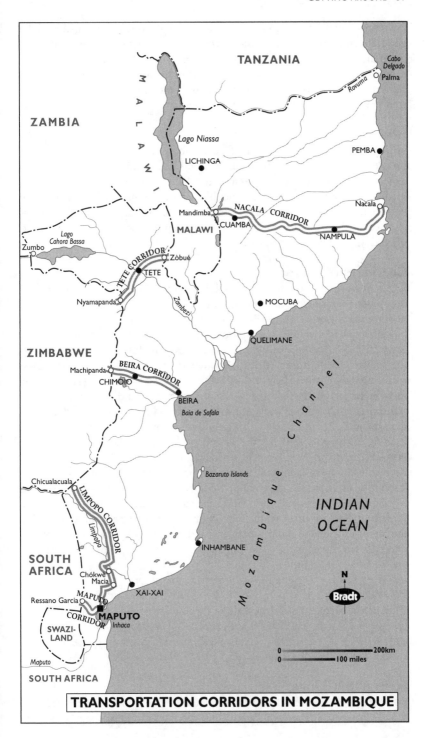

TRANSPORTATION CORRIDORS IN MOZAMBIQUE

point for vehicles going in any given direction, frequently along the road a good 20 minutes' walk from the town centre. What this means is that you generally need to be out of your hotel room at least half an hour before the time you're told that transport leaves. If you're not a morning person, you can alleviate this somewhat stressful scenario by locating the right spot to wait for transport on the afternoon before you travel.

Hitching

Hitching is a viable option south of Vilankulo, where there is a fair amount of private transport, and on the roads between Tete, Chimoio and Beira. It is generally slower in northern Mozambique. Bear in mind that the line between hitching and public transport is rather blurred in Mozambique as elsewhere in Africa: most truck drivers will informally carry passengers for the same fee as charged by buses and *chapas*, and so you should expect to pay for any lift offered to you by a Mozambican.

Corridors of power

While misfortune has hit Mozambique hard in recent years (civil war, droughts, floods, etc), the country can claim one big advantage over its neighbours: its location. For Mozambique is the southern African 'middleman', providing a vital outlet for landlocked countries such as Swaziland, Zimbabwe, Malawi, Zambia and even the Democratic Republic of the Congo, while South Africa, although it boasts the continent's longest coastline, also relies heavily on Mozambican ports. To facilitate the movement of goods from these countries to the Indian Ocean, several transportation 'corridors' exist in Mozambique. The Maputo Corridor serves mainly South Africa and Swaziland; the Beira Corridor links Zimbabwe and Zambia to the port of Beira; the Limpopo Corridor links Zimbabwe to the port of Maputo; and the Nacala Corridor is for Malawi. All of these corridors have railway lines, and the ports of Maputo, Beira and Nacala are the country's three most important. Middlemen always make money, and Mozambique has earned some vital hard currency by selling concessions to foreign investors to manage the railway lines along these corridors, as well as the ports at the end of them. Another vital transportation route, and a popular one with travellers, is the Tete Corridor, which links Zimbabwe to Malawi via the Mozambican town of Tete.

MONEY

The unit of currency is the metical (MT), plural meticais. In mid 2005, US$1 was worth up to around 24,000 MT, depending on where you change money and whether you have cash or travellers' cheques. Meticais come in bills of various denominations, ranging from 10,000 MT to 100,000 MT.

Foreign exchange

Foreign currency can be changed into meticais at banks and private bureaux de change or *cambrios*. For cash transactions, the rates are similar and usually no commission is charged. The recent history of banking in Mozambique reads like a soap opera, with corruption, take-overs and suspicious deaths of leading bankers all being part of the script. Without going into too much detail, the change of most relevance to travellers is that the Banco Commercial do Moçambique (BCM) has merged with the Banco Internacional de Moçambique (BIM). The practical consequence of this merger is that the BCM's services are gradually being taken over by the BIM. At the time of writing, however, branches of the BCM were still operational in almost every sizeable town in the country – and might still be by the time you visit. On the other hand, many of the BCM banks marked on the town maps in this guide might have closed, in which case there should be a BIM somewhere in town providing the services previously offered by the BCM. The reason I mention all of this is because, outside of Maputo, the BCM is the only bank that consistently changes travellers' cheques. The commission on such a transaction is a whopping US$15 no matter how much you wish to change, but you will not normally have a choice. In Maputo, some *cambrios* change travellers' cheques for a more reasonable commission. In mid-2005, some visitors reported difficulty in changing travellers' cheques anywhere in the country. See also *Money Matters* on page 37.

It is relatively straightforward nowadays, at least in the larger towns, to get a cash advance on your credit card. Likewise, ATM machines, which accept major international credit cards, are starting to crop up all over the place. Visa is probably the best card to be carrying; MasterCard is also good; but American Express is less widely accepted.

Along with the BCM and the BIM, the other main banks in Mozambique are the Banco Standard Totta, Banco Austral and Banco de Fomento, the latter of which has branches in Maputo, Beira and Nampula, and might be your best bet outside of the BCM for changing travellers' cheques.

There is a fairly open black market for cash in Mozambique, one that you will practically be forced to use if you arrive in the country overland outside of banking hours. US dollars get the best rate. South African rands are as good as US dollars in and around Maputo, while Zimbabwe dollars can easily be exchanged in Chimoio, Beira or Tete, and Malawi kwacha or Zimbabwe dollars in Niassa and Tete. I would avoid changing money on the street, since there are several con artists about – far better to ask at a hotel, shop or restaurant.

Change

In many African countries, getting change for a large banknote can be a tedious process. In Mozambique, trying to do so can be enough to turn the most phlegmatic soul into a fist-gnashing wreck. Memorably, in Tete, I had to wait an hour to get 40,000 MT change for a 5,000 MT bottle of cola paid for with a 50,000 MT note, and eventually had to buy a second cola (which I gave to a few kids rather than let the guy who served get away with it) to make up the 5,000 MT difference. Obviously, the thing to do is always try to have a good selection of bills at your disposal. If you don't have the right money, check before you pay whether change is available, and if it isn't then suggest that somebody actually finds some before you hand over any money.

Overcharging and bargaining

Tourists to Africa may sometimes need to bargain over prices, but this need is often exaggerated by guidebooks and travellers. Hotels, restaurants, supermarkets and buses generally charge fixed prices and cases of overcharging in such places are too unusual for it to be worth challenging a price unless it is blatantly ridiculous.

You're bound to be overcharged at some point in Mozambique, but it is important to keep this in perspective. Some travellers, after a couple of bad experiences, start to haggle with everyone from hotel owners to old women selling fruit by the side of the road, often accompanying their negotiations with aggressive accusations of dishonesty. It's possible that the whole thing has become something of a vicious circle: if every second tourist you deal with accuses you of overcharging them, the obvious response is to ask an inflated price that you can then drop when the haggling starts. Aggressive posturing may be the easiest way to find out whether you are being overcharged, but it is very unfair on the vast majority of people who are forthright and honest in their dealings with tourists. There are better ways of dealing with the problem.

The main instance where bargaining is essential is when buying curios. What should be understood, however, is that the fact a curio seller is open to negotiation does not mean that you were initially being overcharged or ripped off. Curio sellers will generally quote a price knowing full well that you are going to bargain it down – they'd probably be startled if you didn't – and it is not necessary to respond aggressively or in an accusatory manner. It is impossible to say by how much you should bargain the initial price down (some people say that you should offer half the asking price and be prepared to settle at around two-thirds, but my experience is that curio sellers are far more whimsical than such advice allows for). The sensible approach, if you want to get a feel for prices, is to ask the price of similar items at a few different stalls before you actually contemplate buying anything.

In fruit and vegetable markets and stalls, bargaining is often the norm, even between locals, and the most healthy approach to this sort of haggling is to view it as an enjoyable part of the African experience. There will normally be an accepted price-band for any particular commodity. To find out what it is, listen to what other people pay (it helps if you know the local tongue) and try a few stalls – a ludicrously inflated price will drop the moment you walk away. When buying fruit and vegetables, a good way to feel out the situation is to ask for a bulk discount or a few extra items thrown in. And bear in mind that the reason why somebody is reluctant to bargain may be that they asked a fair price in the first place.

Above all, don't lose your sense of proportion. No matter how poor you may feel, it is your choice to travel on a tight budget. Most Mozambicans are much poorer than you will ever be, and they do not have the luxury of choosing to travel. If you find yourself quibbling with an old lady selling a few piles of fruit by the roadside, stand back and look at the bigger picture. There is nothing wrong with occasionally erring on the side of generosity. (See the section on responsible tourism on page 45 for more about interacting with the local people.)

ACCOMMODATION

Maputo, Vilankulo and Beira have hotels suited to most tastes and budgets, but in other towns hotel standards are generally low and prices high by comparison with many neighbouring countries. Hotels in Mozambique are generally former colonial hotels in various states of renovation or disrepair; it is unusual to come across the sort of cheap local lodgings that are common in countries like Malawi or Tanzania. There are few places in Mozambique where you'll pay significantly less than US$10 for a room in the cheapest pensão.

Organised campsites are mainly restricted to the beaches along the coast south of Beira, and prices tend to be quite high by African standards. Many

MAKING MOUNTAINS OUT OF MOLEHILLS

One thing that never ceased to amaze me about the accommodation in Mozambique was how often so much could be made from so little. A four-star hotel amidst the crumbling colonial buildings of Ilha do Moçambique, for instance, or the hyper-luxurious lodges on the near-deserted islands of the Bazaruto Archipelago. Of all the remarkable feats of Mozambican engineering, however, a farm in Lichinga is perhaps the most noteworthy.

In 1991, a Dutch vet by the name of Mariette came to Lichinga and bought a farm – or rather a piece of land with a lot of goats. During the 1990s, she introduced cows, chickens, rabbits, donkeys, dogs, a bush pig named Julia, and finally, in 1999, a Scottish surgeon named Kate who, like Mariette, had lived and worked in Mozambique during the uncertain times of the civil war. While Mariette continued to occupy herself with the farm, Kate set about transforming Quinta Capricornio (the name preferred to the rather less exotic 'Goat Farm') into one of the most comfortable places to stay in northern Mozambique.

Surprisingly, a concrete tennis court and children's playground were the first things to be built, both sitting somewhat incongruously beside the pigsty and Julia's private residence. Then came two chalets constructed on stilts using wood from the surrounding pine plantation and an ablution block with hot running water stored in a compressor tank heated by hot coals. A solar-powered battery, meanwhile, provides the electricity, while, until recently, contact with the outside world was maintained by a satellite phone. The food in this little world comes from the farm, courtesy of the nearly 500 animals that now populate it, all of it being 100% organic and fresh. 'If it moves, you can eat it,' explains Kate. 'Except if it's Julia,' adds Mariette.

BAGS OF WATER

The oddest custom I encountered in Mozambique was that of dangling several plastic bags filled with water from the awnings above open-air restaurants. Careful inspection showed that the bags were invariably hanging from the supports and not from the awnings, which eliminates the obvious explanation that they are weights to prevent the awning from blowing away. My linguistically impeded enquiries elicited two equally improbable explanations: that the bags were filled with water to keep the air moist (on the hot, humid Indian Ocean?); and that they were there to keep away moths. Well I can't think of a more plausible explanation... I think this falls into the category of 'answers on a postcard, please'.

campsites are part of beach resorts that also have chalet or banda accommodation at hotel prices. There are backpacker-oriented resorts or hostels in Vilankulo and Maputo, and at Tofo Beach and Barra Beach near Inhambane.

Further details of accommodation are included in the regional chapters.

TOURIST INFORMATION

Formal **tourist offices** are few and far between in Mozambique. In fact, the only obvious place where you can go for official, government-sponsored tourist information is the Fundo Nacional do Turismo or FUTUR (1203 Avenida 25 de Setembro, 3rd floor, Maputo; tel: 30 7320; fax: 30 7324; email: dep@futur.imoz.com; web: www.futur.moz.com). The staff are very friendly and helpful, although it must be said that the amount of information available is hardly overwhelming. In Maputo, it would probably be better to head to the backpackers' hostels (Fatima's is best) for the most recent and detailed information for travellers.

Fortunately, there are one or two very good, privately run tourist information centres in Vilankulo, Ilha do Moçambique and Pemba, while the number of lodges and backpackers' resorts along the southern coast is now sufficiently high to negate somewhat the lack of formal tourist offices.

At Wimbe Beach (Pemba) you'll get a lot of help from the Kaskazini bureau – see page 235.

WHAT TO BUY

The north of the country has a craft industry, primarily in making **wooden furniture** of simple but handsome appearance. Other crafts include the well-known **Makonde carvings**. The Makonde are centred around Mueda in the northeast, and here you can get representative items of their work very cheaply. Other places where you might find selections are Nampula, Nacala and Pemba.

Apart from in Maputo, where there are shops specialising in arts and crafts, most of the souvenirs that you'll find on your travels will be sold on the street outside hotels, restaurants and other places frequented by tourists. Even this is a relatively recent development; a few years ago it was difficult to find souvenirs of any description sold anywhere. As elsewhere in Africa, bargaining for souvenirs is expected, although you should conduct such negotiations in a respectful and responsible manner (see *Responsible tourism* on page 46 for further details).

COMMUNICATIONS
Telephone
Mozambique's telephone system is reasonably efficient. From overseas, it's one of the easiest African countries to get through to first time. The international code is +258, and area codes are as follows. However, at the time of writing (August 2005) new digits are being added: see box below.

Beira	03	Maputo	01	Songo	052
Chimoio	051	Nacala	06	Tete	052
Chókwè	021	Nampula	06	Xai-Xai	022
Inhambane	023	Quelimane	04		

The ringing tone is a single short tone followed by a longer pause, and the engaged tone equal lengths on and off. For international calls, dial 00 to get the operator. For directory enquiries, dial 13.

MOZAMBIQUE PHONE NUMBERS SINCE AUGUST 2005

In August 2005 a change to all fixed-line phone numbers in Mozambique came into force, aimed at bringing the numbers into line with the SADC standard of eight digits. It's not completely straightforward, as area codes may or may not be part of the required total of eight; if you get in tangle initially, ask the international phone operator for help.

The area codes given on page 73 haven't changed. The numbers below need to be inserted between the area code and the number of whomever you're phoning. For example for a Maputo number first dial the Maputo area code of 01; then the new addition (below) of 21; and then the number of the person you're calling.

Additional numbers

Maputo	21	Zambezia	24
Gaza (Chokwe)	281	Tete	252
Gaza (Xai-Xai)	282	Nampula	26
Inhambane	293	Niassa	271
Sofala	23	Cabo Delgado	272
Manica	251		

There is a minimum charge of three minutes for telephone calls, whether they are national or international. Telecomunicações de Moçambique (TDM) has offices in almost all towns, where you can make telephone calls and sometimes send faxes and emails. Alternatively, you can use the public telephone booths with cards sold at the TDM offices. The cost of making telephone calls in Mozambique is not excessively high. For instance, calling Maputo from anywhere in the country will cost a little over US$1 for the first three minutes and then about 25 cents per minute. A call to the UK, meanwhile, costs US$4 for the first three minutes and around US$1.50 per minute after that.

There is mobile phone coverage in all of the main tourist centres.

Post

Post from Mozambique is cheap and reasonably reliable, but it is often very slow. Poste Restante letters can be colleted in most large towns, and they should be addressed as in the following example:

Philip Briggs
Poste Restante
Maputo
Mozambique

The current cost of an airmail letter to Europe or North America is around US$1. A quicker service known as *Ultima Hora*, which allegedly takes between three days and one week depending on the destination, is also available for US$2.

PUBLIC HOLIDAYS

In addition to the following fixed public holidays, Good Friday and Easter Monday are recognised as public holidays in Mozambique.

New Year's Day	January 1
Heroes' Day	February 3
Women's Day	April 7
Labour Day	May 1
National Day (Independence Day)	June 25
Victory Day	September 7
Armed Forces Day	September 25
Family Day	December 25

There are also marked commemorative days:

Day of African Unity	May 25
International Children's Day	June 1
Resistance Day	June 16
Assumption of Power by Transitional Government	September 20

In addition, Maputo has a public holiday on November 10.

> ### A BAD EXPERIENCE
> *Dave Armstrong*
> We'd stopped for fuel at a filling station adjacent to a Shoprite. We needed to change some money, and asked around for a bureau de change. However, despite my telling him in no uncertain terms not to, one of my clients (why do they always know better!) ignored my advice and tried to change US$100 on the street. I'd told him that these money-changers are extremely good at palming but he had to find out for himself – and ended up with the equivalent of only US$40. He was not best pleased. For anyone who's stupid or desperate enough to change money this way, I've two pieces of advice: first, don't do it alone (as this client did, while we were filling up with diesel); and secondly make sure that you (and not the dealer) are the last person to count the money before handing over yours, and then keep firm hold of it.

Note that postcards are difficult to find in Mozambique; and when you do find them they are often very expensive and not even of Mozambique.

Email and internet

Teledata is the largest internet service-provider in Mozambique, and for a monthly fee of US$15 computer owners can get access to the internet from anywhere in the country. This has made the setting up of internet cafés – or at least a computer with internet access for the general public – a viable proposition in most of Mozambique's larger towns. The connection times are not always the quickest, and some places are at the mercy of power cuts, but even so, it all seems to work quite well. See the *Useful information* sections for each town for more details.

ELECTRICITY

Electricity is 220V AC at 50 cycles. Two-pin plugs are in use. Stabilisers are required for sensitive devices and adaptors for appliances using 110V. Batteries are useful during power cuts.

MEDIA

The main daily newspapers are the *Noticias* (Maputo), which supports the government, and the *Diario* (Beira). The main weeklies are the *Savana*, the *Domingo* (coming out on Sundays) and the magazine *Tempo*.

English language publications include *Mozambique Opportunities*, for business people, and *Mozambique File*, a monthly news service. South African newspapers are also available in Maputo, normally a day or two old and at a very high price.

Radio Mozambique broadcasts on three channels in Portuguese as well as several local languages. Since 1981 there has been experimental television, TV Mozambique, which broadcasts imported Portuguese and Brazilian programmes alongside Mozambican programmes. There is also an independent station, RTK Television, with an English language bias. Many upmarket hotels pick up the South African channel M-net and other international satellite channels.

MAPS

Backpackers and other travellers who need a good map of Mozambique for hitching or driving purposes should find the following maps quite satisfactory:

Mozambique: Globetrotter Travel Map (New Holland): clear and colourful country, regional and city maps, accompanied by good photographs of Mozambique.
Mozambique (Institut Géographique National): accurate, no-nonsense map published by French geographical institute.
Mozambique Road Map (Ravenstein Verlag)
The *Time Out* map of Mozambique is more readily available than the others, at least in South Africa, but it really is a waste of money – riddled with errors and omitting many important towns.

Health and Safety

HEALTH

written in collaboration with Dr Jane Wilson Howarth and Dr Felicity Nicholson

Mozambique boasts an array of tropical diseases but, although most travellers who spend a while in the country will become ill at some point in their trip, the cause is most likely to be straightforward travellers' diarrhoea or a cold. Provided that you receive the necessary immunisations before you travel to Mozambique, the only major cause for concern once you are in the country is malaria, which can be combated to a large extent by taking sensible precautions (see page 82).

Travel insurance

Travel insurance should be one of your top priorities. This doesn't mean you should buy the dearest and most comprehensive policy you can find, but some degree of health insurance to cover you in case of accident or illness is essential. Most policies offer at least US$1,000,000 in emergency medical expenses, and often a great deal more. They will also pay for you to be repatriated should the need arise. Whether or not you buy additional insurance – for baggage and personal belongings, for example – is up to you; weigh what you stand to lose against what you have to pay.

You can opt either for a tailormade policy, priced according to your destination and the duration of your trip, or a 'multi-trip' policy, which normally covers you for as many trips as you can squeeze into a year provided that none exceeds a certain length. Most travel agents (see page 45) also sell travel insurance. Alternatively, you can arrange it all quickly and easily over the phone with a company such as the UK-based Club Direct (tel: 0800 074 4558; web: www.clubdirect.com).

Travel clinics and health information

A full list of current travel clinic websites worldwide is available from the International Society of Travel Medicine on www.istm.org. For other journey preparation information, consult www.tripprep.com. Information about various medications may be found on www.emedicine.com.

UK

Berkeley Travel Clinic 32 Berkeley St, London W1J 8EL (near Green Park tube station); tel: 020 7629 6233

British Airways Travel Clinic and Immunisation Service There are two BA clinics in London, both on tel: 0845 600 2236; www.ba.com/travelclinics.

Appointments only Mon–Fri 9.00–16.30 at 101 Cheapside, London EC2V 6DT; or walk-in service Mon–Fri 09.30–17.30, Sat 10.00–16.00 at 213 Piccadilly, London W1J 9HQ. Apart from providing inoculations and malaria prevention, they sell a variety of health-related goods.

Cambridge Travel Clinic 48a Mill Rd, Cambridge CB1 2AS; tel: 01223 367362; email: enquiries@cambridgetravelclinic.co.uk; www.cambridgetravelclinic.co.uk. Open Tue–Fri 12.00–19.00, Sat 10.00–16.00.

Edinburgh Travel Clinic Regional Infectious Diseases Unit, Ward 41 OPD, Western General Hospital, Crewe Rd South, Edinburgh EH4 2UX; tel: 0131 537 2822; www.link.med.ed.ac.uk/ridu. Travel helpline (0906 589 0380) open weekdays 09.00–12.00. Provides inoculations and anti-malarial prophylaxis and advises on travel-related health risks.

Fleet Street Travel Clinic 29 Fleet St, London EC4Y 1AA; tel: 020 7353 5678; www.fleetstreetclinic.com. Vaccinations, travel products and latest advice.

Hospital for Tropical Diseases Travel Clinic Mortimer Market Building, Capper St (off Tottenham Ct Rd), London WC1E 6AU; tel: 020 7388 9600; www.thehtd.org. Offers consultations and advice, and is able to provide all necessary drugs and vaccines for travellers. Runs a healthline (0906 133 7733) for country-specific information and health hazards. Also stocks nets, water purification equipment and personal protection measures.

Interhealth Worldwide Partnership House, 157 Waterloo Rd, London SE1 8US; tel: 020 7902 9000; www.interhealth.org.uk. Competitively priced, one-stop travel health service. All profits go to their affiliated company, InterHealth, which provides health care for overseas workers on Christian projects.

MASTA (Medical Advisory Service for Travellers Abroad) London School of Hygiene and Tropical Medicine, Keppel St, London WC1 7HT; tel: 09065 501402; www.masta.org. Individually tailored health briefs available for a fee, with up-to-date information on how to stay healthy, inoculations and what to bring. There are currently 30 MASTA pre-travel clinics in Britain. Call 0870 241 6843 or check online for the nearest. Clinics also sell malaria prophylaxis memory cards, treatment kits, bednets, net treatment kits.

NHS travel website www.fitfortravel.scot.nhs.uk provides country-by-country advice on immunisation and malaria, plus details of recent developments, and a list of relevant health organisations.

Nomad Travel Store/Clinic 3–4 Wellington Terrace, Turnpike Lane, London N8 0PX; tel: 020 8889 7014; travel-health line (office hours only) 0906 863 3414; email: sales@nomadtravel.co.uk; www.nomadtravel.co.uk. Also at 40 Bernard St, London WC1N 1LJ; tel: 020 7833 4114; 52 Grosvenor Gardens, London SW1W 0AG; tel: 020 7823 5823; and 43 Queens Rd, Bristol BS8 1QH; tel: 0117 922 6567. For health advice, equipment such as mosquito nets and other anti-bug devices, and an excellent range of adventure travel gear.

Trailfinders Travel Clinic 194 Kensington High St, London W8 7RG; tel: 020 7938 3999; www.trailfinders.com/clinic.htm

Travelpharm The Travelpharm website, www.travelpharm.com, offers up-to-date guidance on travel-related health and has a range of medications available through their online mini-pharmacy.

Irish Republic

Tropical Medical Bureau Grafton Street Medical Centre, Grafton Buildings, 34 Grafton St, Dublin 2; tel: 1 671 9200; www.tmb.ie. A useful website specific to tropical destinations. Also check website for other bureaux locations throughout Ireland.

USA

Centers for Disease Control 1600 Clifton Rd, Atlanta, GA 30333; tel: 800 311 3435; travellers' health hotline 888 232 3299; www.cdc.gov/travel. The central source of travel information in the USA. The invaluable Health Information for International Travel, published annually, is available from the Division of Quarantine at this address.

Connaught Laboratories PO Box 187, Swiftwater, PA 18370; tel: 800 822 2463. They will send a free list of specialist tropical-medicine physicians in your state.

IAMAT (International Association for Medical Assistance to Travelers) 1623 Military Rd, 279, Niagara Falls, NY14304-1745; tel: 716 754 4883; email: info@iamat.org; www.iamat.org. A non-profit organisation that provides lists of English-speaking doctors abroad.

International Medicine Center 920 Frostwood Drive, Suite 670, Houston, TX 77024; tel: 713 550 2000; www.traveldoc.com

Canada

IAMAT Suite 1, 1287 St Clair Av W, Toronto, Ontario M6E 1B8; tel: 416 652 0137; www.iamat.org

TMVC (Travel Doctors Group) Sulphur Springs Rd, Ancaster, Ontario; tel: 905 648 1112; www.tmvc-group.com

Australia, New Zealand, Singapore

TMVC Tel: 1300 65 88 44; www.tmvc.com.au. Twenty-three clinics in Australia, New Zealand and Singapore including:

Auckland Canterbury Arcade, 170 Queen St, Auckland; tel: 9 373 3531

Brisbane 6th floor, 247 Adelaide St, Brisbane, QLD 4000; tel: 7 3221 9066

Melbourne 393 Little Bourke St, 2nd floor, Melbourne, VIC 3000; tel: 3 9602 5788

Sydney Dymocks Building, 7th Floor, 428 George St, Sydney, NSW 2000; tel: 2 9221 7133

IAMAT PO Box 5049, Christchurch 5, New Zealand; www.iamat.org

South Africa

SAA-Netcare Travel Clinics Private Bag X34, Benmore 2010; www.travelclinic.co.za. Clinics throughout South Africa.

TMVC 113 D F Malan Drive, Roosevelt Park, Johannesburg; tel: 011 888 7488; www.tmvc.com.au. Consult the website for details of eight other clinics in South Africa.

Switzerland

IAMAT 57 Chemin des Voirets, 1212 Grand Lancy, Geneva; www.iamat.org

LONG-HAUL FLIGHTS

There is growing evidence, albeit circumstantial, that long-haul air travel increases the risk of developing deep vein thrombosis. This condition is potentially life threatening, but it should be stressed that the danger to the average traveller is slight.

Certain risk factors specific to air travel have been identified. These include immobility, compression of the veins at the back of the knee by the edge of the seat, the decreased air pressure and slightly reduced oxygen in the cabin, and dehydration. Consuming alcohol may exacerbate the situation by increasing fluid loss and encouraging immobility.

In theory everyone is at risk, but those at highest risk are shown below:

- Passengers on journeys of longer than eight hours duration
- People over 40
- People with heart disease
- People with cancer
- People with clotting disorders
- People who have had recent surgery, especially on the legs
- Women who are pregnant, or on the pill or other oestrogen therapy
- People who are very tall (over 6ft/1.8m) or short (under 5ft/1.5m)

A deep vein thrombosis (DVT) is a clot of blood that forms in the leg veins. Symptoms include swelling and pain in the calf or thigh. The skin may feel hot to touch and becomes discoloured (light blue-red). A DVT is not dangerous in itself, but if a clot breaks down then it may travel to the lungs

Medical kit

Take a small medical kit with you. This should contain malaria tablets and a thermometer, soluble aspirin or paracetamol (good for gargling when you have a sore throat and for reducing fever and pains), plasters (Band-aids), potassium permanganate crystals or another favoured antiseptic, iodine for sterilising water and cleaning wounds, sunblock, and condoms or femidoms. Most antibiotics are widely available in Mozambique, but be hesitant about taking them without medical advice. Depending on your travel plans, it is a good idea to carry a course of tablets as a cure for malaria; recommendations can change so seek specialist advice before travelling. As restaurant meals in Mozambique tend to be based around meat and carbohydrate, some people may like to carry vitamin pills.

Immunisations

Vaccinations against the following diseases are currently recommended for *all* visits to Mozambique. See pages 82–8 for details of other diseases, including malaria, which could be an issue depending on the type of trip you are planning.

Polio, **tetanus** and **diphtheria** vaccinations are normally administered in infancy. This initial protection should be renewed every ten years by a booster injection.

(pulmonary embolus). Symptoms of a pulmonary embolus (PE) include chest pain, shortness of breath and coughing up small amounts of blood.

Symptoms of a DVT rarely occur during the flight, and typically occur within three days of arrival, although symptoms of a DVT or PE have been reported up to two weeks later.

Anyone who suspects that they have these symptoms should see a doctor immediately as anticoagulation (blood thinning) treatment can be given.

Prevention of DVT

General measures to reduce the risk of thrombosis are shown below. This advice also applies to long train or bus journeys.

- Whilst waiting to board the plane, try to walk around rather than sit.
- During the flight drink plenty of water (at least two small glasses every hour).
- Avoid excessive tea, coffee and alcohol.
- Perform leg-stretching exercises, such as pointing the toes up and down.
- Move around the cabin when practicable.

If you fit into the high-risk category (see above) ask your doctor if it is safe to travel. Additional protective measures such as graded compression stockings, aspirin or low molecular weight heparin can be given. No matter how tall you are, where possible request a seat with extra legroom.

Hepatitis A is a viral disease that attacks the liver and usually causes jaundice. Although rarely fatal, this disease can cause serious illness and will certainly terminate your trip. It's a good idea, therefore, to avoid catching it. This is best done by being careful about what you eat and drink, and washing your hands after going to the toilet and before handling food, since the disease can be spread from person to person through faeces and contaminated food and water. The most effective form of protection is the hepatitis A vaccine (eg: Havrix Monodose, Avaxim). The normal course of two injections provides protection for up to ten years; a single dose will be good for about a year. Try to complete the course at least two weeks before you travel. The complete course costs around £100.

Typhoid is caught through the consumption of food or water contaminated with *Salmonella typhi*. The classic symptom of typhoid is a high, sustained fever, although stomach pains, headaches, a pin-point red rash and a loss of appetite are also potential signs that you have typhoid. Since sanitation in Mozambique is sometimes doubtful, vaccination against the disease is a sensible precaution. The preferred method of immunisation is by injection (the less favoured alternative is capsules administered orally), which should be given at least seven days before departure. The vaccine is about 85% effective and lasts for three years.

Meningitis can be caused by a viral or bacterial infection. Viral meningitis is the less serious of the two and normally clears up in about ten days. Bacterial meningitis, however, can be fatal. Several different varieties of bacteria can cause this type of meningitis – an infection of the fluid found in the spinal cord and surrounding the brain – which, in severe cases, can result in brain damage, paralysis and death. Common symptoms include a high fever, thumping headaches and, most classically, a stiff neck. The worrying thing about this disease is the relatively easy way in which it is transmitted. One of the most contagious forms of meningitis is caused by the *Neisseria meningitidis* bacteria, also known as meningococcal meningitis, which is spread through respiratory and oral secretions such as coughing and kissing. Mozambique is not currently considered to be in the 'meningitis belt', so vaccination is not routinely recommended for trips of under two to three weeks. For longer trips, or if you are going to teach children, then the meningococcal vaccine (ACWY) should be taken at least one week before departure. This vaccine lasts for approximately three years.

Yellow fever is no longer a risk in Mozambique itself. However, if you are coming from an infected country (Zambia and Tanzania are the two neighbouring countries where yellow fever is still prevalent), you will require an International Certificate of Vaccination or Revaccination against Yellow Fever. Note that this certificate is not valid until ten days after the date of your last vaccination, after which time it lasts for ten years. The yellow fever vaccine costs around £45.

Malaria

Malaria kills about a million Africans every year. Of the travellers who return to Britain with malaria, 92% have caught it in Africa. The disease is present throughout tropical Africa at altitudes of below 1,800m, and the Anopheles mosquito, which transmits the malaria parasite, is most abundant near the marshes and still water in which it breeds.

For all practical purposes, malaria should be considered to be present throughout Mozambique throughout the year. The only areas from where it is entirely absent are mountainous regions above an altitude of 1,800m, and since few such places exist in Mozambique and those that do can only be visited by passing through malarial areas, similar precautions should be taken wherever you plan to travel. That said, the risk of catching malaria is much higher along the coast or on the shore of Lake Niassa than it is at higher altitudes. The prevalence increases the further north you travel along the coast, and the disease is far more likely to be caught if you visit Mozambique during the wet summer months than if you visit between May and August.

The first step in preventing malaria is to take prophylactic drugs. You can ignore any stories you hear on the travellers' grapevine about it being better to acquire resistance than to take tablets. It is not possible to build up an effective resistance to malaria, and travellers risk death by not taking precautions. It is foolhardy not to take malaria tablets.

The drug currently recommended for visitors spending less than three months in tropical Africa is Lariam (mefloquine). Lariam is generally effective in preventing malaria, although side-effects such as mood swings, visual or hearing disturbances, fits, severe headaches and changes in heart rhythm have been known to occur. Lariam should definitely not be taken by someone with a history of psychological problems, severe depression, diabetes, heart conduction problems or epilepsy. If you don't fall into this category, and you are a non-pregnant adult, Lariam is the recommended drug. Most people do not experience side effects and of those that do, the majority have dizziness, nausea or vivid dreams. These are not medically serious and are not a reason for stopping the drug unless they are unacceptable. More serious side-effects include mood swings, visual disturbances, violent headaches, fits or palpitations. Any of these would be a reason to stop taking the drug and to seek an alternative. If you have never taken Lariam before, it is best to try it two to three weeks before departure to see if it suits you. Alternative prophylactic drugs include **Malarone** and **doxycycline**. Malarone can be used for up to 28 days and is of equivalent efficacy. It seems to have fewer side effects and has the advantage of being taken only one day before departure, daily through the trip and for only one week after leaving the country. Its main disadvantage is the cost, which for some travellers may be prohibitive. A viable alternative is doxycycline. This can be used by epilepsy sufferers (unlike Lariam), but note that roughly 3% of the people who use it develop allergic skin reactions in sunlight. Women taking the oral contraceptive should use an additional form of protection for the first four weeks when taking doxycycline. **Chloroquine** and **proguanil** are now considered to be the last resort, but are still better than nothing. Whatever prophylactic drugs you use, remember to complete the course as directed after leaving the last malarial area, and get into the habit of taking your pills in the evening, preferably after a meal.

Just as important as taking malaria pills is making every reasonable effort not to be bitten by mosquitoes between dusk and dawn. Many travellers assume that simply taking pills gives them full protection against malaria. It doesn't. It stuns me how many travellers wander around at night in shorts and flip-flops in parts of Africa where malaria is prolific. Resistance to prophylactics is widespread in Africa, and the most certain way not to catch malaria is to not be bitten by mosquitoes. This doesn't mean that avoiding bites is an alternative to taking pills – nobody will be able to prevent every potential bite. You should try to do both. (See page 90 for more about avoiding mosquito bites.)

Even if you take your malaria tablets meticulously and take care to avoid being bitten, you might still contract a resistant strain of malaria. If you experience headaches and pains, a general sense of disorientation or flu-like aches and pains, you may have malaria. It is vital that you seek medical advice immediately. Local doctors see malaria all the time; they will know it in all its guises and know the best treatment for local resistance patterns. Untreated malaria is likely to be fatal, but even prophylactic-resistant strains normally respond well to treatment, provided that you do not leave it too late.

If you are unable to reach a doctor, you may well be forced to diagnose and treat yourself. For this reason, it is advisable to carry a cure in your medical kit.

Expert opinion is that the most safe and effective cure available at present is the combination of **Fansidar** and **quinine**. This cure needs to be used in conjunction with a thermometer, so carry one of these as well. The correct procedure is to take two quinine tablets every eight hours until the fever subsides, for a maximum of three days. When the fever subsides, or if it hasn't subsided after three days, take a single dose of three Fansidar tablets. Provided you follow this procedure before the symptoms have become chronic, it is practically 100% effective. Be warned, however, that you should try to drink a lot of water after you take Fansidar. Malarone is also used as a treatment. Four tablets should be taken at the same time of day for three days. No matter which treatment you use, it is no substitute for seeking professional help. So by all means start the course but get yourself to medical help as soon as you can.

Malaria typically takes one to two weeks to incubate but it can take as long as a year (if you are taking tablets prophylactically). This means that you may only display symptoms after you leave Mozambique, for which reason you are advised to complete the prophylactics as directed after returning home. It is all too easy to forget your pills once you are in the everyday routine of life at home, but you should make every effort to remember. If you display symptoms that could possibly be malarial, even if this happens a year after you return home, get to a doctor and, in order that they don't overlook the possibility, ensure that they are aware you have been exposed to malaria.

Finally, if you have a fever and the malaria test is negative (though this still does not exclude malaria), you may have typhoid, which should also receive immediate treatment. Where typhoid-testing is unavailable, a routine blood test can give a strong indication of this disease. (See page 80 for more about typhoid.)

AIDS and venereal diseases

HIV and other venereal diseases are widespread in Mozambique. According to the United Nations Development Programme (UNDP), a massive 14.17% of Mozambican adults are HIV positive. This figure is not quite as high as those in neighbouring countries, but is cause for concern nonetheless, and for extreme caution on the part of travellers. The risks involved in having unprotected casual sex barely need stating. Condoms and femidoms offer a high level of protection against HIV and other venereal diseases, and the additional use of spermicides and pessaries also reduces the risk of transmission.

Hospital workers in Mozambique deal with AIDS victims on a regular basis. Contrary to Western prejudices, health professionals do realise the danger involved in using unsterilised needles, and you are unlikely to be confronted with one in a town hospital or clinic. If, however, you need treatment in a really remote area, where supplies might be a problem, you might be glad to be carrying a few needles and hypodermic syringes.

Other diseases
Bilharzia or schistosomiasis
There is a risk of bilharzia in the rivers and lakes of Mozambique. See the box on pages 86–7 for more details.

Above Maputo city centre with the cathedral in the foreground

Below Close up of Samora Machel from a street mural near the airport, Maputo

Next page Makonde face mask, Nampula

Cholera

Cholera is another disease that occurs in areas of poor sanitation, which includes Mozambique. The main symptom is severe diarrhoea – sometimes accompanied by vomiting – which can cause dehydration and, in acute cases, death. No vaccine against cholera is currently available (the old one is no longer considered to be effective), so the best way to avoid the disease is by paying attention to personal hygiene and being careful about what you eat and drink.

Hepatitis B

Hepatitis B is a serious viral disease that is present in the blood and body fluids of an infected individual. It attacks the liver (like hepatitis A) and can sometimes be fatal. Transmission is by unprotected sexual intercourse, unsterilised needles or through unscreened blood transfusions, which means that the measures recommended to combat HIV (see opposite) apply equally when trying to minimise the risks of catching hepatitis B. The vaccine, administered in three intramuscular doses over a four-week period, provides protection against hepatitis B. The complete course will cost around £80.

Rabies

Rabies can be carried by any mammal. The domestic dog is the species which most often passes it to humans. The most common route of infection is a bite from an infected animal, but a scratch or a lick on an open wound can do it.

The immunisation against rabies is highly effective, but once symptoms appear rabies is incurable, and the way that you die is so horrible that all doctors advise post-exposure vaccine. If you are not immunised and there is any possibility that you have been exposed to a rabid animal, get to a doctor as soon as you can. This should be done as soon as possible, but since the incubation period can be over a month if, for instance, you are bitten on the hand, it's not too late to get this done weeks after exposure. As the incubation period for rabies is determined by the distance between the point of infection and the brain, people who are bitten on the face (as is common with children) have ten days at most and must get help immediately. The message, then, is to be fully immunised against rabies if you intend visiting remote places or handling wild animals. Any wild animals that seem unusually tame should be assumed to be rabid: do not handle them.

All animal bites should be cleaned as protection against general infection. Scrub the wound with soap and bottled or boiled water for five minutes (time it with a watch), then liberally apply povidone iodine or 40% (or higher) alcohol – even gin or whisky will do – or aqueous iodine. This can help to prevent the rabies virus from entering the body, and will guard against wound infection and the very real risk of catching tetanus.

The rabies vaccine consists of three doses over a four-week period. Note that, even if you have been vaccinated against rabies, you will still require at least two post-bite rabies injections. Unimmunised travellers will need a full course of injections plus the expensive rabies immunoglobulin (RIG), which

BILHARZIA OR SCHISTOSOMIASIS
Dr Jane Wilson Howarth

Bilharzia or schistosomiasis is a common debilitating disease afflicting perhaps 200 million people worldwide, but those most affected are the rural poor of the tropics who repeatedly acquire more and more of these nasty little worm-lodgers. Fortunately travellers and expatriates generally suffer fewer problems if they acquire bilharzia because they pick up relatively few parasites and so their burden of worms is less; they are also likely to realise they have bilharzia early and get it treated promptly.

When someone with bilharzia excretes into freshwater, bilharzia eggs hatch and swim off to find a suitable freshwater snail to infest. Once inside the snail, they develop, change and emerge as torpedo-shaped cercariae; these are only just visible to the naked eye, and can digest their way through human or animal skin. This is the stage that attacks people as they wade, bathe or even shower in infected water, and unfortunately many lakes, including Lake Niassa, and also rivers and irrigation canals in Africa carry a risk of bilharzia.

The pond snails which harbour bilharzia are a centimetre or more long; they like well-oxygenated, still or slowly moving freshwater, with plenty of vegetation (waterweed, reeds, etc) for them to eat. The most risky shores will be close to places where infected people use water, where they wash clothes. Winds disperse the cercariae though, so that they can be blown some distance, perhaps 200m, from where they entered the water. Scuba diving off a boat into deep off-shore water, then, should be a low-risk activity, but showering in lake water or paddling along a reedy lakeshore near a village carries a high risk of acquiring bilharzia.

Water which has been filtered or stored snail-free for two days, or water which has been boiled or treated with Cresol or Dettol, is also safe. Covering your skin with an oily insect repellent like DEET before swimming or paddling is also protective.

Cercariae live for up to 30 hours after they have been shed by snails, but the older they are, the less vigorous they are and the less capable of penetrating the skin. Cercariae are shed in the greatest numbers between 1.00 and 15.00. If water to be used for bathing is pumped early in the morning, from deep in the lake (cercariae are sun-loving) or from a site far from where people urinate, there will be less risk of infestation. And afternoon swims will

will set you back around US$800–1,000. Unfortunately, unlike the vaccine, RIG is seldom available in developing countries – another good reason to take rabies vaccine before you go!

Sleeping sickness
This is carried by tsetse flies, which look like oversized houseflies and have a painful but (sleeping sickness aside) harmless bite. Tsetse flies commonly occur in low-lying game reserves throughout tropical Africa. Sleeping sickness

be a much higher risk than an early morning plunge. Since cercariae take perhaps 10–15 minutes to penetrate, a quick shower, or a splash across a river, followed by a thorough drying with a towel, should be safe. Even if you are in risky water longer it is worth vigorously towelling off after bathing: This will kill any cercariae which are still in the process of penetrating your skin.

Only a proportion of cercariae which successfully penetrate will survive and cause disease. Although absence of ealy symptoms does not necessarily mean there is no infection, infected people usually notice symptoms two or more weeks after penetration. Travellers and expatriates will probably experience a fever and often a wheezy cough; local residents do not usually have symptoms. There is now a very good blood test which, if done six weeks or more after likely exposure, will determine whether or not parasites are going to cause problems and then the infection can be treated. While treatment generally remains effective, there are treatment failures and retreatment is often necessay; the reasons for treatment failures are not yet fully understood, but there now may be some drug resistance. Since bilharzia can be a nasty illness, avoidance is better than waiting to be cured and it is wise to avoid bathing in high risk-areas.

Summary points
- If you are bathing, swimming, paddling or wading in freshwater which you think may carry a bilharzia risk, try to get out of the water within ten minutes.
- Dry off thoroughly with a towel.
- Avoid bathing or paddling on shores within 200m of villages or places where people use the water a great deal, especially reedy shores or where there is plenty of waterweed.
- Ideally cover yourself with DEET insect repellent before swimming.
- If your bathing water comes from a risky source, try to ensure that the water is taken from the lake in the early morning and stored snail-free, otherwise it should be filtered or Dettol or Cresol added.

Thanks to Dr Vaughan Southgate of the Natural History Museum, London, and to Dr G B Wyatt of the Liverpool School of Tropical Medicine, for information on bilharzia in Lake Niassa.

has a patchy distribution, and it only occurs within a small limit of the tsetse fly's range: it cannot be considered a real threat to travellers and it's a treatable ailment. In Mozambique, tsetse flies are common in several game reserves: they bite during the day and are attracted to the colour blue.

Ticks and tickbite fever
There are several unpleasant illnesses that can follow a tick bite in Africa, including lyme disease, but the good news is that even if a tick is carrying

disease organisms, it will not inevitably infect you. You are less likely to be infected if you get the tick off promptly and do not damage it.

Remove any tick as soon as you notice it on you (it will most likely be firmly attached to somewhere you would rather it was not) grasp the tick as close to your body as possible and pull steadily and firmly away at right angles to your skin. The tick will then come away complete as long as you do not jerk or twist. If possible, douse the wound with alcohol (any spirit will do) or iodine.

Spreading redness around the bite and/or fever and/or aching joints after a tick bite imply that you have an infection that requires antibiotic treatment, so seek advice.

Diarrhoea and related illnesses

Diarrhoea affects at least half of those who travel in the tropics. The best solution is to stop eating for 24 hours and drink at least three litres a day of clear fluids. After this stick to a very light, plain diet , for example, dry biscuits or boiled potatoes or rice, avoiding heavy greasy foods, spicy foods and alcohol. The bacteria responsible for most diarrhoea and related symptoms (such as the abdominal pains caused by the stomach trying to expel bad food) will normally die within 36 hours if they are deprived of food.

Blockers such as Imodium and codeine phosphate should only be taken if you have no access to sanitation, for instance if you *have* to travel by bus. Blockers keep the poisons in your system, so make you feel bad for longer. They are sometimes useful if bowel cramps persist for more than 48 hours, as can be the case with salmonella poisoning. On the other hand, it is dangerous to take blockers with dysentery (evidenced by blood, slime or fever with the diarrhoea). Really, if diarrhoea or related symptoms persist much beyond 36 hours, the sensible thing to do is consult a doctor or pharmacist. The chances are you have nothing serious, but you may have something treatable.

When you have diarrhoea, it is important to drink a lot. Paediatric rehydration fluids such as Dioralyte and Electrolade are excellent, or you can make your own salt and sugar rehydration fluid (see box). If you are vomiting you can still absorb sipped fluids, and Dioralyte better than most. Sip the drink slowly and avoid anything that is very hot or cold. Try to drink a glass of rehydration fluid every time your bowels open. If you are not eating, you need to drink around three litres of fluid daily in a temperate climate, more if it is hot, you are at a high altitude, or you have fever or diarrhoea. If you are vomiting, do not worry about the quantity you produce – it is never as much as it looks. Dehydration is the only serious complication of diarrhoea and vomiting; provided you keep sipping slowly you will replace sufficient lost fluids, even if you have cholera.

Stomach problems associated with severe flatulence, abdominal distension, stomach cramps and sulphurous belching may well be caused by **giardia**. This is not a serious illness, but it is unpleasant and you will want treatment as quickly as possible. It is best treated with tinidazole. The course comprises four 500mg tablets taken as one dose. This should be repeated after seven days if symptoms persist. You shouldn't touch alcohol while taking treatment for giardia.

TREATING TRAVELLERS' DIARRHOEA

It is dehydration which makes you feel awful during a bout of diarrhoea and the most important part of treatment is drinking lots of clear fluids. Sachets of oral rehydration salts give the perfect biochemical mix to replace all that is pouring out of your bottom but they do not taste nice. Any dilute mixture of sugar and salt in water will do you good, so if you like Coke or orange squash, drink that with a three-finger pinch of salt added to each glass. Otherwise make a solution of a four-finger scoop of sugar with a three-finger pinch of salt in a glass of water. Or add eight level teaspoons of sugar (18g) and one level teaspoon of salt (3g) to one litre (five cups) of safe water. A squeeze of lemon or orange juice improves the taste and adds potassium, which is also lost during a bout of diarrhoea. Drink two large glasses after every bowel action, and more if you are thirsty. If you are not eating, then you need to drink three litres a day plus the equivalent of whatever is pouring into the toilet. If you feel like eating, take a bland, high-carbohydrate diet. Heavy, greasy foods will probably give you cramps.

If the diarrhoea is bad, or you are passing blood or slime, or you have a fever, you will probably need antibiotics in addition to fluid replacement. A three-day course of Ciprofloxacin 500mg twice daily (or Norfloxacin) is appropriate treatment for dysentery and bad diarrhoea. If the diarrhoea is greasy and bulky and is accompanied by 'eggy' burps, the likely cause is giardia. This is best treated with Tinidazole (2g in one dose repeated seven days later if symptoms persist).

If you have diarrhoea with blood or you have a fever, see a doctor for a stool test. Provided that you are taking plenty of fluids, you need not be in a great rush about this, but nor is there any point in delaying: chronic diarrhoea will make it practically impossible to travel anywhere, and if nothing else seeing a doctor will ease your mind.

How to avoid diarrhoea and other food-and-water-borne diseases

There are a great many myths about how diarrhoea is acquired, but most travellers become sick from contaminated food. Salads, especially lettuce, are always a likely source of diarrhoea. Food that is freshly cooked or thoroughly reheated should be safe, and sizzling hot street foods are invariably safer than those served at buffets at expensive hotels. Ice-cream is an ideal medium for bacterial cultures and it is often not kept adequately frozen due to power cuts. Ice may be made with unboiled water, and it could have been deposited by the roadside on its journey from the ice factory.

In any third-world country, you'll hear all sorts of contradictory information about the safety of drinking tap water. In Mozambique, my impression is that you should avoid drinking tap water wherever possible. The best way to purify water is by boiling it: simply bringing it to the boil kills 99% of bugs, and keeping it on the boil for a further two minutes kills everything at altitudes of below 4,500m (which is everywhere in Mozambique). Boiling water is more effective than using iodine, which is in turn more effective than any chlorine-based water-purification tablet.

Outdoor health
Insects
Even if you are taking malaria tablets, you should take steps to avoid being bitten by insects, and by mosquitoes in particular. The most imperative reason for doing so is the increasing levels of resistance to preventative drugs. Whatever pills you take, there remains a significant risk of being infected by malaria in areas below 1,800m. Of much less concern, but still a risk, are several other mosquito-borne viral fevers that either are or else might be present in low- and medium-altitude parts of Mozambique. **Dengue**, the only one of these diseases that is anything close to being common, is very nasty with symptoms that include severe muscle cramps, high fever and a measles-like rash; fatalities are exceptional but medical help should be sought. The other diseases in this category are too rare to be a cause for serious concern. Nevertheless, they are difficult to treat, and some of them are potentially fatal. And it is not only mosquitoes that might carry nasty diseases. **Leishmania**, another difficult-to-treat disease, is spread by sandfly bites. Before you panic, it should be stressed that all these diseases other than malaria are most unlikely to be caught by travellers. I mention them mainly to illustrate that malaria pills on their own do not guarantee your safety against serious insect-borne diseases.

The *Anopheles* mosquito, which spreads malaria, emerges at dusk, as do sandflies and most other disease-carrying mosquitoes. You will thus greatly reduce your chances of being bitten and contracting insect-borne diseases if you wear long trousers and socks in the evening and cover exposed parts of your body with insect repellent, preferably a **DEET**-based preparation such as Repel. While a concentration of 55% DEET is suitable for most adults, you should consider a preparation using 100% DEET (eg: Repel 100) if you are particularly prone to being bitten or are not taking the most effective malaria tablets. Sprays or roll-ons of this sort are not available in Mozambique; bring one with you.

The *Anopheles* mosquito hunts mostly at ground level and it can bite through thin socks, so it is worth putting repellent on your ankles, even if they are covered. DEET-impregnated ankle-bands are also quite effective. When walking in scrub and forest areas, you should cover and spray yourself by day as well; the *Aedes* mosquito, that spreads dengue, is a day-biter. Solid shoes, socks and trousers will, in any case, protect you against snakes, sharp thorns, and harmless but irritating biters like midges.

Like many insects, mosquitoes are drawn to direct light. If you are camping, never put a lamp near the opening of your tent or you will have a swarm of mosquitoes and other insects waiting to join you when you retire. In hotel rooms, be aware that the longer you leave on your light, the greater will be the number of insects with which you are likely to share your accommodation.

Once you are in bed, the most effective form of protection against mosquitoes is a net. Mosquito coils, widely available in Mozambique, will reduce the biting rate, and, even though strains of mosquito have evolved that are skilled at flying in turbulent air, so will a fan. Far better, though, is to carry your own permethrin-impregnated net, which will protect you against everything. Permethrin can also be used on clothing, and it remains effective for several weeks.

To balance the warnings, it should be stressed that the overwhelming majority of insects don't bite people, and of those that do, the vast majority are entirely harmless. Mattresses quite often contain bedbugs and fleas, both of which are essentially harmless.

Sun and heat

The equatorial sun is vicious. Although it is impossible to avoid some exposure to the sun, it would be foolish to incur it needlessly. Tanning ages your skin and it can cause skin cancer. If you are coming to Mozambique from a less harsh climate, let your body get used to the sunlight gradually or you will end up with sunburn. Take things too far, and sunstroke – a potentially fatal condition – may be the result. Wear sunscreen and build up your exposure gradually, starting with no more than 20 minutes a day. Avoid exposing yourself for more than two hours in any day, and stay out of the sun between 12.00 and 15.00. Be particularly careful of sunburn when swimming or snorkelling. A shirt will protect your shoulders and a pair of shorts will protect the back of your thighs.

In hot parts of Mozambique, particularly along the coast, you may sweat more than you normally would. To counter the resultant loss of water and salt, you should drink more than normal and eat extra salt if you develop a taste for it (salt tablets are useless). Prickly heat, a rash caused by sweat trapped under the skin, is a harmless but highly uncomfortable and common problem when people used to temperate climates first enter the tropics. It will help if you wear 100% cotton clothing and splash yourself regularly with water, but avoid excessive use of soap.

Always wear clothes made from natural fabrics such as cotton. These help prevent fungal infections and other rashes. Athlete's foot is prevalent, so wear thongs in communal showers.

Small cuts are inclined to go septic in the tropics. Clean any lesion with a dilute solution of potassium permanganate 2–3 times daily. Antiseptic creams are not suitable for the tropics; wounds must be kept dry and covered.

Dangerous animals

In the past, the dangers associated with African wild animals have frequently been overstated by the so-called Great White Hunters, and others trying to glamorise their chosen way of life. Contrary to such fanciful notions as rampaging elephants and man-eating lions, most wild animals fear us far more than we fear them, and their normal response to seeing a person is to foot it as quickly as possible in the opposite direction. That said, many travel guides have responded to the exaggerated ideas of the dangers associated with wild animals by being overly reassuring. The likelihood of a tourist being attacked by an animal is indeed very low, but it can happen, and there have been a number of fatalities caused by such incidents in recent years, particularly in southern Africa. Frankly, there are so few large mammals left in those parts of Mozambique accessible to tourists that you'd be lucky to see an antelope's hoof print, let alone be charged down by a herd of angry elephants.

One large mammal that may still be a real cause for concern is the hippopotamus, and even then the chances of encountering one of these in Mozambique is slight. The hippo is, however, responsible for more human deaths than any other African mammal. This is not because it is especially aggressive, but because its response to any disturbance while it is grazing is to head directly to the safety of the water, and it will trample anything that gets in its way. You should be cautious around any lake or large river unless you know for a fact that hippo are not present. Hippos are most likely to be out grazing towards dusk, in the early morning, and in overcast weather. The danger is getting between a hippo and the water – it would be most unlikely to attack you if it perceived a clear path to safety – so the risk is greater the closer you are to the shore. You should never walk in reed-beds unless you are certain that no hippos are present. On the other hand, you have little to fear on land by approaching a hippo that is already in the water.

Crocodiles are still present along most large rivers in Mozambique, so in the unlikely event that you decide to go wading in the Zambezi or Limpopo, do ask local advice first. As a rule, any crocodile that lives near human habitation and that is large enough to kill a person will have been dealt with by its potential prey, so the greatest risk is attached to swimming or wading in large rivers away from human habitation.

There are campsites in Africa where vervet monkeys and baboons have become dangerous pests. I am not aware of any such place in Mozambique, but it could happen. It is worth mentioning that feeding these animals is highly irresponsible; not only is it encouraging them to scavenge, but – if the animals become bold to the point where they are potentially dangerous – it may lead to their being shot. If primates are hanging around a campsite, and you wander off leaving fruit in your tent, don't expect the tent to be standing when you return.

Sharks are common along the Indian Ocean coastline, and few if any beaches in Mozambique are protected by shark nets. There is less risk of shark attacks on beaches that are afforded a degree of protection by reefs. In reality, the likelihood of being attacked by a shark is infinitesimal, even on totally unprotected beaches, but there is no denying that the risk exists, and unfortunately there's nothing much you can do to lessen it (except, of course, to stay out of the water).

Snakebite

Although poisonous snakes are present throughout Mozambique, they pose little real threat to humans (in South Africa, where there are just as many poisonous snakes, they kill fewer than ten people every year – fewer than the number killed by lightning!). The reason for this is that most snakes are very shy and secretive, and will move off at the slightest sign of humans. In several years of African travel, I doubt I have seen snakes more than a dozen times, and in all but one instance they slithered off harmlessly.

The one place where you should be conscious of the possible presence of snakes is on rocky slopes and cliffs, particularly where you are scrambling up or down using your hands. This is because snakes respond to seismic vibrations – in most habitats they will sense your footsteps and slither away long before you get near them, but they may not on a rocky slope. You also have a greater danger of cornering a snake, or being unable to get away yourself, in a steep rocky habitat. Finally, rocky areas are the favoured dwelling place of Africa's most dangerous snake, the puff adder. Although this is not a particularly venomous species, it is capable of inflicting a fatal bite. The danger with puff adders is that they are unusually slothful, and the one species of venomous snake that doesn't generally move off in response to human foot treads.

As a general rule, you should wear trousers, socks and solid boots when you walk in the bush. Good boots will protect against the 50% of snakebites that occur below the angle; trousers will help to deflect bites higher up on the leg. If you see a snake, wait to let it pass. If it rises to strike, the common advice is to stand dead still, as snakes strike in response to movement. All well and good, but on the one occasion where a snake reared at me, and twice when I've been with someone to whom this happened, instinct won over logic and the person concerned beetled off as quickly as possible in the opposite direction. This tactic worked perfectly well.

If the worst should happen, don't panic. Most snakes are non-venomous, venom is only dispensed in about 50% of bites by venomous snakes, and it is quite uncommon for a bite to contain enough venom to kill an adult. The chances are that you will not come to any harm. Keep the victim still and calm; wash the wound with soap then wipe it gently with a clean cloth to remove any venom from the skin surface. Remove rings, bangles or watches in anticipation of swelling. If possible, splint the bitten limb, as movement quickens the rate of venom absorption, or if you have a crepe bandage apply this firmly from the end of the bitten extremity towards and over the site of the bite. Keep the bitten part below heart height. The victim should then be taken to a doctor or hospital, where they should be kept under observation. Antivenin will only be administered by a trained heath person if and when signs of envenomation occur. Having a positive identification of the snake will help effective treatment, but you should not attempt to catch it unless you are sure that there is no risk of somebody else being bitten, bearing in mind that even a decapitated head can envenomate.

Finally, note that, after a snakebite, many 'traditional' first-aid measures will do more harm than good:

DO NOT give alcohol or aspirin; paracetamol is safe.
DO NOT cut, incise or suck the wound; suction devices do not work.
DO NOT apply a tourniquet.
DO NOT apply potassium permanganate or ice.
DO NOT PANIC – you are unlikely to have been envenomed.

Medical facilities in Mozambique

There are private clinics, hospitals and pharmacies in most large towns, but unless you speak Portuguese you may have difficulty communicating your needs beyond relatively straightforward requests such as a malaria test – try to find somebody bilingual to visit the hospital with you. Consultation fees and laboratory tests are remarkably inexpensive when compared to those in the West, so if you do fall sick it would be absurd to let financial considerations dissuade you from seeking medical help.

You should be able to buy such commonly required medicines as broad-spectrum antibiotics and Flagyl at any sizeable town. If you are wandering off the beaten track, it might be worth carrying the obvious with you. As for malaria cures and prophylactics, Chloroquine, Fansidar and to a lesser extent quinine tablets can be bought in just about any town, but it is not always so easy to get hold of Paludrine and Larium. That said, it's far better that you carry all malaria-related tablets on you.

If you are on any medication prior to departure, or you have specific needs relating to a known medical condition (for instance, if you are allergic to bee stings or you are prone to attacks of asthma), then you are strongly advised to bring any related drugs and devices with you.

CRIME
Theft

Bearing in mind that there is probably no country in the world that is totally free of crime, and furthermore that tourists to so-called developing nations are always going to be targeted due to their relative wealth and conspicuousness, I would regard Mozambique as a relatively low-risk country so far as crime is concerned. When compared to parts of Kenya and South Africa, mugging is a rarity, and I've never heard of the sort of con tricks that abound in places like Nairobi and Dar es Salaam. Petty theft such as pickpocketing and bag- snatching is a risk in markets and other crowded places, but on a scale that should prompt caution rather than paranoia. Walking around large towns at night felt safe enough to me, though it would be tempting fate to wander alone along unlit streets or to carry large sums of money or valuables. On the basis that it is preferable to err on the side of caution, I'll repeat a few tips that apply to travelling anywhere in Africa:

- Most casual thieves operate in busy markets and bus stations. Keep a close watch on your possessions in such places, and avoid having valuables or large amounts of money loose in your daypack or pocket.
- Keep all your valuables and the bulk of your money in a hidden money belt. Never show this money belt in public. Keep any spare cash you need elsewhere on your person.
- I feel that a buttoned-up pocket on the front of the shirt is the most secure place as money cannot be snatched from it without the thief coming into your view. It is also advisable to keep a small amount of hard currency (ideally cash) hidden away in your luggage so that, should you lose your money belt, you have something to fall back on.

WOMEN TRAVELLERS

Women travellers generally regard sub-equatorial Africa as one of the safest places to travel alone anywhere in the world. Mozambique in particular poses few if any risks specific to female travellers. It is reasonable to expect a fair bit of flirting and the odd direct proposition, especially if you mingle in local bars, but a firm 'no' should be enough to defuse any potential situation. To be fair to Mozambican men, you can expect the same sort of thing in any country, and – probably with a far greater degree of persistence – from many male travellers.

Presumably as a result of Frelimo's pro-feminist leanings, Mozambican women tend to dress and behave far less conservatively than do their counterparts in neighbouring countries; I was surprised at how often I saw what were evidently 'respectable' women drinking in bars and smoking on the street, behaviour that is generally seen as the preserve of males and prostitutes in most other parts of East and southern Africa. I doubt that any Mozambican will be offended by women wearing shorts or other outfits that might be seen to be provocative (Muslims in Mozambique seem far less orthodox than in some other African countries), but revealing clothes *will* undoubtedly attract the attention of males.

Tampons are not readily available in smaller towns, though you should be able to locate them in Beira and Maputo. If you're travelling in out-of-the-way places, it's advisable to carry enough to see you through to the next time you'll be in a large city, bearing in mind that travelling in the tropics can sometimes cause women to have heavier or more regular periods than they would at home.

- Where the choice exists between carrying valuables on your person or leaving them in a locked room I would tend to favour the latter option. Obviously you should use your judgement on this and be sure the room is absolutely secure. A factor to be considered is that some travellers' cheque companies will not refund cheques that were stolen from a room.
- Leave any jewellery of financial or sentimental value at home.

Banditry

Mozambique has a long history of banditry. During the civil war, a significant risk of being held up at gunpoint was attached to driving practically anywhere in the country. This risk has abated in the past few years, but it still exists, though it is probably only of concern to people driving themselves through Mozambique.

Incidents are probably fairly random, and they appear to be related to the car-hijacking syndicates that are rife in South Africa, which means that new minibuses, pick-up trucks and 4WDs are probably at greater risk of being hijacked than are older vehicles and saloon cars. For South Africans, the people most likely to be driving in Mozambique, the risk of armed hijacking is probably less than it would be in Johannesburg.

There are certainly a few precautions you can take against hijacking. The first and most obvious is never to drive at night, and to set off travelling as early as possible so that you have the maximum available time to deal with unexpected car problems during daylight hours. In Johannesburg, most people now drive around with doors permanently locked and windows raised high enough so that nobody can reach in and open the lock – an obvious precaution in an urban context, perhaps less so in rural Mozambique, but one that can do no harm.

Bribery and bureaucracy

For all that you read about the subject, bribery is not the problem to travellers in most parts of Africa that it is often made out to be; and for backpackers in Mozambique it really isn't something to worry about.

There is a tendency to portray African bureaucrats as difficult and inefficient in their dealings with tourists. As a rule, this reputation says more about Western prejudices than it does about Mozambique. Sure, you come across the odd unhelpful official, but then such is the nature of the beast everywhere in the world. The vast majority of officials in the African countries I've visited have been courteous and helpful in their dealings with tourists, often to a degree that is almost embarrassing. In Mozambique, I encountered nothing but friendliness from almost every government official I had dealings with. This, I can assure you, is far more than most African visitors to Europe will experience from officialdom.

A factor in determining the response you receive from African officials will be your own attitude. If you walk into every official encounter with an aggressive, paranoid approach, you are quite likely to kindle the feeling held by many Africans that Europeans are arrogant and offhand in their dealings with other races. Instead, try to be friendly and patient, and to accept that the person to whom you are talking probably doesn't speak English. Treat people with respect rather than disdain, and they'll tend to treat you in the same way.

Mozambique

This gem of the Indian Ocean, Africa's best kept secret until now ... The Bazaruto archipelago offers idyllic, palm lined beaches with a unique African feel. This paradise of Africa offers something for every taste and desire, blue waters and unspoilt coral reefs for fantastic scuba diving, snorkeling, deep sea fishing as well as sand boarding, flying rubber ducks, sunset cruises and not least, upmarket live-a-boards navigating unchartered waters.

12 George St, Bryanston, Johannesburg
PO Box 97508 Petervale 2151
Tel: + 27 11 706 1991 Fax: + 27 11 463 1469
Email: janet@unusualdestinations.com
website: http://www.unusualdestinations.com

UNUSUAL DESTINATIONS

Part Two

The Guide

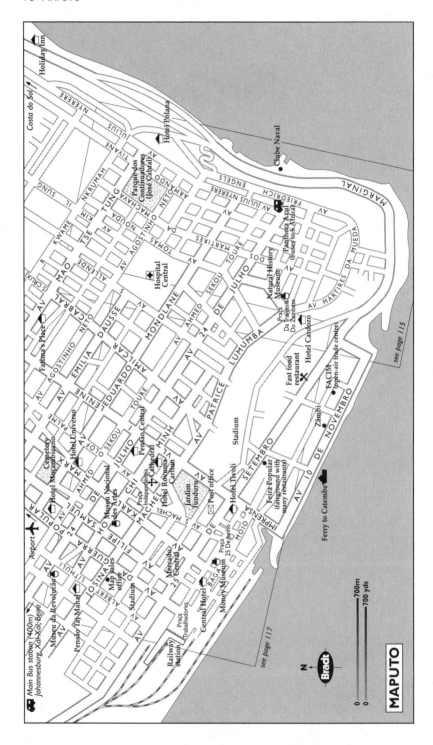

MAPUTO

Maputo

Formerly called Lourenço Marques – or LM for short – Maputo is a bustling, attractive port city with a population of around 1.5 million. Situated in the far south of Mozambique on the Gulf of Maputo (previously known as Delagoa Bay, a corruption of the Portuguese Baía da Lagoa), Maputo lies within 100km of the South African and Swaziland borders, and in addition to being the national capital of Mozambique, it is also the eponymous capital of the country's smallest, most densely populated and most southerly province.

With its wide avenidas and engaging Mediterranean atmosphere, Maputo may come as something of a surprise to anybody expecting a city ravaged by civil war. Certainly it bears little resemblance to the run-down, crime-ravaged slum described to me by several white South Africans – most of whom had not visited Maputo since the 'good old days' of cheap LM prawns, and who were apparently determined to believe the worst of this one-time coastal playground for residents of South Africa's wealthy but landlocked gold-mining regions.

Maputo is a remarkably smart and well-maintained city, just about as clean as you'll find in Africa, with a practically constant supply of electricity, brightly lit pavements and traffic lights that work, freshly painted buildings and well-maintained surfaced roads – not to mention some of the most orderly drivers on the continent. Window-dressing? Well, of course, no amount of paint and tar can obscure Maputo's endemic poverty – but even if it *is* rather trite or dismissive to say that Maputo's poverty struck me as being no greater than that of, say, Nairobi or Addis Ababa, then it seems equally superficial to toe the party line dictating that Maputo should always be written about in terms of civil war and poverty (mingled in with a few tedious and unfavourable comparisons to LM), whereas it's okay to dwell on the more attractive aspects of equally poor cities elsewhere in Africa.

Arrive in Maputo without prejudice and it is, quite simply, a most likeable city – as safe as any in Africa, and with a good deal more character than most. The jacaranda, flame tree and palm-lined avenidas with their numerous street cafés have a relaxed, hassle-free, Africa-meets-Mediterranean atmosphere that is distinctively Mozambican. Along the avenidas are any number of attractive old buildings in various states of renovation and disrepair, dwarfed at times by the rather incongruous high-rise relics of the 1950s and 1960s (LM was something of a laboratory for devotees of the Bauhaus architectural style during this period). Add to these a new crop of office buildings, shopping complexes, hotels and condominiums – with more under construction – and you get the impression that this is a town not only with a memorable past but also a bright future. Maputo has a beautiful location at the mouth of the Matola, Umbeluzi and Tembe Rivers on the Indian Ocean, it boasts a lively nightlife and some of the most vibrant markets in Africa. It is, in short, a compulsive and endlessly rewarding city, and an absolute must on any tourist itinerary of Mozambique. It really isn't all that far from LM in the good old days, except that the absence of apartheid-style laws means that Mozambicans, too, are free to enjoy their capital city.

HISTORY

Delagoa Bay lay to the south of the medieval trade routes used by the Swahili, and there is no particular reason to suppose that the area was ever visited by Muslim sailors prior to the Portuguese era. Nevertheless, the evidence suggests that the bay supported a substantial ocean-going fishing community prior to the 16th century, and also that it was the apex of a local trade network running along the eight navigable rivers that flow into it.

In 1502, the Portuguese captain Luis Fernandes sailed a short distance upriver from what was almost certainly Delagoa Bay, at first thinking he was at the entrance to Sofala. He recorded visiting a sizeable African river port, which impressed him mostly for its numerous cattle – large plump beasts that sold for two copper coins apiece. Once he realised that he was not at Sofala, Fernandes gave the bay the name Baía da Logoa, in the belief that its rivers all originated in an inland lagoon.

The first European to explore the Delagoa Bay was the Portuguese navigator Lourenço Marques, who visited it in 1544 on the instruction of the Captain of Moçambique and Sofala. Marques noted large numbers of elephants in the area, and he found that the natives of the bay were prepared to trade ivory for a few cheap beads. Shortly after this, King João III renamed the bay after Marques. Over the course of the next century, the bay was visited by a Portuguese ship almost every year. Typically, the ship would spend about four months encamped on Inhaca Island, from where it traded for ivory with the local chiefs on the mainland.

During the second half of the 17th century, the Portuguese ivory trade became increasingly centred around the more northerly ports of Kilwa and Quelimane, which meant that Delagoa Bay often went for years without seeing a Portuguese trading vessel. Portugal's partial abandonment of the southern trade opened the way for English and Dutch traders, to such an extent that five British ships were recorded in the bay at one time in 1685.

The earliest attempt to establish a permanent European settlement on Delagoa Bay was not, as you might suppose, initiated by Portugal, but by the Netherlands. In 1721, on the site of present-day Maputo, the Dutch East India

Company established a trading factory and fort, which was abandoned as unprofitable in 1730. Another trading factory was established on Inhaca Island in 1778 by one William Bolts, a British adventurer in Austrian employ. The Austrian settlement was expelled in 1781 when Portugal finally decided to establish a permanent trading post and fort at Delagoa Bay.

In 1781, the Portuguese placed a small garrison on Inhaca Island and set about building a fort on the site of present-day Maputo, but as it turned out, the future capital of Mozambique was to have a less than auspicious start. In May 1782, barely a month after the fort had been completed, the entire settlement burned to the ground. It was quickly rebuilt, but an argument between the newly appointed Governor of Lourenço Marques and local chiefs forced Portugal to evacuate it in 1783. The settlement was reoccupied under a new governor in 1784, and a stronger fortress was built on the site of the modern one, but the garrison of 80 men was plagued by fever and so when three French gunboats arrived in the harbour in October 1796, the Portuguese settlers fled inland. The fortress was reoccupied in 1800, after which time Portugal retained a permanent presence on the bay.

In the early 19th century, Lourenço Marques was a modest and unremarkable trading outpost; in 1825, the only permanent building apart from the fort was a solitary corrugated-iron homestead. Nevertheless, the settlement stood at the centre of a vast trading network, one that spread along the rivers into the present-day provinces of Mpumalanga and KwaZulu-Natal in South Africa. The trade routes to Delagoa Bay were fiercely contested by various local chieftaincies, especially after the great drought of the 1790s initiated an unprecedented and highly militant phase of empire-building among the Nguni peoples of the lowveld. In 1833, Lourenço Marques was razed and its governor killed by Dingane's Zulu army. After 1838, when the Boers defeated the Zulu army at Blood River, the trade routes to Lourenço Marques became the focus of an ongoing battle between the Swazi and Gaza Kingdoms.

In terms of the development of southern Mozambique in general and Lourenço Marques in particular, the most portentious event of 1838 was not the Battle of Blood River but the arrival at Delagoa Bay of the Boer leader Louis Trichardt. The Boers of the Transvaal were eager to open an export route to Delagoa Bay, not only because it was the closest port to the Boer Republic, but also because it would put an end to their dependency on British ports such as Cape Town and Durban. Trichardt died of malaria in Delagoa Bay, but his visit there signalled the beginning of a protracted three-way dispute over the control of what is arguably southeast Africa's finest natural harbour.

The competition for control of Delagoa Bay increased after the discovery of diamonds at Kimberley in 1867 and gold at Lydenberg in 1869. In 1868, the government of the Transvaal claimed that its frontier extended to the coast, a claim that was immediately contested by Britain and Portugal. The result was that the Transvaal and Portugal signed a treaty that not only delineated the modern border between Mozambique and South Africa north of Swaziland, but no less significantly provided for the joint building of a road between the Transvaal and Lourenço Marques.

Unwilling to see the Transvaal establish links with a Portuguese port, Britain immediately and unilaterally annexed the southern part of Delagoa Bay and Inhaca Island to Natal. Portugal called on France to arbitrate over the territorial dispute, and in 1875 it was awarded the entire bay. This was a major blow to the British policy of keeping indirect economic control over the Boer republic – so much so that Britain annexed the Transvaal to its Cape Colony between 1877 and 1881, thereby stalling the development of transport links to Lourenço Marques.

Following the discovery of gold on the Witwatersrand in 1886, Portugal and the Transvaal decided to build a railway line between Pretoria and Lourenço Marques. It was the completion of this line in 1894 that prompted the modern growth of the city. In 1870, Lourenco Marques was a tiny, stagnant trading centre protected by an unimpressive fort. By the turn of the century, the city centre had taken on its modern shape, the port handled roughly one-third of exports and imports from the Transvaal, and the railway line carried over 80,000 passengers annually. On November 12 1898, Lourenço Marques formally replaced Ilha do Moçambique as the capital of Portugal's East African colony. After independence, the city was renamed after the Rio Maputo.

SAFETY

Compared with some other African cities, such as Nairobi, Addis Ababa, Lagos or – dare I say it – Johannesburg, the level of crime in Maputo is relatively low. However, increased tourism brings with it an increase of temptation, and what's safe today may be less safe tomorrow. A recent (normally intrepid) female traveller said that she felt uneasy. Maputo is no different from any other large city (anywhere in the world), and as such is not untouched by the usual urban ills and tourist hazards.

It seems safe enough to walk around main parts of the city in daylight: nobody pays much attention to tourists, and I saw no signs of pickpockets, con artists or other casual thieves on the streets. Crowded places, such as markets and bus stations, should be approached with a degree of caution: don't wear flashy jewellery or carry more money than you need, and try not to keep anything of value in a place where it can easily be snatched. I was comfortable walking on the main roads in the city centre at night – they are very well lit for an African city, and there are plenty of other pedestrians around. But, as in any city, it would be asking for trouble to carry large amounts of money or to use alleys or other unlit roads after dark. At the time of writing, there had been several reports of muggings on the winding roads that connect the Avenida Friedrich Engels to the Avenida Marginal, so this seems a good place to avoid after dark. Check with locals about other dangerous areas when you arrive in Maputo.

If you are travelling to Maputo by public transport, there is a real risk of arriving after nightfall. There are, in my opinion, few riskier or less desirable travel scenarios than wandering around an unfamiliar city at night with your possessions prominently displayed on your back and a map in your hand.

Coming from the direction of Johannesburg, trains arrive in Maputo in the early morning, so no problem there; but if you come by road, spend the night in Komatipoort and give yourself a full day to get to Maputo rather than cross the border after noon. Coming from the north, buses from Beira generally arrive in Maputo after dark; and so I would advise travellers to go as far as Xai-Xai, stay there overnight, and hitch or hop on the first public transport to Maputo the next morning.

There does appear to be a fair amount of property crime in Maputo, particularly against motor vehicles – car parts aren't readily available and so they are subject to a growing shady market. If you are carrying stuff in the back of a pick-up truck, be careful in traffic jams or at traffic lights, as you may be distracted in some way by a couple of people while their friends help themselves to anything that's not secured. You also hear stories, possibly apocryphal, of people grabbing accessories like hubcaps and indicator light covers off cars while they're stalled at traffic lights. It is definitely unsafe to leave an unguarded car parked on the street overnight; don't stay at a hotel unless it can offer you somewhere safe to park you car.

GETTING THERE AND AWAY
By air
See *Getting to Mozambique* on page 49 for details of the international flights that arrive in Maputo. Domestically, LAM has flights to and from Maputo to the following provincial towns: Beira, Vilankulo, Tete, Quelimane, Nampula, Pemba and Lichinga. While Beira and Nampula are served by daily flights, connections to the other towns are less frequent.

The main LAM booking office (tel: 42 6112) is on the Avenida Karl Marx, just off Avenida 25 de Setembro in the heart of downtown Maputo. If you are staying in the Polana district, however, the LAM office on the Avenida Mao Tse Tung opposite the Hotel Polana might be more convenient.

Arriving at Maputo-Mavalane International Airport
There is nothing daunting about arriving at Maputo's international airport, even if it's after dark. The immigration and customs formalities are straightforward and swift, and the amount of hassle from taxi drivers and the like once you've left the terminal building is minimal. Airport facilities include a bank (BCM), bureau de change, post office, snack bar, several small gift shops and various car-rental agencies. If you're leaving Mozambique from the airport at Maputo, it's possible to change your excess meticais back to dollars at either the BCM or the bureau de change. Note that the latter closes at 21.00.

Given that the airport is only about 8km from the town centre, a taxi should not cost you much more than US$10. Alternatively, if you are staying at one of Maputo's more up-market hotels, there will be a courtesy bus waiting for you. Even if you are not a guest at one of these establishments, you could try scrounging a ride – or saying that you are a guest! There is no airport bus as such, although *chapas* do serve the airport. They run along the Avenida de Angola, which ends at Avenida Eduardo Mondlane, one of the city's main east–west thoroughfares (good if you're heading for the Polana district); and they also leave from the roundabout at the end of the Avenida dos Acordos de Lusaka, which is the best route if you want to get to the Baixa. A taxi is probably preferable – especially if you can find someone to share it with – and obligatory if you are arriving at night.

By rail

The train between Maputo and Johannesburg is the only rail service of any interest to tourists that leaves from the imposing Maputo Railway Station next to the port. Trains to Johannesburg leave Maputo at 11.00, arriving the next day at 06.15, and from Johannesburg at 06.10, arriving in Maputo the next day at 11.30. This is considerably longer than the bus journey, although budget travellers will appreciate the advantages of saving on a night's accommodation and arriving in Johannesburg or Maputo bright and early in the morning. There are three classes of travel: first class costs US$17; second class US$13; and third class US$7.

By road

See *Getting to Mozambique* on page 53 for details of arriving in Maputo by bus from South Africa and Swaziland. Going in the opposite direction, the **Panthera Azul** office (tel: 49 8868) is on the corner of Avenida Julius Nyerere and Avenida 24 de Julho. Buses to Johannesburg leave every morning at 08.00, they take about seven and a half hours, and the one-way fare is US$27, for which price you get to travel in a luxurious air-conditioned bus, complete with TV, refreshments and attentive hostesses. Alternatively, minibuses for Johannesburg, Komatipoort and the Mozambican border town of Ressano Garcia leave from next to the large stadium near the Mercado Central. The fare to Johannesburg is about US$20.

The principal domestic destinations accessible by bus from Maputo are Tete, Beira and all of the towns in between. A company called **Oliveira's** runs buses to all of these places, leaving from the Praça 16 de Junho at the end of Avenida 24 de Julho. Most services, including those to Beira and Tete, leave at some time early in the morning (at the time of writing, it was 07.00 for Beira and 06.30 for Tete), while a smattering of buses to points south of Beira (Xai-Xai, for instance) leave in the afternoon. Note that the buses to Beira and Tete will stop somewhere overnight (Maxixe or Vilankulo, for example) before continuing on to their final destination early the next morning. **TSL** is probably the main competition to Oliveira's, with services to the same destinations in buses of a similar standard. Expect to pay around US$15 to Beira, US$18 to Tete, US$9 to Vilankulo, US$6 to Inhambane and US$2 to Xai-Xai. If you're heading to one of the beach resorts relatively close to Maputo (Macaneta, Bilene or Xai-Xai, for example), you could take a *chapa*. These leave when full from a yard on the Avenida de Moçambique, which is the beginning of the EN1 road to Beira. To get to this yard, catch a city *chapa* from next to the Natural History Museum or the Mercado Central going to a Maputo suburb called Jardim.

If you want to hitch northwards, the best place to wait is in front of the Jardim Zoologica (zoo) about 1km along the Xai-Xai road after it branches from the Komatipoort road some 2km out of town.

GETTING AROUND

Taxi cabs are few and far between in Maputo, though you can rely on there always being some at the airport taxi rank, outside the central market, and outside the Hotel Cardoso and Hotel Polana. Taxi fares are negotiable, but you can expect to pay around US$3 for a ride within the city centre and up to US$10 between the city centre and the airport. Buses travel the length and breadth of the city, with major bus stands in front of the Natural History Museum (described simply as 'museu' on the front of buses) and the large markets. You will, of course, probably have absolutely no idea where most of these buses are going, so the best advice is to stay on the main thoroughfares and be prepared to take more than one to get to your final destination. Each ride only costs a few cents.

WHERE TO STAY
Upper range

Nowhere is Maputo's current prosperity more evident than in the number of high-quality hotels that can now be found in the city. Generally speaking, the upper range hotels in Maputo are the best value for money that you'll find in Mozambique. If you feel like spoiling yourself, this is the place to do it.

The **Hotel Polana** (tel: 49 1001; fax: 49 1480; email: res@polana-hotel.com; web: www.polana-hotel.com), which lies on Avenida Julius Nyerere on a low cliff overlooking the Indian Ocean, has been Maputo's most prestigious hotel ever since it opened in 1922. It was designed by the renowned architect Sir Herbert Baker, who also created Cape Town's Mount Nelson Hotel and the Union Buildings in Pretoria, where Nelson Mandela was inaugurated as president of South Africa in 1994. Although it fell into a state of neglect during the years of the civil war, the Polana was renovated with no expense spared in the early 1990s, since when it has reclaimed its status as one of the most elegant and well-run hotels in Africa, combining an Edwardian grace with modern luxuries such as satellite television, air conditioning in all rooms, free internet access, a gymnasium, a gourmet restaurant and coffee shop, and one of the most attractive swimming pools on the continent. Rooms in the main hotel building start at US$150, while those in the renovated section overlooking the sea start at US$195. The **Hotel Cardoso** (tel: 49 1071; fax: 49 4054; email: hcardoso@zebra.uem.mz), opposite the Natural History Museum and also on a cliff, this time with a commanding view over the city centre to the harbour and Catembe, is another Maputo institution, with service and facilities comparable to those at the Polana, and room rates starting at US$135 single and US$150 double. The finest hotel in downtown Maputo (ie: the Baixa) is the **Pestana Rovuma Carlton** (tel: 30 5000; fax; 30 5305; email: reservas.africa@pestana.com; web: www.pestana.com), which, along with the cathedral, dominates the eastern edge of the Praça Independéncia. Every bit as comfortable as the Polana and Cardoso, the Rovuma's main selling point is its location right in the heart of Maputo, a five-minute walk to the shops, restaurants and bars on and around the Avenida 25 de Setembro and only about 15 minutes by foot from the Polana district. Rack rates start from US$98 single and US$122 double, but check for special offers. The new and extremely comfortable **Holiday Inn** (tel: 49 5050; fax: 49 7700; email: himaputo@southernsun.com; web: www.southernsun.com), is Maputo's only beachfront hotel, and of all the hotels in this category it's probably the best value for money, with modern rooms as pleasant and well equipped as you'll find at any Holiday Inn in the world from as little as US$85/single, U$120 double. The **Hotel Avenida** (tel: 49 2000; fax: 49 9600; email: h.avenida@teledata.mz; web: www.hotelavenida.co.mz) has well equipped singles from US$150 and doubles from US$165 (and a remarkable piano bar). Rates in all of the above hotels currently include a sumptuous buffet breakfast. The very new **Hotel VIP Maputo** of the Portuguese VIP Hotels chain (email: hotelmaputo@viphotels.com; web: www.viphotels.com) is close to the FACIM Exhibition Centre. (It's worth knowing that tour operators Unusual Destinations – see page 45 – organise business travel packages to Maputo.) Out of the city and just a six-minute boat-hop across the bay, the comfortable **Catembe Gallery Hotel** (tel: 38 0051; web: www.catembe.net) has just five luxury rooms facing the ocean: from US$70 per person.

Moderate

As the number of hotels at the luxury end of the market continues to grow, so does the number of slightly more affordable establishments. Nowadays Maputo is bulging with very comfortable hotels of around three-star status. Indeed, the **Hotel Terminus** (tel: 49 1333; fax: 49 1284; email: termhot@terminus-hotel.com; web: www.terminus-hotel.com) on a quiet street in the Polana district advertises itself as a 'five-star hotel at three-star prices', and, with most of the facilities of the big fish above , is good value at US$60/single and US$85/double. The Terminus' sister hotel and more or less a carbon copy is the **Hotel Monte Carlo** (tel: 30 4048; fax: 30 8959; email: res@montecarlo-hotel.net; web: www.montecarlo-hotel.net) on Avenida Patrice Lumumba. Also in the same style (ie: for business travellers on a budget), the **Hotel Tivoli** (tel: 30 7600; fax: 30 7609; email: tivoli@teledata.mz) in a good central location on Avenida 25 de Setembro has singles and doubles in the US$60–80 range. It's a friendly place with professional service, and good value. The **Residencial Villa Itália** (tel: 49 7298; fax: 49 1968), between the embassy residences on Avenida Friedrich Engels, feels rather less business oriented than the above hotels in this category, although the rates are similar: US$65 single and US$75 double. The **Hotel Villa das Mangas** (tel/fax: 49 7507; email: villadasmangas@hotmail.com) in the Polana district next to the Geological Museum has compact rooms for US$60/single and US$75/double clustered around a pretty garden with a swimming pool. The **Hotel Escola Andalucia** (tel: 42 3051; fax; 42 2462; email: hotea@isl.co.mz) on Avenida Patrice Lumumba is the training school for Mozambique's hoteliers and has a reputation for excellent service – which perhaps stands to reason. Singles and doubles cost US$45 and US$60 respectively. Other places to stay in Maputo for a similar price include the **Hotel Moçambicano** (tel: 31 0600; fax; 42 3124; email: mozhotel@isl.co.mz) on Avenida Filipe Samuel Magaia, the **Hoyo Hoyo Residencial** (tel: 49 0701; fax: 49 0724) and the **Pensão Martins** (tel: 42 4930; fax: 42 9645; email: morest@isl.co.mz) on Avenida 24 de Julho.

The **Mozaica Guest House** (Av Agostinho Neto 769; tel: 303939, 303965; email: mozaika_guesthouse@hotmail.com; web: www.mozaika.co.mz) is a patchwork collection of eight rooms and one apartment. The ambience is a mix of African, Asian, South American and European influences. It's friendly, funky, fun and inexpensive.

Budget

While business travellers are spoiled for choice when it come to finding accommodation in Maputo, budget travellers – and especially backpackers – are slightly less so. There are currently only two fully fledged backpackers' hostels in Maputo. **Fatima's** at 1317 Avenida Mao Tse Tung is the more established of the two, and should probably be your first port of call for up-to-date tourist information about Maputo – and the rest of Mozambique. The hostel, which is in a private house, has dormitory accommodation from US$4 and private single rooms for US$15. You can also camp in the small garden (which is probably only large enough for two or three tents). There is a well-equipped kitchen, safe parking, and English-speaking staff. The **Base Backpackers** (tel: 30 2723) is at 545 Avenida Patrice Lumumba, and also has dorms for US$7 and private double rooms for US$20. In addition to being the cheapest accommodation in town, both of these places are your best bets if you want to meet potential travel companions or find lifts to points north of the capital.

There are alternative budget options in Maputo which, although not specifically geared to the needs of the backpackers, do offer clean, safe, good-value accommodation. The recently renovated **Pensão Taj-Mahal** (tel: 40 5122; fax: 40 2350) on Avenida Ho Chi Minh has obviously done a lot of work to attract business. The rooms and spacious shared bathrooms are immaculately clean, there is now a restaurant (again, with a very clean kitchen), the manager speaks good English, and the prices are among the best value in town. Singles and doubles are a little under and a little over US$10 respectively. A particularly good choice if you want to be close to the Oliveira's bus station. The **Hotel Universo** (tel: 42 7003; fax: 42 7004) on the corner of Avenida Eduardo Mondlane and Avenida Karl Marx is another place within about a 20-minute walk of the bus station. Showing its age a little with poorly lit rooms and 1960s furniture, it is nevertheless not bad value at US$15 for an air-conditioned double. On the other hand, the **Pensão da Baixa** (tel: 30

8190) on Avenida Filipe Samuel Magaia is possibly the newest hotel in Maputo, with singles with a fan for US$10 and doubles for US$14.50. There are two cheap pensãos on Avenida 24 de Julho. The **Pensão Central** is the cheaper and more basic of the two with singles and doubles with shared bathroom and no fan for US$7.50 and US$12.50 respectively, while the **Pensão Alegre** (tel: 30 7742) is roughly twice the price. Next door to the Alegre, the **Hotel Santa Cruz** (tel: 30 3004; fax: 30 3066) is more expensive still with air-conditioned singles for US$22.50, which includes breakfast but no private bathroom. Maputo's other budget options are in the old town. The **Hotel Tamariz** (tel: 42 2596; fax: 42 8609) on Rua Consiglieri is not exactly cheap at US$28 for singles with a fan and US$38 for doubles, but it does seem to be a well-maintained hotel, and the central location is definitely in its favour. Considerably less appealing are the two places on the bar-lined Rua de Bagamoio. The **Hotel Central** (tel: 30 9254) – not to be confused with the Pensão Central – has no-frills rooms for US$10, while the **Hotel Carlton** is slightly cheaper and better value due to the fact that the rooms have ceiling fans. It might also be worth noting that a dance school and a popular nightclub are directly opposite the Central, which makes it noisy during the day and at night.

WHERE TO EAT

One thing you'll never have to worry about in Maputo is finding a decent meal – there are restaurants everywhere catering to all tastes and budgets. The emphasis is on seafood and Portuguese dishes such as the ubiquitous chicken piri-piri, but there is also a good scattering of specialised places ranging from pizzerias and steak houses to Indian and Oriental restaurants.

If you are in two minds about where to eat, you could do a lot worse than head to the Feira Popular where you'll find some of the capital's finest and most varied restaurants, one next to the other. Arguably the most popular eating place in Maputo is the **Restaurante Escorpião** at the western entrance to the Feira Popular. The menu consists primarily of Portuguese dishes, well prepared, reasonably priced and copious. The coffee here is also very good. The beauty of eating at the Feira Popular is the variety of cuisine on offer. At the **Restaurante Pinga**, for example, you can eat steak tartare and other Gaelic dishes washed down with French wine. Next door to the Pinga there is a good Chinese restaurant, while opposite it the **Restaurante Coqueiro** specialises in food from the Mozambican province of Zambézia. If none of these recommendations appeals, you should have no difficulty finding something else to your taste at the Feira Popular.

Elsewhere, the Polana district is home to some of the most elegant restaurants in Maputo; and Avenida Julius Nyerere is a particularly good place to find many of them. Working south from the Hotel Polana, the **A Grelha Restaurant** serves Portuguese and Italian dishes, the **Restaurante Corte Imperial** is a relatively new place specialising in Malay and Chinese cuisine, the **Bistro** is noted for its roast duckling and beetroot, the **El Greco Pizzeria** is a good place for pizzas, and the **Manjar dos Deuses** has excellent – and pricey – Portuguese food. There are also one or two good restaurants just off Avenida Julius Nyerere. The **Piripiri Restaurant** on Avenida 24 de Julho, for instance, is a popular place for grilled chicken, while the **Sheik Restaurant** on Avenida Mao Tse Tung (which also has a cocktail bar and discotheque) is one of Maputo's more upmarket addresses, serving Chinese and international cuisine. Elsewhere in the Polana district, the **Restaurante O Petisco** next door to the Hoyo Hoyo Residencial has a menu that includes dishes from the Indian state of Goa (ie: curries with a Portuguese influence). A little further up Avenida Eduardo Mondlane, the **Restaurante 1908** with its smartly dressed waiters, colonial-style décor and shady terrace has a certain appeal. The **Café Horóscopo** on Rua Mateus S Mutemba not far from the Hotel Cardoso is obviously tailored to Western taste-buds with toasted sandwiches, continental and English breakfasts, and some of the best milkshakes in Mozambique. Of course, the upmarket hotels in the Polana district – and elsewhere in the city – also have a selection of high-quality restaurants where you can eat very well if you have the money.

Downtown Maputo, or the Baixa, also has its fair share of places to eat. The **Radio Mozambique Restaurant** on the edge of the Botanical Garden is worth mentioning for its pleasant terrace in the leafy surrounds of the garden and its good-value meals. On the other side of the Praça Independéncia, the **Restaurante Impala** has Pakistani and Indian dishes which seem to be popular with people from these parts of the world (always a good sign!). For pizzas and pasta dishes, **Mimmo's** on Avenida 24 de Julho is, along with the **El Greco Pizzeria** in the Polana district, one of the best choices in Maputo. There are also numerous places to eat along Avenida 25 de Setembro. The **Scala** and **Continental**, which face each other on the intersection with Avenida Samora Machel, have a pleasant street atmosphere and are popular meeting places. Both cafés serve tea, coffee, prego rolls, hamburgers, fresh bread and pastries. The more expensive **Ti' Palino Restaurant** does hamburgers, piri-piri chicken and other fast foods.

This section would not be complete without mentioning the Maputo institution that is the **Costa do Sol**. One of the capital's oldest and most popular restaurants, especially at weekends, it lies about 5km north of the city on the coastal road. The restaurant specialises in seafood, which comes in well-prepared and very generous portions. The squid is particularly recommended. There is safe parking for those arriving in their own cars, while city *chapas* leave for the Costa do Sol from the main departure points in the city centre (see *Maputo: Getting around* on page 105).

A number of fast-food outlets have arrived in Maputo over the past few years, with more sure to follow. The South African chain **Steers** is just past the Feira Popular on Avenida 25 de Setembro. You can get the usual McDonald's-style hamburgers, as well as good pizzas, at the adjacent **Debonairs Pizza** (tel: 31 2188), which offers free home delivery. **Mundo's** on the corner of Avenida Julius Nyerere and Avenida Eduardo Mondlane is another popular place, with a pub-style atmosphere and a large menu containing most of the dishes in the fast-food genre (hamburgers, pizza, tex-mex, etc).

There are a number of good **bakeries** in Maputo. I found the best to be the one next to the Hotel Polana, which has excellent cakes, quiches and other sweet and savoury pastries. Note, however, that you cannot eat your purchases on the premises. Other places where you can sit down include the **Pastelaria Nautilus** on the corner of Avenida Julius Nyerere and Avenida 24 de Julho, the **Pastelaria Wimba** near the hospital on Avenida Eduardo Mondlane, and the tea room at the **Cristal Restaurant** on Avenida 24 de Julho.

Of all the **supermarkets** in Maputo, **Shoprite** in the shopping mall of the same name on Avenida Acordos de Lusaka (the road to the airport) has by far the largest selection. Also useful is the supermarket in the Polana district opposite the Café Horóscopo which, although considerably smaller than Shoprite, is open until late in the evenings (past midnight on most evenings).

NIGHTLIFE AND ENTERTAINMENT

Maputo has always had a reputation for being lively by night, and it remains one of the more pleasant African cities for an extended barcrawl. Since the turn of the century, Rua do Bagamoio (formerly Rua Major Araujo) in the old part of town near the railway station has been known to visting sailors as 'Whisky Road' and the 'Street of Trouble', with ten to fifteen bars congregated along its short length. Rua do Bagamoio is rather more subdued now than in former times but it remains an obvious place to start the evening. Perhaps the trendiest bar at the time of writing is **Gypsy's Bar**, which attracts a largely expat clientele and, depending on the mood of the evening, might have dancing. The **Pub-Mundo** next door to Gypsy's has a rather more Mozambican atmosphere; and the **Luso Niteclub** next door to the Pub-Mundo is a cabaret with dancing girls and a small cover charge. Extras inside the club will, naturally, cost… extra. The **Arte Bar** opposite the Hotel Central is a proper discotheque which only really gets going after midnight. Once it does, the music played is mainly of the Western, electronic variety. There is a US$5 cover charge. There is another, larger disco called the **Locomotivo** inside the railway station building not far from Rua do Bagamoio, and two others called **Minigolfe** (with very young clientele at weekends) and **Tara** a little way from the city centre on the road to the Costa do Sol.

Another good, earthy place to hang out, whether you want to drink, eat, shoot pool, make friends, watch a strip show, or ride dodgem cars, is the **Feira Poular** on the east end of Avenida 25 de Setembro. There are literally dozens of bars and restaurants at the fair, as well as a variety of rides and other stalls – you'll find your way around easily enough.

Another good place to drink is at the **night markets**, which are cheaper, friendlier and often more lively than the bars. See the section on markets on page 114 for some suggestions. I didn't feel at all threatened drinking in the markets at night, but it would probably be sensible to carry only as much money as you want to spend.

If you're interested in seeing some live music, the **Ciné Africa** on Avenida 24 de Julho is often the venue when the superstars of African music come to Maputo to give a concert (when I was in town, it was Ismail Lo from Senegal).

On a more regular basis, the **Africa Bar** next to the Ciné Africa has live music at the weekends. The cover charge is US$2.50. The **Cat's Garden** is also on Avenida 24 de Julho, and also has live music at the weekends – this time jazz and blues. The **Centre Culturel Franco-Mozambican** on the corner of the Praça Independéncia also organises concerts and other cultural events (theatre, dance, etc) from time to time.

Maputo's main **theatre** is on Avenida 25 de Setembro next to the Feira Popular, while the capital has several **cinemas** that show relatively recent Western films in their original languages with Portuguese subtitles. Finally, there is a **casino** at the Hotel Polana that is free for guests; otherwise, there is a US$3 cover charge.

ACTIVITIES

Nowadays, there are enough facilities in Maputo to make it possible to indulge most pastimes. There is a **tennis club** in the Botanical Garden which has six courts and changing rooms. The **golf club**, meanwhile, is out towards the Costa do Sol; green fees are only US$6 for 18 holes. There are **swimming pools** at all of the capital's major hotels, and they can be used by non-residents for the payment of a fee (normally something like US$4). The pools at the Polana and the Cardoso are the best. The Hotel Polana also has a **health spa** with a well-equipped **gymnasium** and a **steam room**. Entrance costs US$10 unless you are a member or a guest at the hotel. Like most of Africa, Mozambique is football-crazy, and you can see professional **football matches** at stadiums at Costa do Sol, Desportivo, Machava and Maxaquene.

USEFUL INFORMATION

A magazine called *Mozambique Time Out* contains useful listings of selected restaurants and hotels, with a rough idea of current prices. Published every six months as a supplement to the *Economia* magazine, *Time Out* can be bought for roughly US$3 at most tourist-class hotels as well as at the book shop next to Mundo's and opposite the South African High Commission. There is also a free monthly magazine called *Que Passa* (or *What's On*), which contains one or two useful snippets of information and a lot of advertisements.

The Mozambican **Tourist Office** (tel: 30 7320; fax: 30 7324; email: dep@futur.imoz.com; web: www.futur.moz.com; Mon–Fri 07.30–12.30 & 14.00–17.00) is at 1203 Avenida 25 de Setembro on the third floor. The staff are all very helpful, even if their good intentions are not exactly backed up by a wealth of brochures, maps and other useful information. A better idea would be to visit Fatima's Backpackers on Avenida Mao Tse Tung, where there is a notice-board full of information for travellers – and travellers themselves, whose brains you could pick for up-to-date advice.

Another potential source of tourist information – as well as a good place to book domestic airline tickets if LAM is starting to get you down – are the numerous **travel agents** that have offices in downtown Maputo. A good one is Novo Mundo on the mezzanine floor of the shopping gallery at the Hotel

Rovuma Carlton (tel: 32 9007; fax: 32 9005; email: novomundo@
tropical.co.mz), although there are plenty of others.

Communications and media

The main **post office** occupies an impressive colonial building on Avenida 25
de Setembro. Alternatively, there is a **DHL** office a few doors away. You can
make telephone calls (local, national and international) at the post office or
from the several TDM offices dotted around the city. There are now several
internet cafés in Maputo. The best are the two operated by TDM, one of
which is located in the shopping gallery at the Rovuma Carlton Hotel and the
other in the Polana Shopping Centre. You pay US$3 per hour, although you
don't have to use all of your time in one session. One of the best – and
cheapest – alternatives to the TDM cafés is the British Council (Tue–Fri
10.00–17.00, Sat 09.00–12.30) on a side street near the UK High Commission,
where you can surf for 45 minutes for just US$1.

Only a small selection of English-language newspapers (mostly from South
Africa) and magazines is ever available at the kiosks at the tourist-class hotels.
Somewhat surprisingly, the best selection that I could find was at the relatively
modest Hotel Moçambicano. English-language books and novels, meanwhile,
are even more difficult to come by. The **bookshop** opposite the South African
High Commission and the one at the Polana Shopping Centre are the logical
places to look for them.

There is a **map sales office** in the National Directorate of Geography and
Cartography (DINAGECA) building on Avenida Josina Machel, a block west
of Avenida Guerra Popular. It sells a fair range of 1:250,000 sheets, but few
more detailed maps.

Money

The main branches of Mozambique's banks are in the centre of town either on
or around Avenida 25 de Setembro. This does not mean, however, that you
must come here in order to change money. In the Polana district, for instance,
there are several banks and bureaux de change (*cambrios*) along Avenida Julius
Nyerere where you can change cash and travellers' cheques just as easily. The
cash rate for dollars and rands, whether you are changing them at a bank or a
cambrio, is more or less the same. For travellers' cheques, however, you might
be able to reduce the somewhat prohibitive commission charged by the banks
by changing them at a *cambrio*. For example, the **American Express** office at
the Hotel Polana only charges a 5% commission on travellers' cheque
transactions. A number of the banks in Maputo now have **ATM machines**,
which accept Visa and MasterCard. Alternatively, you can get a credit card
advance at the Standard Bank, although this is a time-consuming and very
expensive (US$35 commission) process. Note that the advance will be paid in
meticais or rands and not dollars. In short, the ATMs are a better bet.

If you prefer to use the **black market** to change money (the financial
incentives for doing so, by the way, are limited), one of the best places for rand
transactions (especially meticais to rands) is next to the stadium where

minibuses leave for Johannesburg. The nearby Mercado Central should also be a good place to change money, although you would be well advised to exercise caution and be vigilant when doing so.

Foreign embassies
Office hours are usually Monday to Thursday 07.30–12.30 and 14.00–17.30, Friday 07.30–12.30 and 14.00–17.00.

Australia Tel: 42 2780
Belgium Tel: 49 0077
Denmark Av 24 de Julho 1500; tel: 30 3413/4/5
France Av Julius Nyerere 2361; tel: 49 1774
Germany Rua Damião de Góis 506; tel: 49 2714; fax: 49 4888
India Av Kenneth Kaunda 167; tel: 49 2437
Italy Av Kenneth Kaunda 387; tel: 49 1605
Japan Tel: 49 1001
Malawi Tel: 49 1468
Netherlands Tel: 49 0031; fax: 49 0429
Pakistan Tel: 49 4265
Portugal Av Julius Nyerere 720; tel: 49 0431
South Africa Av Eduardo Mondlane; tel: 49 1614
Swaziland Tel: 49 2451
Switzerland Tel: 49 2432/2744
UK Av Vladimir Lenine 310; tel: 42 0111/2/5/6/7; fax: 42 1666
USA Av Kenneth Kaunda 193; tel: 49 2797/4146/4482
Zambia Tel: 49 2452
Zimbabwe Tel: 49 0404

Shopping
Crafts and curios
There's a good craft market, the **Mercado Artesanato**, on Praça 25 de Junho every Saturday morning. This is a particularly good place to buy batiks, wood carvings and items crafted from semi-precious stones such as malachite. In recent years, arts and crafts salesmen have responded to the increase in tourist traffic by setting up shop outside the main hotels and other points where tourists tend to congregate. Consequently, the best selection of crafts and curios can be found outside places such as the Hotel Polana, the Hotel Cardoso, the Costa do Sol and the Polana Shopping Centre. All manner of basket work, ranging from reed chairs to book shelves, can be bought from street vendors along the Avenida Marginal and Avenida Julius Nyerere north of the Hotel Polana.

Markets
Maputo boasts several interesting markets. The **Mercado Central** on Avenida 25 de Setembro, housed in an impressive building dating to 1901, is a good place to buy a variety of fresh and frozen fish as well as other fresh produce. The **Mercado do Povo**, on the corner of Avenida Karl Marx and Avenida Ho Chi

Minh, reputedly sells a variety of groceries and vegetables, though we were more impressed by the volume of squawking poultry on sale and still refer to it as the chicken market. At night, the chickens are tucked away, and the market becomes one of the most lively places for a cheap, informal beer in the city centre.

Also in the city centre are several more informal markets, some of them selling stacks of beer and tinned sodas several metres high: one such place is on the corner of Avenida Ho Chi Minh and Avenida Albert Lithuli. But the mother of all booze markets is the **Barracas de Museu** on Rua dos Lusiados, which only opens at night and sells nothing but drink. A warren-like conglomeration of perhaps 100 bars, this is one of the most extraordinary places to drink anywhere in Africa, and is highly recommended provided that you don't carry vast sums of money or valuables on your person.

Further out of town is the main **fish market** on the Avenida Marginal opposite the Club Maritimo. In addition to being the cheapest place to buy fresh fish, this place is of some interest to amateur ichthyologists for the variety of tropical ocean fish that can be seen (even if they are out of their natural habitat). If you're after a good variety of fresh fruit and vegetables, try the **Mercado Janeta** behind the church near the intersection of Avenida Vladimir Lenine and Avenida Mao Tse Tung. It's also a good place for a cheap meal of chicken or fish with rice.

Xipamanine Market, just outside the city centre, is known for its traditional medicines and associated items.

WHAT TO SEE

Maputo lends itself to casual exploration on foot, with several interesting colonial buildings and a buzzing street life. In addition to the two walks described below, it's very pleasant to walk along the seafront along the Avenida Marginal which is usually pretty quiet, with just a few anglers and other promenaders, and a nice breeze through the palms.

Around the Hotel Polana and Natural History Museum

The **Hotel Polana** has for decades been the showpiece of Maputo's hotels, situated in the quarter of the same name, east of the city centre on the rise high above the Bay of Maputo on Avenida Julius Nyerere. The Polana survived the period of revolution in a somewhat run-down condition, but was refurbished by a South African hotel chain in the early 1990s and is now restored to its former status.

Heading south from the Polana, turn off the Avenida Julius Nyerere into the first street to the left and walk along the Avenida Friedrich Engels, which runs high above the coast. The view extends well beyond the Bay of Maputo to the island of Inhaca. One can walk along the Avenida F Engels almost as far as the **presidential palace** (where one should be very careful when taking photographs) and then turn right into the Avenida dos Mártires de Mueda, perhaps even enjoying a coffee in the **Hotel Cardoso** with its fine views of the wide river estuary and the harbour. The open ground next to the hotel has a good view over the city centre.

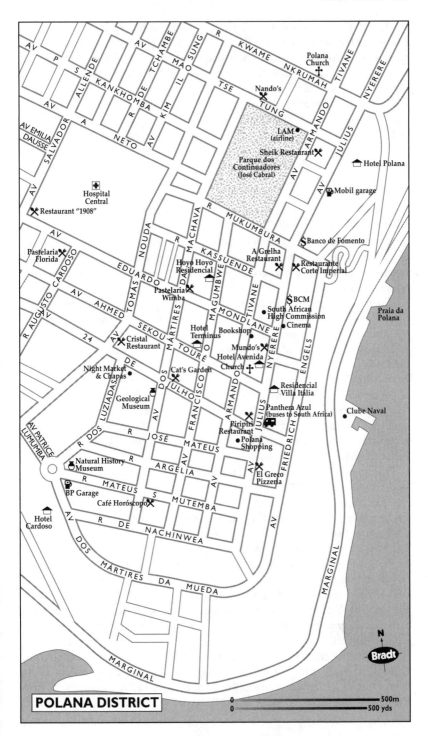

POLANA DISTRICT

0   500m
0   500 yds

N

Bradt

Near the Hotel Cardosa, on the Praça da Travessia do Zambeze, the **Natural History Museum** is housed in a palace built in the Maunelini style (a sort of Portuguese Gothic) and decorated with wonderfully ornamental plaster-work – one of the finest buildings in Maputo. Unfortunately, the collections housed in the museum are somewhat dusty and dilapidated – many of them look like they might have been there since the museum was moved to the building in 1913. One block further on the Avenida Tomás Nduda is the old Maputo synagogue (now the **Geological Museum**). On the Avenida Patrice Lumumba, the **Casa Velha**, with adjoining amphitheatre for open-air performances, is well worth seeing.

The Baixa

The business district of Maputo, the Baixa, is situated at the edge of the wide river to the left and right of the main shopping street, the Avenida 25 de Setembro. Almost all major shops are in or near this street, as are the banks, the airline offices, the main post office, central market, cinemas and the botanical garden. The other busy shopping street is the Avenida Eduardo Mondlane (west end).

The best place to begin a walking tour of the city centre is at the intersection of the Avenida 25 de Setembro and the Avenida Samora Machel, with the Café Continental on one corner and the Scala Restaurant and Cinema Scala, built in 1931, on the other. Walk down the Avenida 25 de Setembro in a westerly direction (away from town) and after the next street to the right you reach the **Mercado Central** (central market), a covered building construted in 1901. It is the prettiest market in Maputo: lively, African and colourful. In addition to vegetables, fruit and everyday household goods, carvings, baskets and other souvenirs are available at the back right-hand side. The surrounding streets have several Asian-owned shops with a decent selection of imported hardware items (flashlights, lanterns, tools, etc).

From here, cross the Avenida 25 de Setembro and walk down the opposite street to the old town. Turning right at the next corner brings you to the Praça dos Trabalhadores, at the centre of which lies a large memorial to Portuguese soldiers killed in World War I. On the edge of the square, the enormous green and white **railway station** is arguably the most impressive building in Maputo, built by an architect of the Eiffel school, designer of the Eiffel Tower in Paris. Once the terminus of the most important railway line in southern Africa, the shortest coastal connection from the industrial areas and gold mines of the Witwatersrand and Johannesburg and the mines of southern Zimbabwe, the opulent, Victorian-style station is little used these days, which gives it a rather sad appearance but does not detract from its importance as an architectural monument.

Close to the railway station lies the entrance to the **harbour**. During colonial times, Maputo harbour was more important to southern Africa than even Durban, a status it seems unlikely to reclaim in the foreseeable future. From the quay, with its huge cranes, there is a view of the ships anchored in the Bay of Maputo.

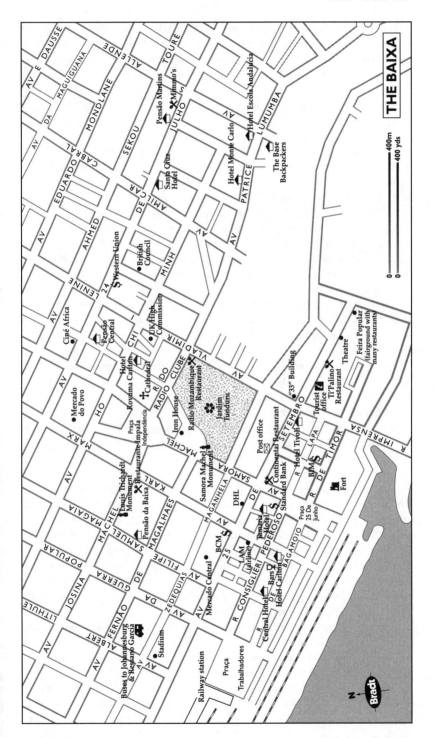

THE BAIXA

Between the station forecourt and the Avenida Samora Machel is the **old town**. Most of the buildings constructed in the late 19th century are quite run down but they still have a certain charm. Many still have either wood or iron filigree and covered balconies, reminiscent of the Creole style of Mauritius and La Réunion, and a few have been restored in recent years. From the station, Rua de Bagamoio – formerly known as the 'Street of Trouble' by sailors who frequented its many bars – leads to Praça dos 25 de Junho via the Central Hotel (the oldest in the city), Carlton Hotel, and several bars.

On Saturdays, the Praça dos 25 de Junho houses a lively and colourful curio market, where you'll see some of the finest batiks on offer in Mozambique. Around the square are situated the **money museum** (Museu da Moeda), the renovated bank building, and the university administration building with a globe on its spire, as well as the fortress, probably the oldest building in Maputo. The **Fortalezada Nossa Senhora da Conceição**, is a formidable red sandstone building enclosing an area of 3,000m² and constructed between 1851 and 1867 on the site of a smaller fort built in the 18th century. Formerly used as a military museum, the fort is not open to visitors at present.

Next, take the main street back to the corner of the Café Continental and Scala and then continue up Avenida Samora Machel to the **Jardim Tunduru** (Botanical Gardens), a public park with many large shady trees. At the top end of the gardens, it is pleasant to sit in the shade and enjoy a coffee or have lunch. To the left of the main entrance gate, on the Praça de Independéncia, is a statue of Samora Machel, the country's first president. Donated by Kim Il-Sung of North Korea, the statue of Machel bears a strange and inaccurate resemblance to Chairman Mao. Also near the main gate is the **Casa de Ferro** (Iron House), a construction of prefabricated metal parts designed by the French engineer Eiffel. Opposite, on the east side of the Tunduru gardens, is the palace in which Paul Kruger, president of the South African Republic, resided after fleeing from British troops at the end of the 19th century and which now houses the Tribunal Supremo.

Continuing up the Avenida Samora Machel brings the tourist to the imposing town hall. On its right is the glistening white **Catholic Cathedral**, a singularly hideous structure that was completed in 1944. The repellent grandiosity of this cathedral doesn't improve when you discover how the labour used to construct it was recruited. The authorities used to pick up teenage girls off the street and have them examined to establish whether they were virgins. If they weren't, they were assumed to be prostitutes and were given the option of paying a fine they couldn't afford, or else working off the fine by providing labour to help build the cathedral.

Perhaps the most surprising monument in the Baixa, worth seeing if only because it is so incongruous, lies on Avenida Josina Machel on the block immediately west of Avenida Karl Marx. The **Louis Trichardt Memorial Garden**, situated on the very spot where this famous Great Trek leader is said to have died of malaria, consists of a stone frieze reminiscent of Pretoria's Voortrekker Monument and a circular pond at the base of which is a ceramic map depicting Trichardt's route from the Cape to Maputo, complete with stylised mosaics of African chiefs in head-dress and bushmen bearing bows and arrows. Alongside the frieze, under the inscription 'They Harnessed the Wilds', the story of Trichardt's trek is told in the sort of messianic tones you might expect of a monument opened in 1968 by the South African Nationalist Minister of Education, one J De Klerk. It's odd enough to find this anachronistic piece of 1960s apartheid chic alive and well in 2001's downtown Maputo, odder still that it has apparently been maintained with meticulous care throughout Mozambique's years of civil war and socialism.

There are several museums in Maputo. Aside from those already mentioned above, tourists interested in the revolutionary history of Mozambique should visit the **Museu da Revolução** on the Avenida 24 de Julho. More interesting, perhaps, is the **Museu Nacional des Artes** on the Avenida Ho Chi Minh, with paintings and sculptures by Mozambique's most famous artists. There's also a cultural centre (**Centro de Estudios Brasileiros**) on Avenida 25 de Setembro, with regular exhibitions and performance arts on Fridays, and an irregular exhibition of various artists at the **Nucleo de Arte**, Rue da Argelia (just off Avenida Julius Nyerere).

DAY TRIPS FROM MAPUTO
Catembe
Separated by a 1km-wide stretch of water, Catembe is Maputo's curiously downbeat twin, and the most obvious day trip from the capital. Decidedly low-rise, Catembe's dusty, unpaved streets could be those of practically any small Mozambican fishing village were it not for the skyscrapers dominating its northern skyline. Catembe is reached from Maputo by a ten-minute ferry ride, leaving from the jetty on Avenida 10 de Novembro at 08.30 and every two hours thereafter, and in the opposite direction every two hours starting at 09.30. To the left of the landing jetty at Catembe there is a pleasant restaurant and small beach. The overland buses to Ponta do Ouro on the border with the South African province of KwaZulu-Natal used to depart from Catembe and as soon as the road is improved, they will probably do so again.

Costa do Sol
The best way to enjoy the sea close to the city is to take a trip from the Polana 5km up the Avenida Marginal to the Costa do Sol restaurant. There is a bus service or one can hitch a ride. From Maputo onwards, one casuarina tree-lined beach after the other lines the coastline. The seabed is very flat, however, and one must wade out a long way to be able to swim. The water is also often cloudy and brown as a result of the river mouth nearby.

In the Costa do Sol restaurant at the end of the street, you can eat well and at a reasonable price.

Matola
This is the greenest industrial area you're likely to have seen. At the end of the Portuguese colonial period, Mozambique was the fourth most industrialised country in Africa. Most of the industries did not withstand the first years of

the socialist People's Republic, and only very few still function properly. The policy of economic reconstruction begun in the late 1980s is intended to change this. You can experience something of the scenery and atmosphere of southern Mozambique if you cross the River Matola from the town.

Matola was outside of the army's protective cordon during the war and consequently it suffered significant damage, so that much of the land is now turned over to agriculture. It is the site of the home and burial place of Chissano, one of Mozambique's leading artists, who committed suicide in 1994. His home, open to the public, contains many of his striking sculptures and carvings, which blend modern and traditional styles.

You can get 'I love Matola' stickers...

Africa Geographic
and
Africa – Birds & Birding

Award-winning magazines
about a continent
worth saving

For subscription details contact:
Africa Geographic/Africa – Birds & Birding
P O Box 44223, Claremont 7735,
Cape Town, South Africa.
Tel: (+27-21) 686 9001. Fax: (+27-21) 686 4500.
E-mail: *wildmags@blackeaglemedia.co.za*
Website: *www.africa-geographic.com*

Maputo and Gaza Provinces

With the exception of the capital and the relatively short stretch of coast between Ponta do Ouro on the South African border and Quissico in Inhambane Province, Mozambique's two most southerly provinces encompass a thinly populated area with little to offer tourists: the vast interior of Gaza in particular is one of the most remote, inaccessible and dry parts of the country.

SOUTH OF MAPUTO

The small block of Mozambican territory that lies to the south of Maputo is rather inaccessible from the capital, the notable exception being Inhaca Island, a popular resort lying in the Gulf of Maputo. The main beach resorts in this area, Ponta do Ouro and Ponta Malongane, both lie close to the South African border and are more easily reached from the South African side than from Maputo. The other potential tourist attraction of this area, the Maputo Elephant Reserve, has been the subject of some big plans for development, although so far none of them have come to fruition.

Inhaca Island

Inhaca is the largest island in the Gulf of Maputo, lying about 35km from the city and 24km from the mainland. The island's name derives from that of the Inhaca chieftaincy, the dominant power on the southern mainland of the Gulf of Maputo in the 16th century. Chief Inhaca offered a hospitable welcome to the Portuguese trader Lourenço Marques, and throughout the 16th century he frequently came to the assistance of shipwrecked Portuguese sailors. From about 1550 onwards, a Portuguese ship would set up camp on Inhaca Island for a few months annually, to trade ivory with the chief's town on the mainland. In 1593, one Portuguese navigator settled on the island for a year before he was murdered and his ship looted by a rival chieftaincy. After 1621, Inhaca fell out of favour with the Portuguese: the ships relocated their annual encampment to Xefina Island and they obtained their ivory from the Tembe chieftaincy on the northern part of the bay.

Inhaca is the most accessible of Mozambique's many offshore islands. It boasts an archetypal tropical island atmosphere, with a couple of good beaches,

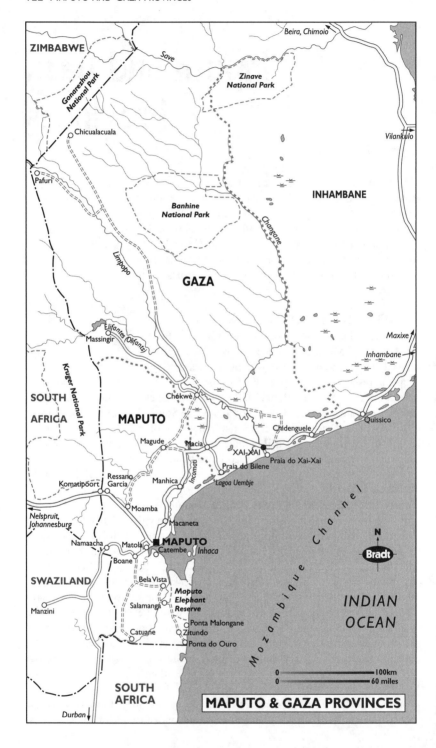

MAPUTO & GAZA PROVINCES

a mangrove-lined north coast, and brightly coloured reefs off the west coast. The reefs of Inhaca are among the most southerly in Africa, due to the water in the gulf being five degrees warmer than elsewhere at this latitude. For those who want to explore the reefs, there is a dive centre operating out of the Inhaca Lodge, which rents scuba and snorkelling equipment. The lodge also organises a variety of day trips.

The island's main tourist focus is Inhaca village, a tiny settlement dominated by the Inhaca Lodge, which has a swimming pool, tree-lined paths and a restaurant. If you have the time, a trip along the north coast to the lighthouse and the Indian Ocean beaches is most worthwhile. The beach directly in front of the hotel is not particularly attractive. If you are prepared to pay the price, a tractor will drive you there. On foot, follow the road to the airport which splits just before the airfield. Take the right fork and follow it along the airport perimeter, and wade through the few small rivers and the swampy mangrove area, which can be flooded at high tide, until you reach the mangrove-free coast and a small village with palm huts where you can buy coconuts. Near the fine old lighthouse is the first of the wide beaches, but it is best not to stop here. Make your way further along the beach over the old coral to the eastern ocean side where there is one beach after the other all along the coast. In each direction the walk takes about two and a half to three hours. If this seems too far, take the tractor out and walk back.

Inhaca has been a centre of scientific research for 65 years. An interesting marine research station lies just to the south of Inhaca village, along with a well-kept museum of natural history. For those with a strong interest in the island's ecology, it's worth trying to get hold of a copy of *The Natural History of Inhaca Island* (edited by Margaret Kalk, Wits University Press, Johannesburg), a 395-page book that includes comprehensive species descriptions of the fauna and flora as well as line drawings depicting the more common species.

Getting there and away
By air
Flights from Maputo to Inhaca Island take barely 15 minutes and cost US$50. Reservations can be made at any travel agent in Maputo or at Pestana Hotels and Resorts (tel: 30 5000; fax: 30 5305; email: pestana_resv_moz@hotmail.com), which owns the Inhaca Lodge and offers flight and accommodation packages to the island.

By boat
At the time of writing (November 2001), the ferry between Maputo and Inhaca that normally departs from the jetty on Avenida 10 de Novembro in Maputo was not in operation. This makes getting to Inhaca Island slightly more complicated and expensive than it could have been – although not prohibitively so. A boat carrying passengers does still leave from the port behind the fort, charging US$25 return for the three-hour voyage to Inhaca Island. It normally leaves Maputo at 08.00 and returns from Inhaca at 16.00, which makes it possible to visit the island in a day trip from Maputo.

In calm conditions, the boat crossing is a most enjoyable experience. As the boat slowly moves away from the coast at Maputo the skyline becomes more and more impressive. After approximately one hour the mountains of Inhaca Island become visible on the horizon, followed gradually by the silhouettes of the palm trees on the neighbouring Ilha Portuguesa.

Where to stay and eat
The four-star **Inhaca Lodge** (tel: 30 5000; fax: 30 5305; email: reservas.africa@pestana.com; web: www.pestana.com) has rooms from US$91/single and US$136/double depending on the season. These prices are on a half-board basis. It's run by the same company – Pestana – as the Rovuma in Maputo. Budget travellers can stay at **Ribeiro's Place**, which has basic reed huts for under US$5, or the **Marine Research Station** (tel: 49 0009) to the south of Inhaca village (although first priority here is given to researchers rather than the general public). Camping is available at **Indigo Bay** for US$6 per person and the **Santa Maria Campsite**, which lies in an attractive and undeveloped corner of the island.

There is a good and expensive restaurant at the Inhaca Lodge, while **Luca's Restaurant** (which also has camping for around US$5) in the village does seafood and vegetarian meals, and is considerably less pricey.

Ilha Portuguesa
The Ilha Portuguesa, opposite the village of Inhaca, is well worth a visit. During Portuguese colonial times it was a leper colony. The island is undeveloped, with a few bushes and palm trees lining idyllic bathing beaches. The beaches tend to be very flat and at low tide large sandbanks become visible. When the tide is unusually low, you can cross the channel between the two islands on foot.

The best swimming beach is the one directly opposite the Hotel Inhaca, but it is dangerous to swim out too far as the current is very strong. You can walk round the Ilha Portuguesa in approximately one to one and a half hours. On the other side of the island from Inhaca a large lagoon forms at low tide, surrounded by wide sandbanks. You can camp wild on the island. A small entrance fee is charged.

You can get there by boat from Inhaca – ask at the lodge.

Maputo Elephant Reserve
This little-known game reserve covers a lake-dotted stretch of coast roughly 30km southeast of Maputo as the crow flies and about 10km north of Ponta Malongane. During the late 1990s, the now late American investor James Blanchard was granted a licence to develop a tourism mega-project, which would have involved restocking and developing tourist facilities at the Maputo Elephant Reserve with a view to combining safari trips with beach holidays at the nearby resorts of Inhaca Island and Ponta do Ouro. This licence was rescinded, however, when Blanchard's estate was unable to demonstrate adequate progress in the development area. At the time of

writing, the Mozambican government was in negotiations with another multi-millionaire, this time a Canadian ecologist named Maurice Strong, to continue where Blanchard had left off. The upshot of all this is that, although the reserve is officially open to visitors, facilities remain severely limited.

The reserve has suffered greatly from poaching in recent years: the 65 white rhinos that were introduced from South Africa have all been killed, and it is thought that many other large mammals including cheetah, leopard and buffalo are now locally extinct. Elephants are still around, though the 1971 population of roughly 350 animals had been reduced to fewer than 60 in 1994. Because the elephants now live in two

Reedbuck

Steenbok

large breeding herds, both of which spend long periods outside the reserve and are very shy, they are unlikely to be seen by casual visitors. Hippos and crocodiles are resident in several freshwater lakes, and small antelope such as red and grey duikers, reedbuck, steenbok and suni are still present in diminished numbers. Bird watching is good, with roughly 350 species recorded, aquatic and coastal scrub species being particularly well represented.

Access to the reserve is by 4WD only, and it is better approached from Ponta Malongane than from Maputo. The resort at Malongone will be able to direct you to the entrance gate. A nominal entrance fee is levied.

Ponta do Ouro and Ponta Malongane

These two beach resorts lie in the far south of Mozambique very close to the border with South Africa. They are very popular with South African fishermen and divers, but rather inaccessible to people travelling on public transport. The small village at Ponta do Ouro has a couple of basic shops, but otherwise the area is very undeveloped except for the holiday resorts at each beach. In July 2001 there was a call for tenders for the construction of a tourism complex in Ponta do Ouro, which would include a 200-room beach resort, yacht marina and golf course. It remains to be seen whether or not these ambitious plans will have been realised by the time you read this.

The beach at Ponta do Ouro is ideal for swimming, surfing, line fishing and various water sports. There are **diving** centres at both resorts where you can hire snorkelling and fishing gear or arrange diving packages. There are five dive sites in total, where lucky divers stand a chance of seeing, amongst other things, zambezis, hammerheads, kingfish, barracuda and potato bass. The surrounding dune forest is potentially good for birdwatching, but there is reportedly still a problem with land-mines so make enquiries before wandering off the beaten track.

Getting there and away

Either resort is best approached from the south via KwaNgwanase in the Maputaland district of the South African province of KwaZulu-Natal. KwaNgwanase can easily be reached in an ordinary saloon car from either Johannesburg or Durban (it is connected by a surfaced road to the N2 between Mkuzi and Pongola) but beyond that a 4WD vehicle will probably be necessary, particularly in the rainy season. After crossing the border, which lies roughly 20km from KwaNgwanase, you'll reach the first intersection after 4km. Turn right here, and then after a further 10km you'll reach a second intersection from where the resorts are signposted. Both resorts lie about an hour's drive from KwaNgwanase, not allowing for the inevitable delays at the border post. The alternative is to drive the 120km to Ponta do Ouro or Ponta Malongane from Maputo with the option of using the Catembe Ferry to get across Maputo Bay. This road is in poor condition and should only be attempted in a 4WD vehicle.

There is sporadic public transport leaving in the direction of either resort from the ferry jetty at Catembe, although you'll probably have to do the trip in stages (Catembe–Salamanga–Zitundo–Ponta do Ouro, for instance); hitching will require a bit of good fortune except perhaps during school holidays, when the main obstacle to an unscheduled visit is that accommodation will almost certainly be booked solid.

Where to stay

The **Ponta do Ouro Beach Resort** – also known as the Motel do Mar (tel: South Africa 012 362 1355; fax: 012 362 1321; email: reservations@ponta.co.za; web; www.pontadoouro.co.za) – has accommodation in self-catering chalets sleeping four people from US$19 per person. If you're looking for something slightly more intimate, try one of the three double rooms at the **Blues Beach House**, a beautifully renovated house on the beach, which costs US$65 per person including breakfast and dinner. There are two guesthouses in the village, **Gracelands** and the much smaller **MGM**; and the **Ponta do Ouro Campsite** at the southern end of the beach has camping from US$5.50 and two-person chalets from US$16. Many of the dive centres based at the campsite, meanwhile, also have accommodation in their respective dive camps, which can be paid for separately or as part of a dive package. Two such centres are the PADI-affiliated **Simply Scuba**, which has a tented camp, and **Dolphin Encountours**, where accommodation is in beachfront chalets.

There is also a well-shaded **campsite** at Ponta Malongane, where pitching your tent will cost around US$10 and two-person rondavels cost from US$25 (without bed linen). There is also a tented dive camp, restaurant and bar.

All of the above-mentioned accommodation can be booked through Mozambique Connection.

THE EN1 FROM MAPUTO TO XAI-XAI
Macaneta

Macaneta is the closest beach resort to Maputo and a popular weekend outing with people working in the capital. The major attractions are excellent game fishing and an attractive, clean beach; the sea here isn't particularly suitable for snorkelling, diving or swimming.

Getting there and away
The unsignposted turn-off to Macaneta lies on the EN1, 37km north of Maputo at a village called Marracuene. The road to the resort is rather sandy and requires a 4WD vehicle. Along the way, you will need to cross the Incomati River by ferry – the trip takes about five minutes and costs US$3 per vehicle. Alternatively, you can catch a boat the whole way downriver to Macaneta Beach for about US$5 per person. The drive from Maputo to Macaneta shouldn't take much longer than a hour. Hitching from Marracuene to Macaneta is easiest at weekends.

Where to stay
The most upmarket option is the **Incomati River Lodge**, which lies on the riverbank in indigenous bush. Accommodation costs US$75 per person per day full board, or US$40 per person self-catering. The **Complexo Turistico Macaneta** consists of a popular restaurant as well as a few chalets and a basic campsite with washing facilities and cold running water. Chalets cost US$60 per unit and camping costs around US$4/site. Booking is rarely necessary. **Jay's Lodge** is on a private beach and it has secluded campsites with hot showers for US$20 per site (up to four people), as well as chalets for US$75–120 per unit. It's advisable to book for Jay's during South African school holidays; this can be done through Mozambique Connection in Johannesburg. If you're stopping at Marracuene, the **Parque de Campismo de Marracuene** on the river has chalet accommodation and camping.

Bilene
The next resort as you head north along the EN1 is Bilene, the former home and burial place of the Gaza chief Shoshangane. Roughly 180km by road from the capital, Bilene overlooks the pretty Uembje Lagoon, which until the floods in 2000 was separated from the Indian Ocean by a large sandbar. Now a channel connects it to the open sea. Bilene's calm waters are popular with watersports enthusiasts, and they offer safe swimming from idyllic white beaches, but the lagoon doesn't offer the good fishing of points further north. As the closest Mozambican resort to Johannesburg, with calm water and beaches that are particularly suitable for family holidays, Bilene tends to be very crowded during South African school holidays, while at the weekends the wealthy of Maputo descend on Bilene to race their cars along the resort's main drag. The rest of the time it's practically deserted.

Getting there and away
The signposted turn-off to Bilene is at the village of Macia, about 150km from Maputo along a well-maintained surfaced road. From Macia, a good 30km surfaced road leads to the main roundabout, about 3km from the beach. There are *chapas* between Macia and Bilene, and hitching should be easy enough, but

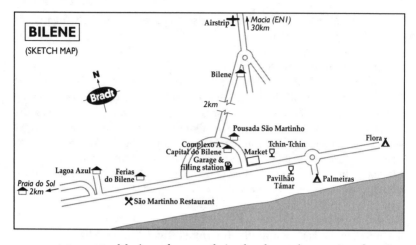

you want to get to Macia early enough in the day to be certain of getting transport on to Bilene. The village boasts a couple of relatively flash restaurants, but nothing in the way of accommodation. A road between Nelspruit in South Africa and Bilene, which bypasses Maputo, is planned for some time in the near future, and there is a small airport with a good runway awaiting the inevitable arrival of charter flights.

Where to stay

The amount of accommodation in Bilene has seen a dramatic increase in the past few years, and now it boasts one of the highest concentrations of tourist facilities in the country. One of the more recent is the newly upgraded **Praia do Sol** (tel mobile: 082 304 319; web: www.pdsol.co.za), a couple of kilometres west of town along a sandy track. Built entirely from local materials in an isolated part of the bush overlooking the lagoon, this place has a slightly magical feel, especially during the quieter periods (ie: outside of the South African school holidays). The rates are US$52 per person, which includes breakfast and a copious dinner, thus making it excellent value and a good choice for single travellers. The **Complexo Turistico Lagoa Azul** (tel: 59006) is just before the turn-off to the Praia do Sol, and has self-catering chalets sleeping four people for a pricey US$85. Better value for money can be found a little way back from the main road in the centre of town. The **Complexo A Capital do Bilene** has air-conditioned rooms with satellite TV for US$30, while the **Pousada São Martinho** (tel: 011 425 1051 South Africa; email: dixie1@global.co.za; web: www.saomartinhomz.com) has similarly priced rooms, or chalets from US$50. The **Hotel Bilene** (tel: 59014) on the main roundabout has air-conditioned rooms from US$42, which is expensive considering it's another 2km or so to the beach. The two campsites in Bilene both occupy attractive spots on the beach. The **Complexo Turistico Parque Flora** – which was a luxurious resort during Portuguese times – is the more secluded. Camping costs US$5, and there are also rondavals from US$15. Meanwhile, the **Complexo Palmeiras** (tel: 082

304372; email: palmeira@bilene.virconn.com) costs US$5 per person per night and has a far greater range of facilities (restaurant, bakery, ice for sale, etc). Both of these campsites are on the eastern side of town.

Where to eat
The **São Martino Restaurant** on the beach at the western end of town is busy during the days serving South African and Mozambican day-trippers. The restaurant at the **Complexo Palmeiras** also has an appealing location, with a terrace overlooking the lagoon, making it the perfect place for a sundowner. Down a path next to the Palmeiras, the **Pavilhão Támar Restaurant** offers a limited selection of Mozambican dishes and, on Fridays and Saturdays, the chance to work off your dinner at the discotheque next door. Back on the main road, again not far from the Palmeiras, the **Tchin-Tchin Restaurant** has a good range of fish dishes and also sells ice-creams. There are also quite smart restaurants at the **Hotel Bilene** and the **Complexo A Capital do Bilene**, the latter of which also has a bakery and the best-stocked supermarket in Bilene.

Activities
The calm waters of the Uembje Lagoon are ideal for snorkelling, canoeing, windsurfing and, when the open sea is too rough, diving (you can see seahorses in the lagoon). Otherwise, there is 22km of reef beyond the lagoon for more serious dives. Whale-watching is also possible from roughly September to the middle of November. All of these activities are available (some free of charge to guests) at the Praia do Sol.

About 15km before arriving at Xai-Xai, you'll see the turn-off for the **Zongoene Lodge** (tel: Maputo 49 9523; email: zongoene@satis.co.za; web: www.satis.co.za/zongoene), a luxurious, self-contained resort about 35km from the EN1 on the Limpopo River delta. Accommodation is in fully equipped chalets, which cost around US$75 per person full board. There is a freshwater swimming pool, and numerous activities, such as snorkelling, fly fishing, deep-sea fishing, four-wheel motorbiking and mountain biking, are available. The lodge even has its own airstrip for fly-in guests.

XAI-XAI
Xai-Xai (pronounced shy-shy) is the name of the capital town of Gaza Province, and also of a popular beach resort 10km out of town. Lying on the north bank of the Limpopo, Xai-Xai was founded in the early 20th century as a satellite port to Lourenço Marques and to service local towns, to which end a narrow-gauge railway was constructed 100km inland during 1909–12.

Being so close to the banks of the Limpopo River, Xai-Xai was hit very hard by the 2000 floods. Locals talk of the lower parts of town being submerged under three metres of water, and landmarks such as the BCM building only just managing to stay above the rising waters. Miraculously, however, once the waters had receded and the buildings dried out, most businesses reopened and continued trading as before.

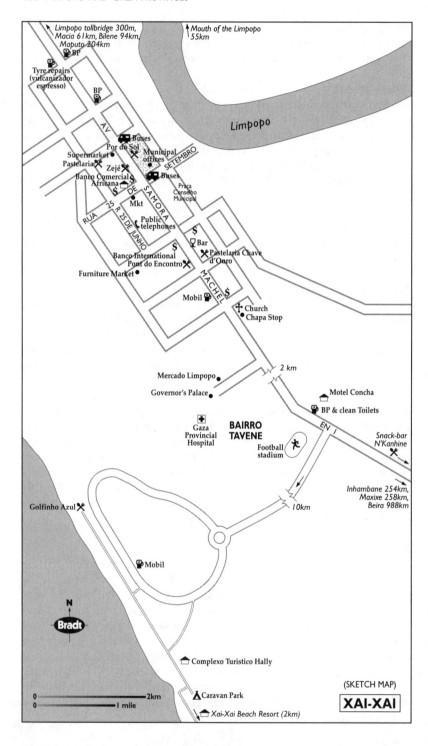

Limpopo tollbridge 300m,
Macia 61km, Bilene 94km,
Maputo 204km
BP

Mouth of the Limpopo
55km

Tyre repairs
(vulcanizador
espresso)

BP

Limpopo

AV

Buses
Por do Sol
Supermarket
Pastelaria
Zejé
Banco Comercial
Africana

Municipal
offices

SETEMBRO

Buses

Praça
Conselho
Municipal

Mkt

S DE SAMORA

RUA 25

R 25 DE JUNHO

Public
telephones

$

$ Bar
$
Pastelaria Chave
d'Ouro

Banco International
Pont do Encontro

Furniture Market

Mobil

MACHEL $

Church
Chapa Stop

2 km

Mercado Limpopo

Governor's Palace

Gaza
Provincial
Hospital

BAIRRO
TAVENE

Football
stadium

Motel Concha

BP & clean Toilets

EN 1

Snack-bar
N'Kanhine

Inhambane 254km,
Maxixe 258km,
Beira 988km

Golfinho Azul

10km

N

Bradt

Mobil

Complexo Turistico Hally

0   2km
0   1 mile

Caravan Park

Xai-Xai Beach Resort (2km)

(SKETCH MAP)

XAI-XAI

Xai-Xai is a fairly nondescript town – the majority of motorised travellers will probably take one look at it and head straight to the beach. To backpackers, it is of interest as a potential stopover along the EN1 and as the springboard for visits to the nearby beach. Those who do find themselves spending a night in town should take a look at the busy little central market, and at the open-air furniture-making market two blocks away. You might also want to take a peek at the brightly painted church on the edge of the town centre. For birders, a stroll along the lush, marshy fringes of the Limpopo might prove rewarding.

The beach, **Praia do Xai-Xai**, is the sort of idyllic stretch of white sand that is so characteristic of Mozambique (you'd get as bored as I would if I attempted to describe every beach in the country). The sea here is renowned for its excellent game fishing, and for the snorkelling and diving possibilities in the many coral reefs lying within 6km of the shore. There are two points of interest on the shore: the ruined Motel Chonguene about 4km east of the campsite, and the Wenela tide-pool roughly 2km to the west of the main road that loops past the beach. The tide-pool is linked to the sea by an underwater tunnel blow-hole, which you should not even think about trying to swim through. Lined by thick coastal scrub as opposed to the palm trees that characterise beaches further north, Praia do Xai-Xai is surprisingly rich in bird life, with the beautiful green and red Livingstone's lourie being a common resident.

Getting there and away
Xai-Xai town straddles the EN1 roughly 215km north of Maputo – your arrival is heralded by the crossing of a large bridge over the impressive Limpopo River. The road between Maputo and Xai-Xai is surfaced in its entirety and there are practically no serious pot-holes to worry about. Regular buses and *chapas* connect Maputo to Xai-Xai. You can pick up a *chapa* to the beach from the main city square, or else you could wander out to the turn-off 2km towards Maxixe and take a *chapa* or try to hitch from there.

The turn-off to Praia do Xai-Xai is clearly signposted on the Maxixe side of town about 200m after the BP garage in front of the Motel Concha. A good surfaced 10km road leads to the main roundabout above the beach. Here, you should take the road to your left down to the beach. After a couple of hundred metres, an unsignposted dirt track to your left leads to the hotel and caravan park.

Where to stay
The cheapest accommodation in town is the **Pensão Africana**, but it's a bit of a dump and poor value for money at US$15/20 single/double. Less central, but much better value and conveniently close to the turn-off to the beach, is the **Motel Concha** (tel: 25099), which has self-contained singles for US$15 and doubles for US$35. There is also a swimming pool, although it was empty when I was there. On the beach, the **Complexo Turistico Hally** (tel: 35003) has double rooms for US$30 including a continental breakfast. You can camp

for around US$5 at the adjacent **Xai-Xai Caravan Park**, or rent a two-person bungalow for US$15. Alternatively, dormitory tents with beds, bedding and mosquito nets are available for about US$9 per person at the **Xai-Xai Diving and Fishing Camp**, which is in a reed enclosure within the caravan park. For more luxurious accommodation, walk about 2km west of the caravan park to the **Xai-Xai Beach Resort**, which is built on a natural slope 15m above sea level. Every one of the self-contained rooms has a private balcony with a sea view.

Beach accommodation is often fully booked during South African school holidays – bookings can be made through Mozambique Connection.

Where to eat
In town, **Restaurante Zéje** serves a variety of fish, chicken and beef dishes in the US$3 to US$5 range, and the waiters speak a bit of English. The **Pastelaria Chaya Doura** serves similarly priced meals, as well as fresh pastries and rolls, and tea and coffee. You can eat inside or on the street. The umbrella-covered veranda of the **Par do Sol Restaurant** looks like it would be a pleasant place for a chilled beer.

Cheap meals are available at the market, as is a wide selection of fruits and vegetables and crusty bread rolls. There is a well-stocked supermarket (frozen meat, pasta, tinned food, wine, beer, fruit juices and most other essentials ranging from margarine to tin foil) on Avenida Samora Machel opposite the Par do Sol Restaurant.

At Praia do Xai-Xai, the best place to eat is the **Restaurante Golfinho Azul**, which serves good fish dishes, chicken and steaks for around US$5–6. There is also a good open-air restaurant in the **caravan park** – the half chicken piri-piri is recommended at US$4.50. The small supermarket attached to the Complexo Turistico Hally is not as well stocked as the one in town.

Useful information
You can exchange money in town at the main branch of the BCM on Avenido Samora Machel. If the rates in town don't look very good, bear in mind that you can pay for practically everything at Praia do Xai-Xai in South African rands, and this will often work out to be cheaper than would paying in local currency.

Xai-Xai Diving and Fishing Camp organises fishing and diving excursions from the beach.

CHIDENGUELE
Just before leaving Gaza Province, about 60km north of Xai-Xai, the EN1 passes the small town of Chidenguele. While there is nothing to detain the tourist in the town itself, the lakes surrounding Chidenguele (Nelson Mandela and his Mozambican wife are rumoured to be building a house on an island in the middle of one of them) are well worth a visit. The birdlife in these lakes includes kingfishers. There is an excellent lodge on the Indian Ocean

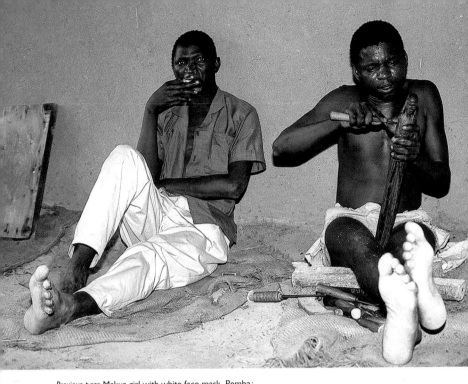

Previous page Makua girl with white face mask, Pemba

Above Makonde carver, Nampula

Below A young tailor operates his sewing machine

coast, 5km from Chidenguele along a sandy track. The **Paraiso de Chidenguele** (tel: 011 782 1026 South Africa; email: wyldsyde@iafrica.com) is built on a sand-dune overlooking the ocean, and the views from its several self-catering chalets are as dramatic as they are far-reaching. The chalets sleep up to eight people and cost a little over US$10 per person. The only other sleeping option in Chidenguele is the **Pousada Numdra**, about a five-minute walk from the EN1. This is also the first – and last – restaurant before you arrive at the Paraiso de Chidenguele.

Stay at the luxurious Indigo Bay Lodge on our 6 day Mozambique Safari and immerse yourself in breathtaking sights coupled with impeccable service. Each of the beautiful 23 chalets has a captivating view of the ocean while maintaining their privacy.

White sandy beaches and emerald green water are just perfect for a few days' relaxation after a busy and exciting safari. Mozambique is easily accessible from Johannesburg or Mpumalanga airports, the flight to Vilanculos is comfortable. We recommend that guests stay at the Indigo Bay and the Marlin Lodge.

See the world with Ker & Downey. Ask about Botswana, South Africa, Zambia, Namibia, Tanzania, Kenya, Rwanda, Uganda and Egypt in Africa. India and Bhutan in South Asia and Ecuador, Peru and Brazil in South America.

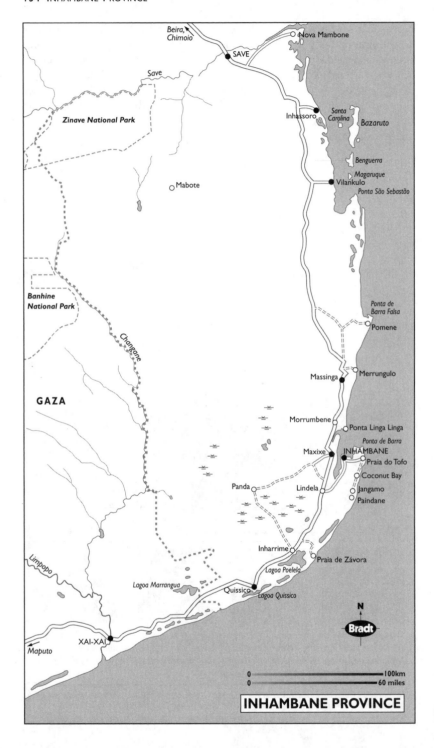

INHAMBANE PROVINCE

Inhambane Province

The long coastal belt of Inhambane Province is the most developed part of Mozambique in tourist terms, boasting a sequence of idyllic and relatively low-key resorts, most of which are practically unvisited except for during the South African, and to a lesser extent Zimbabwean, school holidays.

The main road through this region is the EN1, which more or less follows the coastline from south to north. For most of its length, the EN1 runs between 10km and 100km inland of the coast, but it does briefly skirt the beach at Maxixe township, about 450km north of Maputo. The main towns in this region, running from south to north, are Quissico and the coastal ports of Inhambane, Maxixe, Vilankulo and Inhassoro. Aside from the four coastal towns, there are beach resorts, campsites and backpackers' hostels at Závora, Paindane, Jangamo, Coconut Bay, Tofo, Barra, Linga Linga, Morrungulo, Pomene and on the Bazaruto Islands.

Whereas northern Mozambique boasts a wealth of historical towns and is relatively varied in its landscapes, the south coast is almost entirely of interest for its picture-postcard beaches. This is a great area for snorkelling, fishing, scuba diving and even birdwatching, or just for hanging around on pristine beaches, but it doesn't boast much variety for travellers who aren't equipped for marine activities. If you arrive in Mozambique with a boot full of fishing or diving gear, then practically any beach is worth exploring. For backpackers, the best bets are either Vilankulo or the beaches around Inhambane, where there are inexpensive backpacker-oriented resorts. And if you're not visiting northern Mozambique, then don't miss out on Inhambane, the oldest and most atmospheric town in this part of the country, and one of the most agreeable towns I've visited anywhere in Africa.

The beach resorts along this stretch of coast tend to be booked solid during South African school holidays. During this period, it is advisable to make advance bookings, whether you are camping or looking for a room. A Johannesburg-based company, **Mozambique Connection**, acts as the agency for several of the resorts in this area. See *Tour operators* on page 45 for their contact details. Most South African tourists head straight for one or other of the beach resorts, so school holidays have less effect on room availability in towns such as Maxixe, Inhambane and Xai-Xai, or on the backpacker-oriented resorts.

GETTING AROUND

The EN1 between Maputo and Beira is surfaced for most of its length. The damage inflicted by the 2000 floods has now largely been repaired, although new roadwork projects might slightly disrupt your trip up to Beira at any given moment. There are also surfaced roads connecting the EN1 to Bilene, Praia do Xai-Xai, Inhambane, Tofo, Vilankulo and Inhassoro. The roads to some of the more remote resorts (Závora, Jangamo, Coconut Bay and Morrungulo) are unsurfaced and require 4WD, especially after rain, but with the exception of these places you can explore the region covered in this chapter in an ordinary saloon car. If you're thinking of heading from Inhassoro to Beira or Zimbabwe in a saloon car, read *Beira: Getting there and away* on page 162. Petrol and diesel are readily available at all major towns between Maputo and Vilankulo, but the supply in Inhassoro is rather erratic.

Most areas covered in this chapter are easily explored on public transport. Buses run the length of the EN1 from Maputo to Beira. For long hauls, Oliveira's is regarded as the most reliable operator. It runs a daily service in both directions between Maputo and Beira and Maputo and Tete via Chimoio. Buses heading north leave Maputo at 07.00 and arrive in Beira or Chimoio at around 09.00 the following day. The reason why buses heading north take so long is that they have to overnight at the Save River (or some town before it) in order to cross the poor stretch of road further north in daylight. In other words, you can get from Maputo to anywhere covered in this chapter within one day. In the opposite direction, buses from Beira and Tete leave at 05.00, and usually overnight at Xai-Xai before continuing on to Maputo early the following morning.

For shorter hops, you'll probably have to use the local buses and *chapas* that connect all towns along the EN1. There are also regular *chapas* connecting the EN1 to coastal resorts and towns such as Bilene, Praia do Xai-Xai, Inhambane, Vilankulo and Inhassoro. *Chapas* sometimes run out to the more inaccessible resorts (Jangamo, Coconut Bay and Paindane, for instance), although in these cases it's much better to get them to collect you (more details are given under the relevant section headings).

Once you're out of Maputo, hitching is a possibility; lifts are generally slow in coming, but once you've got a lift it will almost certainly take you all the way to the next town.

QUISSICO

This compact town lies on the EN1 roughly 100km north of Xai-Xai in an area notable for its several deep-blue freshwater lakes. One of the larger lakes lies immediately southeast of Quissico; there is a good view of it from the EN1 as you leave Quissico for Maxixe, and from the municipal building about 200m off the main road. The lake can be reached along a 10km dirt road that leaves the EN1 just outside town. You could probably get there more directly by foot (the shore can't be more than 3km from town as the crow flies, but ask for local advice regarding footpaths – there's no danger of getting lost as the lake lies directly in front of you, but there may be a possibility of land mines if you stray off the established tracks).

Roughly 45km north of Quissico, the EN1 crosses the startlingly beautiful Lake Poelela, reputed to be where Vasco Da Gama first landed in Mozambique in January 1498. You'll get a fair view of the lake from the road, but since there are no facilities in the area and no roads leading to the rest of the lake, the risk of treading on a land mine, however faint, should be viewed as a persuasive deterrent to off-the-beaten-track exploration.

Getting there and away
The surfaced section of the EN1 between Xai-Xai and Quissico is in good condition. Any bus or *chapa* heading between Xai-Xai and Maxixe can drop you off in Quissico, and hitching along this stretch of road should be easy enough.

Where to stay and eat
The only place to stay in Quissico is the **Motel Pousada**, which has double rooms for US$12. There is a restaurant and bar attached to the motel, and you can also eat at the wonderfully named **Restaurante Planet Ran Tan Plan** on the opposite side of the EN1. There's a busy market where you can buy fresh rolls and a variety of fruit and vegetables.

ZÁVORA
Závora has a reputation for being an outstanding spot for snorkelling and game fishing. The signposted turn-off to Závora lies a few kilometres north of the bridge across Lake Poelela. The resort is reached via a sandy 15km road, recommended only if you have 4WD. Camping is available at US$6 per person at the **Závora Lodge**, which also has a few bungalows and beach houses ranging in price from US$45 to US$100 depending on the number of beds and the season. You can book through Mozambique Connection.

MAXIXE
Located at the only point where the EN1 actually skims the coast, Maxixe (pronounced Masheesh) is a popular stopover with people making their way between Maputo and Beira. It is also a useful springboard for travellers heading to Inhambane – the two towns lie on opposite sides of the same 4km-wide bay and are linked by a regular dhow service.

Maxixe is not the most inherently interesting of places: its stark grid-like layout and bustling African market-town atmosphere couldn't offer a greater contrast to the seductive Old World sleepiness that envelops Inhambane. In its favour, Maxixe lies on a pretty palm-lined stretch of coast, offers a good selection of relatively cheap accommodation and food, and the view across the water to Inhambane at dusk is well worth stopping the night for.

Getting there and away

Maxixe straddles the EN1 roughly 450km northeast of Maputo, 235km northeast of Xai-Xai, and 60km by road from Inhambane. The road from Maputo to Maxixe is surfaced in its entirety.

The bus station in Maxixe is conveniently located in the centre of town. You should have no difficulty catching an Oliveira's or a TSL bus to Maputo, with several passing through Maxixe during the course of the day. The best time to wait for them is in the morning at around 07.00. From Maputo, these companies' buses leave the capital at around 07.00, arriving in Maxixe sometime in the early afternoon. The options going the other way towards Vilankulo and Beira are more limited. The preferred bus is the Maputo–Vilankulo express, which passes through Maxixe at around 13.00 and takes about three hours to get to Vilankulo. Otherwise, you will have to catch a stopping bus (one leaves Maxixe at about 08.30), which can take as long as seven hours. Better to take a minibus *chapa*, should you be lucky enough to find one going to Vilankulo.

There are also *chapas* to Massinga and Morrumbene (for Linga Linga) from Maxixe.

Where to stay

You can pitch your tent at the **Campismo de Maxixe** (tel: 30351), which occupies an attractive spot on the bay (although the nearby main road can make it noisy), for US$4 per person. Other accommodation there includes basic thatched bungalows for about US$30. Motorists who are staying elsewhere in Maxixe can make use of the secure parking at the Campismo for US$1.50 per vehicle or trailer. Just before the site, on the left, there's a garage that will change US$ and rand.

The best hotel in Maxixe is the **Hotel Tânia** (tel: 30058), which is on the second floor of a high-rise building opposite the BP garage on the Vilankulo side of town. The rooms are bright, airy and very clean, and some even have hot water. Singles go for US$12.50 and doubles for US$17.50. Although more centrally located and slightly cheaper than the Tânia, and notwithstanding the fact that they have balconies, the rooms at the **Hotel Golfinho Azul** (tel: 30071) roughly opposite the ferry jetty are less inviting. Another option, once again very conveniently located, is the **Oceamo Hotel** (tel: 30097) opposite the bus station, where for just US$5 you get a very clean (and not at all depressing) box-like room with two beds. The **Motel Palmar**, about 1km from the town centre towards Vilankulo, seems reasonable value at US$9 for a self-contained double, but it's not too convenient if you're on foot. Accommodation is in detached cottages, each of which contains two rooms with a shared entrance, so it might be advisable to check the lock on your individual room.

There are also a few rooms at the **Restaurante Pousada do Maxixe**. Doubles cost US$9 (ordinary) or US$13 (self-contained).

Where to eat

The **Stop Restaurant** is probably the best place to eat in Maxixe. It has an unrivalled location overlooking the bay to Inhambane, the food is good, the

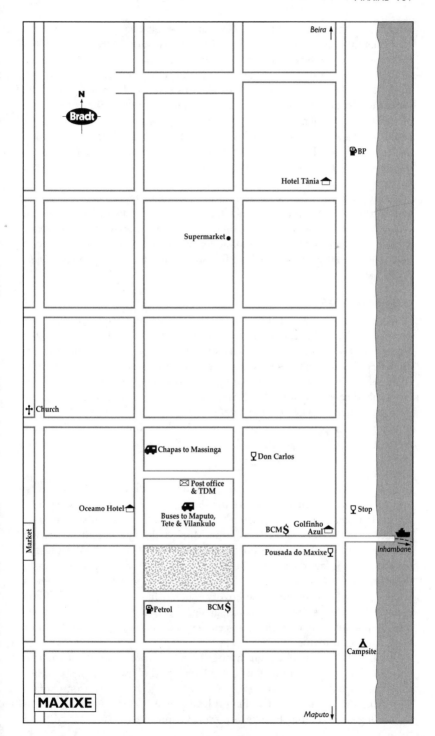

waiters speak English, and it's open early for breakfast, which could be convenient if you're waiting for a bus. The **Restaurante Don Carlos** on the eastern side of the bus station has a similar menu at similar prices (ie: fish, seafood and meat dishes for around US$4) and an inviting Mediterranean bar atmosphere. On the western side of the bus station, the restaurant at the **Oceamo Hotel** serves hearty lunches, catering no doubt to the fair number of weary bus travellers who pass through Maxixe in the early afternoon. You could also eat at the **Restaurante Pousada do Maxixe** – I don't know what the food is like, but I didn't find the musty dining room particularly encouraging. Better, perhaps, to take a drink on the veranda overlooking...the Petromoc filling station!

If you are staying at the Campismo (campsites here have barbecue facilities) and want to prepare your own food, the market has the usual good selection of fresh vegetables and fish, and there is a supermarket with a reasonable selection of imported items, including Western-brand ice-creams, a couple of blocks north of the bus station. Shellfish and the like are probably best bought on the beach.

INHAMBANE

The eponymous capital of Inhambane Province lies on a natural bay formed by a deep inlet at the mouth of the small Matumba River. Inhambane is the oldest extant settlement between Maputo and Beira, and it is without doubt the most pleasant and interesting town covered in this chapter. A spacious layout of tree-lined avenues fringed by several eye-pleasing colonial buildings gives Inhambane a strongly Mediterranean character. It is also a remarkably clean and orderly town, with a strangely subdued Old World atmosphere quite unlike anywhere else I've visited in Africa. In short, Inhambane is definitely worth a visit.

History

Little is known of Inhambane's history prior to the 18th century. It was almost certainly a port of note even before the Portuguese era, and it was visited by several Portuguese traders in the early 15th century. In 1560, Inhambane was selected as the site of a short-lived Jesuit Mission, the first in East Africa, and when the leader of the mission arrived he noted that several Portuguese traders had settled there. By the end of the 16th century it had been incorporated into the Portuguese East African monopoly and had become a regular port of call for Portuguese ivory-trading ships. During the 17th and early 18th centuries, Inhambane was, along with Delagoa Bay (Maputo), the most important trade terminus between the coast and interior of what is now southern Mozambique.

In 1727, the Portuguese Commander Bernado Soares discovered a Dutch vessel trading with the local chiefs of Inhambane. Following this, a punitive expedition led by Domingos Rebello arrived at Inhambane from Sofala, destroying several villages and killing at least two local chiefs as a punishment for trading with another European power. Commander Soares stayed on at

Inhambane, where he built a fort large enough to house a garrison of 50 men. Soares' fort was hardly the most impressive defensive structure (a compatriot remarked that 'it would have been enough for [the Dutch] to have laid eyes on it to capture it'), but its presence evidently discouraged further Dutch trade, and it laid the foundation for a permanent Portuguese settlement.

Although Inhambane was officially recognised as a Portuguese town in 1763, the local ivory trade was in reality dominated by Indians rather than Portuguese, an aberrant situation that dated to the early 18th century when the port had briefly been leased to an Indian trader called Calcanagi Velabo. Inhambane's Christian population numbered only 200 at the end of the 18th century. Remarkably, several of the parish priests appointed at around this time were of Indian extraction! The town rapidly grew in prosperity during its early years (in 1770, the customs revenue raised at Inhambane was almost equal to that raised at Quelimane), not least because it was the first Mozambican port to establish a trade in slaves. Roughly 400 slaves were exported from Inhambane in 1762, a number that had quadrupled by the end of that decade while ivory export figures steadily sank. In 1834, Inhambane was practically razed by Soshangane's Gaza warriors, and most of its traders were killed, but the town soon recovered and by 1858 it had a population of roughly 4,000 (of which 75% were slaves). Even as recently as 1928, Inhambane was the third-largest centre of population in Mozambique, after the capital city and Beira.

Getting there and away

The surfaced 33km branch road to Inhambane is signposted from the EN1 roughly 450km northeast of Maputo, 235km northeast of Xai-Xai, and 30km south of Maxixe. There is a BP garage at the junction town of Lindela.

Although there are regular *chapas* between Lindela and Inhambane, the better way to get to Inhambane by public transport is on a dhow from Maxixe. The two towns are separated by over 60km of road, but they face each other across a bay and are less than 4km apart as the crow flies. Motorised and unmotorised dhows run between Maxixe and Inhambane throughout the day; the cost of a one-way trip is less than US$1. Alternatively, Oliveira's has services to and from Maputo and Inhambane leaving in the mornings from either town. For Vilankulo and Beira, however, you have no choice but to cross over to Maxixe for public transport.

From Inhambane, a good surfaced road covers the 22km to Tofo Beach. The turn-off to Barra Beach is signposted to the left roughly 15km along this road. *Chapas* run on a regular basis from next to the market in Inhambane to Tofo, while the white and red TUCI (Transportes Urbanos da Cidade de Inhambane) buses do the trip less frequently. You'll probably have to hitch or walk the 7km to Barra Beach, or get one of the resorts based there to pick you up at the Tofo junction. It is also possible to get to the resorts south of Inhambane (Coconut Bay, Jangamo and Paindane) by public transport. The turn-off for these beaches is a couple of kilometres out of town on the road that leads to the EN1, and *chapas* depart from the market a few hundred metres before the turn-off. As with

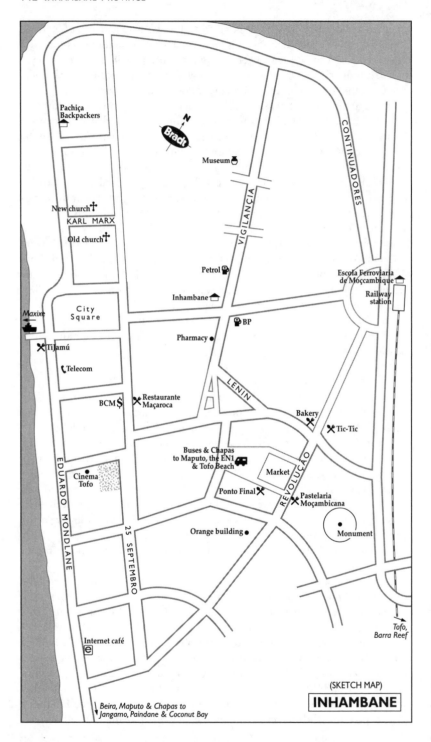

(SKETCH MAP)

INHAMBANE

Barra Beach, the resorts based here can arrange for you to be collected. Pachiça Backpackers in Inhambane is a good place to co-ordinate these lifts.

Where to stay
The **Pachiça Backpackers** (tel: 20565) should be your first port of call when arriving in the Inhambane area. Not only is it a well-run backpackers' hostel with clean dorms and private rooms for US$5 and US$10 respectively, but it also has a wealth of information about what's going on at the surrounding beaches. Moreover, if you want to visit one of the more inaccessible resorts, Isabella, the manager at Pachiça, will try to arrange a lift for you. As if all this wasn't enough, they also have safe parking. After being closed for several months for renovation, the **Hotel Inhambane** was apparently preparing to reopen at the time of writing. It seems that the new-look hotel will be considerably more upmarket than before, with air conditioning and satellite TV in all rooms. If so, expect prices to match. There are also rooms at the **Escola Ferroviaria de Moçambique** (tel: 20781), which occupies a pink building next to the old railway station. Very clean doubles cost US$12.50, with another two beds in an adjoining room separated by the bathroom but no wall.

Where to eat
The **Restaurante Maçaroca** is arguably the smartest in town (where else has cheese and olive starters?), but still not expensive with grilled fish dishes, chicken and chips, and steaks for under US$5. You can also get perfectly satisfactory meals at several places near the market. The **Restaurante Tic-Tic** has your basic chicken, meat and fish dishes for around US$3, all served with fresh rolls from the bakery over the road. You can eat inside or on the small street terrace. The **Restaurante Ponto Final**, on a quiet road next to the market, also has a terrace and a menu more or less identical to the Tic-Tic's. Opposite the market, the **Pastelaria Moçambicana** lacks the variety of cakes and pastries to be found in the bakeries of Maputo but is nevertheless a good place for a prego roll and a cup of tea. The open-air **Ti Jamú Snack Bar** enjoys the finest location of any restaurant in Inhambane – overlooking the bay in front of the jetty. It's just about the perfect place to sit as the sun sets over Maxixe. On Fridays and Saturdays this is also the venue of the local discotheque. Finally, the **Pachiça Backpackers** does good breakfasts (served with 'malaria tea'!) and is reputed for its pizzas.

Useful information
Somewhat ironically for a place so steeped in history and with such a laid-back atmosphere, Inhambane is the only town between Maputo and Beira with a fully-fledged internet café. Download times are not the fastest, but, provided that there's electricity, everything seems to work OK. You'll find it next to the public library on Avenida Eduardo Mondlane, and it costs US$0.60 for 10 minutes.

What to see
Inhambane today is anything but the bustling trade centre that it once was – it is difficult to think of a more sedate town anywhere on the East African coast –

but neither has it fallen into the state of disrepair that sometimes appears to be synonymous with the term 'historical coastal town'. Most of the older buildings are clustered around an open square that lies at the jetty end of Avenida Indepéndencia. Of particular interest is a beautiful 18th-century **cathedral** to the north of the square (with what must surely be deliberate irony, the original cathedral and a more modern church are practically the only buildings on the block-long Rua Karl Marx!). The **seafront** itself is very pretty, particularly at sunset, though it isn't really recommended for swimming. The central **market** on Avenida Revolução is a lively place, with a good variety of vegetables, fish and local crafts on sale. The **museum** on Avenida Vigelença, two blocks north of the Inhambane Hotel, has a random selection of African household items and small exhibits relating to various aspects of Mozambican life, most with explanations in English as well as Portuguese. The museum is open from 09.00 to 17.00, and tourists are expected to make a donation.

The Inhambane area is noted for its seemingly endless stands of tall coconut palms, and although the town itself lacks a good beach, the peninsula on which it lies boasts several, all within 30km of town.

BEACHES AROUND INHAMBANE

Within about a 30km-radius of Inhambane lie several of Mozambique's finest beaches. Some are already well established on the tourist circuit, while others are just starting to be developed. By the same token, some are easy to access by public transport, while others require slightly more effort and organisation. The pay-off for this is, of course, more privacy and seclusion than you'll find at any other resort along the southern Mozambican coast.

Tofo Beach

Tofo Beach lies 22km northeast of Inhambane between the Indian Ocean and the freshwater Lake Pembane. There's a good range of budget accommodation, and more of a party atmosphere than at the quieter resorts south of Inhambane. Dave Armstrong writes: 'The beach is fantastic; it stretches for miles with superb breakers for surfing. Several dive schools offer reasonably priced excursions. Fishing is also available and you can buy freshly landed fish and tiger prawns on the beach. A great area to come and crash for a few days.'

Getting there and away

Chapas to Tofo Beach leave regularly from next to the market in Inhambane. Large white and red buses also do the trip. Hitching along the paved road between Inhambane and Tofo should be easy enough.

Where to stay

Hotel Marinhos (tel: 29015), the only hotel at Tofo, sits directly on the beach at the place where chapas from Inhambane arrive. En-suite rooms with fan and hot water cost from US$30/single and US$50/double, and some have sea views. Over the road, the **Centro Turistico Ferroviaro** (tel:

29020) is slightly cheaper. **Casa Barry** (web: www.casabarry.com), under new management in 2005, has four-person chalets for around US$40, clean facilities, decent snacks, and a new campsite due to open in late 2005. The relaxed **Bamboozi Backpackers** (web: www.bamboozi.com) lies in a coconut grove 1–2km northward along the beach, with camping, and rates ranging from around US$10 in a basic hut to $55 upwards for a 3-bedded chalet or honeymoon suite. Partying is good here. Plenty of other smaller beachside places are opening up; take your pick.

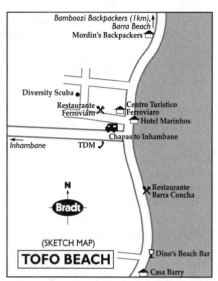

Map labels:
Bamboozi Backpackers (1km),
Barra Beach
Mordin's Backpackers
Diversity Scuba
Restaurante Ferroviáro
Centro Turistico Ferroviaro
Hotel Marinhos
Chapas to Inhambane
Inhambane   TDM
N
Bradt
Restaurante Barra Concha
(SKETCH MAP)
Dino's Beach Bar
TOFO BEACH
Casa Barry

Where to eat
Even though it lacks a beachfront location, the **Restaurante Ferroviáro** is probably the best place to eat at Tofo Beach. The menu includes a variety of imaginative dishes, many of them cooked with coconut, for around US$10, plenty of vegetarian choices, and good breakfasts. The restaurant at the nearby **Hotel Marinhos** offers Mozambican and Portuguese fare, as well as the unquestionable draw of a beach terrace. However, you can't beat the view from the restaurant at **Bamboozi Backpackers**, which is perched on top of a sand-dune overlooking the ocean. The menu contains good old-fashioned traveller-style food such as pancakes, omelettes and curries. Back in the centre of town, the **Restaurante Barra Concha** is directly on the beach, as is **Dino's Beach Bar**, which serves various cocktails and rents out snorkelling and other equipment for watersports (windsurf boards, boogie boards, etc).

Barra Beach
About 5km before you reach Tofo Beach, a fork in the road leads to Barra Beach, which lies a further 7km down a sandy track. If you intend to stay at either of the two accommodation options at Barra, let them know and they'll pick you up at the Tofo junction. The **Bar Babalaza** at the junction serves pizzas and various other meals and drinks.

The **Barra Lodge** (tel: 20561; email: barra@pixie.co.za; web: www.barralodge.co.za) has self-catering cottages sleeping six from US$58, beach houses from US$33 per person and camping from US$4.50 per person. They have facilities for horse-riding on the beach. **Barra Reef** (South Africa tel: 011 803 3356) is the other campsite at Barra Beach, lying at the very north of the peninsula, past the freshwater Lake Malongue. Close to some swamps and near a reef that offers good snorkelling, the resort has camping from US$3.50 per person. Facilities include flush toilets, hot showers and electricity.

Jangamo, Paindane and Coconut Bay

Much more secluded than Tofo and even Barra, the beaches to the southeast of Inhambane are the ones to head for if you really want to get away from it all but don't want to make the arduous slog up to the coastal areas of northern Mozambique.

Getting there and away

Most of the resorts based at these beaches will be quite happy to collect you provided that you let them know when you'll be coming. Pachiça Backpackers in Inhambane is a useful intermediary in this respect. Alternatively, *chapas* from Inhambane run along the very sandy 24km-road that leads to these beaches. The turn-off is a couple of kilometres out of town on the branch road to the EN1, and *chapas* depart from the market a few hundred metres before the turn-off. Going in the opposite direction, you should have no problem finding a ride back to the main road.

Where to stay

The **Jangamo Beach Resort** (tel: 013 7901013 South Africa; email: daphs@yebo.co.za; web: www.geocities.com/daphnesza) is the pick of the bunch. There are several attractive chalets of various sizes, most with panoramic views of the Indian Ocean, as well as single and double rooms with communal bathroom. The cost works out at around US$11 per person, whether you are in a room or sharing a chalet. The restaurant serves three meals a day, and the quality of the food is very high. Similar facilities are available at the neighbouring **Guinjata Bay** (tel: +27 (0)83 283 6918 South Africa), the **Coconut Bay Resort** about 15km to the north of Jangamo, and the **Paindane Beach Resort** (tel: 011 734 5970 South Africa; email: dolfish@hixnet.co.za) about 5km to the south. You can also camp at Paindane for around US$6 per person.

Activities

There is excellent diving at several reefs off this part of the Mozambican coast. The best known is Manta Reef, described as a 'manta ray cleaning centre', where, in addition to manta rays, you can see turtles and various other reef fish. Sightings of whale sharks are also a distinct possibility in open waters, while divers might hear the plaintive moans of humpback whales between about September and the middle of November. There are dive centres at all of the resorts, but the best is the **Pisces Dive Centre** (web: www.divemozambique.com) at the Jangamo Beach Resort. One of only three PADI-affiliated centres in Mozambique, this school offers dive packages for qualified divers, as well as the various PADI courses for beginners and those who would like to improve their skills. The best snorkelling, meanwhile, is at the reef on the point in front of the Paindane Beach Resort.

THE EN1 FROM MAXIXE TO VILANKULO

There are three other coastal resorts lying to the east of the EN1 as it heads north towards Vilankulo, arguably the country's major tourist centre.

Ponta Linga Linga

Facing Inhambane on a peninsula on the northern side of the Bay of Inhambane is the small village of Linga Linga, accessible by dhow from Morrumbene on the EN1. Yet another good spot for diving, Linga Linga has a backpackers' resort called **Funky Monkeys**, which has dormitory accommodation and camping for around US$5. It also does meals.

Morrungulo

Lying roughly 100km north of Maxixe, the resort of Morrungulo is reached via a signposted 13km dirt road, which leaves the EN1 about 7km north of Massinga town. It can normally be reached in an ordinary saloon car, but the branch road is very sandy in parts and so a 4WD is preferable.

The **Morrungulo Beach Resort** has camping for US$8 per person, and there are a few very smart self-catering cottages costing US$120 per unit for up to four people. Facilities include organised scuba diving and deep-sea fishing excursions, and you can also rent snorkelling equipment. There is another, slightly cheaper, campsite called **La Rosa Camping**, though there is not as much shade here as there is at the Morrungulo Beach Resort.

The Zambia Reef in Morrungulo is known for its outstanding soft and hard corals.

Pomene

The turn-off for the resort of Pomene is about 12km from Massinga. From there, it's 50km or so along a sandy track to the **Pomene Lodge**, which has more or less the same facilities at the same prices as those at the Morrungulo Beach Resort. The diving here, as elsewhere, is very good.

VILANKULO

This small but sprawling town, which lies roughly 700km from Maputo and 500km from Beira, is the focal point of tourism in Mozambique. Indeed, Vilankulo is something of a melting pot, containing at any one time its fair share of backpackers, upmarket travellers, and South African and Zimbabwean family holidaymakers. Consequently, Vilankulo has as diverse a range of accommodation and other tourist facilities as you'll find in Mozambique, and it is also the easiest place from which to access the islands of the Bazaruto Archipelago. All of this has made Vilankulo the most popular – if not the most attractive – place to stop between Maputo and Beira.

Getting there and away
By air
LAM flies to Vilankulo from Maputo on most days of the week. The LAM office is at the airport, which lies about 2km off the road linking Vilankulo to the EN1. See page 51 for details of flights to Vilanculo by Pelican Air (from Jo'burg), Charlan Air (from Lanseria) and Swazi Express (from Durban).

By sea
See *Bazaruto Archipelago: Getting there and away* on page 153 for information on how to get to and from Vilankulo and the islands by boat.

By road
Vilankulo lies 20km east of the EN1 along a good surfaced road. The misleadingly signposted turn-off is roughly 220km north of Maxixe – you'll know that you're there when you pass a BP garage to your left and then shortly afterwards reach a large intersection around which lies a cluster of small shops. Take the fork to the right.

Coming directly from Maputo on public transport, the best options are the express buses run by Oliveira's and TSL, which arrive in Vilankulo in the late afternoon just before it starts to get dark. Buses between Maputo and Beira also stop in Vilankulo, where they normally spend the night. This means that in order to catch the bus to Beira you'll have to be at the bus station as early in the morning as 04.00. The express bus back to Maputo leaves at around 05.00. *Chapas* leave when full from next to the market, most of them heading south towards Maxixe. If you miss the bus to Beira, you are probably better off taking a *chapa* to the EN1 and doing the trip in stages by catching whatever transport is heading north, or hitching.

Where to stay
Vilankulo's lukewarm charm and lack of a decent beach are made up for by the wealth of accommodation options that exist for visitors of all budgets. The more expensive lodges are on the beach about 2km north of Vilankulo's main thoroughfare. **Dugong Beach Lodge** (tel: +27 11 234 1584) has just 10 luxuriously appointed framed tented rooms with private patios. Facilities include a freshwater swimming pool and a full range of watersports. Viewing may include turtles, flamingos and pelicans. The Lodge is located in the Vilanculos Marine Coastal Sanctuary, 30,000 hectares of marine and wildlife territory. Rates are from US$250 per person, full board. The **Vilankulo Beach Lodge** has prices ranging from US$50 to US$85 per person, including breakfast and dinner. A few hundred metres before the Vilankulo Beach Lodge, the **Aguia Negra** (tel: 021 8471160 South Africa; email: am01@bushmail.net) has accommodation in attractive, tepee-like chalets from US$45 per person, which includes a good cooked breakfast and use of a small swimming pool. There is also a library where you can read or exchange books. Another kilometre or so before the Aguia Negra, the **Casa Rex** (tel: 82048; email: casarex@teledata.mz) has well-decorated, breezy rooms from US$52.50/single and US$70/double. There are only five of them, however, so you should try to make a reservation. This lovely little place has a good restaurant with plenty of fresh, well-cooked food. Since the closure of the Hotel Dona Ana (the pink building next to the port) in August 2000, **Bimbi's** is the best hotel in Vilankulo, even though its location in a side street off the main road is not particularly in its favour.

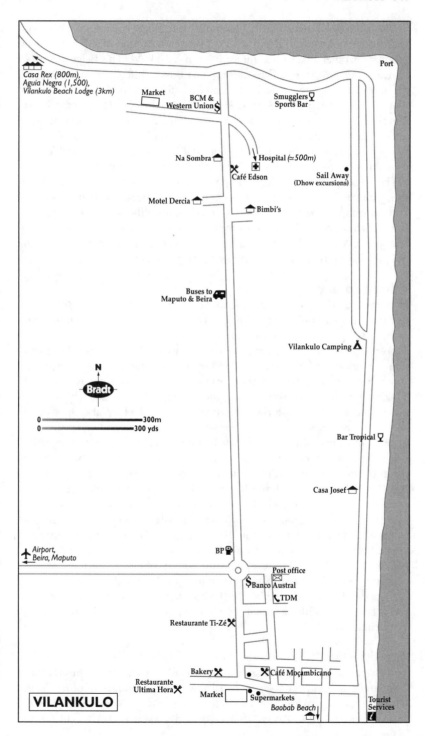

Casa Rex (800m),
Aguia Negra (1,500),
Vilankulo Beach Lodge (3km)

Port

Market

BCM &
Western Union $

Smugglers
Sports Bar

Na Sombra

→ Hospital (≈500m)

Café Edson

Sail Away
(Dhow excursions)

Motel Dercia

Bimbi's

Buses to
Maputo & Beira

Vilankulo Camping

N

Brandt

0 ————————— 300m
0 ————————— 300 yds

Bar Tropical

Casa Josef

Airport,
Beira, Maputo

BP

Post office

Banco Austral

$

TDM

Restaurante Ti-Zé

Bakery

Café Moçambicano

Restaurante
Ultima Hora

Market

Supermarkets

Baobab Beach

Tourist
Services

VILANKULO

The **Baobab Beach** (email: 2baker@bushmail.net) has been popular with backpackers but we've had bad reports of it recently (mid-2005). There is no shortage of other budget accommodation in Vilankulo. The Belgian-run **Na Sombra** (tel: 82090; email: nasombra@go.to; web: http://go.to/nasombra) on the main road not far from the beach is probably the best, with clean, comfortable rooms with a fan for US$11/single and US$15/double. The nearby **Motel Dercia** is also worth a try if the seven rooms at the Na Sombra have been taken. Otherwise, there are a couple of Mozambican-run places on Vilankulo's south-facing beach. **Casa Josef** (tel: 82140) is good value at US$12.50 for doubles with mosquito net and a clean, spacious, shared bathroom. The round huts directly on the beach at the **Bar Tropical**, meanwhile, are cheaper, more basic and, given their proximity to the popular bar, not as peaceful as the rooms at the Casa Josef. You can camp a little further along the beach at the **Vilankulo Camping**. The cost of each site depends on its distance from the beach, with the cheapest starting at around US$3.50. This might change, however, if the rumours are true and the campsite has in fact been taken over by new management.

Where to eat
In terms of setting and quality of food, the restaurant at the **Casa Rex** is hard to beat. Whether you're in the dining room with its crafted wooden furniture or the lush garden overlooking the bay, there's a relaxing, slightly colonial atmosphere that you don't find at too many places in Mozambique. Lunch and dinner menus cost US$10 and US$15 respectively, while individual dishes are about US$7. At the other end of the scale – but still good – is the **Restaurante Ti-Zé** next to the market, where you can get chicken and chips for an unbeatable US$2. The nearby **Restaurante Ultima Hora** also does simple Mozambican dishes, which you can eat in a pleasant courtyard under the shade of coconut palms. The **Café Moçambicano**, once again close to the market, is the place for coffee and pastries, while the restaurant at the **airport** is reputed for its quality snacks, which include stuffed crab and toasted sandwiches. The **Aguia Negra** and the **Vilankulo Beach Lodge** both have good restaurants, as does the **Na Sombra**, which does barbecues at the weekends.

A large number of the South Africans who visit Vilankulo tend to migrate to the **Smugglers Sports Bar** in the evenings to play pool, watch rugby and cricket matches, eat overpriced South African-style food and, of course, drink beer. To facilitate such revelries, the bar stays open until 02.00. The Mozambican alternative to Smugglers is the **Bar Tropical**, which sits directly on Vilankulo's south-facing beach. Busy at most times of the day and night, you'll find most of the action at the weekend disco, which gets going late on Friday and Saturday nights.

Activities
The Bazaruto Archipelago is dealt with in detail on pages 152–7, but for those who would like to get a taste of the islands with the minimum of hassle and without spending an arm and a leg, the three-day dhow safaris offered by the Vilankulo-based **Sail Away** (email: www.dhowsafari.com) might be the

answer. You travel in motorised dhows, camp on Benguerra Island, and visit Benguerra, Bazaruto and Magaruque Islands over the three days. This all costs US$40 per day, which includes food and camping charges but not the national park entrance fee.

More conventional activities such as diving, fishing, catamaran trips, windsurfing and canoeing are available at the dive centre at the Aguia Negra, while Tourist Services can arrange some off-beat day trips to nearby saw mills, gas works and de-mining operations.

Useful information

Unusually for Mozambican towns (even the touristy ones), there is an excellent source of tourist information at **Tourist Services** (email: margie@teledata.mz) on the beach roughly parallel with the market. Run by Margie, a South African woman who has been living in Vilankulo for a number of years, this is your one-stop shop for information about Vilankulo and the surrounding area (including the Bazaruto Archipelago), transport to the islands and day trips to nearby points of interest.

Since the recent arrival of a telephone line in Vilankulo, Margie has plans to start an **internet café**. By the time you read this, such plans may or may not have been realised.

The **Banco Austral** opposite the road leading to the EN1 is the best place to change cash and get an advance on your Visa card, the latter of which incurs a very reasonable US$5 commission. To change travellers' cheques (with the usual US$15 commission) you must go to the BCM on the main road near the beach. There is also a **Western Union** office at the BCM.

INHASSORO

Heading north along the EN1, Inhassoro is the final mainland coastal resort before the road veers inland for the 450-odd kilometre trip via the Save River to Beira. Much smaller than Vilankulo, but with a similarly sprawling layout, Inhassoro has an attractive beach and low-key atmosphere that could, in the right mood, keep you lingering on for days.

Unfortunately, Inhassoro was somewhat trashed by the 2000 floods. It lies on a slope, and when the floodwaters swept over the town they washed many of the beachfront houses into the ocean. The campsite at the Hotel Seta was also damaged.

Getting there and away

Inhassoro lies 13km from the EN1 along a good surfaced road. The turn-off is 50km north of the turn-off to Vilankulo. Buses between Maputo and Beira stop at Inhassoro.

Where to stay and eat

The **Hotel Seta** is an attractive, well-run and surprisingly inexpensive place lying in large, wooded grounds above the beach. It has self-contained doubles for US$20 as well as more basic doubles using clean communal toilets and showers for US$12. The attached campsite costs around US$3 per person. There is a good restaurant and well-stocked bar attached, and safe parking on the property.

About 1km from the hotel, adjacent to the bus station, the **Complexo Salema Mufundisse Chibique** has double rooms for US$12 and serves filling meals for around US$3.

BAZARUTO ARCHIPELAGO

The Bazaruto Archipelago consists of a string of small sandy islands lying roughly 15–25km from the mainland north of Vilankulo and south of Inhassoro. One of the few parts of Mozambique that was safe to visit during the closing years of the civil war, the Bazaruto Islands have developed an upmarket package-based tourist industry that functions in near isolation from the rest of the country. Most visitors to the islands fly directly there from Johannesburg without ever setting foot on the Mozambican mainland.

The archipelago, gazetted as a National Park in 1971, consists of five main islands. The three largest islands were formerly part of a peninsula that is thought to have separated from the mainland within the last 10,000 years. The largest and most northerly island is Bazaruto itself: 30km long, on average 5km wide, and boasting a few substantial freshwater lakes near its southern tip. South of this are Benguerra, the second-largest island, and the much smaller Magaruque, the latter almost directly opposite Vilankulo. The smallest island, Santa Carolina, is a former penal colony covering an area of about 2km² roughly halfway between Bazaruto and the mainland. The fifth island, Bangue, is only rarely visited by tourists.

With their white palm-lined beaches, the islands of the Bazaruto Archipelago are everything you would expect of Indian Ocean islands. They are of great interest to birdwatchers. Roughly 150 species have been recorded, including several that are rare or localised in southern Africa, for instance green coucal; crab, sand and Mongolian plovers; olive and blue-cheeked bee-eaters; and a variety of petrels, gulls and waders. Lesser flamingoes seen on the islands come from a nearby breeding colony, the only one known to occur in eastern Africa south of Lake Natron in Tanzania.

An estimated 45 reptile and amphibian species occur on the islands, including two endemics. The freshwater lakes on Bazaruto and Benguerra support a relic breeding *Bushbuck* population of crocodiles, while the shores of the islands are nesting sites for at least three types of turtle including the rare loggerhead. Mammals present include the localised suni antelope, red duiker, bushbuck and samango monkey. An endemic butterfly species is found on Bazaruto Island.

However, the main attractions of the islands lie off their shores. The surrounding sea, warmed by the Mozambique Stream, is crystal clear and its reefs support a variety of brightly coloured fish, making the area one of Mozambique's finest snorkelling and diving destinations. There are well-established diving centres on the north of Bazaruto Island and on

Benguerra Island. Visitors to the islands frequently see marine turtles, humpback whales, and bottlenose, spinner and humpback dolphins, as well as large game fish such as marlins and barracudas. The islands are also renowned for their game fishing (see box on page 156).

The Bazaruto area supports what is probably East Africa's last viable population of the the endangered dugong. This large and exclusively marine herbivore is a member of the family Sirinia, along with the manatee of the Atlantic Ocean, and its closest terrestrial relatives are elephants and hyraxes. The name Sirinia, a reference to the Sirens of Greek legends, has been given to this family of marine animals because they are considered to be the most likely candidate for the source of the mermaid myth. Dugongs were formerly widespread and abundant in the Indo-Pacific region, and as recently as the early 1970s groups of four to five were commonly seen in places like Inhambane, Angoche and even near Maputo. Dugongs have suffered a drastic population decrease in the past few decades, probably because so many individuals are trapped in fish nets. They are now threatened with extinction except in the seas around northern Australia and the Arabian Gulf.

The Bazaruto Islands have a long history of human occupation. Prior to the Portuguese occupation of the coast, the islands were almost certainly the site of East Africa's most southerly Muslim trading settlements. By the middle of the 16th century, the islands were lorded over by Portuguese traders, and the surrounding sea was known for producing high-quality pearls. The first formal Portuguese settlement was established in 1855, on Santa Carolina. Initially an ivory trading post, the island was later used as a penal colony, but it was evidently abandoned by the beginning of the 20th century. Interesting historical relics include a ruined 19th-century fort on Magaruque and a fully intact but non-operational 100-year-old lighthouse on Bazaruto.

Getting there and away
By air
Because tourism to the Bazaruto Islands has developed in relative isolation from that on the mainland, the overwhelming majority of visitors fly to the islands from South Africa as part of a package organised by the lodge they are staying at. People visiting one of the islands as a self-contained trip out of South Africa are thus advised to contact the various lodges mentioned below or a travel agent to find out what sort of packages are currently available. It is also possible to fly to Benguerra Island from Vilankulo by seaplane for US$65 one way. Bookings can be made at Tourist Services in Vilankulo.

By sea
If you are staying at one of the lodges on the Bazaruto islands, motor boat transfers (which usually cost extra) can be arranged from Vilankulo, as can safe parking on the mainland. Hiring your own motor boat will cost around US$120 per boat, and is only really an option if you are in a sizeable group. Once again, contact Tourist Services for more details. Independent travellers on a tighter budget will probably prefer to get to and from the Bazaruto islands

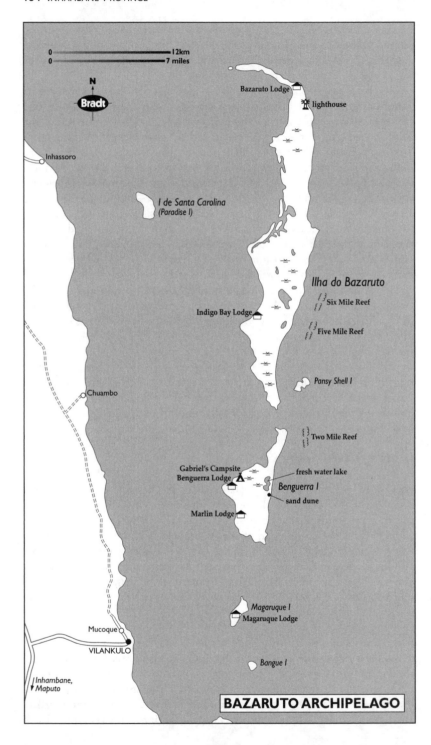

0 ———————————— 12km
0 ———————————— 7 miles

N

Bradt

Inhassoro

I de Santa Carolina
(Paradise I)

Bazaruto Lodge

lighthouse

Ilha do Bazaruto

Six Mile Reef

Indigo Bay Lodge

Five Mile Reef

Chuambo

Pansy Shell I

Two Mile Reef

Gabriel's Campsite
Benguerra Lodge

fresh water lake

Benguerra I

sand dune

Marlin Lodge

Magaruque I
Magaruque Lodge

Mucoque

VILANKULO

I Inhambane,
↓ Maputo

Bangue I

BAZARUTO ARCHIPELAGO

by dhow. Motorised dhows are obviously quicker and more reliable than the wind-assisted variety. These leave from the port at Vilankulo and Gabriel's Campsite on Benguerra Island when there are sufficient numbers to make a trip worthwhile. Expect to pay up to US$10 for the one-hour voyage to Benguerra. Dhows with sails cost roughly half the price and take at least twice as long provided that the wind is favourable. Day trippers who want to be sure of getting back to the mainland on the same day might consider hiring a dhow. The Vilankulo-based Sail Away charges US$40 per day for a fully equipped and crewed motorised dhow.

From the mainland, Bazaruto and Santa Carolina Islands are best reached from Inhassoro. Motor boats to these islands can be arranged at the Hotel Seta, which also has safe parking for motorised travellers.

National park fees

People visiting the islands of the Bazaruto Archipelago must pay an entrance fee because the area is a national park. Those staying at the upmarket lodges will be charged US$10, which may be automatically added to their accounts. Backpackers and other such travellers who are staying at the campsite on Benguerra Island should present themselves to the park rangers, who pass by from time to time, and pay a fee of around US$5 (although this is rumoured to increase in the near future).

Benguerra Island

Benguerra Island lies 14km from Vilankulo and is 11km long and 5.5km wide, which makes it the second-largest island in the archipelago. With two upmarket lodges, a campsite and natural attractions including freshwater lakes with crocodiles, sand-dunes and an island vegetation (coconut palms, milkwood trees, mlala palms, cashew trees, casaurina trees, etc) that supports an impressive range of birdlife, Benguerra is also the most visited island in the archipelago. The most popular time for birders to visit Benguerra is October and November, when wading birds stop on the island during their annual north–south migration. At this time you can see flamingos, green coucal, crab plovers, mangrove kingfishers and the very rare blue-throated sunbird. Meanwhile, other species such as olive bee-eaters can be seen all year round.

Where to stay and eat

The best place to stay on the island is the **Benguerra Lodge** (tel: +27 (0) 11 4520641; fax: +27 (0) 11 4521496; email: benguerra@icon.co.za; web: www.benguerra.co.za), which has just undergone a major refurbishment (July 05). Peeping out from behind the trees on the island's western shore, Benguerra Lodge is intimate and has a rich East African/Arabic feel – both in its décor, and in the food, largely comprising freshly caught seafood. The two Honeymoon Suites (each with its own private deck and dip pool/jacuzzi) and the 11 private ensuite chalets merge naturally into the surrounding indigenous forest and are only a moment's walk from the sandy beach. For especial luxury and privacy there is an exclusive villa, set apart from the rest of the Lodge, with

GAME FISHING AND DIVING FROM BENGUERRA ISLAND
Bob de Lacy Smith

The Bazaruto area offers some of the most challenging game fishing in southern Africa. Large black and striped marlins are regularly taken between October and December. Prior to the civil war, specimens weighing in the region of 500kg were caught off the islands, and the recent record is more than 400kg. Sailfish can be caught throughout the year, with July and August being the best months for these fine fighters. The largest specimen so far is 55kg. Other game fish to be taken include tuna, all types of bonito, wahoo, king and queen mackeral, dorado, rainbow runner, prodigal son, giant barracuda and several species of kingfish including the mighty giant trevall (*Caranx ignoblis*).

Saltwater fly-fishing has also taken off in the area and regular clinics are held where experts pass on their knowledge to novices. The sport has a growing following and conditions on the islands are ideal. The much sought bonefish occurs in the area, and specimens of up to 8.2kg have been caught by local fishermen, though they have so far evaded the rods of fly-fishermen.

For divers, Two Mile Reef has several interesting dive sites with a maximum depth of 20m. These reefs are completely unspoilt and teem with fishes ranging from tiny coral fish to the mighty potato bass and brindle bass. Manta rays and whale sharks can also be seen by lucky divers. There are many other undived reefs in the area, notably the untouched reefs at Cabo Sebastão, which offer the experienced diver opportunities to go deeper than 20m.

two double bedrooms, a private lounge/dining area with personal chef, and private swimming pool. Rates are from US$395 per person on a full board basis.

Also on the island's western shore, the **Marlin Lodge** (tel: +27 12 543 2134; fax: +27 12 543 2135; email: reservations@marlinlodge.co.za; web: www.marlinlodge.co.za) has 21 chalets, all built on stilts with wooden decks, reed walls and thatched roofs. The ensuite rooms (in four different categories) have private verandas and are connected by elevated walkways from the back, with a wooden walkway leading down to the beach directly in front of each unit. There's a swimming pool, good recreation areas, and a friendly atmosphere where guests can choose to be involved in activities or to remain secluded and private. Children of all ages are accepted, and the staff are professional. Rates are from US$178 to US$350, depending on room category.

The vast majority of independent travellers who visit the Bazaruto Archipelago stay at **Gabriel's Campsite**, which is on the beach about 1km north of the Benguerra Lodge. Camping costs US$7 and two- and three-person chalets go for US$15, which might seem a little pricey before you check out the alternatives. There is a small restaurant.

Bazaruto Island

The 30km strip of land that forms Bazaruto Island lies about 30km from Vilankulo. Ecologically similar to Benguerra Island, this island also attracts its fair share of tourists. The **Bazaruto Lodge** (tel: 30 5000 Maputo; fax: 30 5305; email: reservas.africa@pestana.com; web: www.pestana.com) on the northern tip of the island is run by the same group that owns the Rovuma Carlton in Maputo and the Inhaca Lodge on Inhaca Island, and is of a similarly luxurious standard with accommodation in fully equipped bungalows on a half-board basis from US$145/single and US$214/double. At the other end of the island, the **Indigo Bay Island Resort** (formerly Sabal Bay Lodge) was opened in August 2001 after being completely renovated by its new owner. On the west side of the island in a protected bay, it has 24 beach chalets, 24 bay-view rooms and two suites, all with softly fringed thatched roofs to blend with the natural surroundings. It's a beautiful place that really works – the 50 rooms are so well spaced that there's still an impression of intimate seclusion. Facilities are comprehensive: they've even gone to the amazingly painstaking lengths of shipping several horses over to the island for the guests' amusement. Chalets start at US$322 per person. It's run by Rani Resorts (tel: +27 11 467 1277; email: reservations@raniafrica.co.za; web: www.raniresorts.com).

The other islands

There is currently nowhere to spend the night on the other Bazaruto islands. Lying about 12km from Vilankulo, **Margaruque Island** is the closest island to the mainland and the logical place for a day trip. It takes anywhere from one to three hours to walk round it. The 100-room hotel on **Santa Carolina Island** (also known as Paradise Island) was formerly the most popular place to stay on the islands, but is now in a derelict state with no immediate plans for renovation. The most southerly island in the archipelago is the uninhabited **Bangue Island**, which is basically just a sand-dune in the ocean.

NAMIBIA • THE CAPE • BOTSWANA • ZAMBIA • ZIMBABWE • MALAWI • TANZANIA • MOZAMBIQUE • RWANDA

Visiting Mozambique's Islands?

We arrange superb trips to the **Bazaruto & Quirimba Archipelagos** for individuals or groups, and can combine these islands with trips in the rest of Africa.

Our team of experts are independent and know the islands and the lodges there from personal experience. We can advise you on all the alternatives, and help you to

choose what's right for your trip. Then we'll organise it for you smoothly and efficiently, and charge you the same or less than if you had booked the trip yourself directly.

See our website or contact us now for our award-winning Africa brochure.

Then you can plan a superb trip to Mozambique and beyond – at an unbeatable price.

Tel: +44 (0) 20 8232 9777
Fax: +44 (0) 20 8568 8330

Email: info@expertafrica.com
Web: www.expertafrica.com

EXPERT AFRICA

A Sunvil TRAVEL COMPANY

AITO

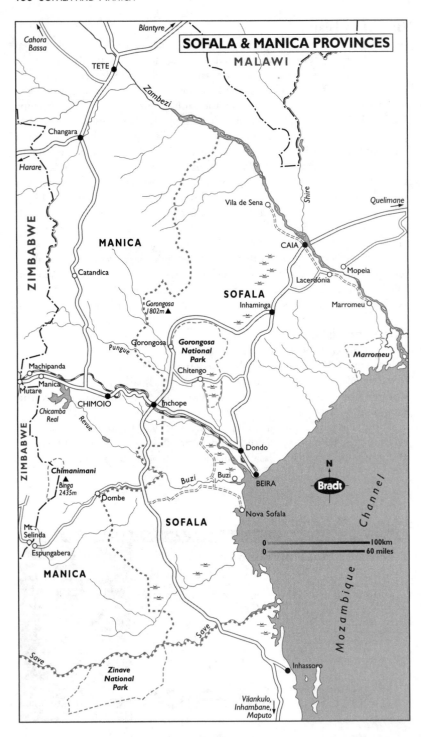

SOFALA & MANICA PROVINCES

Sofala and Manica

The central Mozambican provinces of Sofala and Manica are bordered by the Save River to the south, Zimbabwe to the west, the Indian Ocean to the east, Tete Province to the northwest and the Zambezi to the northeast. This is an area of relatively limited interest to travellers, and the two provinces have been lumped together largely because they are connected by one of the most important routes in Mozambique, the so-called Beira Corridor between Mutare in Zimbabwe and the Indian Ocean port of Beira.

The interior of central Mozambique has a long history, largely because of its strategic importance to the Swahili gold trade in medieval times. For centuries, the Zambezi Valley formed the main trade corridor between the coastal port of Sofala and the goldfields of present-day Zimbabwe. Settled by Muslim traders in the 15th century, the Zambezi Valley later became the first part of the East African interior to be permanently settled by the Portuguese. Many of the region's modern towns were founded even before the Portuguese occupation of the coast. Manica, for instance, stands on the site of the Masekesa gold fair, which operated intermittently from pre-Portuguese times until it was overrun by Nxaba's Nguni warrors in the 1830s, while Tete and Sena on the Zambezi were both founded by Muslims and then occupied by Portugal in the 16th century. Alluring as this may sound on paper, few visible traces of the region's more antiquated settlements remain.

The Beira Corridor assumed a high level of regional importance during the years of civil war, when it was protected by the Zimbabwean army and was just about the only part of Mozambique that allowed for a reasonably safe passage. Along the Beira Corridor, Chicamba Real Dam is an attractive enough spot but of no more than passing interest, while Chimoio, the capital of Manica Province, is affably unremarkable. To the north of the Beira Corridor, Gorongosa National Park is sadly depleted of game, and both the national park and neighbouring Mount Gorongosa suffer from inaccessibility and a lack of accommodation or camping facilities. Perhaps the most interesting place in either of these provinces is Beira itself, a city which has acquired a bad name with travellers but which I thoroughly liked and enjoyed.

GETTING AROUND

The main roads in this part of the country are all surfaced and in reasonably good condition, and the Beira Corridor can be driven in its entirety in any vehicle. Aside from a few temporary dirt diversions, you can cruise along most of the Beira Corridor at around 80km/hour, keeping an eye open for the very occasional pot-hole. The Tete to Chimoio road is in a similar condition. The only other routes likely to be used by visitors are the dirt road between Chimoio and Selinda on the Zimbabwe border, which requires 4WD, and the road north from Inchope to Gorongosa, which, although in bad shape, is surfaced and thus should be navigable in any vehicle. There are plenty of buses and *chapas* connecting the various towns along the Beira Corridor.

BEIRA

Beira, the capital of Sofala province, is the country's second-largest city and its most important port. It is also quite possibly the most unpopular city in southern Africa, at least so far as travellers are concerned. Before arriving in Beira, I had received reports of an unfriendly, depressing, war-damaged slum, with nothing to see and a high incidence of crime against tourists, from travellers who had removed the city from their itineraries for precisely these reasons. So, when I finally arrived in Beira, I was expecting the worst.

As it turned out, the city was yet another Mozambican victim of unjustified bad publicity and travellers' Chinese whispers. For Beira is a town with character. OK, so it *is* rather run-down, though it appears to me that this is more through neglect than any direct war damage – certainly it bears no comparison to Kampala when I visited it shortly after the end of Uganda's civil war – and the city centre itself is rapidly being restored to something approaching its pre-war condition. There is, of course, a great deal of poverty in Beira, but then so is there in any city in the so-called developing world, the difference being one of prominence: along with Maputo, Beira is one of the few places in Africa to have high-rise slums. As for the reported crime and unfriendliness, all I can say is that I felt perfectly safe wandering around the city centre at night, and I didn't notice any hostility.

What Beira does have is a definite atmosphere, determined by its sticky Indian Ocean air, a quite preposterous mix of mismatched architectural styles, and a buzzing street and café life focused around the attractive city square and the bars in the grid of roads near the railway station and port. It's a thriving, pleasant city, and with a bit of common sense I don't think there's anything to fear security-wise. Don't let the bad reports put you off.

History

The region around Beira was the medieval gateway to the African interior. For centuries prior to Portuguese occupation, the region's most important trading centre was Sofala, situated about 50km south of present-day Beira amongst the shallow waterways and impermanent sandbars that characterise the stretch of coast near the mouth of the Buzi River. Founded in the 9th century AD, Sofala formed the main link between the inland trade route to the gold mines of

Karangaland and the prosperous city of Kilwa (in southern Tanzania), as well as being an important trading centre in its own right. By the 15th century it probably had a population of around 10,000.

In 1500, Sofala was visited by Sancho de Toar, who recognised its pivotal role in the gold trade. Five years later, Portugal erected a small fort and trading factory at Sofala. Although this was done with the permission of the local sheikh, Portugal rapidly set about establishing its own local trade network, bypassing the Muslim traders. Within a year of its foundation, the Portuguese fort was attacked without any marked success by the sheikh and his allies. Portugal responded by killing the sheikh in a punitive attack, and installing a puppet ruler in his place.

The Portuguese occupation of Sofala evidently coincided with a northward migration of the main chieftaincies of Karangaland and a corresponding shift in the main inland trade routes. Combined with the increasing dominance of ivory over gold as a trading commodity, this shift in trade routes caused Sofala to diminish in importance. As early as 1530, the main captaincy of the coast was shifted from Sofala to Mozambique Island. By the 17th century, Sofala was a neglected backwater, with the token Portuguese occupancy largely to prevent the fort from falling to a rival European power. By the 1750s, the stone buildings of the Portuguese quarter were partially submerged, and Sofala was more or less left in the hands of a few Muslim traders. By the time that modern Mozambique came into being, Sofala's permanent buildings had mostly disappeared beneath the sea, and the ancient port was passed over in favour of Chiluane as the local administrative centre. The stone fort at Sofala was dismantled and its bricks were used to build Beira Cathedral.

Beira itself is one of Mozambique's more modern cities, founded in 1884 on the sandy, marshy shore near the mouth of the Pungue River as a base of operations for the rich *prazero* Joaquim Carlos Paiva de Andrada. In the late 1880s, the British imperialist and founder of Rhodesia, Cecil John Rhodes, attempted to annex the Beira area, but his attempts at warmongering garnered no support from the British government and in 1891 the area was formally incorporated into Mozambique. The town centre was laid out in 1887, and at the same time a permanent garrison was installed. Beira was granted city status in 1894. Serious development of the port started in 1891, when it was leased to Andrada's Mozambique Company, and it accelerated after 1898 following the completion of Rhodes' railway line to Rhodesia.

In its early days, Beira was a scruffy shanty town with a reputation as the most drunken, lawless settlement in Africa. At the start of the 20th century, the city boasted some 80 bars and a population of only 4,000, roughly a quarter of which consisted of Europeans, mostly of Portuguese or British origin. The town did not have the most amenable of settings: the company that built the railway line to Rhodesia lost 60% of its European staff to malaria in two years, and the surrounding area was so untamed that lions were frequently seen walking through the main street. The sand on which the town was built was so deep that 40km of trolley lines had to be laid to allow residents to transport goods to their homes. The trolley lines later served as public transport, before they were torn up in 1930.

Beira's rapid expansion was curbed after rail links were completed between Rhodesia and South Africa in 1903. Nevertheless, the figures produced by the 1928 census show that by this time Beira was well established as the country's second city, with a population of almost 23,694 – more than half that of Lourenço Marques, and well over double that of the next-largest town in Mozambique. The city today has a population of around 300,000.

Getting there and away
By air
There is an international airport at Beira, which has LAM flights to and from Johannesburg (Tuesdays, Thursdays and Saturdays) and Harare (Tuesdays and Thursdays). Domestically, LAM flies between Beira and Maputo on a daily basis. There are also regular flights to and from Beira and Nampula and Quelimane (which might be something to consider if you want to avoid the very time-consuming and uncomfortable road trip between Beira and Quelimane). The LAM booking office (tel: 30 2213) is near the Praça do Metical, while the airport is about 15km from the city centre. It's easy to get either to or from the airport by public transport. From the city centre, catch a *chapa* from the bus station; from the airport, walk the 100 metres or so to the main road where *chapas* pass by on a regular basis. Alternatively, a taxi should cost between US$7.50 and US$10.

By sea
There are no formal passenger-boat services linking Beira and Mozambique's other coastal towns. However, Quelimane could be a realistic destination to reach by sea. My enquiries at the port unearthed a cargo boat that apparently leaves Beira at 05.00 on Tuesday mornings. The fare is US$7.50 and the voyage normally takes about 24 hours. Treat this as an indication that such a trip is possible rather that a guarantee that you can get from Beira to Quelimane by boat on Tuesdays. On the other hand, closer destinations such as Buzi are readily accessible by boat. Enquire at the port for departure times.

By road
From the south
The road heading north from Inhassoro to Beira has a few very bad stretches – nothing to worry about if you are driving a 4WD or using public transport, but a potential problem if you are driving a saloon car. It is important to get an early start, as the full 450km drive from Inhassoro to Beira will take at least ten hours, longer if you have a flat tyre or any other technical problem, and you most certainly do not want to be driving on this road after dark (aside from the risk of banditry, you'd almost certainly drive into a pot-hole sooner or later). If you don't think you can make it all the way in a day, you could cut an hour off the trip by staying at one of the rooms attached to the roadside bar in Pande, a small settlement about 10km south of the Save River – there is no other accommodation that I know of between Inhassoro and Beira.

From Inhassoro to the Save River there is an excellent surfaced road, which you can cruise along at a comfortable 80km/hour or so. After crossing the Save (and paying the nominal toll-fee), for the next 100km or so the road is in the process of being resurfaced by a Swedish-funded project. At the time of writing, the job had only been half done, and vehicles were obliged to use the dirt lanes on the side of the new road. Provided that you take it slowly and choose your tracks carefully, you should have few problems negotiating this section of the EN1.

The worst bit of road begins roughly 50km north of the Buzi River and it continues until about 30km before Inchope, the village at the junction of the EN1 and the Beira Corridor. This stretch probably only covers about 30km, but even in a 4WD it will take longer than an hour to get through. Heavily mined during the civil war, there are several patches that are badly pot-holed. If it hasn't rained for a few days, you can get through in just about any car, provided that you have reasonable clearance and that you drive very slowly (at low speed, there's no real danger of damaging a tyre or rim, but there are countless opportunities for cracking an unprotected sump, which means that you need to be very conscious of the height of the centre of the car in relation to the wheels). The situation changes from week to week, and the best place to seek current advice is at the Hotel Seta in Inhassoro, but broadly speaking, and a week of unseasonal weather excepted, a saloon car should get through during the dry winter months (May to September) but it may have problems in the wet summer months.

If you are using public transport, the best thing to do, whether you're heading to Beira directly from Maputo or from somewhere in between, is to catch one of the buses that travel the whole way between Maputo and Beira. These stop at all large towns along the way, but unlike local buses they don't stop at every possible opportunity to pick up passengers. The recommended bus service is Oliveira's, which leaves Maputo at 07.00, overnights at Vilankulo or the Save River to avoid crossing the worst stretch of road in the dark, and normally arrives in Beira before 12.00 the following day. You can check exact timetables and prices at the booking office at the Praça 16 de Junho in Maputo. The full trip costs US$15. Another recommended service is TSL, which leaves Maputo at roughly the same time as the Oliveira's bus.

In the opposite direction, Oliveira's and TSL buses from Beira to Maputo leave at 05.00 and, because they will have crossed the bad stretch of road by midday, they will sometimes continue driving until they reach their final destination – generally late at night. Then again, they frequently stop for the night at Xai-Xai, continuing on to Maputo the next morning and arriving at a much more sociable 07.00.

From the west

The road connecting Beira to the Zimbabwean town of Mutare via Chimoio is in good condition, and the 300km trip shouldn't take longer than four hours in a private vehicle. There is also a good road connecting the Beira Corridor to Tete; the junction is roughly halfway between Chimoio and Manica.

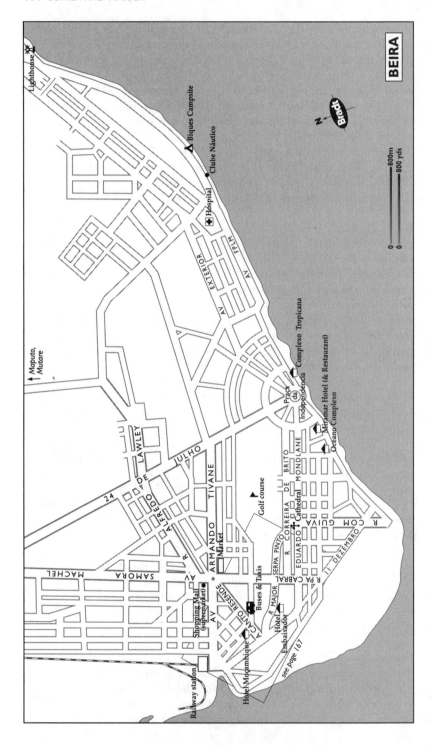

Coming from Mutare or Tete on public transport, it is emphatically worth avoiding arriving in Beira in the late afternoon or evening. If there's any danger of this, I suggest that you spend a night in Chimoio, then catch the first public transport to Beira the next morning. *Chapas* to Beira leave Chimoio from the bus terminus opposite the railway station. In the opposite direction, *chapas* and buses to Chimoio leave Beira from the central bus station on Rua Daniel Naputina. There are regular *chapas* between Chimoio and Machipanda on the Zimbabwe border – watch out for thieves. Hitching is a realistic possibility along the Beira Corridor.

From the north
There are no bus services covering the 1,055km road that connects Nampula to Beira via Quelimane. Your options are to spend the best part of a week on the back of various trucks (covered in further detail in *Quelimane: Getting there and away* on page 189) or to fly. If you are thinking of driving this stretch, a 4WD is essential and you should check whether the ferry across the Zambezi is operating.

Orientation
Arriving by bus, your trip will terminate either at the central bus station near the traffic island on Rua Artur Canto Resenda, or else at the market on the junction of Avenida Samora Machel and Avenida Armando Tivane. If the former, not only are you centrally positioned but there are also usually a few private taxis at the traffic island. If the latter, you'll feel like you've been abandoned in the middle of nowhere, but in fact you're only five minutes' walk from the town centre – walk across Avenida Samora Machel and follow Avenida Armando Tivane for about 100m and the first road to your left is Rua Artur Canto Resenda, which after an odd little kink and about 200m will bring you to the central bus station.

The city centre is divided in two by a mangrove swamp called the Chiveve, which is crossed by several bridges, including one at the city centre end of Rua Artur Canto Resenda between the central bus station and Praça do Metical, the main banking square. To the south and east of the Chiveve is the old town, with many houses dating from the turn of the century, the main city square (Praça da Municipalia), the Mercado central, the main post office, and a number of hotels and restaurants.

Where to stay
Considering that Beira is Mozambique's second city, the accommodation options are somewhat limited. There are one or two choices in each category (ie: upper range, moderate and budget), although not much room for manoeuvre if you are overly selective about where you stay. The **Hotel Moçambique** (tel: 03 32 5011) in the high rise building with the Total wall fresco just off Rua Artur Canto Resenda is still one of the best hotels in Beira despite the opening of a new business-class hotel in 1999. Air-conditioned, self-contained rooms with hot water, television and buffet breakfast are

US$59/single and US$77/double. This compares favourably with the aforementioned competition, the **Hotel Tivoli** (tel: 32 0006; email: h.tivoli-beira@isl.co.mz), which is in the road behind the Moçambique and charges an extra US$20 or so for similar, albeit slightly newer, rooms. The **Hotel Embaixador** (tel: 32 3121; fax: 32 3788) on Rua Major Serpa has perhaps the greatest variety of rooms in Beira, with standard singles from US$35, suites from US$70 and air-conditioned apartments from US$85. The smaller **Hotel Infante** (tel: 32 6603) on Rua Jaime Ferreira, meanwhile, is clean, pleasant and conveniently located. Large, carpeted, self-contained doubles with a fan, telephone and small balcony start at US$24. One of the best-value hotels in Beira has to be the **Hotel Miramar** (tel: 32 2283; fax: 32 9558), which lies one block behind the seafront restaurant of the same name near the Praça da Independencia. Self-contained singles cost only US$10 (US$12.50 with air conditioning), while air-conditioned doubles are also good value at US$17.50. Also on the seafront, this time about 2km east of the Praça da Independencia, is the **Biques Campsite** (tel: 31 3051), which seems to be where most of the independent travellers who visit Beira hang out. Camping costs US$4 per person, or you can rent basic caravans (with no bedding) for US$14. There is a well-stocked bar and a restaurant serving Mozambican and international dishes such as hamburgers and pizzas. The few pensãos to be found in Beira are, quite frankly, not up to much. The **Pensão Beirense** on Rua Luis Inacio is cheap and very basic with doubles for US$7.50, while the **Pensão Sofala** next to the bus station is even more modestly priced at US$7 for a double (US$5 for a single). Rooms at the other bus-station pensão, the **Pensão Messe** (tel: 32 8875), have a fan and TV and therefore cost almost double the price of those at the Sofala, although I fancy that travellers would gladly swap the TV for a working shower.

Where to eat

In most respects, Beira's merits and demerits may well be a subjective matter, but few would deny that it boasts a remarkable selection of good, reasonably priced restaurants. Top of the list is the **Restaurante Pique-Nique**, which lies in the southwest corner of the city centre opposite the disused National Cinema. The service and food here wouldn't look out of place in a European city: some might say that the red-velvet carpet, crushed flock wallpaper, and tuxedoed English-speaking waiters seem something of an affectation, but my opinion where Mozambique is concerned is that you should enjoy your comforts where you can afford them. In any case, what counts is the food, which is excellent and not too expensive at around US$5–7 for a main course.

In the same league is the **Arcádia Restaurant** on Rua Poder Popular. Alternatively known as Johnny's Place, after its founder Johnny Kamamis, the Arcádia has been one of Beira's top restaurants for over three decades and no visit to the city would be complete without a meal there. You can eat inside, or at a table on the street, and, again, the prices are not prohibitive. The emphasis is on seafood, although there is also a selection of South African dishes, cooked breakfasts and – a rarity in Mozambique – vegetables.

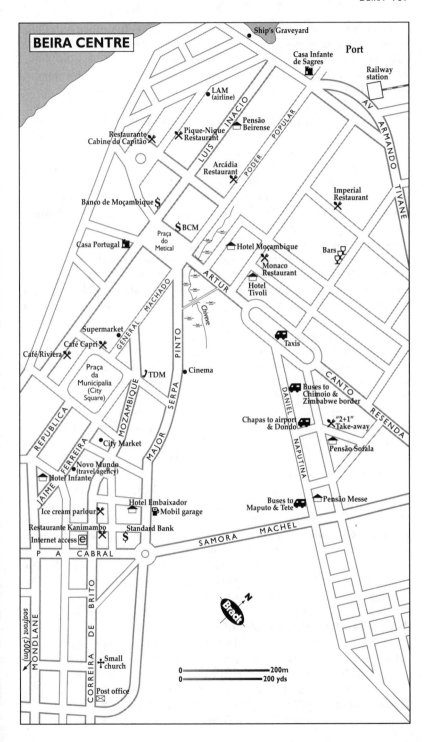

BEIRA CENTRE

Ship's Graveyard

Port

Casa Infante
de Sagres

Railway
station

LAM
(airline)

Pensão
Beirense

Pique-Nique
Restaurant

Restaurante
Cabine do Capitão

LUIS INACIO

PODER POPULAR

Arcádia
Restaurant

Imperial
Restaurant

Banco de Moçambique $

$ BCM

Praça
do
Metical

Casa Portugal

Hotel Moçambique

Bars

Monaco
Restaurant

ARTUR

Hotel
Tivoli

Chiveve

Supermarket

Taxis

Café Capri

Café Riviera

Praça
da
Municipalia
(City
Square)

GENERAL MACHADO

SERPA PINTO

TDM

Cinema

CANTO RESENDA

Buses to
Chimoio &
Zimbabwe border

DANIEL NAPUTINA

Chapas to airport
& Dondo

"2+1"
Take-away

MOZAMBIQUE

REPUBLICA

MAJOR

City Market

Pensão Sofala

FERREIRA

Novo Mundo
(travel agency)

Hotel Infante

JAIME

Hotel Embaixador

Mobil garage

Buses to
Maputo & Tete

Pensão Messe

Ice cream parlour

Restaurante Kanimambo

Internet access

Standard Bank

SAMORA MACHEL

P A CABRAL

N
Bradt

CORREIRA DE BRITO

DE

seafront (500m)

MONDLANE

Small
church

Post office

0 ———————— 200m
0 ———————— 200 yds

The **Restaurante Imperial** near the railway station has a good reputation, and the menu and prices are similar to the Arcádia. The huge speakers hanging from the walls, however, suggest that this is perhaps not the place for a quiet romantic dinner. Also recommended in this part of town is the **Restaurante dos CFMC**, which lies within the station building and is known for good game meat and local dishes.

Less central, the **Miramar Bar and Restaurant** is on the seafront a few hundred metres west of Praça da Independencia. The sea-facing veranda is a pleasant place to down a couple of beers as the sun sets, and the food is of a similar standard and price to the Arcádia. About a block further west, and also overlooking the beach, the **Complexo Oceana** has a popular disco, a sports bar, and good meals East of the Praça da Independencia and still on the seafront, the **Complexo Tropicana** and the more venerable **Clube Náutico** are both popular ex-pat hangouts, especially at weekends. In addition to restaurants specialising in seafood, both of these places have swimming pools. There is also a good seafood restaurant in town near the Praça do Metical called the **Restaurante Cabine do Capitão**, which has a street terrace, an air-conditioned dining room and waiters decked out in ludicrous sailor uniforms. For Chinese food, you could try the **Restaurante Kanimambo** next to the Hotel Embaixador.

If you're looking for something cheaper, try the **2+1 Take Away** opposite **Pensao Sofala**, which does a variety of basic meals for about US$3 and tangy prego rolls and burgers for US$1. Primarily a take-away, there are a couple of tables where you can sit outside, and I found it a reliable spot for a chilled soda break in my meandering through town.

For a lingering breakfast or afternoon tea, there's a choice of two *Salaõ de chá* on Praça da Municipalia, the air-conditioned **Café Capri** and the **Café Riviera**. These places serve fresh bread, a range of pastries, and tea and espresso coffee. The Capri also has a little kiosk selling imported chocolates and other tempting odds and ends.

If you're putting together your own food, the Mercado Central is also on Praça da Municipalia, and there's a good supermarket just off the square on Rua General Machado next to the Capri. By far the largest supermarket, however, is Shoprite, which is the principal store in the shopping mall next to the main roundabout on Avenida Samora Machel.

There's an ice-cream parlour tucked away on an alley behind the Hotel Embaixador. In addition to ice-cream, it serves syrupy fruit juice and sells a variety of imported chocolates and biscuits.

Nightlife and entertainment

The main concentration of **local bars** is in the triangle of roads between the railway station and Rua Artur Canto Resendo. It's follow-your-nose stuff: there are at least ten bars in this area, and sooner or later you'll stumble into the one that's for you. The most popular **discotheque** in this area is at the Restaurante Imperial, although Beira's best-known nightspot is the Complexo Oceana, whose weekend disco has been around since the 1960s.

There is a brand new big-screen cinema on Avenida Major Serpa Pinto, which shows relatively recent Western films in their original languages with Portuguese subtitles. Admission costs just over US$1. Of the several **swimming pools** to be found in the city, the municipal pool opposite the Hotel Moçambique is the most central, while the one at the Clube Náutico is the most pleasant. The pool at the Complexo Tropicana is a bit too green and murky for my taste.

Useful information

The Beira office of the well-regarded **travel agent** Novo Mundo (tel: 32 9007; fax: 32 9005; email: novomundo@tropical.co.mz) is on Rua Jaime Ferreira. If the LAM booking office is getting you down, this is a good place to book domestic – and international – airline tickets.

The **post office** in Beira is identified by a red flag above the entrance of an anonymous block of flats in the southeastern part of town. **Internet** access, meanwhile, is available at a computer shop called Worldeyes (Mon–Sat 09.00–midday & 15.00–20.00), which is a couple of blocks behind the Hotel Embaixador. There is only one computer, and the charge is US$6 per hour or 2,000 meticais per minute.

There are three or four of the usual **banks** dotted around the Praça do Metical. There is also a branch of the Banco de Fomento at the Hotel Embaixador.

What to see

If you like your entertainment to come planned and packaged, there isn't an awful lot to occupy yourself with in Beira, but it's a pleasant city to explore with several notable buildings and an attractive seafront. The city centre boasts an intriguing mixture of architectural styles, ranging from early-20th-century colonial buildings – many in an advanced state of disrepair – through 1950s constructions in the Bauhaus style to some bizarre and ostentatious modern buildings

A good place to start any exploration of the city centre is Praça da Municipalia, which is ringed by old colonial buildings, notably the marble Municipal Hall, with a tile mural of Sofala castle, and the old fort and jail, which now serves as the city market. A short walk away, on Rua Luis Inacio at the corner of Praça do Metical, the red-brick Casa Portugal is one of the best surviving examples of a turn-of-the-century Portuguese dwelling, even if it is in a considerable state of disrepair. Praça do Metical, named after the country's currency, is appropriately ringed by banks housed in buildings of various vintages.

From Praça do Metical, walk up Avenida Poder Popular to the recently restored Casa Infante Sagres, a fine old colonial building covered in mosaic murals. About 200m to the left of the Casa Infante Sagres, the Ship's Graveyard (not to be confused with the actual port) contains the rusty hulks of several cargo ships, some of which are apparently inhabited. To the right of the Casa Infante Sagres, a short and bumpy dirt road leads to Praça dos

Trabalhadores (Workers' Square), the port, and the adjacent railway station. Completed in 1966, the railway station has been described in the tourist literature as 'one of the most beautiful modern buildings in Africa' and by my favourite correspondent, Andrew Chilton, as 'a hideous example of imperial overlord modern school architecture'. Full marks to Andrew on this, I'm afraid.

Return to Praça da Municipalia and follow Avenida Republica into Avenida Eduardo Mondlane. A short distance along the road (just off the city centre map), the Beira Cathedral is in my opinion the most beautiful building in the city, erected between 1907 and 1925 using stones taken from the Portuguese fort at Sofala. There is a pretty chapel along the same road, as well as one a block up on Rua Correia de Brito. In addition to housing Beira's main cluster of old ecclesiastic buildings, this part of town was formerly the most upmarket residential area, and there are several pleasing old houses, some beautifully maintained, others utterly derelict.

A brisk 30-minute walk along Avenida Eduardo Mondlane, some of which is under a canopy of overhanging trees, brings you out at Praça da Independencia, a large open circle on the seafront. From here, you can follow Avenida 27 de Abril back towards town, with the crumbling seafront wall to your left – possibly taking a drink or meal break at the Miramar Restaurant, an open-air place facing the sea a few hundred metres down the road from Praça da Independencia – then walk up Rua 11 de Dezembro back to the city centre.

Further afield, the site of the historic city of **Sofala** lies at the southern end of the bay, approximately 40km from Beira, on a lovely tropical beach. Today little remains of the former glory of Sofala, once the gateway to southern Africa. Sofala is accessible by road from **Buzi**, which is famous in its own right as being the location of a huge factory known as the Buzi Company, a vestige of colonialism and the old forced labour or *chivalo* system. Buzi can be reached by small boat (*chata*) or, more safely, by ferry from the port at Beira.

THE BEIRA CORRIDOR

The strategic importance of the Beira Corridor, which consists of a 300km-long railway line and a parallel road and oil pipeline, grew after Zimbabwe achieved full independence in 1980, leaving South Africa and Namibia as the last bastions of white rule in Southern Africa. Zimbabwe and the various other states neighbouring South Africa formed the SADCC (Southern Africa Development Co-ordination Conference), with the declared aim of reducing the region's economic dependence on the apartheid regime. For landlocked countries such as Zimbabwe, Zambia and Botswana, a crucial factor in achieving this goal was to have access to a sea port that was not under South African control.

Beira was the obvious choice, due to its proximity to the Zimbabwe border. However, by the mid-1980s, years of neglect had caused Beira's harbour to silt up to the point where it was practically unnavigable, while the rail link to Zimbabwe had become a regular target for terrorist attacks by Renamo. The Mozambican national army was too weak to protect against these attacks, and so Zimbabwe's defence forces took responsibility for defending the Beira Corridor. After large amounts of foreign aid were used to make Beira harbour operational, Zimbabwe and Zambia steadily increased their imports via Beira during the late 1980s – although neither country ever came close to being independent of the South African transport system. See *Corridors of power* on page 68 for more about Mozambique's transportation corridors.

Gorongosa Mountain and National Park
written in collaboration with Paul Ash
The Parque Nacional de Gorongosa extends over the brachestygia-covered plains north of the Beira Corridor to the southeastern base of Mount Gorongosa. Formerly regarded as one of southern Africa's finest wildlife reserves, attracting over 12,000 visitors a year, and with more game than the much larger Kruger National Park in South Africa, the area became a central battleground when Renamo had its headquarters near Mount Gorongosa, and there is now little wildlife left. The park still looks very run down. Having said this, the Parque Nacional de Gorongosa is the flagship of Mozambique's wildlife rehabilitation projects. Since the end of the war, a lot of work has been done to reopen the park to visitors. Countless landmines have been lifted, bridges repaired, and the lodge rebuilt. Animals have also started to return now that the gunfire and slaughter has stopped. Game numbers are still low, but nothing is extinct. Birding is excellent, especially around the campsite. Anti-poaching programmes have been surprisingly successful, and although the wildlife is still quite shy, it is generally thought that an extensive restocking programme will not be necessary. Sightings of lions and buffaloes have increased, a herd of sable antelopes still survives despite being decimated by poachers in the early 1990s, and a 75-strong breeding herd of elephants roams the park at will.

The 1,862m high **Mount Gorongosa**, which lies outside of the synonymous national park, is an isolated massif rising almost 1.5km above the surrounding plains. Covered in montane forest, Gorongosa has acquired something approaching legendary status with South African birders as the only place south of the Zambezi where the attractive and vociferous green-headed oriole can be seen. It also supports a variety of other interesting forest birds, though as things stand it's a destination suitable only for dedicated and self-sufficient birders. The best way of getting up Mount Gorongosa is with a ranger/guide from the Chitengo Safari Lodge. Prices are negotiable, and you will have to provide him with food.

Note that there is a US$15 entrance fee to visit the park, plus US$15 per vehicle per day, and that it is closed during the rainy season from late October to early April when the floodplains are inundated and impassable.

Getting there and away
The surfaced 62km road to Gorongosa town leaves the main road through the Beira Corridor at Inchope. The unsurfaced turn-off to Gorongosa National Park departs eastwards from this road about 40km towards Gorongosa. To get

to Mount Gorongosa, continue along the tar road until it terminates at Gorongosa town, then ask to be shown the rough motorable track that passes the southeastern base of the mountain. There are some very rough footpaths up to the forest zone. It would be unrealistic to explore this area without a 4WD, a tent, and sufficient food.

Once in the park, it may be possible to hire a 4WD and driver for around US$20 per person per day to take you on game drives.

Where to stay
The bungalows at the **Chitengo Safari Lodge**, which was attacked heavily during the civil war, are currently being used by trainee park rangers. You can camp at the lodge, however, for around US$7.50 per person (bring your own tent). There is no food at Chitengo, so you'll have to bring your own supplies. The shower blocks and toilets have been repaired, but don't expect anything as luxurious as hot water.

Chimoio
The capital of landlocked Manica province, and Mozambique's fifth-largest city, Chimoio is the archetypal small southern African town. Portuguese signposts aside, there is nothing about Chimoio (pronounced Shimoio) that is distinctively Mozambican; in fact, with its fresh mid-altitude climate and drearily uniform grid of streets, you could as easily be in Zimbabwe or Malawi, countries that have in common a distinct lack of towns with any discernible character.

Chimoio may not be the sort of town you'd make a special effort to see, but it's agreeable enough, and its location, roughly 40km from the junction of the Beira Corridor and the Tete road and 100km from the Zimbabwe border, makes it a route focus of sorts, and the obvious place to spend a night if you enter Mozambique from Mutare late in the day. The only real tourist attraction around Chimoio is Cabeca de Velho, a vast granite outcrop shaped like an old man's face in repose. Visible from the city centre, and less than 3km away as the crow flies, the outcrop might make a rewarding day's walk – there are reportedly good views from the top.

Getting there and away
There are regular *chapas* and buses between Chimoio and Beira, taking roughly three hours, and also between Chimoio and the border taking about half that time. Oliveira's buses between Maputo and Tete all stop at Chimoio, and there are also regular buses running directly between Chimoio and Tete. Note that no passenger trains stop at Chimoio.

Where to stay
The only accommodation in the city centre is the unsignposted **Pensão Flôr do Vouga** (tel: 22469) at 670 Avenida 25 de Setembro. The rooms are quite large, nicely furnished and of reasonable value at US$15 for a double. There is only one single, at US$9. About 2km out of town on the Beira road, the

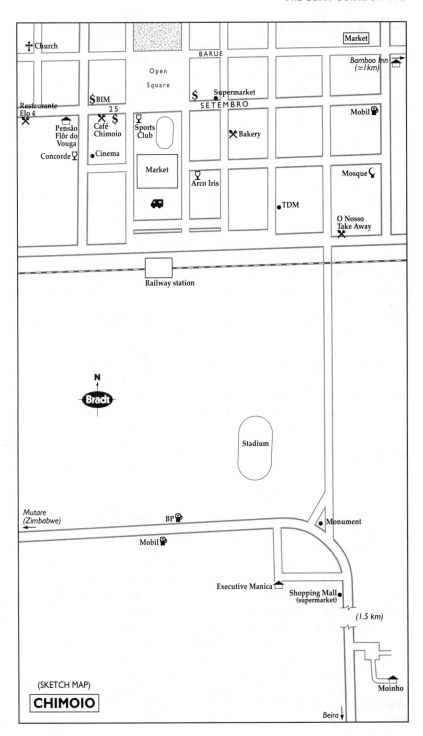

(SKETCH MAP)

CHIMOIO

Motel Moinho (tel: 24762) is not a bad alternative. The main building of this hotel, shaped like a mill, contains a ground-floor bar and restaurant and a few eccentrically shaped rooms on the first and second floors. There is also a row of more conventionally rectangular rooms at the back. All rooms are self-contained with hot showers, and they cost US$20/double. There is safe parking. If you're coming on public transport from Beira or the south coast, you could ask to be dropped at the turn-off to the motel before you reach the town centre. Otherwise, it's a 30-minute walk from the bus station. Follow the main road out of town across the railway line with the stadium to your right for about 400m until you hit the intersection with the main Beira–Mutare road. Here you must turn left, towards Beira, until after about 1.5km you'll see the hotel signposted to your left (and the windmill rising above the surrounding shrubs and trees). The motel is about 400m from here, next to a pleasant reed-hut village.

Another affordable option, and considerably more central, is the **Bamboo Inn**, which is noisy and basic but very friendly and cheap at US$5/double. To get there, walk up to the small market (top right corner of the accompanying map), then turnleft out of town, follow a bend in the road and continue on for about ten minutes.

Probably the final option if you're on foot is the **Executive Manica Hotel** (tel: 23190; fax: 23129), a business-class hotel lying about 200m off the main Beira–Mutare road. Self-contained rooms with air conditioning, satellite TV and telephone cost US$70/82.50 single/double, and facilities include a good restaurant, safe parking and a swimming pool. There is a campsite, the **Palhota de Chicoteco**, about 5km along the road to Zimbabwe, and you can get basic rooms for around US$10 at the **Centro de Formacão da Cruz Vermelha** or Red Cross (tel: 23409) 4km from the town centre.

Where to eat
If you're staying at the **Motel Moinho,** look no further – the food here is excellent, reasonably priced at around US$4 to US$5 for a main course, and the portions are immense. There's also a nice bar in the main building.

In town, the liveliest place to eat is the **Sports Club Bar** next to the small stadium, which serves a variety of meat, fish and chicken dishes for around US$4. Further west on Avenida 25 de Setembro, the **Café Chimoio** has pizzas, sandwiches, milkshakes and an impressive range of fizzy drinks, juices and milk-based drinks. The hacienda-style décor at the **Restaurante Elo 4** belies its good-quality Italian cuisine, while the **Restaurante Quintal** (still on Avenida 25 de Setembro) is known for its pizzas. For snacks and fast food, the **O Nosso Take Away** on the other side of the railway track as you enter the town centre has a good selection of salads, sandwiches and the like, and is very cheap. There are now better bakeries in town than the **Arco Iris**, a small *salaõ de chá* opposite the market, although it remains a good place for a cup of tea. The market sells a reasonable range of fruit and vegetables, and there is a large Shoprite supermarket about 1km from the town centre on the road to Beira.

Useful information

If you've just entered from Zimbabwe, a priority will probably be to exchange some foreign currency, which you can do at the main branch of the BCM on Avenido 25 de Setembro or at the private Bureau de Change on the same road. Around the market, you'll find plenty of people willing to change cash – in this part of Mozambique, Zimbabwe dollars will get you the best rate, but be warned that there are some slick operators around. At weekends, there are sometimes concerts in the small stadium next to the market.

Chicamba Dam

Lying between Chimoio and the Zimbabwe border is an area of thick brachestygia woodland and undulating hills with good views of the Vumba Mountains to the south. In the middle of this distinctively African landscape lies Chicamba Dam, remarkable as much as anything for being the only functional tourist attraction in the Mozambican interior south of the Zambezi. Chicamba Dam is popular with bass fishermen (the resort is often full during Zimbabwean school holidays) while the surrounding wooded hills have an isolated, low-key charm, and would be of great interest to bird-watchers. Otherwise there's not a great deal to say about the dam – there are dozens of similar places in South Africa and Zimbabwe – except that it's a more inherently attractive stopover than Chimoio, and that it might make for a welcome mid-altitude break from the sweaty coast for backpackers who are covering the whole of the coastline. If that sounds like damnation with faint praise, let me put it this way: I could happily have spent a week relaxing and birding in the area, and just as happily have lived my life without ever seeing Chicamba Dam.

Getting there and away

The dirt turn-off to the Casa Msika Motel is clearly signposted from the main road through the Beira Corridor roughly 47km from Chimoio and 20km from Manica. The resort lies about 5km from the main road.

Where to stay and eat

The **Casa Msika Motel** (tel: 22675) lies on the lake shore. It has chalets costing US$24/double and a campsite where you can pitch a tent for US$2.50 per person. There is a restaurant and bar on a raised wooden platform on the edge of the lake.

Mount Binga

The country's highest mountain is not difficult to climb but it is not easily accessible from the Mozambican side. The 2,436m-high mountain is situated in the Chimanimani Mountains right on the Zimbabwe border and from the Zimbabwe side it is easy to reach.

In order to climb Mount Binga, start at Mutare in Zimbabwe, then go 150km south to the small town of Chimanimani. From the town there is a good dirt road to the entrance of the Chimanimani Mountain Park, where

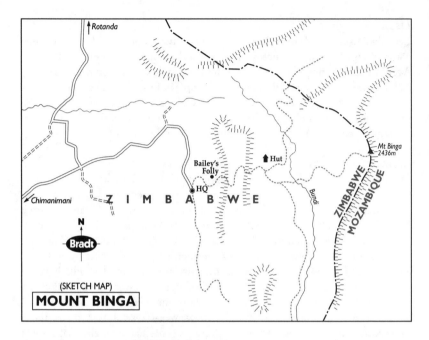

there is a campsite with showers and toilets as well as the park headquarters. The normal route to the hut via Bailey's Folly takes one to one and a half hours without a pack, and about two hours with a pack. The hut is situated above a spectacular high-lying valley surrounded by the Chimanimani mountain ridge. From the hut to the summit takes about another two and three-quarter hours.

The climb down to the floor of the valley is splendid, under trees with wide spreading branches. After this you cross the very picturesque Bundi stream and then climb to the small ridge followed by the final stretch up to the summit. The view from the summit stretches beyond the descending mountains of the Mount Binga Massif well over Mozambique.

MOZAMBIQUE CONNECTION TRAVEL

For all your travel requirements contact the SPECIALISTS

mozcon.com tel: 0027 11 803 4185 res@mozcon.com

Tete Province

The province of Tete in western Mozambique must rank as one of the most peculiar relics of the colonial carve-up of Africa: a wedge-shaped Portuguese territory protuding into what was formerly the British Central African Protectorate. Today Tete is bordered by Zimbabwe to the west, Zambia to the north, and Malawi to the east. Only the short southern border is shared with other parts of Mozambique.

Looking at a map, one would probably consider Tete to be a part of northern Mozambique. In reality, the province and its eponymous capital city have much closer economic links and are more easily accessed from the south, largely because they are isolated from the four provinces of the northeast by Malawi and the Shire River. Tete's virtual separation from the rest of Mozambique and its importance as the most straightforward route between Blantyre and Harare have resulted in several other mild anomalies; for instance, considerably more English is understood in Tete itself than in any other town in Mozambique.

Tete probably sees more traveller through-traffic than the rest of Mozambique's provinces combined, once again a function of its location as opposed to any great inherent charms. Practically every traveller who crosses between Malawi and Zimbabwe uses the so-called Tete Corridor (the road which bisects Tete and which was known during the civil war as the 'Gun Run') but very few spend even one night in Mozambique, let alone explore the province. Tete town is also the main gateway to southern Mozambique for travellers coming from Malawi.

As seen from the window of a bus between Blantyre and Harare, Tete is not the most inviting of areas: a dry, dusty badland covered in puny acacia scrub and punctuated by the occasional small thatched village, which only makes you wonder how anybody can live in this harsh, arid climate. Lying at a low altitude on the south bank of the Zambezi, the town of Tete manages to be both dusty and almost intolerably humid. As seen in the harsh light of the day, it's a town with little to no aesthetic appeal, though in the softer light of the evening the old town and riverbank take on an altogether more pleasant hue.

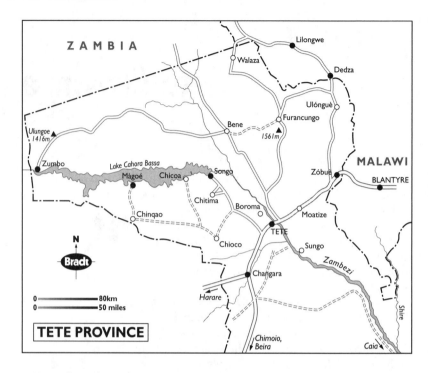

TETE PROVINCE

Away from the main road, Tete Province boasts at least one worthwhile and straightforward excursion in the form of the vast Cahora Bassa Dam and the nearby town of Songo – the latter with a remarkably fresh highland climate after the claustrophobic humidity of Tete. More off the beaten track, but also of interest, is the attractive mission at Boroma, which lies on the west bank of the Zambezi some 60km upriver from Tete.

TETE

The eponymous capital of Tete Province, often and with some justification claimed to be the hottest town in Mozambique, is situated on the southwest bank of the Zambezi roughly 650km upriver from its mouth and at an altitude of only 175m above sea level. Remarkably, the large suspension bridge at Tete is the only permanent crossing of the Zambezi anywhere in Mozambique, hence the town's importance as a regional transport hub. Tete today is quite modern in both appearance and outlook. The city expanded greatly in size and population during the construction of Cahora Bassa Dam, and it is now one of the largest towns in the Mozambican interior, with a population of around 50,000.

History

Tete is a settlement of some antiquity. Even before the Portuguese arrived in East Africa, it lay at the junction of the Zambezi and three of the four main trading routes from the Sofala area into the African interior. The site of the modern town was probably occupied by Muslim traders in the 15th century, when it formed the main link between the coast and the gold fairs of Karangaland. Tete was settled by a few Portuguese adventurers in 1531, and by 1630 it supported around 20 *mazungo* households.

Contemporary reports suggest that Tete was rather makeshift in appearance until around 1767, when it was made the seat of administration for the Zambezi Valley and a garrison of 100 soldiers was posted there on a permanent basis. By the end of the 18th century, Tete's city centre consisted of roughly 30 stone houses enclosed by a 3m-high wall, as well as a hospital, trade factory, governor's residence and council building.

Getting there and away
By air
LAM has flights between Tete and Maputo, Lichinga, Beira and Quelimane. The LAM booking office is on Avenida 24 de Julho between the Pensãos Alves and Central, while the airport is 5km out of town towards Zóbuè. Any bus travelling between Tete and Moatize, a small town 20km to the east, can drop you at the entrance to the airport. Buses to Moatize leave Tete from in front of the Hotel Zambeze.

By road
Tete will be the first port of call for travellers who are visiting southern Mozambique from Malawi. A good surfaced road connects Blantyre to Tete via Mwanza and Zóbuè – in a private vehicle, the 225km drive shouldn't take more than three hours, allowing for delays at the border. Using public transport, the simplest way to get to Tete is with one of the daily buses between Blantyre and Harare, but you could also do the trip in hops.

A scenic and well-maintained surfaced road connects the Tete and Beira Corridors. This 270km road branches southwards from the Tete Corridor at Changara, 95km from Tete on the road towards the Zimbabwe border, and it connects with the Beira Corridor 270km further south, roughly 20km west of Chimoio (the capital of Manica Province). Oliveira's and TSL run daily buses between Tete, Chimoio and Beira, and there are also regular *chapas* along this road.

When you are ready to leave Tete, you'll find that buses to Chimoio, Beira and Songo leave from the terminal on Avenida 25 de Junho, *chapas* to Beira and Chimoio leave from in front of the Hotel Kassuende, *chapas* to Songo and Chitima leave from opposite the Hotel Kassuende, and *chapas* to Zóbuè on the Malawi border leave from in front of the market near the slaving fort.

Where to stay
The accommodation options in Tete are limited to a reasonable selection of satisfactory hotels and a campsite: nothing out of this world; but then again, nothing too awful. The newest and most expensive place to stay is the **Motel Tete** (tel: 23498), which is on the main road to Beira (the EN103) just before you get into town. Air-conditioned, self-contained doubles overlooking the Zambezi River cost US$60, which, probably due to the

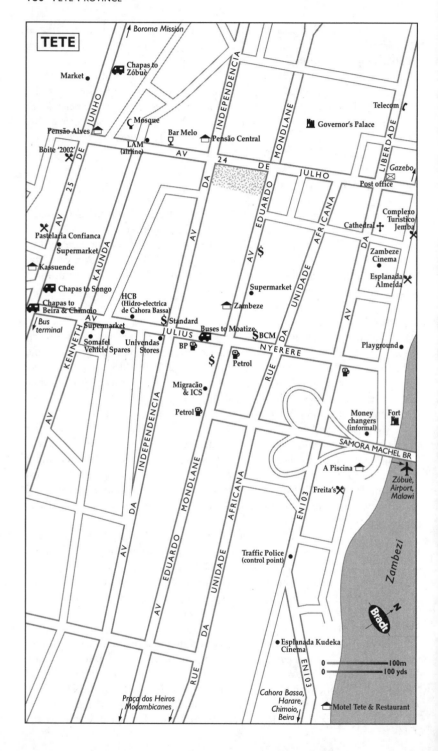

Previous page 18th-century church at Quelimane

Above The Church of Senhora Baluarte at Ilha do Moçambique is the oldest European building in the southern hemisphere

Below A private mosque sits among the reedhouses on the outskirts of Lichinga

view, is considerably more than you'll pay at the various other establishments in town. This is not to say that there's anything wrong with the view from the rooftop terrace of the seven-storey **Hotel Zambeze** (tel: 23100), the tallest building in Tete, although the rooms are a little jaded compared with those at the spanking new Motel Tete. You can get an air-conditioned double at the Zambeze for around US$20, which seems to be the going rate in this town. At least it is at the **Pensão Central** (tel: 22523) and the **Pensão Alves** (tel: 22523), two places near the market, which also have more basic rooms for around US$10. The Central might be a better bet since it was the more recent to open and is under the same management as the excellent Restaurante Freita's (see below). Also near the market, the **Hotel Kassuende** (tel: 22531) seems overpriced at US$30 for a double with air conditioning. For campers, the popular Piscina Complex near the river has closed; the Jesus E Bom campsite is across the bridge on the right; but probably the best option is to ask at the **Motel Tete** for permission to park by the river at the back of the Motel. It's not advertised, but some travellers did it recently (mid-2005) and report being charged US$5 per person on hard standing with hot showers and decent toilets.

Where to eat
Whatever else it may lack, Tete certainly has an above average selection of restaurants and bars, most of which run along the riverfront. Set back from the river at the southern end of town, the **Restaurante Freita's** is probably the best in town, with a wide selection of dishes ranging from pasta and pork to the more predictable chicken and fish. The chips here are particularly good, and the chicken piri-piri is also strongly recommended. Most dishes cost less than US$5. The all-night disco on Fridays and Saturdays is the most popular in Tete.

On the riverfront north of the bridge, the **Esplanada Almeida** is a pleasant place for a cold beer, but the food is relatively ordinary and, judging by the smell, it's positioned right next to a popular ablution spot.

Attractive flowering gardens and relatively fresh air conspire to make the **Complexo Turistico Jemba** the best place to enjoy a sundowner in full view of the Zambezi. It has a varied menu, and is perhaps the only place in Tete that serves pizzas. There's a loud disco in the complex at weekends, though far enough away from the bar and restaurant that it's not too intrusive.

The **Pastelaria Confianca** on Avenida 25 de Junho is a good place to enjoy a relaxed, varied breakfast. In addition to a selection of pastries, doughnuts, fresh bread and espresso coffee, the Pastelaria stocks chilled fruit juice and refrigerated chocolates, and it serves good burgers, prego rolls and egg or cheese sandwiches.

Most of the hotels mentioned above serve meals, but they're ordinary by comparison with the proper restaurants. The two exceptions might be the **Motel Tete**, which serves outstanding breakfasts, and the **Pensão Central**, which has established a good reputation for its evening meals. When it hasn't been flooded by heavy rains, the restaurant at the top of the **Hotel Zambeze** might also be worth checking out for the view.

What to see

Tete is, in all honesty, a town of limited interest to tourists, and for many its few attractive qualities will be outweighed by the oppressive humidity of the Zambezi Valley. The old part of town is not without a certain decrepit charm: there are some beautiful old houses here, though most are in urgent need of restoration. The oldest building in town is the disused cathedral, which reportedly dates back to 1563. The most unlikely building is a domed gazebo on the riverfront, presumably where the Portuguese colonists enjoyed their sundowners. Also worth a look is the old slaving fort near the municipal market, though it now protects a couple of water tanks so it may be difficult to get inside, and a second fort on the riverfront below the bridge.

An attractive feature of Tete is the row of bars and restaurants that lines the riverfront – this is, after all, the one place in Mozambique where the Zambezi is readily accessible to casual visitors, and even if the riverbank around Tete itself is somewhat denuded of natural vegetation, it would be a shame to visit Mozambique and not spend at least one evening drinking in sight of Africa's fourth-largest river. More adventurously, you could ask around to find a fisherman to paddle you along the river in a dugout: the papyrus beds near the town support a good variety of birds, and you wouldn't need to go more than 1km or so upriver to stand a good chance of seeing hippos and crocs.

The large, multi-span suspension bridge across the river is the only bridge in Mozambique that spans the Zambezi; it was built in the late 1960s.

Tete is reputedly Mozambique's hottest town – which is a good reason to relax, enjoy the surroundings and sightsee slowly.

BOROMA MISSION

One of the most interesting excursions out of Tete is to Boroma, site of one of the country's most attractive missions. Boroma was an important source of alluvial gold even before Portuguese times, though it had been exhausted long before the mission was founded in 1891. The centrepiece of the mission is a large and beautiful church on a hill overlooking the river, abandoned by the missionaries shortly after independence, but recently reoccupied by an Italian priest. The Boroma area is also a good place to see hippos and crocs, and it should offer good birdwatching.

Getting there and away

A few vehicles run between Tete and Boroma daily, generally leaving Tete before 08.00. To pick up transport to Boroma, follow Avenida 25 de Junho out of town past the old slave fort and market for five to ten minutes until you see a large blue signpost pointing to Boroma. The point where vehicles wait is about 100m past this signpost, immediately after the road bends to the left. The road to Boroma should only be attempted in a 4WD, and it may be closed due to flooding after heavy rain.

Where to stay

There is no formal accommodation at Boroma, and with an early start it would be easy enough to visit the mission as a day trip out of Tete. If you have a tent, you should be allowed to pitch it near the mission.

CAHORA BASSA DAM

Situated on the Zambezi in the north of Tete Province, Cahora Bassa Dam is the fifth-largest dam in the world and it dams one of Africa's ten largest bodies of water, covering an area of 2,660km². Construction of the 300m-wide and 160m-high concrete wall started in 1969 and, despite Frelimo's attempts at sabotage, it was completed in 1974.

Cahora Bassa is potentially Africa's largest supplier of electric power and a vital source of foreign revenue for Mozambique. The five turbines, housed in a rock-hewn cavern of cathedralesque dimensions, have a total capacity of 2075MW, roughly ten times the power requirement for the whole of Mozambique. When the dam was built, the idea was that it would supply large amounts of hydro-electric power to South Africa. Sadly, by the end of the civil war only two of the dam's turbines were still functional, and no electricity from Cahora Bassa had reached South Africa since part of the power line was destroyed by Renamo in 1986. Nowadays, since the rehabilitation of the dam in 1997 and the beginning of construction of a new plant some 70km downstream of Cahora Bassa, Mozambique can expect to earn a considerable amount of its foreign exchange from the export of electricity to South Africa and other neighbouring countries.

Now partially submerged, the Cahora Bassa Rapids were the obstacle that prevented Livingstone's Zambezi Expedition from opening up the Zambezi as 'God's Highway' into the African interior, and which led to the explorer turning his attention to the Shire River in what would eventually become the British enclave now known as Malawi. Covering a distance of roughly 80km, and marked by two near-vertical drops of 200m, the rapids had been known to the Portuguese and other traders for several centuries before Livingstone arrived at the Zambezi – the phrase 'Cahora Bassa' means 'where the work ends' in the local dialect, a reference to the fact that rapids were an impassable obstacle for boatsmen sailing up the Zambezi.

Livingstone had used a path that arched around the rapids in the course of his epic trans-African hike, the journey that preceded and inspired the Zambezi Expedition, so it is something of a mystery why he never thought to look at the rapids for himself, and steadfastly dismissed local advice that they would be impassable. Even when his boat, the *Ma-Robert*, was confronted by the rapids on November 9 1858, Livingstone refused to believe they couldn't eventually be surmounted, though he was finally persuaded of this in November 1860, when he attempted to ascend the rapids with five dugout canoes, a number of which overturned, taking many of the expedition's notes and drawings with them.

Probably the first person to navigate the rapids was a rather enigmatic and obscure figure remembered in the annals of the Royal Geographic Society by the name of Mr F Monks (though his real surname was evidently Foster). In 1880, Monks made a solo canoe trip between the confluence of the Gawayi and Zambezi Rivers and the port of Quelimane. Although he left no substantial journal of this trip, he did leave behind an impressively accurate topographical map of the Zambezi and several of its tributaries as far downriver as Tete. Monks disappeared into the African interior a few years after this, never to be heard of again. As a footnote, the first people known to have kayaked the full length of the Zambezi from its source near the borders of Zambia, Zaire and Angola are two young British travellers, Rupert FitzMaurice and Justin Matterson, who did the trip to raise money for charity towards the end of 1996.

An interesting story associated with Cahora Bassa is that of the legendary silver mines of Chicova, which were shown to Portuguese explorers in the early years of the 17th century. In 1617 and 1618, the period when Madeira occupied the fort at Sena, an estimated 450kg of silver was brought there, allegedly from Chicova. The odd thing is that the mines were 'lost' shortly after Madeira left Sena, and despite the attempts of several fortune hunters since, they have yet to be relocated. If the mine ever did exist, then it's probably now submerged by Cahora Bassa, or close to its southern shore.

The closest town to the dam, **Songo**, was purpose-built in the style of a Portuguese village while the dam was under construction. By 1974 it had a population of almost 15,000. Located in the cool, breezy highlands immediately south of the dam, Songo is well worth visiting in its own right, with a spacious layout and green, flowering gardens that blend attractively into the surrounding woodland. The approach road to Songo is one of the most spectacular in Mozambique, and the well-wooded, boulder-strewn hills that surround the town offer a refreshing contrast to the humid air and stark landscape of Tete. The Songo area also promises excellent birdwatching, and there are plenty of roads along which you can explore it (though do bear in mind that straying from roads could be risky; this part of Mozambique was heavily mined during the civil war).

Travellers cannot visit the dam without authorisation. It is straightforward enough to get authorisation once you arrive in Songo, but it would nevertheless be a better idea to get a *credençial* in advance (you can do this at the HCB (Hidro-electrica de Cahora Bassa) office on Avenida 25 de Junho in Tete), if only because visitors who arrive at Songo without permission may be required to leave their passports at the police checkpoint about 5km before the town for the duration of their stay. Alternatively, contact Mr Nhamposa, HCB's chief of Public Relations at Songo (tel: 82221/2/3/4).

Getting there and away

Songo lies 150km from Tete along an excellent surfaced road. The turn-off to Songo is roughly 25km from Tete along the road towards the Zimbabwe border. It isn't signposted but it's the only major junction along this stretch of road. The drive from Tete to Songo can comfortably be done in two hours in a private vehicle.

Buses travel between Tete and Songo twice a day. In theory, these buses leave Tete at 08.00 and 14.00, but this timetable is evidently not adhered to with any rigidity. If you miss the bus, a few *chapas* leave for Songo daily from in front of the Hotel Kassuende. You could also take a *chapa* to Chitima (marked on some maps as Estima), a small town at the base of the mountains about 15km from Songo, and pick up a lift to Songo from there.

Where to stay and eat

The **Pousada Sete Mentes**, the only hotel in Songo, is a pleasant and reasonably inexpensive place with a good restaurant. The restaurant at the airport serves really good chicken and chips for US$4.

At the dam itself, the **Ugezi Tiger Lodge** has fully equipped A-frame huts and safari-style tents for the increasing number of fishermen who are attracted to the Cahora Bassa Lake for its abundance of fish (species include tiger, chessa, beam, cornishjack and vundu). There is another fishing lodge at **Màgoé**, west of Songo, roughly at the middle point of the lake's southern shore.

There is also a very basic resthouse in Chitima. It isn't signposted, but it's easy enough to find since it's right behind the bar where *chapas* stop to pick up passengers.

ZUMBO

Lying on the Zambian border at the confluence of the Zambezi and Luangwa Rivers, Zumbo was once an important gold fair, said to have been founded in 1715 by Francisco Pereira, a Goan trader and refugee from the Rozvi attack on Dambarare. By 1750, a lively trade in gold with the Rozvi had led to Zumbo becoming the largest Portuguese town on the Zambezi, with a Christian population of almost 500 including 80 Europeans. By 1764, when it was granted municipal status, Zumbo was possibly the most prosperous settlement in Portuguese Africa.

Zumbo's decline can be linked to the political tensions that gripped the upper Zambezi area in the late 18th century, combined with the great drought that started in 1895. After being attacked several times, Zumbo was fortified in 1801, and at the same time a Portuguese garrison moved in. This was not enough to prevent further attacks and so the town was evacuated in 1813. The fair was reoccupied in 1820, but following the resurgence of drought conditions and the looming threat of the Ngoni after they deposed the Rozvi dynasty in 1836, Zumbo was permanently abandoned by Portugal.

In 1859, the British explorer Richard Thornton passed through the ghost town that had once been described as the metropolis of the whole trade of the rivers. Thornton recorded seeing the ruins of some 200 stone houses lining the riverbank over a distance of 3km. A more recent report confirms that a fort of unknown antiquity, built around a 500-year-old fig tree, was still in use at Zumbo during World War II. Though Zumbo is well off any beaten track today, it may well be of interest to self-sufficient travellers with private transport – and if anybody does head out this way, I'd be most interested to hear about it.

steppes travel

travel beyond the ordinary

Steppes Travel is a travel company unlike any other, for those seeking something out of the ordinary.

We organise tailor-made journeys exclusively for you.

Our consultants are travel specialists with expert, first-hand knowledge of Mozambique and the African continent.

Whether you want to go on safari, explore the unspoilt coastline, experience the amazing diving and snorkelling off the Bazaruto Archipelago or discover the richness of Mozambique's cultural heritage, Steppes Travel can take you there.

And in style and comfort. We represent some of the world's most exclusive hotels and lodges - and Mozambique is no exception.

We have visited, and personally recommend, only the best accommodation in Mozambique, from luxury safari lodges to the most private and stylish beach or island hideaways...

- Benquerra ● Marlin Lodge ● Indigo Bay ● Vamizi
- Nkwichi Lodge ● Dugong Lodge ● Maputo Hotels
- Quilalea ● Londo Lodge ● Pemba Beach Hotel
- Matemo ● Medjumbe ● Lugenda Bush Camp
- Rongui ● Macaloe

Call us to arrange a tailor-made journey to Mozambique on

01285 650011

www.steppestravel.co.uk

AFRICA ASIA CENTRAL & SOUTH AMERICA

Zambézia

Zambézia, in central Mozambique, is the most populous province in the country, and the most agriculturally rich, with many areas receiving an average rainfall of around 2,000mm. Paradoxically, this province also suffers from what are possibly the worst transport links in Mozambique, and despite its pivotal position it is only likely to be visited by travellers who are making their way overland between Beira in southern Mozambique and Nampula in the north.

The overland trip from Beira to Nampula is among the most taxing in Mozambique, and most travellers will choose to punctuate it with a stay at Quelimane, the capital of Zambézia. Fortunately, this ancient river port is, relentless humidity aside, one of the more pleasant cities in the country, with surprisingly good tourist facilities and easy access to the nearby beach resort at Zalala.

Apart from Quelimane, Zambézia has little to offer travellers. The attractive town of Milange is only likely to be visited by travellers entering Mozambique from Malawi. A more accessible part of the western highlands of Zambézia is the area around Gurué, a spacious small town with a beautiful situation at the base of Mount Namuli, Mozambique's second-highest peak.

QUELIMANE

Quelimane is Mozambique's fourth-largest town, with a population of roughly 140,000. The settlement that eventually became Quelimane was founded on the north bank of the Qua-Qua River after it was discovered that this relatively small waterway was linked to the Zambezi by a channel that emerged near modern-day Mopeia. For centries, the Qua-Qua offered safe and easy access to the Zambezi, at least when compared to the vast and labyrinthine Zambezi Delta to its south, but the channel connecting the two rivers silted up during the great drought of the 1820s and has since fallen into disuse.

History

Quelimane was almost certainly founded by Muslim traders, probably at around the same time as Tete and Sena. The first Portuguese trading factory at Quelimane was established in 1530, and the town appears on Portuguese

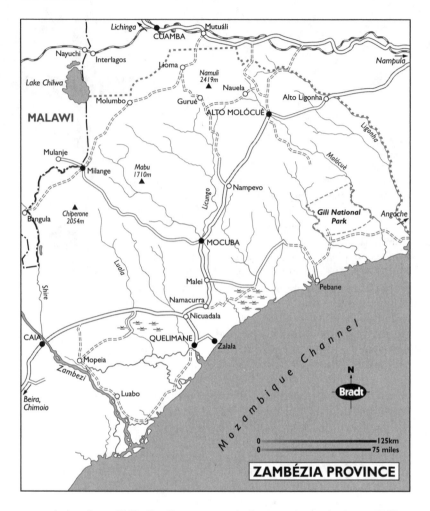

ZAMBÉZIA PROVINCE

maps dating from 1560. Quelimane grew in importance as the ivory trading routes up the Zambezi replaced the older gold-trade routes out of Sofala. Reports dating to the 1590s depict it as an attractive small town, surrounded by plantations and protected by a wooden fort.

Like many other coastal settlements, Quelimane benefited greatly from the growth in the slave trade during the latter part of the 18th century. It also became a major supplier of food to Mozambique Island during this period. Quelimane's oldest stone buildings date to the 1780s, and in 1812 the town was made a separate Captaincy with its own customs house. By the 1820s, Quelimane was the most important slaving port in East Africa, but its municipal status was discontinued in 1826 due to the lack of government control over the free trade in slaves. The main results of this action were that the local slave trade was driven underground, and that many visiting ships avoided Portuguese settlements altogether, preferring to enter into clandestine trade with Muslim settlements elsewhere on the coast. Quelimane nevertheless remained a prosperous settlement, mainly through its importance as a supplier of agricultural produce. David Livingstone was officially appointed the British Honorary Consul to Quelimane in 1858, even though his main interest in the town was as a base from which to explore the Zambezi.

Getting there and away
By air
You can fly between Maputo and Quelimane on every day of the week. LAM also connects Quelimane to Beira, Nampula and, less frequently, Tete. The LAM booking office (tel: 21 2800) is on Avenida 1 de Junho, while the airport is about 3km north of the centre. About half of the 4WDs parked outside the airport are actually taxis, and you should be able to negotiate a ride into town for about US$3.

By sea
Although there are no formal passenger boat services linking Quelimane to other coastal towns, you might be able to get a ride on a cargo vessel as far as Beira. If this option is of interest – perhaps to avoid the arduous journey by land – get your face known at the port just in case a boat happens to be making the trip when you want to go.

By road
If you are driving from Beira to Quelimane, prepare yourself for at least a day of ruts and pot-holes, relics of intense mining during the civil war. Twelve hours for the 450km journey is good going, and very strenuous. The condition of the road means that a 4WD vehicle is a necessity, especially during the rainy season.

There is no public transport along most of the road between Beira and Quelimane, so you'll probably be dependent on getting a lift with a truck and you should expect this to take the best part of two days with an overnight stop at Caia. From Beira, take any vehicle heading towards Chimoio and ask to be dropped at Dondo, 28km west of Beira. Once you have found the huge crowd of people sitting by the northbound road that branches from the Beira Corridor at Dondo, you will know that you have found the right departure point. When eventually a truck arrives, be prepared for a scramble and then, once aboard, switch off for the 10–15-hour journey to Caia, the small village on the south bank of the Zambezi near the confluence with the Shire River.

There is no bridge at Caia, but a vehicle ferry crosses back and forth throughout the day between 06.00 and 18.00. You will probably have to overnight at the river before picking up transport to Quelimane the next day. Either you can bed down in the huge truck yard with the other passengers, or else you can stay in the peculiar and very hot and stuffy double-storey reed hotel on the north bank of the river. The only other accommodation along this road is a pensão at Inhaminga, a small town 85km south of Caia where there is also a large mission. Inhaminga is the obvious place to break up the trip if you're not in a rush.

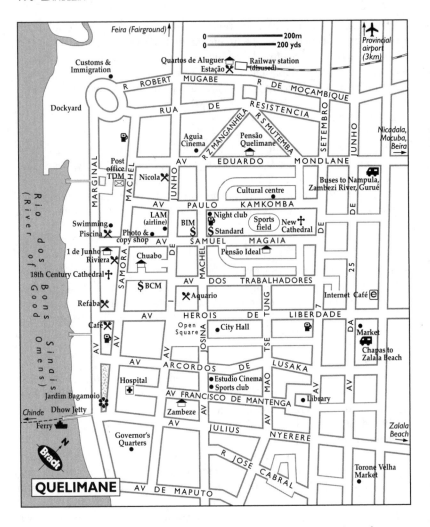

At the time of writing, travellers were starting to mention the new Gorongosa road as an alternative way of getting to Caia. From Beira, take a *chapa* along the Beira Corridor to Inchope, where there is a heavily pot-holed branch road to the town of Gorongosa. At Gorongosa, the newly surfaced road begins – or at least it will do just as soon as it is formally opened. For the time being, however, vehicles must drive on dirt tracks beside the road, and should be able to reach Caia in about seven hours. Hitching is certainly possible, although it must be said that traffic is thin.

Travellers covering the road between Quelimane and Beira from north to south should first take a bus from Quelimane to the Zambezi River: a relatively painless three-hour journey. If you're lucky (or unlucky!), you might find a bus going straight to Beira, in which case brace yourself for a very long trip.

For motorised travellers, there are a couple of potentially interesting diversions from the Caia area. To the east, a rough road follows the course of the Zambezi about 50km downriver to Lacerdónia (formerly known as Chupanga), where Mary Livingstone, wife of David Livingstone and daughter of Robert Moffat, was buried in the mission grounds. This road continues eastwards from Lacerdonia to the village of Marromeu on the fringes of the Zambezi Delta.

Roughly 50km upriver of Caia, the rather remote outpost of Vila de Sena was formerly one of the two most important Portuguese outposts on the Zambezi, and it quite possibly stands on the same site as the trading post of Seyouna mentioned in a 12th-century Arab document. The 3,660m-long railway bridge at Sena, completed in 1935, was the longest bridge in the world at the time it was built, and it would still be the longest bridge in Africa had it not been sabotaged by Renamo during the civil war. The Sena Bridge is unusable at the time of writing, but I understand that it will eventually be rebuilt.

Getting to Quelimane from the west and north is rather more straightforward. From Milange on the Malawi border there is at least one *chapa* daily to Mocuba on the main Beira–Nampula road. From Nampula, there are regular buses and *chapas* to Quelimane, most of which stop overnight at Mocuba. There's plenty of transport between Mocuba and Quelimane.

Where to stay
The last thing that you'd expect to find in Quelimane is a plush tourist-class hotel, but that's precisely what the **Hotel Chuabo** (tel: 21 3181; fax: 21 3812) is. One of the most upmarket hotels in northern Mozambique, the eight-storey Chuabo has self-contained rooms with air conditioning, satellite TV and fridge for US$85/single and US$140/double, most of them with views over the river and old cathedral. The next most comfortable option is the **Quartos de Aluguer**, an Italian-run place next to the railway station where you can get compact and very new rooms with private bathroom, air conditioning and TV for US$30. The **Hotel Zambeze** (tel: 21 5490) on Avenida Acordos de Lusaka is centrally located and has good-value rooms for US$12.50/single and US$17.50/double. Even better value is the clean and friendly **Pensão Ideal** (tel: 21 5423), in a pink building more or less opposite the new cathedral on Avenida Filipe Samuel Magaia. Doubles here start at a mere US$7, and even the air-conditioned rooms with private bathroom are only US$15. The **Hotel 1 de Julho** at the river end of Avenida Filipe Samuel Magaia is also perfectly satisfactory, with doubles priced at US$12.50 and US$17.50 depending on whether or not you want air conditioning. Bringing up the rear is the **Pensão Quelimane** (tel: 21 2359), a rather grand-looking white building on Avenida Eduardo Mondlane, which charges a rather inflated US$17.50 (US$25 if you're on the ground floor) for rather ordinary self-contained rooms.

Where to eat
The **Pastelaria e Salão de Chá Riviera**, a building with reflective-glass windows on the corner of Avenidas Samora Machel and Filipe Samuel

Magaia, must rank as the best place to eat in Quelimane. There is a comfortable air-conditioned dining room, as well as tables on the street outside; and the food (fresh spongy chocolate cake, a variety of pastries and sandwiches, good hamburgers, chicken and chips, etc) is of a high standard.

Another good place to eat, especially if you fancy a pizza or something else Italian, is the **Restaurante da Estação** next to the railway station.

Also very pleasant is the **Restaurante Refaba** on the riverfront next to the night market. There's generally a good breeze here, and although the food is standard Mozambican fare (chicken, meat or fish with chips for around US$4–5) the portions are substantial and the quality is well above average.

The restaurant on the eighth floor of the **Hotel Chuabo** is worth a try, though you should check the menu at the ground-floor reception to see what's on offer – generally a selection of three or four different meals, with a good chance of something unusual like prawn curry or pork cutlets. Meals cost around US$5. The view from the restaurant is exceptional.

The **Piscina** (Swimming Pool) opposite the Hotel 1 de Julho serves chilled beer and cheap if unexciting meals, and you can take a table on the roof, where there's a good breeze.

The **Café Nicola** serves beer and simple snacks such as prego rolls. There's also reasonable food at the **Hotel Zambeze** and ice-cream at the open-air **Restaurante Aquario** facing the main square. Note that many of the restaurants in Quelimane are closed on Mondays.

Entertainment
The limited entertainment options in Quelimane include a **cinema** (showing Bollywood films) and a sports club (where you can watch **basketball matches**) on Avenida Josina Machel, and a murky green municipal **swimming pool** opposite the Hotel 1 de Julho, which costs US$2.50 to use.

Useful information
If you were surprised to find an upmarket hotel in a town such as Quelimane, you will be even more astonished to hear that there is also a well-organised and exceedingly cheap **internet café** just north of the market at the Instituto do Magistério Primário or IMAP (Mon–Fri 07.00–20.00, Sat 09.00–12.00). There are several computers, connection times are reasonably quick, and it only costs US$1.50 per hour (or 500 meticais per minute).

Banks in Quelimane include the BCM next to the Hotel Chuabo (where you can also find a **Western Union** office), and the BIM Expresso on the corner of Avenidas Josina Machel and Filipe Samuel Magaia (which has an ATM machine).

What to see
Quelimane today has a more modern and low-rise appearance than you might expect. There is no old town as such: most of the older-looking buildings in the city centre evidently date to the early 20th century, and we couldn't see any trace of the old forts and customs house. Built in 1776, the old waterfront

cathedral is still in reasonable condition, though it has fallen into temporary disuse (except as a breeding ground for some impressively large rats) due to a leaky roof. Nevertheless, it remains an appealing building, and the caretaker will probably let you poke around inside if you ask. There are several old plaques on the wall and floor, including five tombstones marking the graves of former priests. The night market next to the cathedral is also worth visiting – a couple of dozen reed-and-bamboo bars surrounding a rather incongruous and normally empty discotheque.

ZALALA

Zalala Beach, 27km from Quelimane, is the obvious place to head for if you want to break up the slog between Beira and Nampula in relatively rustic surrounds. The surfaced road to Zalala passes through one of the most extensive coconut-palm plantations in Africa, and the wide sandy beach itself offers good swimming and surface.

No more than 100m from the beach, the **Complexo Turistico Kassi-Kassi** (tel: 212302, fax: 213599) consists of several chalets, each of which has two double bedrooms for around US$20 per unit. These could be full over the weekend, so ring first. Alternatively, you can camp in the grounds for US$2.50 per tent. There's decent food and expensive beers in the restaurant.

To get to Zalala, follow Avenida Julius Nyerere out of Quelimane city centre. The road to Zalala is unsurfaced immediately as you leave the city centre, but the tar starts about 1km towards Zalala near a cemetery. In a private vehicle, you can't go wrong if you just stick to the surfaced road. If you're looking for a lift, the best place to wait is opposite the cemetery. There are regular *chapas*, which leave from the market, and it's easy enough to hitch, especially at weekends.

ALONG THE QUELIMANE–NAMPULA ROAD

The 525km road connecting Quelimane to Nampula is in poor condition for most of its length, though the last 100km or so before Nampula has been freshly tarred in the past five years. As things stand, you really need a 4WD to cover this road, or at least a vehicle with good clearance, and the full journey will probably take eight to ten hours. Plenty of buses and *chapas* cover this road, though few make it the whole way through in a day. Vehicles travelling from Quelimane to Nampula generally overnight at Alto Molócuè, 187km before Nampula, while vehicles travelling from Nampula to Quelimane generally overnight at Mocuba, 148km before Quelimane.

Mocuba

Mocuba is a nice, airy town at a sufficiently high altitude to stay relatively cool. It is mostly of interest to travellers as the junction of the road between Nampula and Quelimane, and the road west to Milange on the Malawi border. Vehicles to and from Quelimane stop in the market place, those to and from the north stop at the bridge at the north end of town. To get to Milange, you need to take the dirt road parallel to the tarred road just past the UN

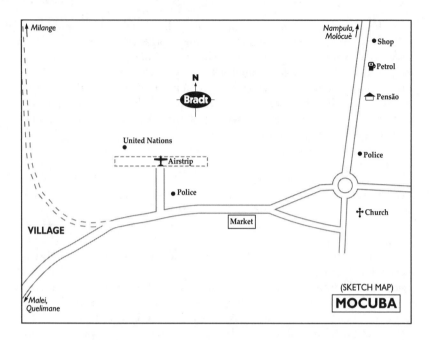

airstrip. This then turns right and heads northwest. It's quite easy to miss. The accommodation options in Mocuba include the rather run-down and decidedly overpriced **Pensão Cruzeiro** (US$15/double) and the **O Sitio Restaurant** on the wide avenue parallel to the main road, which has clean rooms.

Alto Molócuè

This dusty, scruffy small town sprawls around the Molócuè River exactly halfway between Mocuba and Nampula. The leafy administrative part of town, situated on a hill overlooking the north bank of the river, has a few interesting buildings dating to the early 20th century, notably a very pretty church, a peculiar house that was evidently converted from a fort, and a run-down town hall with a large and decidedly pointless parking area in front of it. The hotels, restaurants and municipal market are in the small commercial centre, clustered around a triangular town 'square' to the south of the river about 500m from the administrative centre.

The best accommodation is at the **Pensão Santo Antonio**, where you have the choice of a clean double room with a fan and private balcony for US$10 or a self-contained double with a fan and fridge for US$25. The **Pensão Fambo Uone** is rather scruffy by comparison and no cheaper at US$10 for a spacious double without a fan. The food at the Santo Antonio isn't up to much, but there's an anonymous bar and restaurant about 50m from the square in the opposite direction to the market that has much better food. A limited range of fresh fruit is on sale at the market, and there's a good bakery between the market and the square.

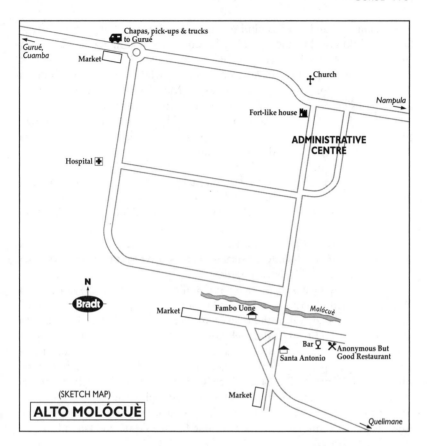

Vehicles heading towards Nampula or Quelimane leave Alto Molócuè from the square in the commercial centre. Vehicles heading to Gurué via Nauela leave from the traffic circle about 500m out of town along the road that passes the church.

GURUÉ

The highland town of Gurué makes for an interesting off-the-beaten-track diversion from the main road between Quelimane and Nampula. Situated amongst rolling hills and tea plantations at the base of the 2,419m-high Mount Namuli, Mozambique's second-highest peak, Gurué has the highest rainfall of any town in Mozambique and an atmosphere quite unlike that of any other part of the country. Gurué would look and feel pretty tropical if you arrived there fresh from the European winter, but after a few weeks on the muggy coast of Mozambique it has a wonderfully fresh and invigorating climate.

Getting there and away

Gurué can be approached in two ways from the Nampula–Quelimane road, either directly from Alto Molócuè via Nauela along a little-used but reasonably well maintained and very beautiful 80km road, or else from Nampevo via Errego along a 125km road that is reportedly in better condition though not as scenic. In a private vehicle, the direct route from Alto Molócuè is the better option if you're coming from the direction of Nampula, while the Nampevo route is better if you're coming from the direction of Mocuba. Using public transport, there's considerably more traffic along the road from Nampevu to Gurué.

The road to Gurué via Nauela is considerably quieter, but passes through some of the most attractive scenery in Mozambique: dense, green brachystegia woodland, rolling hills, and some monumentally contorted granite outcrops. Nauela itself is an intriguing place, with a small fort and large church as well as a few terminally run-down colonial buildings. The surrounding countryside is very beautiful. There's no accommodation, but you should be fine with a tent. One option, then, would be to take a lift as far as Nauela (a few vehicles go here daily from Alto Molócuè) and spend some time there before trying to find transport on to Gurué. Coming from Quelimane, you can find buses going directly to Gurué. There is also direct transport to Gurué from Milange on the Malawian border.

The best way to approach the town if you're coming from the north is via Mutuáli, which is on the Nampula–Cuamba railway line. Trucks bound for Gurué await the arrival of the train from Cuamba (which usually pulls into Mutuáli at around 07.00), although you can't bank on there being transport when the train from Nampula arrives at about 13.00. If you don't see any trucks at the departure point beside the old tank next to the railway station, remain on the train all the way to Cuamba and catch it back to Mutuáli the next morning. Going in the opposite direction (ie: Gurué–Nampula), trucks leave very early in the morning from Gurué (01.00–02.00) so that they can connect with the train as it passes through Mutuáli at around 07.00 en route to Nampula.

Where to stay and eat
The Austrian-run **Pensão Gurué** (tel: 91 0050; email: construart.pp@ teledata.mz) has self-contained rooms with running water from US$14, and you can camp for US$4 per tent. Indeed, the owner of the Pensão Gurué is taking great strides to improve tourist facilities at Gurué, and this is the best place for up-to-date tourist information about what's going on in Gurué during your visit. Internet access is also available at the pensão. There are one or two more basic pensãos in town, including the **Complexo Sanzala**, the **Pensão Namuli** and the **Pensão Monte Verde**. If you're travelling in a group, you might consider renting a house such as the one owned by the BCM that is used to accommodate visiting employees. Enquire at the bank for details.

The best food in Gurué is probably served at the **Pensão Gurué**. Meals cost between US$3–4, and there are dishes for vegetarians. The nicest location, meanwhile, is that at the **Restaurante La Brisa**, which is in a garden. There is a **Tanzanian-run snack bar** on the main square, which serves popcorn and ice-cream, as well as one or two other largely unexceptional restaurants and bars in town. The weekend discotheque is held at the **Café Domino**.

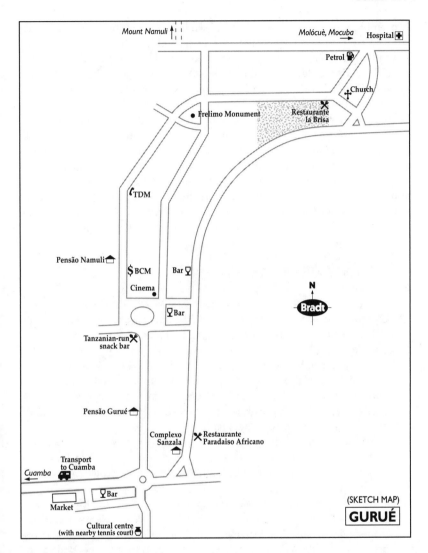

Mount Namuli

Molócuè, Mocuba

Hospital

Petrol

Church

Frelimo Monument

Restaurante la Brisa

TDM

Pensão Namuli

BCM

Bar

Cinema

Bar

N

Bradt

Tanzanian-run snack bar

Pensão Gurué

Complexo Sanzala

Restaurante Paradaiso Africano

Transport to Cuamba

Cuamba

Bar

Market

(SKETCH MAP)

GURUÉ

Cultural centre (with nearby tennis court)

Activities

There are occasionally **concerts** at the Cultural Centre just to the left of the road to Cuamba, while the ex-pat community in Gurué has constructed a **tennis court** next door to while away the time. This is strictly speaking a private facility, although you might be able to use it if you can find the correct person to ask.

The Gurué area is promising **walking** country. The sizeable town centre sprawls along the higher contours of a small hill offering great views up to Mount Namuli and down to a wood-lined dam. Several roads lead out of town among the tea plantations and to the footslopes of Namuli, where there are still a few well-maintained estate properties. As is the case elsewhere in

Mozambique, a degree of caution is advised before attempting any serious off-road walking – mines may well remain a risk, and you should certainly check out the situation before attempting to ascend the slopes of the mountain. One good day walk would be to follow the road to Alto Molócuè out of town for roughly 5km, where there is a large, isolated and apparently abandoned old church standing on a hill.

It takes only about one hour to reach the summit of Mount Namuli. However, those contemplating this trip should budget on it taking three days: one to walk to the foot of the mountain via Muresse (5–6 hours from Gurué); one to climb up and down the mountain; and another to walk back to Gurué. The Pensão Gurué has a small hut at the foot of the mountain where you can camp, and can also provide guides and porters. Note that before attempting to climb Mount Namuli you should contact the local chief (*regulo*) for instructions about routes, the weather and other factors that might have a bearing on your trip.

A GOOD EXPERIENCE

Dave Armstrong

We're forever hearing (in many cases validly) about corrupt police, extortion and robbery. However, we had a pleasant experience at one of Mozambique's many roadblocks. Our clutch had been deteriorating for a few days and, as the policeman waved us on, the vehicle stalled for the umpteenth time. We got out to push it to the roadside and the policeman strolled over. We explained the problem and lifted the bonnet. He glanced casually into the engine and immediately spotted where our clutch fluid was leaking. It looked very serious but he said he had a 'friend' who could help us.

This was where we expected the 'but it will cost you millions of meticais', but it never came. He reached into his pocket for a cellphone, dialled, spoke briefly, and told us someone would be with us shortly.

About 20 minutes later a battered car turned up containing two guys (one very drunk) and two small boys. The younger of the two guys (sober) didn't speak English but the policeman showed him the problem. He said via the policeman that he could fix it but needed to get a spare part. He demanded the equivalent of US$125. We had no alternative but to hand over the cash and off he went, leaving his drunken partner and two kids as collateral. Half an hour later he returned with the part, a receipt and change; then spent a further thirty minutes fitting the part. When he'd finished, the vehicle started and the clutch worked perfectly. He asked for nothing in payment but we happily gave him US$50 as without his help our trip would have come to an abrupt end. As for the policeman – he refused to take any payment, saying he was pleased he had been able to help. We managed to persuade him to take a couple of T-shirts as a thank-you.

Niassa Province

Sometimes referred to as the Siberia of Mozambique, Niassa
is the country's driest and least densely populated province,
but also one of its most scenic and climatically pleasant.
The western border of the province is dominated
by Africa's third-largest body of water, the 585km-
long Lake Malawi, still called by its colonial name, Lago
Niassa in Mozambique, and by the wild, brachystegia-
covered mountains that form the eastern escarpment of
the Great Rift Valley.

Although few travellers currently explore Niassa,
the province is the main gateway into Mozambique for
people coming from Malawi, with border crossings by
rail between Liwonde and Cuamba, by road between
Mangochi and Mandimba, and by boat between Likoma and Cóbuè. The rail
crossing in the south of the province is the one currently favoured by most
travellers, many of whom then take a train straight out of Niassa to
Nampula. However, as more people become aware of the road and boat
crossings further north in the province, and facilities on the lake shore
improve, Niassa may yet realise its enormous potential for relatively off-the-
beaten-track exploration.

Oddly, Niassa is more accessible from neighbouring Malawi than it is from
other parts of Mozambique. There are only two access roads to Niassa from
elsewhere in Mozambique. The reasonably well maintained 310km
unsurfaced road between Cuamba and Lichinga, the provincial capital, is the
more accessible route, covered by several *chapas* and buses daily. The rough
750km road between Pemba and Lichinga via Montepuez and Marrupa is only
suitable for self-sufficient 4WD drivers, though it could make for an exciting
hitching trip for patient backpackers.

CUAMBA

Cuamba is an important route focus, lying at the junction of the railway line
between Malawi and the coast of Mozambique, and the main roads north
through Niassa and south via Gurué to Quelimane. Considering that it is
currently many people's introduction to Mozambique, Cuamba is a pretty
humdrum sort of place; a dully uniform grid of flame-tree lined avenidas
salvaged from complete anonymity by the granite hills that surround it. In

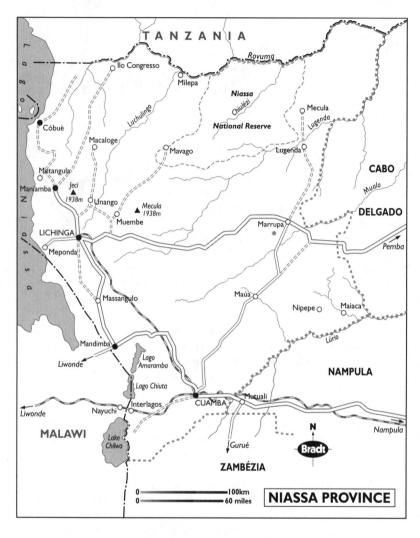

TANZANIA

Rovuma

Ilo Congresso

Milepa

Niassa
Chiulézi

National Reserve

Cóbuè

Macaloge

Mavago

Mecula

Lugenda

Lugenda

CABO

Métangula

Jeci
1938m

Manjamba

Unango

Mecula
1938m

Muembe

Muolo

DELGADO

Marrupa

LICHINGA

Meponda

Pemba

Massangulo

Maúa

Nipepe

Maiaca

Mandimba

Lúrio

Liwonde

Lago
Amaramba

Lago Chiuta

NAMPULA

Liwonde

Nayuchi

Interlagos

CUAMBA

Mutuali

Nampula

MALAWI

Lake
Chilwa

Gurué

N

Bradt

ZAMBÉZIA

0 ———— 100km
0 ———— 60 miles

NIASSA PROVINCE

its favour, Cuamba is a relatively young and hip town due to the presence
of some 150 students who study at the agricultural college based there, and
as a result there are more bars than you would expect in a town of such a
size. Another notable feature of the town is that it has its own electricity
supply, derived from a hydro-electric scheme established in 1988 with
Norwegian aid.

Getting there and away

Many travellers enter Mozambique from Malawi using the rail service
between Liwonde and Cuamba. A train leaves Cuamba on Mondays,
Wednesdays and Fridays at 04.30 for the border town of Interlagos. The
journey takes roughly six hours.

A daily passenger train also operates between Cuamba and Nampula. In either direction, the train leaves at around 06.00, takes about eight hours and costs less than US$3. The seats are reasonably comfortable and the service isn't prohibitively crowded. That said, it's advisable to buy a ticket a day in advance and to arrive at the station at around 05.00 to be certain of getting a seat.

Minibuses leave for Mandimba and Lichinga early in the morning from the opposite side of the railway track to the town centre. Be there at around 05.00 to be sure of getting the quickest transport. You can still reach these destinations later in the day, although you'll have to rough it on the back of a truck or in a *chapa*. If the train from Nampula arrives on schedule at around 14.00, there should be some buses waiting outside the railway station to take arriving train passengers on to Lichinga. The 310km trip between Cuamba and Lichinga takes about six to eight hours in a bus, a bit longer in a truck or *chapa*.

By public transport, Gurué is best reached by a combination of train and *chapa* (see *Gurué: Getting there and away* on page 196). If you have your own transport and are not travelling during the rainy season, there is a short cut to Gurué, which crosses the River Lúrio and takes only two hours.

People who are driving their own vehicle between Cuamba and Nampula might think about using the route through Gurué and Alto Molócuè – it's a longer road, but much more scenic. Otherwise, most of the unsurfaced road between Cuamba and Nampula is well maintained, the only bad stretch being that around the town of Lúrio.

Where to stay

While Cuamba's charms are somewhat debatable, there's no denying that the town's accommodation in generally very good value. The possible exception is the **Hotel Vision 2000** (tel: 62632; fax: 62713; email: h-vision2000@teledata.mz) on the eastern side of town, the place where most of the business travellers, aid workers and tourists who visit Cuamba tend to end up. Even the cheapest rooms with fan and private bathroom seem overpriced at US$30, although maybe the lack of running water and the power cut in the middle of the hot, humid night that I was there were exceptional. On the plus side, this is a good place to meet other travellers and to find lifts to Lichinga and Malawi. The restaurant isn't bad either. To be fair, the Vision 2000 also owns the adjacent **Residencial Formosa**, which is aimed more at travellers on a tight budget. Singles here are US$7.50 and doubles US$15. Next to the Vision 2000 – and probably its main competition – is the considerably more economical **Pensão São Miguel**, where singles and doubles start at US$9 and go up to US$11.50 for rooms with a fan, TV and private bathroom. Also very cheap – albeit a little more basic than the São Miguel – is the clean and friendly **Pensão Namaacha** on the main square, where you can get a double for only US$5. The balcony overlooking the square is also a good place to while away the afternoons and evenings. Elsewhere, the **Pensão Cariacó** has doubles with

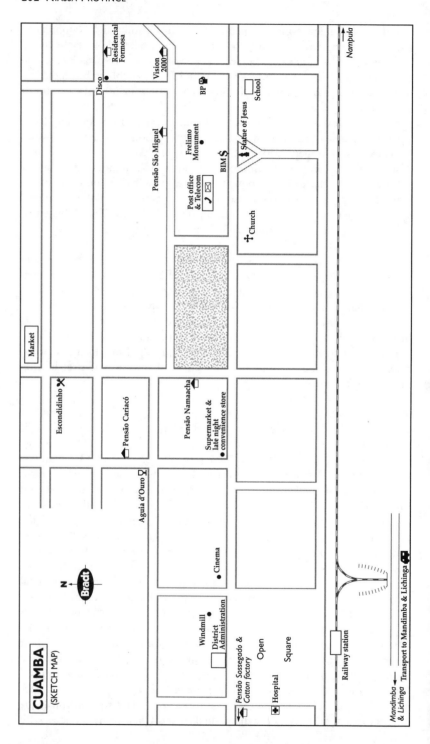

mosquito net from US$7, and the **Pensão Sossegado** opposite the cotton factory is presumably the preferred lodging of the factory's visiting employees. Basic rooms start at US$5.

Where to eat

The restaurant at the **Hotel Vision 2000** has a small selection of dishes, which come in generous portions, while the **Restaurante São Miguel** has the standard fare and a small bakery selling fresh bread. At the time of writing, the 'in' place with Cuamba's movers and shakers (ie: the students) was the **Aguia d'Ouro**, a bar-restaurant with fluorescent lighting and loud music. Perhaps more a place for a cocktail and a game of pool than a quiet meal, the restaurant does serve some decent snacks, as well as all of the usual dishes. Likewise, the bar at the **Restaurante Escondidinho** seems to be more promising than the restaurant itself.

There is a good supermarket near the main square. After the main shop has closed, the adjoining convenience store stays open until late in the evening.

Useful information

The main **bank** in Cuamba is the BIM opposite the statue of Jesus on the eastern side of town. You can get advances on your Visa credit card, and there is also an ATM machine.

Note There is a disused airstrip on the other side of the railway track from the town centre. While you can walk freely up and down the runway, you should not turn off it to inspect the apparently deserted control tower and aeroplane hangar. This is, in fact, an army barracks, and you risk arrest, three hours of futile questioning by hard-nosed military men, another three hours of questioning by the police, confiscation of your passport, and a subsequent 'fine' to get it back, should you choose to wander about in this area. Heed this advice, for I write it from personal experience!

MANDIMBA

Situated on the Malawi border almost exactly halfway between Cuamba and Lichinga, Mandimba is notable mostly for being the best place to cross between Malawi and Mozambique by road (see *Getting to Mozambique* on page 56). In other respects, it is a thoroughly nondescript town, sprawling messily along the main road for a kilometre or so. Mandimba's one saving grace is the unusually cheap and pleasant resthouse, the **Pensão Massinga**, just after the pyramid on the right coming from Cuamba, where double rooms cost under US$10 and the generally good restaurant serves some of the best *chambo* (lake fish) in Mozambique. The **Bar Ngame** also has rooms, although they are more expensive than those at the **Pensão Massinga**. There is good birdwatching about 5km out of Mandimba.

Buses travelling in either direction between Cuamba and Lichinga generally stop at the market in Mandimba between 09.00 and 10.00. Should you arrive in Mandimba from Malawi between 10.00 and 14.00, you will still stand a good chance of catching a lift in either direction on the back of a truck. If you arrive later than that, expect to spend the night in Mandimba.

MASSANGULO

This atmospheric small town lies about 2km off the main Cuamba–Lichinga road, roughly 65km north of Mandimba. Situated at the base of a pretty mountain, and dominated by an extraordinary mission church, Massangulo could be an attractive place to spend a couple of nights, particularly if you like walking. The **Yaileka Resthouse** behind the market has cheap if rather basic rooms. Most vehicles heading between Cuamba and Lichinga don't divert to Massangulo, but you can ask to be dropped at the signposted turn-off and walk from there – it shouldn't take longer than 30 minutes.

LICHINGA

Formerly known as Vila Cabral, Lichinga is the capital of Niassa and the main gateway to the Mozambican shore of Lago Niassa. Lichinga lies at an altitude of 1,277m on the plateau to the east of the lake, giving it a refreshingly breezy climate. Fringed by the unusual combination of exotic pine plantations and more characteristically tropical vegetation such as mango trees and leafy plantains, Lichinga has a markedly different atmosphere to any other of the large towns in Mozambique. Indeed, without being spectacular in any way, Lichinga has a seductive atmosphere that might end up enticing you to stay slightly longer than you had planned.

Getting there and away
By air

You can fly between Lichinga and Maputo with LAM on most days of the week, although these flights go via either Tete or Nampula and Beira. The LAM booking office is not far from the Praça do Liberados, while the spanking-new airport opened in September 2001 is about 7km from the town centre along the road to Metangula. You should have no problem hitching – indeed you might not have a choice.

By road

The unsurfaced road between Cuamba and Lichinga is generally in good condition. Minibuses to Mandimba and Cuamba depart at around 05.00, as does the bulk of the other transport leaving Lichinga (eg: *chapas* to Meponda and Metangula, and trucks to various towns around the Niassa National Reserve). If you arrive later in the day, you might have a long wait before you find transport going your way – and I didn't find hitching along the Metangula road particularly rewarding. Buses, *chapas* and trucks leave from in front of the central market.

Where to stay

The best accommodation in Lichinga has been the **Quinta Capricornio** (tel: 20159; email: quintakate@hotmail.com), about 800m through the pine

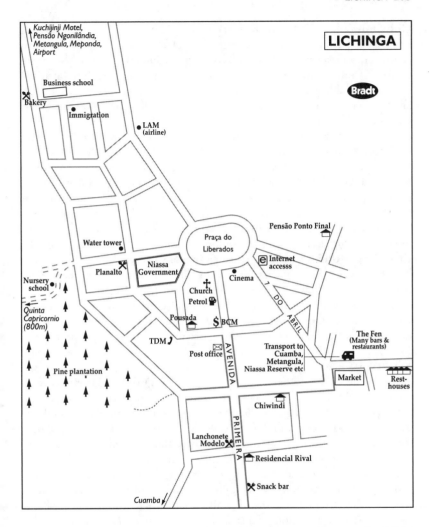

Kuchijinji Motel,
Pensão Ngonilândia,
Metangula, Meponda,
Airport

Business school

Bakery

Immigration

LAM
(airline)

LICHINGA

Bradt

Pensão Ponto Final

Water tower

Praça do
Liberados

Internet
accesss

Planalto

Niassa
Government

Cinema

Nursery
school

Church

Petrol

Quinta
Capricornio
(800m)

Pousada

BCM

TDM

The Fen
(Many bars &
restaurants)

Post office

Transport to
Cuamba,
Metangula,
Niassa Reserve etc

Pine plantation

AVENIDA

1 DO ABRIL

Market

Rest-
houses

Chiwindi

Lanchonete
Modelo

PRIMEIRA

Residencial Rival

Snack bar

Cuamba

plantation on the western edge of town (see *Making mountains out of molehills,*
page 71). At the time of writing we've just heard that it's closed, we hope
only temporarily. Otherwise there are two well-equipped chalets sleeping up
to four people, with another, larger, house under construction. The
communal ablution block has hot running water, and you can camp in the
farm's quiet, pine-scented grounds. If all of this whets the appetite, the
prices will have you foaming at the mouth with anticipation: US$10 per
person for bed and breakfast and US$3 to camp (tents can be borrowed if
you leave a deposit). This is certainly one of the not-to-be-missed
accommodation options in Mozambique, and it is essential to book ahead if
you want to be sure of getting a chalet. Elsewhere in town, the
accommodation has radically improved over the past five years or so. For
instance, recent renovations and a decrease in prices has done the **Hotel**

Chiwindi (tel: 20920) near the market absolutely no harm at all. In fact, it has changed from the worst- to the best-value place to stay in the town centre almost overnight. Clean and comfortable singles start at US$5, going up to US$8 if you want a private bathroom. The nearby **Residencial Rival** is also reasonable value, with self-contained singles and doubles for US$7.50 and US$9 respectively. The bucket showers allegedly come with hot water, which is no trivial thing on Lichinga's occasionally chilly nights. There are one or two other options next to the market, including the friendly, family-run **Rest House Will Senjewe** (tel: 20034) with basic singles for a mere US$3, and the similar **Rest House Anexo** next door. The **Pensão Ponto Final** (tel: 20912) in a side street not far from the Praça do Liberados is a popular place, with clean, self-contained, motel-style double rooms for US$15. A little further from the centre on the road to Metangula is the labyrinthine **Pensão Ngonilândia**, with its US$5 rooms all joined by interconnecting doors with the communal bathroom in the middle, and the **Kuchijinji Motel** (tel: 20336) a further 4km or so down the road, which has doubles in smart little houses for US$13. There is also a conference centre here, but no restaurant or other facilities.

The Pousada Lichinga, at one time the only place to stay in town, was closed for renovation at the time of writing; and the large building site next door will eventually be an upmarket hotel. When, exactly, is a matter for conjecture.

Where to eat

As with the accommodation, the food at the **Quinta Capricornio** is without doubt the best to be had in Lichinga. This is perhaps not surprising since virtually all of the ingredients come from the farm itself. The basic principal is that 'if you can see it walking around, you can eat it', which means that you can order goat, chicken, beef and even rabbit dishes, all of which come in huge portions. The farm also makes its own smoked sausage, jams, canned stews and soups, and these are for sale. In town, you should head for the Fen (the Lichinga equivalent of the Feira Popular in Maputo) directly opposite the central market, where you'll find probably the highest concentration of restaurants in northern Mozambique. The jewel in the Fen's crown is the **Restaurante Chambo**, where you can hobnob with local dignitaries and enjoy the fullest menu, the best service (and the cleanest toilets) of any restaurant in the town centre. While the Chambo is the most upmarket establishment in the Fen, there are many other places offering tasty, perfectly hygienic food for around US$2 per dish. Some places don't have food but are open to drinkers until the early hours of the morning. Elsewhere in town, there are one or two relatively uninspiring snack bars, such as the very central **Restaurante Café Planalto** and the **Snack Bar Residencial Rival** next to the hotel of the same name. Roughly opposite the Residencial Rival, the **Lanchonete Modelo** sells fresh bread, although Lichinga's best bakery is perhaps that opposite the business school on the road to Metangula, where you can get bread, croissants and assorted buns.

Useful information
Internet access is available at the public library just off the Praça do Liberados from 12.30–13.30 and 17.30–19.00. It costs US$1 for 15 minutes, and there is only one computer.

Lichinga has long had the reputation of being the best place in Mozambique to change US dollars in cash into meticais, and I suppose that the rate is ever so slightly better than elsewhere – although you'd have to change an awful lot of dollars for it to make a real difference. The best **bank** to change cash and travellers' cheques is the typically chaotic BCM on Avenida Primeira. Note that travellers' cheque transactions incur the usual US$15 commission.

It is possible to **rent 4WD vehicles** in Lichinga for around US$100 a day. Enquire at the Quinta Capricornio for more details.

LAGO NIASSA (LAKE MALAWI)
Lake Malawi is the third-largest lake in Africa, measuring 585km from north to south and up to 100km from east to west. The bulk of it lies in Malawi itself, but large stretches of the eastern shore are territorially part of Mozambique and Tanzania. During colonial times, Lake Malawi was known as Lake Nyasa and Malawi was called Nyasaland. For some reason this colonial name has remained unchanged in Tanzania and Mozambique, where the lake is still known respectively as Lake Nyasa and Lago Niassa.

Lago Niassa is a remarkable body of water, lying at the southern end of the Rift Valley system, an immense geological scar that cuts through Africa all the way from the Red Sea in the north. Much of the lake is hemmed in by the dramatically mountainous Rift Valley escarpment, which in places towers more than 1km above its waters. Its thrillingly clear water probably protects a greater variety of fish than any other lake in the world. At least 500 fish species have been recorded – a greater tally of freshwater species than for the whole of Europe and North America – and it is thought that a similar number of species still await formal scientific discovery. Lake Malawi is particularly notable for its amazing variety of cichlids, a group of highly colourful fish that look after their offspring by holding them in their mouths until they are large enough to fend for themselves.

For people who are visiting Mozambique as part of a longer trip through Africa, the Mozambican stretch of the lake offers little that cannot be done more easily and cheaply in the better developed Malawian sector. The attraction of this part of the lake is that it is still really off the beaten track, so that there remains a genuine sense of exploration attached to visiting it. Another feature of the eastern lake shore is that, because it faces west, it is the best place to see the dramatic sunsets for which the lake is famous.

There are three points of access to Lago Niassa. Meponda lies almost directly east of Lichinga along a good 65km road, so is the easiest place to get to from the provincial capital. Metangula has better facilities than Meponda but is roughly 120km from Lichinga. Cóbuè is another 80km north of Metangula, and of note mostly as the best place to cross between Malawi and Mozambique over the lake.

The more adventurous traveller might be interested to know that there are walking paths between Meponda, Metangula and Cóbuè. The stretch from Meponda to Metangula, for instance, will take about three days for a good walker, who should carry enough food and water to last the whole trip. Note that these sandy paths are not particularly suitable for bicycles.

The best and quickest way of travelling along the Mozambican shore of Lago Niassa is by the Malawian ferry, which does a circuit of the lake twice a week. On Saturday mornings it arrives in Metangula from Nkhotakota on the Malawian side of the lake, from where it continues on to Cóbuè, the Likoma Islands and finally Nkhata Bay back on the Malawian side. On Tuesdays it does the same trip in reverse, arriving in Metangula in the early afternoon. The immigration office in Metangula sends people to meet the boat, so those arriving from Malawi can get their passports stamped. Otherwise, this formality can be done at the immigration office in Lichinga.

Meponda

This is the closest lakeshore settlement to Lichinga. Little more than a glorified village with a few mostly derelict concrete buildings, Meponda lies on an attractive sandy beach that arcs for a kilometre or more below low wooded hills. At present there is no formal accommodation at Meponda, although rumours of the imminent construction of a lodge have been persisting for some time. For now, there would be nothing stopping you from camping on the beach or, if you don't have a tent, from sleeping under one of the open-sided reed shelters in the beachfront salão de chá, which also serves beers, sodas and basic meals such as fish and chips or chicken and rice.

To get to Meponda, follow the Metangula road out of Lichinga for about 5km until you reach the signposted turn-off, from where it's 60km to Meponda. The descent to the lake passes through tall brachystegia woodland and several small villages where you will see several examples of the distinctive huts and raised grain stores that are characteristic of Niassa. Public transport to Meponda leaves from the market in Lichinga. The trip takes about two hours.

Metangula

The largest settlement on the Mozambican shore of Lago Niassa (which isn't saying a great deal), Metangula was formerly the main slave terminus on the eastern side of the lake, the counterpart to the slaving emporium of Nkhotakota in Malawi. Today, Metangula is rather an out-of-the-way place, consisting of a small town centre with a few shops and a run-down pensão. More attractive than staying in Metangula itself would be to head 8km along the lake shore to Chiwanga, where there is a beach resort called the **Centro Turistico Cetuka** (tel: 34000) with a few reed huts on the beach for US$9/double (ask for the one with the window that opens on to the lake), as well as a bar, and a restaurant that sometimes has *chambo*.

There is a good 90km road from Lichinga as far as Maniamba, then a rougher 28km road to Metangula; a 4WD vehicle is required. To find a truck heading this way, go to the market in Lichinga, preferably before 05.00. You will probably have to walk the 8km from Metangula to Chiwanga.

Cóbuè

The small town of Cóbuè lies on a beautiful part of the Lago Niassa shore, roughly 80km north of Metangula and facing Likoma Island, a Malawian territory surrounded by Mozambican waters. There is a place to stay at Cóbuè called the **Hotel Santo Miguel**, with rooms for around US$10.

About 10km south of Cóbuè, on the shores of the lake, the secluded and low-impact **Nkwichi Lodge** (tel: 0088 16 315 73694; email: info@mandawilderness.org; web: www.mandawilderness.org) lies in an idyllic spot. It has just seven chalets, built of local wood, stone and grass thatch, tucked among the trees that fringe the lake's sandy shore.

As well as swimming, snorkelling, boating and exploring, you've the chance to visit farms and friendly local communities. The Manda Wilderness Community Trust (a registered UK charity) works closely with Nkwichi to ensure that the local people benefit from the growth of responsible tourism in their area. Numerous projects (the building of wells and schools, agriculture, horticulture...) have been undertaken.

The Trust also manages the Manda Wilderness Game Reserve, which was set up to protect and manage a 100,000ha community reserve on the shores of the lake. In 2005, Manda was a finalist in the Conservation section of the World Travel and Tourism Council 'Tourism for Tomorrow' awards.

By staying at the lodge, guests contribute to environmental conservation and community development. A stay provides wages for up to 50 local members of staff. Their salaries support up to 15 members of each one's direct families. Thus by coming to the lodge you can touch the lives of as many as 750 local people.

The 2006 rates start from US$160 per person sharing ($210 single) for full board, and increase in peak seasons.

Coming from the south, there are infrequent trucks between Metangula and Cóbuè, but the more comfortable mode of transport is by fishing dhow. If all goes well and the winds are favourable, the journey should take around eight hours at a cost of about US$2. Coming from Likoma Island in Malawi, dhows formally act as public transport to Cóbuè, taking about an hour to make the 10km crossing.

It is permitted to visit Cóbuè from Likoma for up to 24 hours without a Mozambican visa, but a visa *is* required for a longer stay, or if you plan to travel further afield in Mozambique. At the time of writing, visas must be obtained in advance (this can be arranged at the high commission in Lilongwe or the consulate in Blantyre).

NIASSA NATIONAL RESERVE

Although it remains a trip for the adventurous and hardy traveller, a visit to the Niassa National Reserve is considerably less problematic than it was a few years ago. Nowadays, there are places to stay at all three of the 'buffer zones' around the reserve – Mavago District, Unango District and Cóbuè town –

and you can hire guides to take you to the places where you are most likely to see animals. These animals typically include monkeys, baboons, jackals, warthogs, buffaloes, wild dogs and various types of antelope. On a good day, you might also see elephants, hyenas and lions. Note that the chances of seeing animals are probably higher in the buffer zones than they are at the official entrance to the reserve at Mecula, where the level of human traffic, although by no means high, is more substantial than in the buffer zones. By the same token, also note that the animals that you'll see in Niassa are not as used to humans as those at the region's more developed national parks and are therefore potentially much more dangerous than they could be.

Where to stay

Located in a 4,000km² private concession in Luwire, the Lugenda Bush Camp is due to open in 2006 so we can't give first-hand details here. It's in the Lugenda Wildlife Reserve (www.luwire.com), a reserve of around 7500km² along the east bank of the Lugenda River bordering the Niassa Reserve. With just four luxury East-African-style tents tucked into the vegetation along the river bank, the focus in this remote and exclusive destination will be on personalised service and game drives. Its own airstrip will provide fly-in access from Pemba. Rates will start from US$379 per person sharing (US$549 single) in the low season, including full board, air transfer to/from Pemba and scheduled safari activities. The camp is run by Rani Resorts (tel: +27 11 467 1277; email: reservations@raniresorts.com; web: www.raniresorts.com).

Other than at Cóbuè (see page 209), the remaining accommodation in the buffer zones consists of camping, which normally costs US$10. You can rent tents at the Quinta Capricornio in Lichinga for US$2 per day plus a US$10 deposit. There is a small resthouse in Mavago which has basic rooms for US$3. For more information about the other accommodation and safari options available at Mavago, contact wilderniass@teledata.mz or call the following satellite phone number: 00 881 631 418 423. Guides also cost US$10 per day; their food is extra.

Getting to Cóbuè has been covered on page 209. There are decent enough roads to Mavago (via Muembe, where there is a good restaurant) and Unango (which leads eventually to Macaloge). Trucks plying these routes leave from in front of the market in Lichinga, although their frequency is, to say the least, unpredictable.

South of the Niassa National Reserve, on the road from Cuamba to Marrupa, the mission at Maúa and the even more remote mission at Nipepe both have beautiful churches decorated in traditional style. The Marrupa area is reportedly rich in game, and for some years there has been tentative talk of running safaris into the area . Maiaca, near the border with Nampula Province, is another good location for spotting wild animals, principally elephant, buck and hyena. Camping is possible by the river, a subsidiary of the Lúrio.

Nampula Province

Bounded by the rivers Lúrio to the north and Ligonha to the south, the province of Nampula is comprised largely of open savannah broken up by any number of isolated and imposing rocky outcrops, mesas and plateaux. The provincial capital, also called Nampula, is the largest and most prosperous city in northern Mozambique, and an important route focus – it would be practially impossible to travel through northern Mozambique *without* stopping over in Nampula at least once.

Historically, the most important town in Nampula Province is Ilha do Moçambique (Mozambique Island), which was the Portuguese capital in East Africa for almost four centuries prior to 1898, when it was superseded by Lourenço Marques. For those with a historical bent, Ilha do Moçambique is without doubt the most alluring travel destination in Nampula, if not in the whole of Mozambique: an absorbing and atmospheric warren of dense alleys and beautiful colonial buildings, many of which date to the earliest years of the Portuguese occupation.

Nampula boasts few other tourist attractions. The rocky outcrops that dominate the landscape reputedly offer some of the best free-face rock climbing in southern Africa, but pending further tourist development, this is of academic interest to anybody but experienced and fully equipped rock climbers. The Indian Ocean port of Nacala, roughly 100km north of Ilha do Moçambique, has largely superseded the older port in economic terms but it is of limited interest to visitors – the nearby beach at Fernão Velosa is highly rated by snorkellers. Also of interest is the ancient Muslim port of Angoche, situated on one of the finest beaches in the country and boasting a small turn-of-the-century 'old town'.

NAMPULA

Nampula is the commercial heart of northern Mozambique, a relatively lively and prosperous city with good shops and reasonable facilities for visitors. An important transport hub, Nampula is likely to be visited at some point by most people who travel through northern Mozambique. Otherwise, it is of limited interest to visitors – a southern African everytown, which, the linguistic

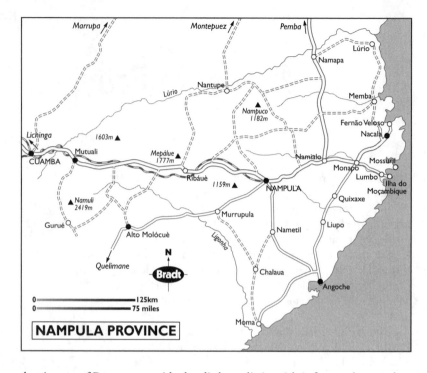

NAMPULA PROVINCE

dominance of Portuguese aside, has little to distinguish it from a dozen other similarly sized towns in Zimbabwe or Malawi.

Getting there and away
By air
LAM has flights linking Nampula and Beira on every day of the week. On most of these days, the plane stops in Beira, while Nampula is also connected to Quelimane, Lichinga and Pemba by air. The LAM booking office (tel: 21 2801) is in the town centre, while the airport is about 4km out of town and about 1km off the road to Nacala. There are no taxis, but you should be able to hitch or get a ride into town for around US$2.

By road
Nampula is connected by a surfaced road to Pemba, Nacala and Ilha do Moçambique. The stretch between Nampula and Namialo, the turn-off for Pemba, is in a sorry state, and the 87km will take you about two hours. The road north to Pemba, on the other hand, is in excellent condition, and you can quite easily cruise along it at 100kmph. The remainder of the road to Nacala is only slightly better than the Nampula–Namialo stretch, while the road to Ilha do Moçambique once you get past Monapo is fine. The route that runs more or less parallel to the railway line from Nampula to Cuamba is unsurfaced but in good condition, except for the stretch around the town of Lúrio where 4WD will definitely be required. 4WD is also recommended if

Above The hills outside Gurue, with Mount Numuli in the background

Below Children in reed homesteads

Above Fishermen at Vilankulo

Below Dhows near the ferry at Maxixe,
where boats are boarded for Inhambane

you want to drive between Nampula and Quelimane, although the 100km of the road closest to Nampula has been resurfaced.

By public transport

The best option for backpackers who are heading to Nampula from Niassa Province or Malawi is the recently installed daily rail service between Cuamba and Nampula. Trains leave in either direction at about 06.00 and take roughly eight hours. The seats are comfortable, though you risk having to stand for at least part of the way if you don't arrive at the station an hour or so before the train departs. Tickets cost less than US$3 for the whole trip. The alternative to the trains is to go by road via Gurué – an interesting and scenic trip covered more fully on page 196.

There is plenty of transport between Nampula and Pemba, Nacala and Ilha do Moçambique. The best option to Pemba is the daily Transnorte bus, which leaves in either direction at 04.00 sharp. There is also a daily bus to Nacala, leaving at the same time. All *chapas* and buses between Nampula and Pemba, Nacala or Ilha do Moçambique leave from and arrive in Nampula at the junction of Avenida Paulo Samuel Kamkama and Avenida de Trabalho. If all goes well, the bus journey to Pemba should take around eight hours, while the trips to Ilha do Moçambique and Nacala are more like four hours.

There is at least one bus daily in either direction between Nampula and Quelimane. Buses heading to Quelimane generally stop overnight at Mocuba and buses heading to Nampula stop overnight at Molócuè. It is also possible to do this trip in hops using the regular *chapas* that connect Nampula to Molócuè and Mocuba, and Mocuba to Quelimane. Most transport along this road, including the bus, leaves Nampula at around 05.00. The best place to wait for vehicles is at a stop situated, with the obliqueness that seems to be characteristic of Mozambicans where public transport is concerned, about 20–30 minutes' walk from the railway station and town centre along the Quelimane road. In other words, to be sure of getting a seat on the bus to Quelimane you need to be out of your hotel room by 04.15 at the latest.

Where to stay

Perhaps as vindication of its status as the commercial hub of northern Mozambique, Nampula has accommodation to suit all budgets. Top of the pile is the **Hotel Tropical** (tel: 21 2232; fax: 21 6359), which has cornered the international market (hence the flags outside). Comfortable, air-conditioned rooms with television and hot water cost US$55/single and US$80/double, which includes breakfast. The **Hotel Lúrio** (tel: 21 7528), just round the corner from the Tropical, is run-down and overpriced by comparison. Prices start at US$25/single and US$40/double for self-contained rooms with just a fan. There is a television room on the first floor which, with its sombre, 1950s-style, plastic-covered armchairs, reminded me of an old people's home.

The remaining accommodation options in Nampula are all pensãos. However, while in most Mozambican towns you can generally count on anything described as a 'pensão' not being too expensive, this isn't necessarily so

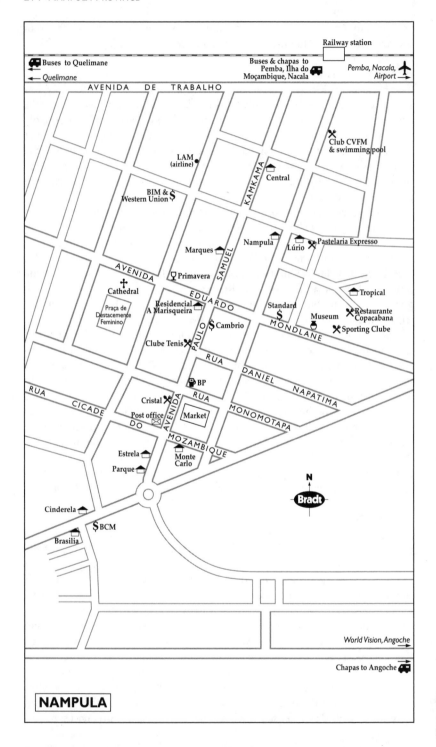

Railway station

Buses to Quelimane

← Quelimane

Buses & chapas to
Pemba, Ilha do
Moçambique, Nacala

Pemba, Nacala,
Airport →

AVENIDA   DE   TRABALHO

Club CVFM
& swimming pool

LAM
(airline)

KAMKAMA

Central

BIM &
Western Union

Nampula

Lúrio

Pastelaria Expresso

Marques

SAMUEL

Primavera

AVENIDA

Cathedral

Tropical

Praça de
Destacemente
Feminino

EDUARDO

Residencial
A Marisqueira

Standard

Museum

Restaurante
Copacabana

Cambrio

PAULO

MONDLANE

Sporting Clube

Clube Tenis

RUA

DANIEL

NAPATIMA

BP

RUA

Cristal

MONOMOTAPA

RUA

CICADE

Post office

AVENIDA

Market

DO

Estrela

MOZAMBIQUE

Monte
Carlo

Parque

N

Cinderela

Bradt

BCM

Brasilia

World Vision, Angoche →

Chapas to Angoche

NAMPULA

in Nampula. Working along Avenida Paulo Samuel Kamkama from north to south, the **Pensão Marques** (tel: 21 2527) has air-conditioned rooms with television and running water for US$30. The **Residencial A Marisqueira** (tel: 21 3611) struck me as better value, if only because the rooms, which are otherwise similar to those at the Marques, also have a fridge. Singles are US$17.50 and doubles US$24. The **Pensão Estrela** (tel: 21 4902) also has singles for a reasonable US$15, but they don't have air conditioning. Meanwhile, the **Pensão Brasilia**, just beyond the roundabout at the end of Avenida Paulo Samuel Kamkama, charges a rather exorbitant US$37.50 for more or less what you get at the other upmarket pensãos. Which brings me to the town's budget options. On the face of it, US$10 might seem like a lot to pay for a large, bare room at the **Pensão Cinderela** across the road from the Brasilia, especially since the rooms have no fans and the shared bathroom comes with a bucket shower. Give this place a chance, however, and you'll find that it's clean, friendly and really not that bad value after all. Moreover, if you make a fuss about the fan, they'll find you one from somewhere. The nearby **Pensão Parque** (tel: 21 2307) is similarly priced and has running water. Even cheaper at US$4/single and US$7.50/double – and surprisingly clean and airy for the price – is the **Pensão Central** (tel: 21 2519), a stone's throw from the railway station. The **Residencial Monte Carlo** (tel: 21 2789) opposite the market is considerably worse value for money, with no fans, no private bathrooms and no running water in rooms that cost US$14; while the **Pensão Nampula** is undeniably cheap, undeniably dingy, and best given a very wide berth.

Where to eat

Probably the best place to eat in Nampula, both in terms of choice of food and ambience, is the **Restaurante Copacabana** opposite the Hotel Tropical. The vast menu includes typical Mozambican dishes such as *matapa*, vegetarian meals, pizzas and pasta dishes, none of which is hugely expensive. The restaurant at the **Hotel Tropical** also has a good selection, and you can choose to eat in the air-conditioned dining room or on the cosy terrace outside. Another good choice is the **Clube Tenis**, which has a smart, pleasant outdoor restaurant serving everything from steak and chicken to prawns at reasonable prices; dishes start at around US$5. An attraction for some will be the weekend discotheque. The **Sporting Clube** next to the museum also has several outdoor tables. The menu is more limited than the Clube Tenis, but the food is still very good and relatively inexpensive. The **Club CVFM** has an air-conditioned restaurant, which, although the food is nothing special at around US$5 for most dishes, does offer some relief from the humidity in hot weather. The club's swimming pool has a high diving board and lies in peaceful bougainvillea draped gardens. Entrance to the pool costs US$1.50. The **Pastelaria Expresso** next to the Hotel Lúrio is probably the best place for bread and pastries, although there is nowhere to sit down to eat your purchases. The **Oasis Snack Bar** next to the Pensão Central also sells bread and cakes – as well as popcorn, ice-creams, hamburgers and other fast foods – and does have tables and chairs. The **Bar Primavera** on the corner of Avenida Eduardo

Mondlane close to the cathedral is a small but popular drinking place with a coffee machine and a few tables on the street. There is a small **supermarket** next to the Standard Bank on Avenida Eduardo Mondlane, which has a reasonable selection of imported items and also sells apples and pears.

Useful information

The Banco de Fomento or the private bureau de change, both of which are on Avenida Paulo Samuel Kamkama, are probably your best bets for changing **money**, since the BCM (the only other option for foreign exchange) is not particularly central. Meanwhile, there is a **Western Union** office and an ATM machine, which apparently accepts Visa, at the BIM. There is a posh **pharmacy** (with automatic doors!) next to the Standard Bank on Avenida Eduardo Mondlane.

What to see

The main cluster of older buildings is focused around the Praça de Destacemento Feminino, but of these only the early-20th-century cathedral vaguely warrants a second look. Of greater interest is the Museu Nacional de Etnologia (Tue–Sat 14.00–16.30, Sun 10.00–16.30; donation expected), which has a good ethnographic collection dominated by a number of old musical instruments and some very weird face masks. The Makonde co-operative behind the museum is a good place to see Makonde carvers at work and to buy or (for a small negotiable fee) photograph Makonde masks and carvings. Just outside Nampula lies a large basalt outcrop resembling a profile of a face looking at the sky. Known as 'the old man', local legend has it that this outcrop materialised upon the death of an old king of Monomotapa in 1570.

NAMIALO

The small town of Namialo lies at the junction of the main road between Nampula and Pemba and the turn-off to Nacala and Ilha do Moçambique. Travellers heading between Pemba and either Nacala or Ilha do Moçambique may well choose to spend a night in Namialo, whether they've come from Pemba and feel like a meal and a wash before continuing their travels the next day, or they are heading to Pemba and want to catch the Transnorte bus that leaves from Nampula at 04.00 and passes through Namialo at around 08.00.

If you do spend a night in Namialo, the **Pousada Hotel** on the main road has large, slightly run-down double rooms for a reasonable US$7.50. Remarkably, given that it is an archetypically dusty and unappealing African junction town, Namialo boasts a couple of good restaurants. The **Restaurante Tropical**, the unsignposted green building about two blocks from the Pousada along the main road towards Nampula, serves large, tasty helpings of fish or chicken and chips for around US$4, and it has a fridge stocked high with beers, sodas and imported cartons of fruit juice. The newer restaurant around the corner is apparently even better.

All public transport in and out of Namialo stops at the bus station roughly opposite the Pousada.

MONAPO

Monapo lies 38km east of Namialo and roughly 3km before the roads to Nacala and Ilha do Moçambique part way. Monapo is noted for its cashew factory – it's a good place to buy them cheaply – but there is no obvious reason why you would want to spend a night here, and so far as I'm aware, nowhere to stay if you do.

ILHA DO MOÇAMBIQUE

The town of Moçambique, on the small coral island of the same name, is not only the oldest European settlement in East Africa, but arguably also the most bizarre. Declared a UNESCO Cultural Heritage Site in 1992, Ilha do Moçambique, known to locals simply as Ilha (pronouned *ilia*), must surely rank as northern Mozambique's most alluring travel destination both for its singular atmosphere and for its wealth of beautiful old buildings.

Linked to the mainland by a 1.5km-long single-lane causeway, the crescent-shaped island measures a mere 2.5km from north to south and is at no point more than 600m wide. Despite its small size, the island supports a population of roughly 7,000, and as the most important Portuguese settlement on the East African coast for the best part of four centuries, it boasts several of the oldest extant colonial buildings in the southern hemisphere.

History

Ilha do Moçambique was, like Sofala and Angoche, an important Muslim trading centre even before the Portuguese landed on the east coast of Africa. The island's name is probably derived from that of Moussa Ben Mbiki, said by some to have been the incumbent sheikh when Da Gama first landed there in 1499, and by others to have been the founding father of the island's Muslim settlement.

Prior to the Portuguese occupation, Mozambique Island was renowned as a centre of ship building; in 1502, a Portuguese navigator, Vincente Soares had a boat assembled there. Portugal occupied the island in 1507, two years after it occupied Kilwa and Sofala, and immediately built a hospital, church and small fort. With its long tradition of boat building, and easily defendable position at the junction of the East African coast and the all-important route to India, Mozambique Island soon became the focus of Portuguese naval activities and the most important stopover for Portuguese ships waiting for the monsoon winds. This rapid rise to prominence caused Portugal to abolish the Captaincy of Kilwa in 1513. In 1530, the Captaincy of Sofala was renamed the Captaincy of Moçambique and Sofala, and the island effectively became the capital of Portuguese East Africa, a status it was to retain for close on four centuries.

By the mid-16th century, some 70-odd officials, ranging from a judge and doctor to priests and soliders, were listed on the official payroll of the island. Depending on how many ships were docked at the island, it supported up to 1,000 Portuguese at any one time. Food was in short supply, and although some was imported from the Comoros islands and Madagascar, many provisions were bought through the Muslim traders who

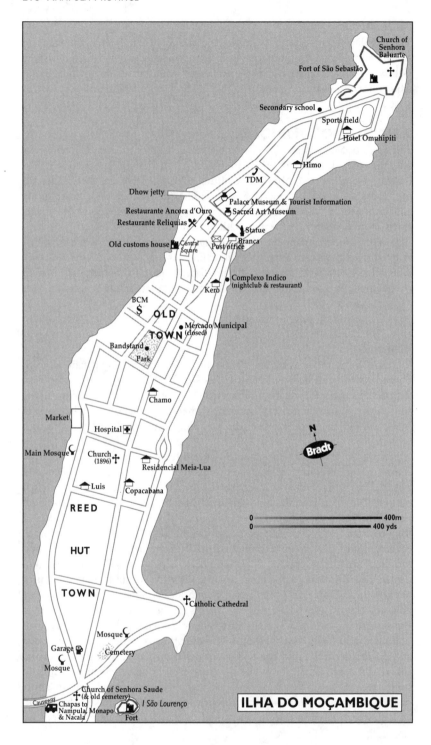

ILHA DO MOÇAMBIQUE

had abandoned the island for Sancul on the facing mainland following the Portuguese occupation.

Mozambique Island was the site of the earliest battle between European powers to take place in Africa, when the Netherlands attempted to seize it as an East African base for the Dutch East India Company in 1607/8. The island was also attacked by Omani Arabs in 1671 and by France in 1793–97. Mozambique Island was the most important port south of Mombasa from the early 16th to late 19th centuries. It probably peaked in prosperity during the 18th century, when it handled some 70% of the ivory exported from the Mozambican coast.

Mozambique Island began a slide into economic decline during the late 19th century. This phenomenon was rooted in two causes: the general southward drift of the economy towards Lourenço Marques and the Portuguese 'discovery' of the far superior natural harbour at nearby Nacala. The declining importance of the island was acknowledged as early as 1898, when it was superseded as national capital by Lourenço Marques, even though it was still handling roughly 20% of the total goods shipped out of Mozambique. As recently as 1928, Mozambique Island was still one of the five largest urban centres in the country, supporting a population of 7,000. However, it was by this time losing even its local economic significance, following the completion of the more modern port at Nacala. In 1935, the reins of local government were moved from the island to the new provincial capital of Nampula.

Ilha do Moçambique may now be something of a backwater, but it is also one of the few old towns in Africa that has by and large kept its historical appearance. Portuguese architecture dominates, though very few buildings on Ilha do Moçambique are in the expansive classical style seen at somewhere like Ibo, most probably due to the small size and dense population of the island. Among the more interesting buildings are the fortress of São Sebastão, the former governor's palace, and the Church of Senhora Saude.

The old town, a maze of narrow alleys lined with fading whitewashed buildings and little changed in shape since the late 18th century, has a mood not unlike that of some of the older Swahili island towns of the Tanzanian and Kenyan coast: Lamu, say, or even more strikingly the old quarter of Mombasa. An unexpected factor, but one that serves only to underline Mozambique's kinship with the rest of the Swahili coast, is the overwhelming Muslim presence. Every historical source that I'm aware of states that the Muslim population was forced to relocate to the mainland during the four centuries when Mozambique Island was the Portuguese centre of operations in East Africa. Probably the Muslims drifted back across to the island after the capital was moved to Maputo in 1898; possibly even more recently, in the wake of what was effectively the Portuguese evacuation of Mozambique in 1975. Whenever and however it occured, the Muslim reoccupation of the old town has created a strong but possibly rather deceptive sense of historical continuity, one which has the effect of reducing four centuries of Portuguese occupation to something of a passing episode.

Getting there and away

There are regular buses between Nampula and Ilha do Moçambique. Going in the opposite direction, you might have to do the trip in stages: Ilha to Monapo to Namialo to Nampula, for instance. To get to Nacala, your best bet is to get off at the junction just before you arrive at Monapo; and for Pemba, you should make your way to the junction at Namialo. Most of the transport out of Ilha do Moçambique leaves between 05.00–07.00 and 10.00–12.00 from next to the causeway.

Where to stay

The old hotel, the Pousada do Moçambique, has been transformed into the four-star **Hotel Omuhipiti** (tel: 61 0101; fax: 61 0105), which opened in May 2001. There is something slightly surreal about staying at such a new and luxurious place, surrounded as you are by so much antiquity. On the other hand, this might just be its greatest attraction. All of the self-contained rooms have hot water, air conditioning and TV, with singles costing US$65 and doubles US$75.

A couple of pleasant new guesthouses are the **Escondidinho** (tel: 610057), which has a pool and rooms from US$30 en suite and US$20 with a shared bathroom; and **Patio de Quintalinhos** (tel: 610090; www.mozambiqueguesthouse.com), near the mosque on the west side of the island, with rooms from US$20 to 35 including continental breakfast.

The rest of the accommodation on Ilha do Moçambique is in private houses. You can locate them by consulting the map on page 218. Rather than deal with each of these places individually, I have chosen to list them below. This is because they are all pretty identical: most have two or three clean rooms, normally with a fan, and access to a bathroom, kitchen facilities and sometimes a communal sitting room.

Mascamolo aka **Casa Dinho** Tel: 61 0107. US$15/single, US$25/double; with air conditioning.
Casa Himo Tel: 61 0673. US$15/single, US$20/double.
Casa Branca Tel: 61 0076. US$10/single, US$20/double.
Residencial Meia-Lua Tel: 61 0163. US$10/single, US$17.50/double.
Casa Chamo Tel: 61 0044. US$10/single, US$15/double; with breakfast.
Casa Kero Tel: 61 0034. US$10/single, US$15/double; with breakfast.
Copacabana US$5 per person.
Casa Luis aka: **The Private Garden** US$5 per person.

It is also possible to camp for under US$5 at the **Camping Casuarinas** on the mainland side of the causeway. There is also a restaurant.

Where to eat

Most people would say that the **Restaurante Reliquias** near the Palace Museum is the best place to eat on the island (not that there's a great deal of competition). Indeed, the interior décor, the tables outside overlooking the sea, and the exotic menu boasting of curries with coconut rice, *matapa* with cashew nuts and various other dishes that I can't spell, does bode well for a pleasant meal. However, when I ate there they only had fish stew, it took ages to arrive, and the Portuguese owner snapped at me when I expressed my overall disappointment at the quality of the food. This said, the other diners seemed to be reasonably happy. The restaurant at the **Hotel Omuhipiti** is the logical alternative to the Reliquias. The menu is considerably less extensive (at least on paper!), although what they do is well prepared, tasty enough, and not too expensive. If neither of these appeals, the **Complexo Indico** on the island's east-facing beach has reliable dishes in the US$4–5 range. There is also a lively disco here on Fridays and Saturdays from about midnight onwards.

The other places on the island are what one would describe as 'local restaurants'. The best is probably the **Restaurante Ancora d'Ouro** opposite the Sacred Art Museum. There's nothing sacred about the food, however, although you can't really complain when fish and chips cost only US$1.

The **Café Museu** at the tourist information centre is a good place for a coffee, especially if it's not too windy for some tables to be set up outside overlooking the square. The **kiosk** opposite the Residencial Meia-Lua, meanwhile, is probably the best that you'll find in the way of a convenience store on the island.

Useful information
The **Tourist Information Centre** (tel/fax: 61 0081) at the Palace Museum is one of the best tourist offices that you'll come across in Mozambique. Run by the dynamic Japanese wife of the curator of the museum, the information – both practical and cultural – on Ilha do Moçambique is carefully laid out in brochures, with a huge map of the island on the wall to put it all into context. You can also find English-speaking guides to show you around the island, as well as buy various handicrafts and specialist books about Ilha do Moçambique. The cherry on the cake is a pot of free condoms next to the postcards.

The **post office** is near the central square, while you can make **telephone** calls at the TDM building next to the Palace Museum.

If you have to change **money** while on the island, there is a BCM in the old town. Note, however, that they don't change travellers' cheques.

What to see
São Sebastão
Dominating the northern tip of the island, the **fortress of São Sebastão** has often been described as the most formidable fortress in Africa. Measuring up to 20m high, it was built with dressed limestone shipped from Lisbon between 1546 and 1583 as a response to the Turkish threat of 1538–53. The shape of the fort has changed little over the intervening centuries, though all but one of the three original gates, the one beneath the buttress of Santa Barbara, was filled in before 1607, and its condition is remarkably similar to that described by the English sailor Henry Salt in the 1800s. The fortress was in active use as

recently as the liberation war, when it was used as a Portuguese barracks. It remains in remarkably good condition, and its wells are still the only source of fresh water on the island.

There must be few other buildings that have played such a decisive role in shaping the course of history as has Sao Sebastão. On March 29 1607, nine Dutch ships appeared off the shore of Mozambique Island, causing the Portuguese inhabitants to withdraw to the fort. The Dutch navy landed on the island and occupied it for about a month, but, unable to capture the fort, it withdrew on May 13. A year later, the Dutch returned to Mozambique Island with a formidable fleet of 13 ships carrying 377 guns and 1,840 men. Again, they seized the island, and again, three months after landing, they were forced to withdraw, incapable of capturing the fort.

Had São Sebastão been a less imposing fortress, it is almost certain – given that Portugal was by this time a waning naval power – that Mozambique Island would have become the Dutch East India Company's East African base, with incalculable ramifications on the eventual course of events that shaped modern Southern Africa. In all probability, a Dutch victory in 1607 would have signalled the end of Portugal's influence in the region. Furthermore, with Mozambique Island as its African base, it is unlikely that the Dutch East India Company would ever have founded the filling station on the Cape of Good Hope that was eventually to become Cape Town and give birth to the Afrikaner nation.

The fortress of São Sebastão has witnessed several other important events in Mozambican history. In Febrary 1618, the acting Captain of Moçambique and Sofala was stabbed fatally on the steps of the fort by his eventual successor, a culmination of the ongoing intrigues that surrounded the three-yearly appointment to this most profitable of the various postings available in Portugal's Indian Ocean empire. In 1671, an Omani naval attack on Mozambique Island followed a similar course of events to the earlier Dutch attacks, as the Omanis occupied the island for several weeks but were unable to drive the Portuguese out of the fort – an outcome that had a strong influence on the modern-day boundary between Mozambique and Tanzania.

Apart from São Sebastão, the only 16th-century building to have survived to the present day is the **Church of Nossa Senhora Baluarte**, which lies within the fortress. Built in 1522, this small church is the oldest standing European building in the southern hemisphere. The main body of the church has changed little since the 16th century, though the covered porch and pulpit both date to the 18th century. The eminent archaeologist James Kirkman, writing about 30 years ago, remarked that Senhora Baluarte is notable for its several gargoyles as well as a Manoeline frieze around the roof and the Royal Arms of Portugal situated above the entrance, but these features seem either to have been removed in the interim or else they are obscured by the lamentably run-down condition of the building. On the floor of the church, a stone plaque marks the tomb of the Portuguese Bishop of Japan, who was buried there in 1588. There are several other graves of bishops outside the main building, dating from between 1592 and 1969. Several human bones of unknown origin are stored in a box in the church.

The old town

The island can be divided into two parts: the old stone town or museum zone to the north and the reed-hut zone to the south. Most of the historical buildings lie in the old town, which has changed little in shape over the past 300 years.

When the Dutch evacuated Mozambique Island in 1607, they burned the old town to the ground, destroying the old Muslim quarter as well as two churches and the hospital, and sparing only the Portuguese-held fortress of São Sebastão and the church that is protected within its walls. In 1671, the Omani Arabs again razed much of the old town following their short-lived occupation of the island, for which reason the only extant 17th-century building in the old town is the former **Jesuit College of São Paulo**. Situated near the jetty, this large red building with its impressive spire was constructed in 1619. It served as a college until 1763, when it was converted to a governor's palace following the decision to make the Viceroy of Moçambique independent of the Goan colonial government.

Now a museum, the **former palace** is a fascinating place to explore. The original church, which was formally opened in 1640, is worth looking at for its garish pulpit, a cylindrical wooden protusion decorated with some beautiful carvings of the apostles, below which is a chaotic assemblage of rather less lovable but arguably more compelling creatures, evidently a mixture of gargoyles, angels and dragons. Also notable is the copper-plate altar and the dozen or so religious paintings that decorate the otherwise-bare walls. The courtyard separating the church and the former palace also has several large statues, for some reason painted in a loud shade of green.

The interior of the former palace is a revelation. The 20-odd rooms are all decorated in period style, I would imagine with the furniture left behind when the governor moved to Lourenço Marques, though it's perfectly possible that some of it was collected from other old homes on the island. In addition to any number of four-poster beds and antique chairs and tables, most of which is Goan in origin, the rooms are liberally decorated with vases and other porcelain artefacts from China. There is something strange and disorientating about walking from the ostentatious riches of the palace back out into the dusty, run-down alleys of the old town.

The most remarkable artefact in the palace is the large tableau that hangs in the banquet hall, a depiction of one of the shipwrecks, which, in the 16th century alone, stranded or killed many thousands of Portuguese along the coast of East Africa. The right-hand side of the tableau depicts a ship being swirled into the clouds, while on the beach a solitary grey-bearded mariner, the picture of thirst and exhaustion, is desperately dragging his tired limbs towards shade. On the left half of the tableau, a group of semi-naked Portuguese maidens sits in a circle below the trees, subjected to the secret scrutiny of two Africans whose wide-eyed expression could easily be interpreted as a sign of curiosity, but in my opinion is more likely to signal recognition of an easy meal. If, as seems probable, this tableau is of some antiquity, then it is a remarkably resonant testament to the fears, prejudices and bravery of these first Europeans to settle in East Africa, one that is somehow made more vivid by its touches of the fantastic: a line of wooden crosses has already been erected on the beach below the still airborne ship, while the maidens' breasts, dangling unnaturally from below their armpits, are spared the immodest realism of nipples. Fascinating as the island's old buildings are, this tableau offers the one real glimpse into the minds of their constructors: pale, God-fearing immigrants who for all their cruelty, greed and arrogance were evidently haunted by the fear and horror of shipwrecks and the African 'savages' that surrounded them. The Palace Museum is open from 08.00–12.00 and 14.00–17.00. There is no entrance fee, although you are encouraged to make a donation.

Situated right next to the former palace, the **Sacred Art Museum** is housed in the former Church of the Misericordia. Translating roughly as the 'House of Mercy', the Misericordia was a religious organisation, nominally charitable in its aims and blessed with a notable gift for raising revenue through bequests and later from a large *prazo* in Zambézia. The church that houses the Sacred Art Museum served as the island headquarters of the Misericordia from when it was built in 1700 until the organisation was disbanded in 1915, and the majority of artefacts it contains are the former property of the church. I found it difficult to get very excited about the dozens of statues of saints displayed in the museum, especially after having spent some time in the palace next door. The most unusual artefect is a Makonde carving of Jesus. It would be interesting to know when and how this statue was acquired, since it is very different in style and subject to any other Makonde carving that I've seen.

Also of interest in the old town is the gateway and cannon on the main square near the palace, and the rather risible statue of a 15th-century Portuguese captain on the waterfront between the palace and the Hotel Omu-hipiti. Roughly where the old town merges into the reed-hut part of town, the **hospital** is housed in a large and very grand whitewashed 18th-century building, which formerly served as the administrative headquarters of the colonial government.

Around the causeway

On the southern end of the island, not far from the causeway, the **Church of Senhora Saude** is the third-oldest building in Mozambique. A rather plain building, founded in 1633, Senhora Saude reportedly underwent extensive renovations in 1801, which makes it difficult to say how much of the original church is intact. The interior has a haunting atmosphere, created as much as anything by the psychedelic array of mosses that colour the wall behind the crucifix. The cemetery in which the church lies is one of the oldest on the island, with many hundreds of tombstones marking Christian, Muslim and Hindu graves.

Facing the Church of Senhora Saude, the island of **São Lourenço** consists of a tiny, mushroom-shaped coral outcrop that can be reached on foot at low tide. The small island is entirely taken up by a 17th-century fort, now rather overgrown but still in good shape with several cannons in place. If you want to walk across, check the tides in advance, since the island is accessible by foot for no longer than an hour. Despite the presence of a couple of rusty iron ladders in front of the fort, the best way to climb up to the island is through a gap in the coral overhang, which can be reached by walking around the right side of the island for about 100m.

Also of interest in this part of town is the whitewashed **Catholic Cathedral**, an 18th-century building that stands on a palm-covered peninsula about 500m northeast of São Lourenço. On the beach in front of the cathedral, shipbuilders still practise the craft for which Ilha do Moçambique was famous even before the Portuguese arrived.

On the mainland about 5km from the causeway and signposted along the main road towards Nampula is a **war cemetery** containing the graves of 80 soldiers kiiled at Lumbo fighting the Germans in 1918.

MOSSURIL

This small town on the mainland facing Ilha do Moçambique is of interest to travellers as the best place to pick up dhow transport to Angoche and other nearby coastal centres. It is also close to one of the few beach resorts in this part of Mozambique, the **Complexo Chocas-Mar**, which has rondavels on the beach for around US$25 and a good restaurant. If you do head out to this area, it's worth making a visit to the nearby town of **Cabaceira**, where you can see the 18th-century Church of Nossa Senhora de Remedios and the remains of a fort of similar antiquity. The turn-off to Mossuril is signposted from the main road between Monapo and Ilha do Moçambique. There are a few *chapas* daily between the turn-off and Mossuril, where you will have to pick up another vehicle covering the 25km road to the Complexo Chocas Mar.

NACALA

The modern port of Nacala is situated on the deep and attractive Bay of Fernão Veloso roughly 70km north of Ilha do Moçambique as the crow flies. Connected by rail to Malawi, Nacala is a port of some regional importance and it has been maintained largely through the use of Malawian and Zambian capital. The town is of little interest to travellers, though I did find the relatively bustling atmosphere in the compact, modern town centre to be somewhat refreshing after the air of stagnation that hangs over Ilha do Moçambique.

Getting there and away

Nacala is connected to Nampula by a good surfaced road, which branches from the main road to Pemba at Namialo, 87km from Nampula, and from the road to Ilha do Moçambique near Monapo, 38km past Namialo and 64km before Nacala.

At least two buses daily travel directly between Nampula and Nacala, leaving in either direction at around 05.00. There are also several *chapas* covering this route daily, though you may have to change vehicles either at

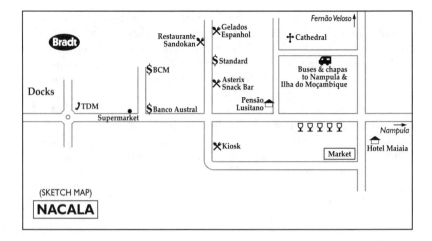

(SKETCH MAP)
NACALA

Monapa or Namialo. All transport towards Nampula leaves Nacala from the main road opposite the Hotel Maiaia.

Coming from Pemba, the best thing to do is catch the Transnorte bus towards Nampula and disembark at Namialo, from where there is plenty of transport through to Nacala. If you are heading from Nacala to Pemba, I would recommend you to catch a *chapa* to Namialo, spend the night there, and then pick up the Transnorte bus coming from Nampula when it passes through Namialo at around 06.00.

To cross between Ilha do Moçambique and Nacala, take any vehicle heading towards Monapo and ask to be dropped at the junction of the Nacala and Ilha do Moçambique roads, which lies roughly 3km east of Monapo.

Where to stay

Despite persisting and somewhat bizarre rumours of a backpacker's hostel in Nacala, there are in fact only two places to stay in town. The **Hotel Maiaia** (tel: 52 6827) stands in the place of the old Hotel Nacala. Owned by the same group as the Hotel Omuhipiti on Ilha do Moçambique, standards at the Maiaia are similarly high. Self-contained rooms with hot water, air conditioning and TV cost US$60/single and US$70/double, which includes breakfast. More down-at-heel accommodation is available at the unsignposted **Pensão Lusitano**, a couple of blocks down the hill from the Maiaia. The rooms are clean, basic and sensibly priced at US$7.50/single and US$15/double, and are just about good enough to be a legitimate alternative to the town's more expensive hotel.

There is actually another place, the **Pensão Selva**, about 2km up the hill in the 'cidade alta' ('uptown') – as opposed to the 'baixa' ('downtown') where the other two hotels are located – although I can't think of a compelling reason to stay there.

Where to eat

The **Restaurante Sandokan** is the best place to eat in Nacala. Dishes are US$4 upwards, and the dining room has attractive furnishings and is air-conditioned. Over the road, the **Gelados Espanhol** has all the usual snacks and pastries, although you really come here for the ice-creams, banana splits and milkshakes. The restaurant at the **Hotel Maiaia** is also worth a try. Otherwise, there are one or two snack bars – the **Asterix Snack Bar** with its rather limited egg-and-chips menu is probably the most salubrious – and a few bars flanking one side of the market.

FERNÃO VELOSO

Roughly 15km from Nacala, there is good snorkelling and diving off the beach at the entrance of the Bay of Fernão Veloso. There are regular *chapas* to this beach from Nacala, and once there you'll find a South African-run operation called **Fim do Mundo** (tel: 52 0017), which has dormitory accommodation for US$5, rooms for US$20, chalets for US$25 and camping for US$2.50. There is also a restaurant and a small swimming pool, as well as a very highly regarded dive school, which runs trips to some of the country's more off-the-beaten-track dive sites. To get there, follow the road to the beach and, just before you reach the military camp, take the sandy track to the left.

ANGOCHE

This ancient trading town on the mouth of the Mluli River is thought to have been founded in the 15th century by an offshoot of the ruling family of Kilwa. Following the reorientation of gold mining in the interior during that century, Angoche became the terminus of a new trade route from the Sena on the Zambezi. Like the Querimba Islands, Angoche became an important refuge for Muslim traders in the early years of the Portuguese occupation of the coast. The town enjoyed a boom period between 1505 and 1511, during which time the route from Sena assumed increasing importance to Muslim traders as a clandestine way of getting gold to the coast without Portuguese knowledge. It has been estimated that the town's population stood at around 10,000 during this period. In 1511, Angoche was bombarded by Portuguese ships and burned to the ground, and its sheikh was taken into captivity. The town slid into relative obscurity when ivory replaced gold as the major trading commodity along the coast, and it's trade links were dealt something of a death blow after Barreto's army massacred the Muslim traders at Sena in 1572.

Angoche's revival is linked to the slave trade in the early 19th century. By 1830, it had become a thriving trade centre, and it assumed even greater importance after slavery was abolished by Portugal and the trade went underground. Because Angoche is difficult for large ships, it was easy for the Muslim traders to avoid detection by the British boats that starting policing the coast in 1842. In early 1847, a Portuguese warship attempted to impose an anti-slaving treaty on Angoche, but was driven away. Later in the same year, Britain and Portugal bombarded the town from the sea, but despite causing great damage to its buildings, they were unable to occupy it. Angoche finally fell to Portugal in 1862, following a bloody battle which caused the leading trader, a Muslim called Mussa Quanto, to flee into the interior. The town has since sunk into relative obscurity, though it remains the local administrative centre.

Angoche today see few visitors, but it would be a worthwhile diversion for travellers with enough time. Surprisingly, there is nothing in the run-down old town that dates to before the turn of the century, but it is not without atmosphere and the long, wide beach is very attractive. Basic accommodation is available at the Pensão Oceania, where it is also possible to arrange dhow trips to some of the nearby islands. You can also rent bungalows for around US$15.

Angoche is connected to Nampula by a 170km-long unsurfaced road, for which a 4WD vehicle is strongly recommended. At least one bus daily covers this road, leaving Nampula at 05.00 sharp, as do a few trucks, which also generally leave in the early morning. The bus and *chapa* stop for Angoche is a good 20–30-minute walk from the town centre, so I would advise you to be out of your hotel room by 04.15. To get to the bus stop, follow Avenida Paulo Kamkama south to the large traffic circle just after the Pensão Parques. Here you must turn right for about 100m then left immediately after passing the BCM and before the Pensão Brasilia. Follow this curving road for about 500m until you hit a T-junction, where you must turn left. Roughly 1km along this road, you'll notice the World Vision office to your left – the stop is shortly after this and you'll see plenty of people waiting there.

Nine luxury private villas on a tiny uninhabited Indian Ocean island – magnificent sea views and sandy beaches

Unparalleled natural beauty and complete exclusivity

Multi-lingual staff ensure your five-star comfort, well-being and relaxation

Gourmet dining with Mozambican cuisine influenced by Portugal and Goa

Located in the Quilálea Marine Sanctuary in the remote and beautiful Quirimbas Archipelago

"Quilálea" comes from a Swahili word for "sleep". Sleep and dream happily on our magical island!

The undiscovered island

Tel: +258 272 21808
mobile: +258 82326 3900
email: info@quilalea.com
web: www.quilalea.com

Cabo Delgado

14

Cabo Delgado (which roughly translates as Cape Thin) is Mozambique's most northeasterly province, bounded by the Rovuma River and Tanzania to the north, an Indian Ocean coastline of roughly 300km to the east, the Lúrio River and its beautiful falls to the south, and Niassa Province to the west. The provincial capital, Pemba, is set on the third-largest bay in the world. It's a pleasant enough coastal town, and the obvious focal point of tourism in Cabo Delgado. Once remote and little-visited, it now gets a growing amount of fly-in tourism from South Africa and Dar es Salaam; but still its attractions can't compare with those of Ibo (see page 235), an ancient town and island that forms part of the Quirimba Archipelago (see *Quirimbas National Park*, page 230). Also of interest in Cabo Delgado is Mueda (see page 243), the unofficial capital of the Makonde Plateau, and the attractive small port of Palma (page 244), which is also the main springboard for the little-used route between northern Mozambique and southern Tanzania.

The main ethnic group in Cabo Delgado is the Makua. In and around Pemba, you'll frequently see Makua women wandering around with what appear to be white masks, the result of plastering their faces with a white paste or *mussiro* made from the bark of a particular tree. Surprisingly these have no ritual or other non-cosmetic significance. The white paste is merely a skin softener, serving a similar purpose to the face masks used (but generally in private) by many Western women. Interestingly, there's a similar custom in the Comoros, 200km away.

GETTING AROUND

Cabo Delgado can be approached from three directions: Tanzania to the north, Niassa Province to the west and Nampula Province to the south. The latter is the most straightforward, since Pemba is connected to Nampula town by a reasonable surfaced road and regular public transport.

In a private 4WD, it may become possible (when/if the road is improved...) to drive to Pemba from Niassa via Marrupa and Montepuez, bearing in mind that some river crossings become impassable after heavy rain. No public transport covers this route, and hitching can be very slow.

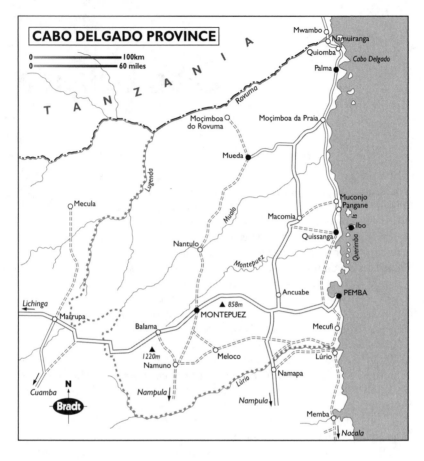

CABO DELGADO PROVINCE

0 ═══════════ 100km
0 ═══════════ 60 miles

From the north, access by private vehicle is now possible thanks to a motorised ferry that began taking vehicles across the Rovuma River in June 2000, but some parts of the road are in very poor condition. For more details on travel from Tanzania, see *Getting to Mozambique* on page 59.

From Pemba, a Mecula bus departs daily at 06.00 for Nampula and Moçimboa (the stop is behind Osman's supermarket). To continue to Mueda, get off at Aussi (Owassi) where the road forks to Moçimboa, then take a *chapa* for the last 35km to Mueda. The unsurfaced road connecting Pemba to Quissanga, the departure point for dhows to Ibo and the other islands of the Quirimba Archipelago, is currently in a bad state of repair.

QUIRIMBAS NATIONAL PARK

The **Quilálea Marine Sanctuary**, the first protected marine area in the Quirimbas Archipelago (see page 244), was set up by a private company – and endorsed by the government – in 2001, around the islands of Quilálea (35 hectares, 55km north of Pemba) and Sencar (75 hectares). In June 2002, and partly because of the sanctuary's success, the 500,000ha **Quirimbas**

National Park was created, containing both the archipelago and a part of the mainland. Its coastal border runs from just north of Pemba to just south of Medjumbe Island. The project of a park in the Quirimbas had – because of the region's very high biodiversity, great scenic beauty and important history – been under intermittent discussion since the 1970s. The Park's headquarters are on Ibo Island.

The Worldwide Fund for Nature or **WWF** (web: www.wwf.org and www.wwf.org.mz) is heavily involved in the Quirimbas Park. Its website is a good source of ongoing information. The overall goal of the park, in this beautiful but ecologically fragile area, is 'to conserve the diversity, abundance and ecological integrity of all physical and biological resources in the park area, so that they may be enjoyed and used productively by present and future generations'. Nor is nature the only beneficiary. One of the park's six associated aims involves contributing to 'the economic and social well-being of the park's ancestral inhabitants by promoting sustainable resource use strategies, by developing ecologically sensitive livelihood options and by prioritising their interests in the economic opportunities deriving from the establishment of the park'.

PEMBA

Formerly known as Porto Amélia (after the French princess Maria Amélia d'Orléans, who married King Don Carlos I and became the last Portuguese queen), Pemba – the capital of Cabo Delgado Province – is a relatively modern town by coastal standards. Lying on the site of a failed Portuguese attempt to build a colony in Cabo Delgado in 1857, the modern town was founded in 1904 as an administrative centre for the Niassa Company. By the late 1920s the old town centre had more or less taken its present shape, and it supported a population of over 1,500. More recently, Pemba was largely untouched by both the liberation and civil wars, despite being in one of the most unsettled provinces, and it is generally less run-down in appearance than most Mozambican towns.

Pemba town is situated on the tip of a peninsula on the southern side of Pemba Bay, a huge and semi-enclosed natural harbour. The beaches are wide, sandy and clean, and lined with palm trees. A coral reef protects the beach and guarantees safe swimming as well as good snorkelling. Pemba has enormous potential as a tourist resort, though it is currently rather off the beaten track and likely to remain so until such time as airfares from Maputo drop.

Pemba's modern town centre is a rather bland place, but it's worth walking down to the old town centre near the port, where a small grid of roads lined with run-down colonial buildings is fringed by a very attractive and remarkably neat reed-hut village called Paquitequete. Built on sandy ground that sometimes floods at high tide, this was Pemba's first settlement, and its inhabitants are largely Muslim. Also of interest is the Makonde wood-carving co-operative on Avenue Chai about 1.5km from the main road (Avenue 25 Setembro) to Wimbe Beach.

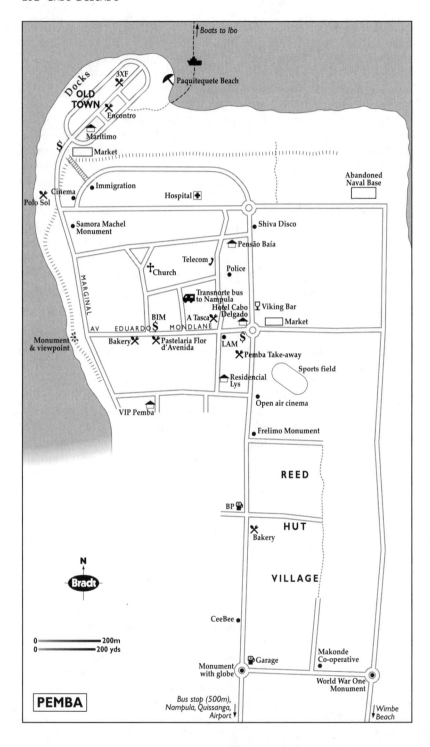

↑ Boats to Ibo

Docks
3XF
OLD
TOWN
Encontro
Marítimo
Market
Paquitequete Beach

Abandoned
Naval Base

Immigration
Hospital
Cinema
Polo Sol
Samora Machel
Monument

Shiva Disco
Pensão Baía
Telecom
Church
Police
Transnorte bus
to Nampula
Hotel Cabo
Delgado
Viking Bar
BIM
A Tasca
Market
Monument
& viewpoint
Bakery
Pastelaria Flor
d'Avenida
LAM
Pemba Take-away
Residencial
Lys
Sports field
VIP Pemba
Open air cinema

MARGINAL

AV EDUARDO MONDLANE

Frelimo Monument

REED

BP

HUT
Bakery

N

Bradt

VILLAGE

200m
200 yds

CeeBee

PEMBA

Garage
Makonde
Co-operative
Monument
with globe
World War One
Monument

Bus stop (500m),
Nampula, Quissanga,
Airport ▼

Wimbe
Beach

The best time to visit Pemba is from April to October, when the cooling trade winds blow. In the rainy season, the monsoon blows from the northeast, which can make the beach very unpleasant. Pemba is the most easterly place using Central African Time (the same as South Africa) so daybreak is very early (04.15 in midsummer) and the sun sets before 18.00 most of the year.

Getting there and away
By air
LAM flies between Maputo and Pemba daily. From Johannesburg, LAM flights are on Wed and Fri, leaving at 08.40 and arriving in Pemba at 13.40 with a one-hour stop at Maputo. Return flights to Johannesburg leave Pemba on Wed and Fri at 13.30 and reach Jo'burg at 18.30 with a stop in Maputo. There's also a Sunday flight leaving Pemba at 14.30 and arriving Jo'burg at 19.00. Currently LAM offers South Africans a promotional fare Jo'burg–Pemba–Jo'burg of around US$480. There are daily LAM flights (not Fri or Sun) to/from Dar es Salaam: return fare US$332.

Air Corridor flies Maputo–Pemba on Mon and Wed with a stop in Beira; also Pemba–Maputo on Tue and Sun with a stop in Beira and connecting to Johannesburg.

The airport lies about 3km out of Pemba on the Estrada National 106 or Airport Road. There are taxis and Moti Rent-a-Car, but no buses into town; however, it's easy enough to hitch a lift. Larger hotels have courtesy buses to meet flights. The Pemba Beach Hotel and the Quilálea Lodge have ground staff to help transfer their clients, and may also secure reduced fares on LAM flights.

By boat
The quickest route from Pemba to Ibo Island is to go by road to Quissanga and then take a dhow – see *Ibo Island: Getting there and away* on page 240). A cheaper – and much slower – alternative is to ask about dhows leaving for Ibo Island and Moçimboa da Praia from Paquitequete Beach, five minutes' walk from the old town. With favourable winds, the voyage to Ibo takes around 12 hours. There's a passenger ferry service between Dar es Salaam and Mtwara, near to the Mozambican border; from Mtwara public transport runs to the border ferry and thence to Moçimboa da Praia.

By road
The 420km road between Nampula and Pemba is surfaced for most of its length and should be passable in practically any vehicle at any time of year. Watch out for pot-holes, especially between Namialo and Nampula. The drive should take around four to five hours.

The Mecula Bus Company runs a regular daily service throughout the province; a bus leaves Pemba for Nampula at 06.00 from a bus stop on the Nampula or Airport road (Estrada National No 106) about 500m past the turn-off to Wimbe Beach; and leaves Nampula for Pemba at 06.00 from in front of the railway station. Most other traffic covering the whole route leaves at around 05.00.

There are other buses between Nampula and Pemba but nothing (except taxis) goes as far as Wimbe Beach. Buses seem to have scheduled stops of 20 minutes or so at Namapa, where there's a bar with a fridge and a toilet at the back, and at Namialo on the junction to Ilha do Moçambique.

Where to stay

There is a fair choice of accommodation in the town centre. A good source of information is the tourism services company Kaskazini (see *Useful information*, page 235). For budget travellers, the best place is the **Pensão Baía** (tel: 272 20153) on Avenida I Maia in the new town centre; its clean and reasonably pleasant doubles with fan cost from US$20. (Note that camping on the beach isn't allowed.)

There are several mid-to-lower-range hotels. Of these, the **Hotel Cabo Delgado** (tel: 272 20558/9, 272 21522) has reasonable rooms (upwards of US$30) but could do with a lick of paint. The **Residencial Lys** (tel: 272 20951; email: sulemane@teledata.mz) on Rua Forças Populares is also a bit shabby at the edges. Also see Wimbe Beach, below. A new place on a peninsula just north of Pemba and south of the Quirimbas National Park is **Londo Lodge** (tel: 258 7221048; email: info@londolodge.com; web: www.londolodge.com), with five traditionally built luxury villas and four bush villas. Guests will be met at the airport and taken across Pemba Bay to the lodge by either powerboat or traditional dhow. Activities include snorkelling in the bay's coral reef and guided bush and nature walks. Rates (US$250–325) vary according to season, with special offers for longer stays.

Where to eat

Restaurants in Pemba are opening and closing almost overnight, so check the current scene when you arrive. (Also see *Wimbe Beach*, page 235.) At the top of the hill leading down to the old part of town is **Restaurant 556**, a typical South African sports bar serving a good selection of steak, wine and beer. The **Samar Restaurant**, a Portuguese-style restaurant on the left behind the old Viking, has a good-value range of traditional dishes, seafood and daily specials. The **Pastelaria Flor d'Avenida**, opposite the BIM on Avenida Eduardo Mondlane, serves cakes, coffee, cold drinks and light meals all day and night; while the **Kappa Kappa Bakery**, next door, sells good fresh bread. For a treat, head about 20km south of Pemba on the Mecufi road to the **Upeponi** beach bar and restaurant in Murrebué, for freshly caught fish and chicken grills on an unspoilt beach.

The **market** (for fresh fruit and bread) in the new town centre is downhill from the main traffic circle. Nearby are a few bars with relatively cheap beers. The main market, built in 1941, is in the old town centre. Mbanguia market in sprawling Natite neighbourhood is Pemba's largest, with everything from live chickens to fresh fruit and household goods. There are plenty of **grocery stores** and **supermarkets**; try Osman Yacob's supermarket on the way into town, Gastronomia on Avenida Eduardo Mondlane and Casa Nilsa in the old part of town.

Useful information
Kaskazini
An excellent source of information about Pemba and Cabo Delgado is **Kaskazini Tourism Services** (tel: +258 272 20371, +258 82 3096990; email: info@kaskazini.com; web: www.kaskazini.com). Launched in 2003 to promote tourism in the whole of northern Mozambique, it represents a range of operators and can provide services and activities including accommodation, car rental, diving, fishing, watersports, bush exploration, cultural events and full tailor-made holiday packages. The website is particularly helpful and informative. Kaskazini's office is at Wimbe Beach; or, if you're in Pemba and need help, give them a call and they'll come to you.

Practicalities
Most of the **banks**, services and shops are on the central Avenida Eduardo Mondlane. There's a **post office** in the port area with poste restante facilities and another round the corner from the Hotel Cabo Delgado. **Pharmacies** are Farmacia Nova on the main avenue, Farmacia Carlos Lwanga behind Osman Yacob's supermarket and Farmacia Pemba in the old town. There are public **card-phones** all over town. Artes Maconde (shown on the town plan under its old name CeeBee) offers phone, fax and **internet** services; the cheapest internet access in Pemba is at the TDM booth by MCel, on the corner of Avenida Eduardo Mondlane and 25 Setembro as you arrive in the Avenida. Several **car rental** companies have 4WDs and 2WDs available; rates are generally high. **Taxis** with meters are based in the town centre. Petty theft is quite common, so look after your belongings.

WIMBE BEACH
Most tourists visiting Pemba stay at Wimbe Beach, about 6km from the town centre. To get to Wimbe from there, follow the Nampula road out of town towards the airport for about 1km, then turn left at the junction marked by a traffic circle in the middle of which lies a monument with a large globe at its base. After a few hundred metres, passing the Makonde Co-op to your left, you'll reach the waterfront and a very large traffic circle with a monument to soldiers who died in World War I. Turn right here and follow the beachfront road for another 4–5km before arriving at Wimbe. There's no public transport along this road, only taxis, but it shouldn't be difficult to hitch a lift.

Where to stay
The new **Pemba Beach Hotel** (email: pembabeach@teledata.mz; web: www.pembabeach.com), opened in 2002, has all you would expect of its 'deluxe' status, including attractive architecture, ocean-facing rooms with balconies and terrific views, pool, gardens, tennis, conference facilities, a yacht marina, a fully equipped dive centre and a good range of watersports. Double/twin from US$223 per person, single from US$301, including buffet breakfast, airport transfer and taxes (increasing in peak seasons). There are also eight self-catering villas. Reservations must be made through Rani Resorts'

head office; tel: +27 (0) 11 467 1277; email: reservations@raniresorts.com. The **Complexo Turistico Caracol** (tel: 272 20147; web: www.centroturisticocaracol.com) has simple, clean, comfortable, ensuite beachfront units with air conditioning and a sea view (not all have hot water) across the road from Wimbe Beach, at US$50–100 depending on size, including airport transfers. The **Nautilus Beach Resort** (tel: 272 21520) has thatched bungalows on the beach (not all are ensuite or have hot water) at US$75–130 or so, depending on size and facilities, so best check it out before booking. It has a casino and dive shop, as well as a Dive Centre called CI Divers (tel: +258 82 6822700), run by owner Pieter Jacobs, that can arrange scuba excursions and the hire of snorkelling equipment and kayaks.

There are various **self-catering** options, with prices from around US$60 upwards per unit – contact Kaskazini (above) for the latest details. One such is the very small **Complexo SAL** (tel: +258 272 20134, +258 82 7048310), 15m from the restaurant Aquila Romana: air conditioned, hot water, mini kitchen with fridge/freezer, safe parking. Single from US$65; double from US$80.

Where to eat
The **Restaurante Mar de Sol** (good for drinks and snacks) is next door to the Nautilus Beach Resort. Close by is the picturesque **Pemba Dolphin** serving fresh seafood on the beach; it also has a popular bar for drinks, cocktails and fresh juices. **Restaurante Wimbe,** 100m down the beach, has a popular disco at weekends. At the southern tip of Wimbe, the Italian **Aquila Romana** has a good selection of pizzas and pastas. A few hundred metres beyond the end of the beach, **JPS** is a local restaurant specialising in grilled chicken and seafood – either order in advance or be prepared to wait a while. **A Rita**, a popular and reasonably priced Portuguese restaurant (closed just now but likely to reopen), is across the road from the beach, as is the little **Super Wimbe** with traditional Mozambican food.

IBO ISLAND
The small town of Ibo lies on the island of the same name, part of the Quirimbas Archipelago. Ibo is one of the most ancient settlements in Mozambique, and after Ilha do Moçambique (generally called just '*Ilha*' in Mozambique) is arguably the most fascinating and atmospheric town in the country. By mainstream tourism standards, Ibo is still one of Africa's best-kept secrets. Access and tourist facilities are improving steadily, however, and the increasing number of visitors who do make the effort to get there may well regard it as the highlight of their time in Mozambique.

Ibo today is run-down but utterly compelling: a strangely haunting backwater that in my experience of Africa compares only to Kilwa Kivinje on the south coast of Tanzania. The abandoned palaces and villas have lapsed into disrepair, the clay tiles falling off the roofs and the walls slowly being strangled by layers of moss and undermined by the vast sprawling tendrils of strangler figs. The exposed rag coral walls and fading whitewash of the crumbling buildings give the town a washed-out pastel air that is strangely at odds with

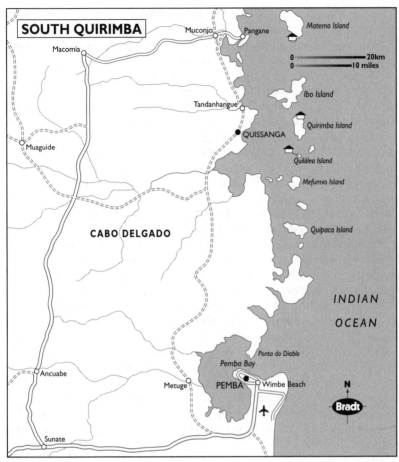

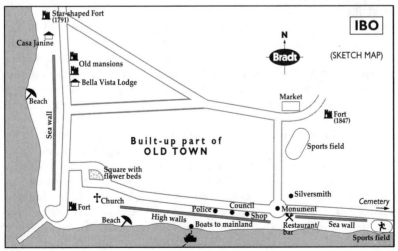

the deep-blue tropical sky and the bright-red flame trees, and the lush greenery that lines the streets in which mangrove kingfishers sing at dawn.

In my opinion at least, it is the most alluring off-the-beaten-track excursion in northern Mozambique. If there is an obvious point of comparison it is Ilha do Moçambique, but Ibo is far from being a miniature of *Ilha*; which may have been the Portuguese capital for four centuries, but the cluttered alleyways of its town centre are evocative more of the Muslim world than of anything European. Paradoxically, Ibo, which was frequently a base for clandestine Muslim trade during the Portuguese era, has an uncluttered and overwhelmingly Mediterranean character, its wide roads lined with opulent high-roofed buildings boasting classical façades and expansive balconies supported by thick pillars. Ibo is also in a more advanced state of decay than Mozambique – but this could be changing. Several new rehabilitation projects are at planning stage, while some have already obtained funding and are under way. By the time you read this guide there may be visible results.

Ibo Island is located in a region of great scenic beauty, high biodiversity of worldwide significance, and some of the most unspoilt, unexplored and important island reef ecosystems in the Indian Ocean. It has a rich history and culture that blend indigenous Africa with Arab and Portuguese influences. Ibo Island also falls within – and is the headquarters of – the newly created **Quirimbas National Park** (see page 230). A number of organisations and investors have identified the importance of Ibo's history, culture and biodiversity, and community and conservation projects are already under way. For example a new community tourism programme, an agricultural market garden project and a silversmiths' programme will be run and managed from the new Ibo Island Lodge (see advertisement on page 250), and can be visited by the Lodge's guests as well as by day visitors to Ibo. Also a research project on the history of Ibo has been set up and should be completed in mid-2006.

History

Little is known about the Quirimbas' history prior to the arrival of the Portuguese, but they were certainly occupied by Muslim traders well before the 15th century, and they are assumed to have formed an important link in the medieval coastal trade network between Kilwa and Sofala. The Quirimbas were originally known to the Portuguese as the Maluane Islands, after a type of cloth that was manufactured on the islands from pre-Portuguese times until well into the 17th century.

At the time the Portuguese first landed in the area, it seems that the main trading centre in the archipelago was on Quirimba Island immediately south of Ibo. This island became the main refuge for Muslim traders from Kilwa after that city was occupied by Portugal in 1507. Because the Muslims of Quirimba refused to trade with Christians, Portugal attacked the islands in 1523, killing some 60 Muslims, burning down the town, and looting large amounts of ivory and other merchandise. However, this massacre had little long-term effect in subduing the Muslim trade, so Portugal attempted to gain control over the islands by more devious means of leasing them to Portuguese citizens.

By the end of the 16th century, seven of the nine largest islands in the archipelago were ruled by Portuguese traders and the other two by Muslims. Islanders were forced to pay a tribute of 5% of their produce to the island's ruler, as well as a tithe to the church. At this time, Ibo had become the most important town on the islands. A description dating from 1609 reveals that Ibo was substantially fortified, and that the islands were reasonably prosperous and a major source of food supplies for Mozambique Island. By the 18th century, *prazos* had been established on all the main islands, and the archipelago was lorded over by two *mazungo* (white-skinned) families, the Meneses and Morues.

Ibo came into its own in the second half of the 18th century, as the major supplier of slaves to the sugar-plantation owners of France's Indian Ocean Islands. Portugal resented the prosperity of the islands' independent traders and, fearing that the islands might fall into Omani or French hands, granted Ibo municipal status in 1763. By the end of the 18th century, Ibo is thought to have been the second most important Portuguese trading centre after Mozambique Island. It was still an important trading and administrative centre when it was leased to the Niassa Company in 1897, but the shallow, narrow approach to the island wasn't suitable for modern ships and so the Niassa Company relocated its base to Porto Amélia (Pemba) in 1904 and Ibo gradually went into decline. Ibo today supports a population of fewer than 5,000, most of whom speak a Swahili dialect (Kimuani).

As with several other old Mozambican towns, it is hard to establish the age of many of Ibo's buildings. The dates on tiles and a few buildings seem to place much of the town centre in the early 19th century. Many buildings along the semi-fortified southern waterfront are even older, such as the medium-sized fort on the southwestern tip of the island, the **Fortim de S José**. It was the first fort built (in 1760) by the Portuguese, but fell into disuse when the *Fortaleza de S João Baptista* was built.

Next to this fort, and facing the colourful town square, is the large whitewashed **Church of Our Lady of Rosaria**. Services are held there once a month. According to one source, the church was built in 1580, but I couldn't find anyone to let me inside so didn't see anything to confirm this. At the time it struck me as unlikely that a church of this size would be built at a time when only a few Portuguese had settled on the islands. However, since visiting Ibo I've read that Dominican missionaries were busy on the Quirimbas in the late 16th century (their records claim 16,000 converts by 1593), which lends some credence to a date of 1580. On the basis of appearance alone I would have guessed Ibo's church to be roughly contemporaneous with the late-18th-century cathedrals at Inhambane and Quelimane, but still it may have been built on the site of an older church. Maybe the new Ibo history research project (or more knowledgeable readers) will clarify this. Beside the church are about 15 children's graves.

The most interesting building in Ibo, and one of the best preserved, is the **Fortaleza de S João Baptista**, a large, star-shaped fort to the northwest of the town centre, complete with a dozen or so cannons and ringed by a grove of tall palms. Built in 1791 to protect the island from French invasion from the island of Réunion, this fort was used as a prison into the 1970s – it's said that the ramparts are haunted by the ghosts of Mozambicans who died there while incarcerated by the Portuguese. The fort no longer appears to have any formal use, but its entrance is occupied by some traditional silversmiths who'll happily allow you to watch them at work without expecting you to buy anything. A nominal entrance fee is charged.

Another fort, **Fortim de Santo António**, dating to 1825, lies at the back of the town near the market; there's a good view over the town from the top or (if you dare climb it) from the nearby water tower. If you walk east along the waterfront past this fort, passing a volleyball field to your left, you eventually come to an interesting old graveyard. Apparently some relics of pre-Portuguese times also exist in the town, including two ancient mosques and an Arab fortress, but I saw no trace of these.

Getting there and away
By air
The flight by light aircraft from Pemba to Ibo Island is breathtaking. Subject to availability, daily scheduled flights leave Pemba for various private island resorts, and stop en route at Ibo to drop off or pick up passengers. You can book these with WildLife Adventures (page 32), with Kaskazini Tourism Services in Pemba (page 235), or via Mario (tel: +258 82 316 5010). The current fare from Pemba to Ibo is US$75 one way. If you're in a group maybe you could charter a plane – ask Kaskazini for details.

By road/boat
Ibo is the only island you can visit easily without being booked into a private resort, and quite a few people travel there by road and then by dhow. In a private vehicle, the best way to Ibo from Pemba is to drive to Quissanga on the mainland opposite the island, and catch a boat from there. The unsignposted turn-off to Quissanga lies about 25km along the road to Nampula, to the right as you come from Pemba. Quissanga is upwards of two hours' drive from this turn-off. Currently the unsurfaced road is passable only in a 4WD. Once at Quissanga, ask directions to Tandanhangui (Tandangangy), a small fishing village reached by a 5km road (turn left at the top of the hill when you see the sea), which might well prove testing to vehicles without 4WD. At Tandanhangui you'll have to ask around about dhows to Ibo. You can leave your vehicle at your own risk at the Ibo Island Lodge (formerly Bella Vista Lodge, see *Where to stay*, page 241) compound for about US$2 per day.

For travellers without vehicles, the most straightforward way of getting to Ibo is with the South Africa-based WildLife Adventures, which operates a vehicle and boat transfer between Pemba and Ibo Island. This can be organised via either WildLife Adventures (page 32) or Kaskazini (page 235).

By public transport, you should find a couple of vehicles a day going from Pemba all the way to Tandanhangui. They leave from the bus stop on the

Nampula (25 do Setembro) road about 500m past the junction to Wimbe Beach. Dhows between Tandanhangui and Ibo take up to two hours each way provided that you arrive at high tide (they don't sail at low tide) and the winds are favourable.

The other way of getting to Ibo is with one of the dhows that run between Pemba and Moçimboa da Praia. The problem is that these have an erratic schedule dictated by the combination of tides, winds and demand, so you'll simply have to ask around; in Pemba, the best place to do this is Paquitequete Beach, five minutes' walk from the old town. The trip from Pemba to Ibo takes at least 12 hours, quite possibly longer, and there's no food, water, cover or toilet facilities on the dhow. You may prefer asking around to try to organise a private lift to Quissanga.

Where to stay and eat

At the time of writing, the **Bella Vista Lodge**, owned and run by WildLife Adventures (see page 32), is on the verge of major refurbishment, due for completion in mid-2006, so we can't give first-hand details of what it will be like by the time you read this. The current lodge, already popular with tourists, occupies a fully restored 120-year-old colonial mansion on the main waterfront road. Bedrooms are simply furnished but comfortable, extremely spacious and clean: from US$60 per person (2005 rates). The upgraded lodge will be spread over three rehabilitated mansions, all more than a century old, with luxury as the keynote. Its name will change to **Ibo Island Lodge** (see page 250). Plans include guided walks and introductions to the culture and history of Ibo Island, as well as a full range of water-based activities and excursions. Community projects already operate from the lodge to ensure that local people benefit from the development of tourism; see website www.iboisland.com for details of these. Rates for 2006 start from US$210 per person, including breakfast, dinner and activities. Contact WildLife Adventures for bookings and for details of specials and packages that include flights and transfers. For updates on the lodge's refurbishment check website www.wildlifeadventures.co.za.

As is the case on Ilha do Moçambique – albeit on a far greater scale – the other accommodation options on Ibo Island are in private houses. The address best established with travellers is **Casa Janine** (aka: Villa Ruben), the home of a Frenchwoman who used to live on the island and now runs a small restaurant and bar in Pemba. Located in an attractive spot near the *Fortaleza de S João Baptista*, double rooms with fan and mosquito net cost US$25, and you can camp in the garden for around US$5. Meals can also be prepared as long as you order well in advance, and cost US$5–10.

Food can be a bit of a problem on Ibo if you don't eat at the Ibo Island Lodge (formerly Bella Vista). At the restaurant and bar near the Trabalhadores Monument you need to pre-order (and it's often closed). The nearby market has little other than a few mangoes, stale bread and biscuits, and warm cans of coke. In theory, you shouldn't find it hard to get hold of fresh seafood cheaply (1kg of prawns can cost as little as US$2 on Ibo) but in practice you may have to ask around to find out when the fishing boats are coming in that day. As with everything on Ibo, tides dictate the day's activities, so it's best to start asking around first thing in the morning so that you can find somebody to locate what you want and prepare it for you. Things like potatoes and rice are probably best brought over from Pemba.

Excursions from Ibo

The best option is to organise a **dhow trip** out of Ibo, on which you stand a good chance of seeing dolphins, turtles and other large marine creatures, including (from July to November) humpback whales. Ibo Island Lodge offers dhow excursions and safaris, as well as a canoe trip through some beautiful old **mangroves**. With your own snorkelling equipment, you could explore the wreck or have a great dive around the lighthouse, though ask local advice about tides as the currents can be dangerous at times.

Quirimba Island, just south of Ibo, has a couple of old Portuguese houses on a former *prazo* estate as well as a large coconut plantation, 350 head of cattle, a small coffee orchard and a good 1km grass runway, but you'll need to check whether the owners currently accept visitors.

At very low tide it's possible to cross from Ibo to the mainland on a narrow strip of sand, but the track is confusing and you *must* have a competent local guide if you want to walk it.

ELSEWHERE IN MAINLAND CABO DELGADO
Pangane

This pleasant beach spot is on the mainland about halfway between Pemba and Moçimboa da Praia. As well as the usual seaside activities – it's easy to hire a boat to explore the surrounding reefs – the Pangane area has significant (but often elusive) populations of large mammals such as buffalo, elephant and lion. To get there from Pemba, follow the Nampula road west for 87km to the junction town of Silva Macua (shown on some maps as Sunate), then take the main Moçimboa da Praia road northwards for 100km as far as Macomia, where you turn right on to the R528 to Muconjo (aka Mucojo). You'll reach Muconjo after roughly 50km, then it's another 2km to Pangane Beach. Even without private transport, you should be able to get from Pemba to Pangane in a day if you make an early start. The best way is probably to take the Mecula bus towards Macomia. If hitching, you shouldn't have to wait too long for a lift to Macomia, but there's less transport from there through to Muconjo.

An attractive newcomer here is **Guludo Base Camp** (web: www.guludo.com) on a 12km beach. The tented accommodation has mosquito nets and open-air bathrooms. Daily rates (2005) start from around US$204 per person, full board (no single supplements) – lower for longer stays and higher at peak season. Of this, 5% goes to a regeneration programme working in Guludo and the National Park. Activities include diving, snorkelling, elephant tracking and bush walks. Transfers to/from Pemba, Ibo and Matemo Island can be arranged. The **Pangane Acampamento** is an attractive campsite with good toilets and showers. Its basic reed huts cost upwards of US$5 per person, or you can camp for less. **Casa Chung** (aka Casa Suki) is a Chinese-owned compound and shop near the fish market; it has rooms with bedding for upwards of US$10 and can also prepare inexpensive meals.

Mueda

Mueda is the principal town on the Mozambican part of the Makonde Plateau, the only part of the country not to have been conquered by Portugal at the start of World War I. Even after the Plateau was quelled in 1919, the Makonde people for whom it is named retained a tradition of resistance. This was intensified after an infamous massacre on June 16 1960, when Portuguese soldiers fired on an officially sanctioned meeting of peasant farmers in Mueda, killing an estimated 600 people. Partly in reaction to this massacre, though also because of their proximity to the Tanzanian border, the Makonde gave Frelimo strong support during the war of liberation. Most of the plateau was under Frelimo control after 1964, though Mueda itself remained in Portuguese hands. After the operation known as Gordian Knot, in which 350,000 Portuguese soldiers drove Frelimo underground in Cabo Delgado, roughly 300,000 people in the Mueda area were resettled into *aldeamentos*, collective villages that were wired off to prevent contact with Frelimo. Needless to say, the fact that many of these were arbitrarily placed in arid areas did little to help Portugal win the hearts of Cabo Delgado's people.

The **Makonde** of northeastern Mozambique and southeastern Tanzania are among Africa's best-known craftsmen, and their intricate carvings follow a tradition dating back several hundred years. Makonde society is strongly matrilineal, and the carvings in their purest form celebrate a cult of femininity. The carvers are always male and the carvings are mother figures carried for protection. Oral history links the origin of the carving tradition to the Makonde's original occupation of the plateau. The progenitor of the first Makonde, so tradition goes, was a genderless being living alone in the bush who one day carved a statue in the shape of a woman, left it outside his hut overnight, and awoke to find it transformed into flesh and blood. The carver, apparently also transformed from his formerly genderless state, married the woman and they conceived a child, which died three days after its birth. They moved to higher ground, and again they conceived, and again the child died after three days. Finally they moved to the top of the plateau, and the woman gave birth to a child who became the first Makonde.

Traditional Makonde carvings typically depict a stylised figure of a woman, sometimes with children, but the subject matter of the carvings has diversified greatly in the past three decades. Like any dynamic art form, Makonde carvers have responded to fresh input, particularly in Tanzania. In Mozambique, a good place to see carvings is at the co-operatives in Nampula and Pemba, and of course around Mueda itself. If you want to see the carvers in action, you need to get out to the villages, which is still where most of them work.

A Mecula bus serves Mueda from Pemba (see *Getting around* on page 229). From Pemba by *chapa*, it's four hours to Macomia, then six hours more (including diversions) to Mueda; each leg costs US$3. There's frequent transport to/from Moçimboa da Praia, but getting to/from Moçimboa do Rovuma on the Tanzanian border may take a few days.

There is a basic but acceptable pensão in Mueda: **Pensão Ntima** (tel: 272 84022). Rooms cost upwards of US$10 per person. Water for washing and flushing toilets may come in a bucket.

Moçimboa da Praia

Moçimboa da Praia is the springboard for travellers heading through to Tanzania, and one of the few places in Mozambique where educated people tend to speak English as well as, or instead of, Portuguese. It's also where you'll find Mozambique's northernmost post office and the last petrol station before Mtwara in Tanzania.

A Mecula bus runs there from Mueda; the road is tarred all the way. Vehicles also go from Pemba. If you want to get to Palma, walk 500m north of the Pemba/Mueda stop.

There's a small French-run pensão, **Natalie** (tel: +258 82 4396080; email: natalie@teledata.mz), overlooking the mangroves: three ensuite rooms with running water, each with one double and one single bed. When we last checked it, the **Pensão Mahometana Magid** in the town centre was colourful and quite comfortable, except for cockroaches in the bathrooms. There are also one or two other places to stay on the coast about 2km east of the town centre.

Palma

This small but beautiful town lies on an attractive natural harbour that is thought once to have been a mouth of the Rovuma River. The government buildings and hospital are up on the hill, overlooking a coconut-palm-fringed lagoon and private residences by the sea. Unfortunately, as elsewhere, the beach near the houses is used as a toilet.

The unsurfaced road from Moçimboa to Palma should only be attempted in a 4WD. From Palma, you can continue to Namuiranga (or Namoto) on the Mozambican side of the Rovuma River. The journey is through thick bush, and in a *chapa* it will take around three hours to cover 40-odd kilometres. If you're exceptionally lucky you may spot wild elephants, leopards and packs of wild dogs, but don't count on it! Wildlife is shy in mainland Mozambique.

The rather basic **Hotel Palma** is situated beside the sea.

THE QUIRIMBAS ARCHIPELAGO

The Quirimbas Archipelago consists of 32 small islands strung out along the Mozambique coast, and stretches almost 400km northwards from Pemba to the town of Palma. Its total area is 750,639 hectares. In 2002 it became a part of the Quirimbas National Park (see page 230). Composed of fossil coral rock, the islands are lushly vegetated and the surrounding shallows support extensive mangrove swamps and a wide range of wading birds. The islands also protect an important breeding colony of sooty terns and a variety of turtles: hawksbill, green, loggerhead and leatherback.

It's on these small islands that new luxury resorts are now being built, conforming strictly to the needs of this beautiful but ecologically fragile area. They're so new (in some cases not yet open) that we can't always give first-hand information, but as far as possible we quote websites so that readers can follow progress for themselves.

There no organised public transport in the area, so you'll be dependent on lifts from local boats or on boats (or helicopters) belonging to the lodges. A good starting-point for information is the Kaskazini tourist office in Pemba (see page 235).

Quilálea Island

You can stroll round the whole of tiny (35 hectare) uninhabited Quilálea in well under an hour. It's a remote speck of ancient coral reef on which have been built nine spacious and secluded luxury thatched villas, each on its own outcrop overlooking the sea. The **Quilálea Island Resort** (tel: +258 272 21808, +258 82 326 3900; email: quirimbas@plexusmoz.com; web: www.quilalea.com) opened in November 2002 and is highly rated by both tour operators and guests, who've called it 'a jewel in Africa' and 'an instant classic'. Also see page 228. Rates in 2006 start from US$375 per person (no single supplements apply) and include all meals, snacks and picnics, snorkelling, and use of non-motorised boats and canoes and dhow excursions within the Quilálea Marine Sanctuary. The house reef is just a few flipper-strokes from the beach. Additional activities include big-game fishing, PADI dive courses and excursions to other islands. Access is via helicopter from Pemba to Quirimba Island and thence by boat to Quilálea, or by helicopter direct to the island. The air transfer is free for guests staying seven nights or more.

Quilálea Island and nearby Sencar Island are located in the beautiful and ecologically important **Quilálea Marine Sanctuary**, established in 2000 and the first protected marine area in the archipelago (see also *Quirimbas National Park* on page 230). Since its inception and the banning of local fishing in the area, marine life has been increasing. Turtles nest on the beaches, dugongs are often sighted, and humpback whales shelter in the channel from July to January before journeying south. More than 375 different species of fish have been identified in the sanctuary area, giving snorkellers a rare and colourful treat. The shores of Quilálea are particularly rich in seashells.

Matemo Island

Northward from Quilálea is Matemo Island, just 8km long and 3km wide with lush vegetation and palm groves. It's home to the **Matemo Island Resort**, opened at the end of 2004. The 24 compact and well-appointed chalets, decorated in vibrant colours, have satellite television, minibars and phones. A freshwater pool and a full range of watersports are available, plus sunset cruises and excursions to other islands. Access is via light aircraft from Pemba, 95km to the south: a hop of about 20 minutes. The 2006 rates start from US$343 per person sharing and US$464 single including air transfers. This is one of the resorts in Mozambique managed by Rani Resorts (tel: +27 (0) 11 467 1277; email: reservations@raniresorts.com; web: www.raniresorts.com).

Medjumbe Island

This tiny island (1.1km by 350m) north of Matemo has a variety of bird species including the black heron; its waters contain marlin, sailfish, dogtooth tuna, mackerel, various species of kingfish, and bonefish. The **Medjumbe Island Resort** should open in early 2006, with twelve secluded air-conditioned chalets with mini-bars, satellite television and tea/coffee-making facilities. Medjumbe is a slightly steeper island than some others and the chalets are 10m up from the beach. It also is run by Rani Resorts; 2006 rates and contact details are as for Matemo, above.

The Maluane Project

The Maluane area in the far north of Mozambique consists of three islands, a coastal strip and a 33,000ha wildlife reserve. The Cabo Delgado Biodiversity and Tourism Project, initiated in 1998 and known more simply as the Maluane Project, is a partnership between the Zoological Society of London (see www.zsl.org for a fact sheet), the Mozambique government, the local community and donors worldwide. Its objective is to conserve and develop the Maluane area, whose marine wildlife includes turtles, humpback whales, whale sharks, dugongs, dolphins, manta rays, giant clams, over 350 varieties of reef fish and 30 different genera of coral. The mainland hosts elephant, lion, buffalo, hippo, leopard, wild dog, various antelope and monkey species, and multiple birds.

The project has strong environmental and community links; it is both a sustainable low-impact tourism initiative and a scientifically based conservation programme. Ongoing funding will come from international donors and luxury adventure tourism. Work has started on three eco-friendly luxury island lodges (on Vamizi, Rongui and Macaloe islands); two mainland safari camps will come later. **Vamizi Island Lodge** is scheduled to open around the end of 2005, with **Rongui Island Lodge** and **Macaloe Island Lodge** following sometime in 2006. Construction should start later in 2006 on the Lake Macungue Safari Lodge, on the mainland within the Maluane wildlife reserve.

Vamizi Island Lodge will offer 12 very spacious luxury ensuite chalets set into the thick deciduous woodland fringing the shore, with thatched roofs, polished wood floors, four-poster beds and private verandas overlooking 8km of white sandy beach. The island is 1.5km by 12km. For more details see website www.maluane.com or check out the tour operators listed on pages 44–5, several of whom (Expert Africa, Rainbow, Steppes, Unusual Destinations...) cover Vamizi.

Appendix

Sally Crook

LANGUAGE

Mozambicans speak Portuguese in a more sing-songy way than the Portuguese themselves, and their speech is much easier to understand than the guttural string of consonants Europeans use. There are two renderings of the verb 'to be'. *Ser* (*sou, é, somos, são*) is more or less for characteristics or permanent states, and *estar* (*estou, está, estamos, estão*) for temporary states. Many words can be guessed from English or Spanish and some Spanish speakers get along quite well with a mixture of *português* and *espanhol*, popularly known as *portanhol*. Examples include many words ending with -ion in English and -on in Spanish which are similar in Portuguese but end in -ão (plural usually -ões) – *televisão, razão* (reason), *verão* (summer).

Take care, though, for some similar Spanish and Portuguese words have completely different meanings: *Niño* (Spanish = child) versus *ninho* (Portuguese = nest); *pretender* means 'intend' rather than 'pretend' (*fingir*) and it is best not to describe an ordinary man as *ordinário* as this implies he is common or vulgar.

Asterisks (*) denote words derived in or specific to Mozambique or Africa.

Pronunciation

ã + a followed by m	nasal (similar to 'ang').	o or ó	o when stressed (as in hot)
c	ss before i or e; k elsewhere	ou	o sound (as in both or window)
ç	ss	õ + o followed by m	nasal (similar to 'ong').
cc	ks	qu	k before i or e; kw elsewhere
ch	sh		
g	soft j before i or e; hard g elsewhere	s	z or sh (at end of syllable)
j	soft j (as in French)		
lh	ly (as in Spanish ll)	x	sh or s
nh	ny (as Spanish ñ)	z	soft j
o or ô	oo when unstressed		

Double vowels are pronounced separately:

compreendo	compree-endo
cooperação	coo-operassaoo

Greetings

Good morning	*Bom dia*	How are you?	*Como está* [komo shta]
Good afternoon	*Boa tarde*		
Good evening/ night	*Boa noite* (meeting as well as taking leave)	I am well	*Estou bem* [shtow be(ng)] (or a reply to *como está* might be *bom obrigado / boa obrigada* = I am good, thank you)
Hello	*Hola*		
Goodbye	*Até logo* (until later)		
What is your name?	*Como sé chama?*		
My name is	*Chamou me* [shamow mu]		

Basic phrases

Please	*sé faz favor* (or *por favor*)	What's this (called)?	*Como se chama isso?*
		Who?	*Quem?*
Thank you	*obrigado/a* (I'm obliged)	When?	*Quando?*
		Where?	*Onde?*
You're welcome	*de nada* (ie: 'it's nothing' – reply to thank you)	From where?	*Donde?* (contraction of *de onde*)
There is no	*não há* (or *falta*)	Where is	*Onde fica /é / está?*
Excuse me	*disculpe* (or *perdone me*)	Do you know	*Você sabe?*
		I don't know	*Não sei*
Give me	*dê me*	I don't understand	*Não compreendo* (also *não percebo*)
I like to	*eu gostou de…*		
I would like	*(eu) queria*	Yes	*Sim*
How?	*Como?*	No	*Não*
How much?	*Quanto?*	Perhaps	*Talvez* [talvej]
How much (cost)?	*Quanto custa / é isso?*	Good	*Bom / Boa* (m/f)
What?	*(O) Que?*		

Food and drink

beef	*carne de vaca*	dinner	*jantar*
beer	*cerveja*	drink (noun)	*uma bebida*
bon appétit	*bom apetito*	drink (verb)	*beber*
bread	*pão*	eggs	*ovos*
breakfast	*matabicho* (★ lit. 'kill beast')	fish	*peixe* [payshy] or *pescado* (as food)
cake	*bolo*	fizzy soft drink	*refresco*
cassava, manioc	*mandioca*	juice, squash	*sumo*
coffee	*café*	lunch	*almoço*
bean	*feijão* (*feijoada* = a dish of rice, beans and pork)	maize beer	*byalwa* (★)
		maize, mealies	*milho*
		maize porridge	*vuswa* (★) or *nsima* (★ in the north [nsheema])
chicken	*frango* (as food)		
chips, french fries	*batatas fritas*		

meat	*carne*	rum (local)	*cachaça*
milk	*leite*	snack	*merenda* or *lanche*
pasta	*massa* (NB *pasta* =		(elevenses)
	file or briefcase)	spirits	*aguardente*
pork	*carne de porco*	sweet potato	*batata doce*
potato	*batata*	tea	*chá*
restaurant	*restaurante*	to eat	*comer*
rice	*arroz*	water	*água*

Other useful words

a little (not much)	*pouco/a*	large	*grande*
a lot (very, much)	*muito/a*	lorry, truck	*camião*
aeroplane	*avião*	malaria	*malária, paludismo*
after	*depois (de)*	market	*mercado*
bank	*banco*	money	*dinheiro*
bathroom, toilet	*casa de banho*	mosque	*mesquita*
battery (dry)	*pilha*	mosquito net	*mosquiteiro*
bed	*cama*	mountain	*montanha*
before	*antes (de)*	never	*nunca*
block (of buildings)	*quarteirão*	night	*noite* [noyty]
boarding house	*pensão*	nightclub	*boite* [booat(y)]
book	*livro*	nothing	*nada*
bus	*machimbombo* (★)	now	*agora* [agwara]
	autocarro (Portuguese)	on the beach	*na praia*
car	*carro*	railway	*caminho de ferro* (n)
casualty department	*banco de socorros*		*ferroviário/a* (adj)
change	*câmbio*	rain	*chuva*
child	*criança*	river	*rio*
church	*igreja*	road	*estrada* [shtrada]
city, town	*cidade*	sea	*mar*
cold/hot water	*água fria/quente*	shop	*loja*
(hard) currency	*devisas*	small	*pequenho/a*
day	*dia*	street, road, highway	*rua*
diarrhoea	*diarréia*	swamp, marsh	*pântano*
doctor	*médico*	today	*hoje*
dry season	*estação seca*	tomorrow	*amanhã*
enough	*bastante*	to hurt (or ache)	*doer*
fever	*febre*	to swim	*nadar*
film (roll of)	*película*	toilet paper	*papel higiênico*
hill	*colina*	too much	*demais/demasiado/a*
hospital	*hospital*	train	*comboio*
hotel	*hotel*	travellers cheques	*tcheques de viagem*
house	*casa*	village	*aldeia*
hut	*palhota*	yesterday	*ontem*
ill	*doente*	you	*você* (polite, formal),
lake	*lago*		*tu* (familiar)

Numbers

Each part of a cardinal number is changed to ordinal when referring to a place in a sequence (eg: 2,112th = two thousandth hundredth tenth second), so it is simpler to call the 11th floor of a building *andar numero onze* than *o decimo primeiro andai*, for instance. For days of the month only the first is an ordinal number (first of May, but two of May etc). Therefore, one can get by with only the cardinal numbers and *primeiro/a* (= first).

1	*um/uma*	9	*nove*	60	*sessenta*
2	*dois/duas*	10	*dez*	70	*setenta*
3	*três*	11	*onze*	80	*oitenta*
4	*quatro*	20	*vinte*	90	*noventa*
5	*cinco*	21	*vinte e um/uma*	100	*cem*
6	*seis*	30	*trinta*	1,000	*mil*
7	*sete*	40	*quarenta*	1,000,000	*milhao*
8	*oito*	50	*cinquenta*		

IBO ISLAND LODGE

Virtually unknown to the outside world and undisturbed for centuries there is a place where time has stood still. This place is Ibo Island. Nestled in the awesome **Quirimbas Archipelago National Park** of northern Mozambique, Ibo is the most fascinating, idyllic and beautiful island you could dream of visiting. **Ibo Island Lodge** encompasses three magnificent mansions each over one hundred years old and overlooking the ancient waterfront.

★ Just 12 luxury air conditioned en-suite rooms boast antiques and handcrafted furniture ★
★ Romantic dining features the freshest of sea food served at the roof-top restaurant ★
★ Guided activities present a remarkable journey through the history of Ibo ★
★ Guided mangrove excursions showcase outstanding bird and marine life ★
★ Sea kayak, swim or snorkel in clear blue waters amongst breathtaking scenery ★
★ Visit Ibo's pristine sandbank beach (only accessed by boat and totally private) ★
★ Cultural and community projects ★
★ Traditional sailing dhow safaris and heavenly, de-stress Ibo inspired massage ★

Ibo Island Lodge offers a unique journey to an era long forgotten!

Contact us for specials, flights and packages combining
Ibo Island with all neighbouring islands and resorts.

Ibo Island Lodge Central Reservations:
PO Box 30661, Tokai, 7966.
Cape Town, South Africa.
Tel: ++ (27 21) 702 0643 Fax: ++ (27 21) 702 0644
E-mail: info@iboisland.com   www.iboisland.com

Appendix

FURTHER READING
History and background

Malyn Newitt's *A History of Mozambique* (Wits University Press, South Africa, 1995) is probably the best single-volume history of an African country that I've ever come across. Clocking in at roughly 600 pages, it is authoritative, up-to-date, stimulating and highly readable – I'd go so far as to say that nobody with more than a passing interest in Mozambique's colourful history should visit the country without reading it. I'm not certain how easy it will be to locate this book outside South Africa, but if you are having problems you can contact Wits University Press directly at PO Wits, Johannesburg, South Africa; tel: 011 484 5907; fax: 011 484 5971; email: wup@iafrica.com.

For those requiring greater detail on a particular period, books that I found to be both useful and readable included three by Eric Axelson, namely *Portuguese in East Africa 1488–1600, Portuguese in East Africa 1600–1700* and *Portugal and the Scramble for Africa 1875–1891* (all Wits University Press), as well as Allen and Barbara Isaacman's *Mozambique: From Colonialism to Revolution 1900–1982* (Westview Press 1983). For wider coverage of the Karonga Kingdoms and Manomotapa, a recommended read is David Beach's *The Shona and Zimbabwe 900–1850* (Heinemann 1980).

Some of the better books covering more recent events in Mozambique are William Finnegan's *A Complicated War* (University of California Press 1992), Joseph Hanlon's *Mozambique: Who calls the shots?* (James Currey 1991) and Alex Vine's bang-up-to-date *Renamo: From Terrorism to Democracy in Mozambique* (James Currey, revised and updated edition 1996).

Michael Main's *Zambezi: Journey of a River* (Southern Book Publishers 1990) is an emininently readable introduction to practically every aspect of southern Africa's largest watercourse, with solidly researched material on the region's history and a wealth of obscure anecdotal detail about some of the more eccentric characters who have been associated with the Zambezi.

According to the cover blurb of Kerry Swift's *Mozambique and the Future* (Don Nelson Publishers 1974), its author was the last journalist to conduct a comprehensive tour of Mozambique before the 1974 coup in Portugal. Notwithstanding a few reservations about assertions such as 'South Africa ... appears to be sincere in her promises of sovereign independence for the Homelands', not to say the author's evident admiration for the gung-ho antics of the Portuguese officers he encounters along the way, this book does offer an interesting and plausible on-the-spot snapshot of Mozambique during the closing stages of the liberation war.

Something of a companion piece to Swift's book – though infinitely better – is Nick

Middleton's *Kaleshnikovs and Zombie Cucumbers: Travels in Mozambique* (Phoenix 1994), which offers a similar snapshot of Mozambique twenty years on, during the closing stages of the civil war and shortly after the signing of the 1992 Peace Accord. Hanging out with NGO workers rather than generals, Middleton punctuates his languid and often very funny travelogue with some pithy insights into the detrimental effects of the Western aid industry, a clear background to the civil war, and some fascinating stuff on the occultism that lies close to the surface of rural life in Mozambique – along with Newitt's *History* this book would top my list of recommended reading.

Other books that I consulted during the course of my research were Lawrence Green's *Harbours of Delight* (Howard Timmins 1969), a lively and anecdotal travelogue covering most of Africa's main harbours; Genesta Hamilton's *In the Wake of Da Gama* (Skeffington & Son 1951), which covers Portuguese exploration up to 1729; CF Spence's rather dry *Mozambique: East African Province of Portugal* (Howard Timmins 1963); the *Lourenço Marques Guide* (edited by Carlos Alberto Viera da Silva); and James Kirkman's excellent survey of the important old buildings of the Swahili coast *Men and Monuments on the East African Coast* (Willmer Brothers 1964).

Also worth reading is Sally Crook's *Viva Mozambique* (Starling Books 1996), which gives a personal account of the author's six years of living and working in the country.

The definitive annotated bibliography of books about Mozambique is *World Biographical Series No 78: Mozambique* (Clio Press 1987), edited by Colin Darch and Calisto Pacheleke.

Field guides

Any of several field guides to the mammals of southern Africa will be close to comprehensive for Mozambique. My first recommendation would be Chris & Tilde Stuart's *Field Guide to the Mammals of Southern Africa* (Struik Publishers, South Africa, 1988).

For birders, several field guides to Southern African birds are available, and these include all species recorded in Mozambique south of the Zambezi. In my experience, Kenneth Newman's *Birds of Southern Africa* (Southern Book Publishers, South Africa) remains the most useful book in the field, but Ian Sinclair's *Sasol Birds of Southern Africa* (Struik Publishers, South Africa) is also very good. The renowned *Robert's Birds of Southern Africa* is a bit bulky in some circumstances, but it gives far more detailed species descriptions and it's the only guide with continental distrubution, a useful feature if you're birding north of the Zambezi.

There is no readily accessible, affordable and portable guide to the birds of northern Mozambique, where you could see a few dozen species not recorded south of the Zambezi. Serious birders heading this way are strongly urged to carry Ber van Perlo's *Illustrated Checklist to the Birds of Eastern Africa* (Collins 1995), which illustrates and briefly describes every bird recorded in Tanzania, Kenya, Uganda, Ethiopia and Eritrea. The book includes distribution maps as far south as the Tanzania–Mozambique border, so it's fairly easy to establish which species are likely to extend their range into northern Mozambique.

For divers and snorkellers, it might be worth getting hold of a copy of Kenneth Bock's portable *Guide to the Common Reef Fishes of the Western Indian Ocean and Kenya Coast* (Macmillan 1978) or J L B Smith's rather more bulky *Sea Fishes of Southern Africa* (Central News Agency 1965).

Fiction

Mozambique has reputedly produced a fair body of African literature, though as it is all written in Portuguese it is not readily accessible to English speakers. Highly recommended, and readily available in book shops in Maputo, is the collection *Short Stories from Mozambique* (Cosaw Publishers 1995), an anthology of 20-odd stories edited and for the main part translated by Richard Bartlett.

Maps

Backpackers and other travellers who need a good map of Mozambique for hitching or driving purposes should find the following maps quite satisfactory:

Mozambique: Globetrotter Travel Map (New Holland): clear and colourful country, regional and city maps, accompanied by good photographs of Mozambique.
Mozambique (Institut Géographique National): accurate, no-nonsense map published by French geographical institute.
Mozambique Road Map (Ravenstein Verlag)
The *Time Out* map of Mozambique is more readily available than the others, at least in South Africa, but it really is a waste of money – riddled with errors and omitting many important towns.

Internet
General
Africa News On-line www.africanews.org. The best pan-African news agency on the internet.
Music www.mediaport.net/Music/Pays/mozambique/index.en.html. Comprehensive listing of Mozambican CDs – which you can also purchase online.
Ilha do Moçambique www.ilhademo.net. Dedicated to Mozambique Island, with some decent photographs of the island's most important buildings.
Time Out www.timeout.co.mz. Nothing to do with the English publication of the same name, this site has arguably the most detailed practical information for travellers to Mozambique. There is a strong bias towards the southern provinces, and some of the information might not be particularly up-to-date.
Mozambican Constitution www.richmond.edu/~jpjones/confinder/MOZ.htm. Just to prove that these days you really can find anything on the web, here's the complete English translation of the 1990 Mozambican Constitution.
2000/01 Floods www.oxfam.org.uk/atwork/emerg/mozflood01.htm. With news of how Mozambique has been getting back on its feet after the 2000 and 2001 floods.
Mozambique News Agency www.poptel.org.uk/mozambique-news. The English website of the Mozambique News Agency. Probably the most comprehensive and up-to-date Mozambique-related news on the web, although sometimes it can be a little too detailed for the casual observer.
Northern Mozambique www.go2africa.com/mocambique. A reasonable travel portal with basic information for visitors to Mozambique and, unlike many such sites, pages about areas in the less travelled northern part of the country.

Mozambique news and links

The following sites all contain Mozambique-related news stories in English, as well as links to other sites relevant to Mozambique:

www.mozambique.mz
www.allafrica.com/mozambique
www.mozambiquenews.com

Tourism

The websites of the tour operators listed on page 45 give information about the areas they cover.

World Travel Starts at Stanfords
Maps and Guides for all corners of the World
Stanfords Flagship Store
12–14 Long Acre, Covent Garden, London, WC2

Other Stanford Stores:

Stanfords at British Airways Travel Shop: 156 Regent Street, W1

Stanfords at The Britain Visitor Centre: 1 Regent Street, SW1
(Maps and Books of the UK and Ireland only)

Stanfords at the Scottish Tourist Board: 19 Cockspur Street, SW1
(Maps and Books of Scotland only)

Stanfords in Bristol: 29 Corn Street, Bristol, BS1

International Mail Order Department
Tel: 020 7836 1321 Fax: 020 7836 0189

www.stanfords.co.uk

Bradt Travel Guides

Africa by Road Charlie Shackell & Illya Bracht
Albania Gillian Gloyer
Amazon, The Roger Harris/Peter Hutchison
Antarctica: A Guide to the Wildlife
  Tony Soper/Dafila Scott
Arctic: A Guide to Coastal Wildlife
  Tony Soper/Dan Powell
Armenia with Nagorno Karabagh Nicholas
  Holding
Azores David Sayers
Baghdad Catherine Arnold
Baltic Capitals: Tallinn, Riga, Vilnius, Kaliningrad
  Neil Taylor et al
Bosnia & Herzegovina Tim Clancy
Botswana: Okavango, Chobe, Northern Kalahari
  Chris McIntyre
British Isles: Wildlife of Coastal Waters
  Tony Soper/Dan Powell
Budapest Adrian Phillips/Jo Scotchmer
Cameroon Ben West
Canary Islands Lucy Corne
Cape Verde Islands Aisling Irwin/
  Colum Wilson
Cayman Islands Tricia Hayne
Chile Tim Burford
Chile & Argentina: Trekking Guide
  Tim Burford
Cork Linda Fallon
Costa Rica Larissa Banting
Croatia Piers Letcher
Cyprus see *North Cyprus*
Dubrovnik Piers Letcher
Eccentric America Jan Friedman
Eccentric Britain Benedict le Vay
Eccentric California Jan Friedman
Eccentric Edinburgh Benedict le Vay
Eccentric France Piers Letcher
Eccentric London Benedict le Vay
Eccentric Oxford Benedict le Vay
Ecuador: Climbing & Hiking in
  Rob Rachowiecki/Mark Thurber
Eritrea Edward Denison/Edward Paice
Estonia Neil Taylor
Ethiopia Philip Briggs
Falkland Islands Will Wagstaff
Faroe Islands James Proctor
Gabon, São Tome & Principe Sophie Warne
Galápagos Wildlife David Horwell/Pete Oxford
Gambia, The Craig Emms/Linda Barnett
Georgia Tim Burford
Ghana Philip Briggs
Hungary Adrian Phillips/Jo Scotchmer
Iran Patricia L Baker
Iraq Karen Dabrowska
Kabul Mini Guide Dominic Medley/
  Jude Barrand

Kenya Claire Foottit
Kiev Andrew Evans
Latvia Stephen Baister/Chris Patrick
Lille Mini Guide Laurence Phillips
Lithuania Gordon McLachlan
Ljubljana Robin & Jenny McKelvie
Macedonia Thammy Evans
Madagascar Hilary Bradt
Madagascar Wildlife Nick Garbutt/
  Hilary Bradt/Derek Schuurman
Malawi Philip Briggs
Maldives Royston Ellis
Mali Ross Velton
Mauritius, Rodrigues & Réunion Royston Ellis/
  Alex Richards/Derek Schuurman
Mongolia Jane Blunden
Montenegro Annalisa Rellie
Mozambique Philip Briggs/Ross Velton
Namibia Chris McIntyre
Nigeria Lizzie Williams
North Cyprus Diana Darke
North Korea Robert Willoughby
Palestine, with Jerusalem Henry Stedman
Panama Sarah Woods
Paris, Lille & Brussels: Eurostar Cities
  Laurence Phillips
Peru & Bolivia: Backpacking and Trekking
  Hilary Bradt/Kathy Jarvis
Riga Stephen Baister/Chris Patrick
River Thames, In the Footsteps of the Famous
  Paul Goldsack
Rwanda Janice Booth/Philip Briggs
St Helena, Ascension, Tristan da Cunha
  Sue Steiner
Serbia Laurence Mitchell
Seychelles Lyn Mair/Lynnath Beckley
Slovenia Robin & Jenny McKelvie
South Africa: Budget Travel Guide Paul Ash
Southern African Wildlife Mike Unwin
Spitsbergen Andreas Umbreit
Sri Lanka Royston Ellis
Sudan Paul Clammer
Switzerland: Rail, Road, Lake Anthony Lambert
Tallinn Neil Taylor
Tanzania Philip Briggs
Tasmania Matthew Brace
Tibet Michael Buckley
Uganda Philip Briggs
Ukraine Andrew Evans
USA by Rail John Pitt
Venezuela Hilary Dunsterville Branch
Vilnius Gordon McLachlan/Neil Taylor
Your Child Abroad
  Dr Jane Wilson-Howarth/Dr Matthew Ellis
Zambia Chris McIntyre
Zanzibar David Else

Bradt Travel Guides Ltd
+44 (0)1753 893444   www.bradtguides.com

Index

Page numbers in bold indicate main entries, those in italics indicate maps.